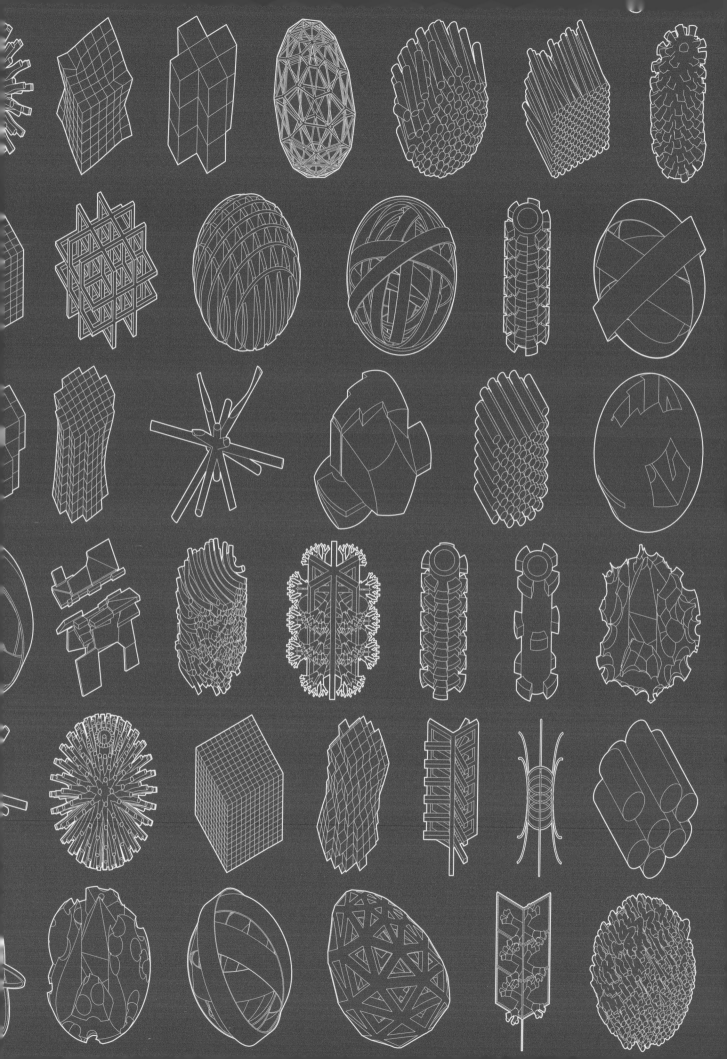

ARCHITECTONICS AND PARAMETRIC THINKING

COMPUTATIONAL MODELING FOR BEGINNING DESIGN

Frank Jacobus
Angela Carpenter
Rachel Smith Loerts
Antonello Di Nunzio
Francesco Bedeschi

Taylor & Francis Group

NEW YORK AND LONDON

Designed cover image: Frank Jacobus

First published 2023
by Routledge
4 Park Square, Milton Park, Abingdon, Oxon OX14 4RN

and by Routledge
605 Third Avenue, New York, NY 10158

Routledge is an imprint of the Taylor & Francis Group, an informa business

© 2023 Frank Jacobus, Angela Carpenter, Rachel Smith Loerts, Antonello Di Nunzio, and Francesco Bedeschi

The right of Frank Jacobus, Angela Carpenter, Rachel Smith Loerts, Antonello Di Nunzio, and Francesco Bedeschi to be identified as authors of this work has been asserted in accordance with sections 77 and 78 of the Copyright, Designs and Patents Act 1988.

All rights reserved. No part of this book may be reprinted or reproduced or utilized in any form or by any electronic, mechanical, or other means, now known or hereafter invented, including photocopying and recording, or in any information storage or retrieval system, without permission in writing from the publishers.

Trademark notice: Product or corporate names may be trademarks or registered trademarks, and are used only for identification and explanation without intent to infringe.

British Library Cataloguing-in-Publication Data
A catalogue record for this book is available from the British Library

Library of Congress Cataloging-in-Publication Data
A catalog record has been requested for this book

ISBN: 978-1-032-18052-6 (hbk)
ISBN: 978-1-032-18053-3 (pbk)
ISBN: 978-1-003-25263-4 (ebk)

DOI: 10.4324/9781003252634

Typeset in Swis721
by Frank Jacobus, Angela Carpenter, and Rachel Smith-Loerts

This book has been prepared from camera-ready copy provided by the authors.

CONTENTS

Author Biographies, Acknowledgments

1   **Logics**   **1**

     Introduction   3
     The Power of Parametric Thinking   9
     Invisible Parametrics   18
     Architectonics and Parametric Thinking   28
     Customization's Parametric Play   39
     Classical Architecture as Parametric Construct   50
     Parametric Thinking and Sustainable Design   57
     Fabricating Parametric Thinking   64
     Spatial Computing, Artificial Intelligence, and the Future of Parametric Design   74

2   **Elements**   **82**

3   **Constructions**   **106**

     3.1 Frame Objects   108
     3.2 Plane Objects   136
     3.3 Solid Objects   166
     3.4 Hybrid Objects   190

4   **Morphologies**   **226**

     Index   **302**

ARCHITECTONICS AND PARAMETRIC THINKING

COMPUTATIONAL MODELING FOR BEGINNING DESIGN

This book is an approachable guide for students and professionals to learn parametric modeling through the lens of architectonics, allowing readers to pair fundamental ideas about architecture with parametric thinking.

Architectonics and Parametric Thinking begins by clearly positioning the potentials of parametric design through a series of chapters written by leaders in their respective industries. This helps to situate the vast potential of parametric softwares, allowing the reader to understand the full range of what is made possible by working computationally. Following this theoretical introduction, the book presents a manual that walks readers through the step-by-step construction of parametric modeling scripts built through an architectonic lens using clear, compelling diagrams. Each of these diagrams provides textual accompaniment that describes how each new portion of the script is transforming the algorithm as a whole, as well as diagrams that show the physical transformation that is taking place as a result of the script's evolution.

Parametric modeling is radically transforming the design disciplines and will become the primary way designers generate new products moving forward. Written and expertly designed for architecture students and professionals, this book provides an interactive approach to teaching the basics of parametric thinking in relation to architecture and design.

AUTHOR BIOGRAPHIES

Frank Jacobus is an award-winning artist, educator, and principal architect of SILO AR+D. He has completed residential and institutional projects across the United States. SILO's architecture is recognized nationally and internationally with design awards and was selected recently as an *Emerging Voice* by the Architectural League of New York, and as a *Next Progressive* by Architecture Magazine. Frank's other book projects include "Archi-Graphic: An Infographic Look at Architecture", "The Visual Biography of Color", and "The Making of Things: Modeling Processes and Effects in Architecture".

Angela Carpenter is the Fabrication Labs Manager at the Fay Jones School of Architecture and Design Build Lab. Angela oversees the facility and integration of building-focused courses taught at all scales. She provides expertise and instructional support in digital fabrication techniques and procuring specialized equipment. Angela has taught as a Visiting Assistant Professor and Instructor in advanced Design-Build studios and Additive Manufacturing. Her experience has allowed for developing multi-scale investigations in material manipulation and construction advancements.

Rachel Smith Loerts is a Visiting Instructor at the Fay Jones School of Architecture and Design. After working four years as a project designer for multiple architecture firms, Rachel spent six years managing Digital Fabrication Laboratories. As manager she facilitated student and faculty digital fabrication processes for design studios, seminars, fabrication research, and community outreach programs. During this time, she was awarded the Tau Sigma Delta Silver Medal for her commitment to developing student fabrication knowledge.

Antonello Di Nunzio is a freelance architect and programmer who develops innovative tools for more environmentally conscious architectural design. He has more than six years of practical experience as consultant and open-source developer in the AEC industry. He worked at Accenture as senior programmer, and collaborates with the University of Arkansas Rome Center and with different companies such as Sinergi Integrated Building Sciences as environmental simulation specialist for LEED. Currently Antonello works mainly with Ladybug Tools LLC as an application developer to innovate the AEC industry.

Francesco Bedeschi is an architect and an educator. Since 2003 Francesco is an Adjunct Professor of Architecture at the University of Arkansas Rome Center and since 2019, he has taken the role of Director. In 2007-2008 Francesco became connected with the green building movement in the United States. He is now a member of the Green Building Council Italia where he currently serves on the executive board. Since 2010 he has collaborated with SINERGI Integrated Building Sciences.

ACKNOWLEDGMENTS

Special thanks to all of the students who contributed to this book and its hundreds of diagrams. Without your efforts this visual content would not have been possible. It is for students and young practitioners like yourselves that we decided to create this text in the first place. Thanks goes to the following students specifically who spent countless hours line weighting, diagramming, and putting up with our nit-picking:

Emily Kloostra, Thomas Rohrbach, Camila Salgueiro, Madison Smith

Thanks also to the students who helped us by checking the Rhino/Grasshopper scripts to ensure that all the wires where plugged in correctly and that we had not made any other definitional mistakes. They are, in alphabetical order: Abigail Archibald, Rylee Ball, Haley Czeschin, Jared Davenport, Raqual Gamboa, David Hoff, Nicholas Hurley, William Langston, Maggie Lee, Andrew Mardell, James Muse, Hailey Pease, Whitley Raney, Aspen Regan, Evan Roberts, Claire Sanders, Kerrigan Servati, Jeffrey Simmons, Morgan Solomon, and Katherine Voss.

Thanks also to the University of Arkansas and the **Fay Jones School of Architecture and Design** for dedicating resources to this effort and supporting us in this multi-year endeavor.

Finally, thanks to our colleagues from around the country for giving us feedback regarding the work and the theory that supports it. Our hope is that this book finds its way into the hands of design students who want to discover more about the nature of parametric thinking and how it can contribute to a beautiful and sustainable built environment.

1 LOGICS

The **LOGICS** section of this book consists of a series of chapters which set up the argument for the relationship between architectonics and parametric thinking as well as the uses of parametric tools generally. These chapters include descriptions of what is implied by the term *architectonic* as well as what is meant by the term *parametric*. They include descriptions of effect and what it means to iterate an architectonic construct. They also include descriptions of how parametric and architectonic thinking have been used historically and are currently used in the design disciplines today. For instance, a chapter on parametric thinking in classical architecture sets up the argument that these approaches are not new to our disciplines but instead form the foundation upon which western design disciplines are built. A chapter on parametric modeling with respect to new fabrication methods affords you a glimpse into the use and importance of the basic principles of parametric modeling and how this type of thinking and operating impacts contemporary construction methods. These and the other chapters in this section serve to provide a backdrop as to how the tools and techniques covered in the book have become widely used methods in design practice.

INTRODUCTION

Frank Jacobus

This book teaches parametric thinking and modeling through the lens of architectonics. With that description there are already two words presented, *parametric* and *architectonic*, that may serve to confuse rather than clarify. While the book's chapters will provide more in-depth definitions of what is meant by *parametric* and *architectonic*, it is valuable to start with an abbreviated definition of each.

When we say *parametric*, we are referring to a process or way of thinking wherein a system, an ordered aggregation of forms and spaces, is thought of in terms of relationships between quantifiable, changeable properties. These properties are thought of as *parameters*. Working parametrically using digital computational tools has radically changed design processes globally. In a non-parametric environment, the drawn lines of an object, like a window for instance, must be manually redrawn if the window size changes. In a parametric environment, the window is still often drawn with lines, but those lines are encoded with dimensional properties that can easily be changed simply by typing in a new width and height, rather than by redrawing the entire window assembly. This change can happen locally, to a single window, or globally, to all windows within a defined set. This is perhaps the most basic example of parametric modeling, but when one imagines having to redraw hundreds of windows, or thousands of various objects within any building design, they can understand the incredible time savings that occurs when these elements can be automatically updated with just the click of a few buttons.

The word *architectonics* means many different things to many different people. It originates from the Greek *arkhitekton*, which itself is from *arkhi*, meaning chief and *tekton*, meaning builder, carpenter. When one digs even deeper into these roots, they find *teks*, which means to weave or fabricate.[1] For the purposes of this text, we view architectonics as architectural form's underlying syntactic structure. In other words, architectonics implies a primary set of architecture's formal rules, an understanding of its fundamental elements, how they come together, and to what effect.

The pairing of architectonics with parametric thinking and modeling within this book is done for a number of reasons. First, both of these phenomena deal with the inherent quantifiable characteristics of a thing. For instance, a planar object, which is a foundational architectonic type, can quickly evolve into a frame-like object with a simple dimensional change in one direction.

That simple dimensional change, which is an evolution in the object's parameters, has radical implications with respect to how we construct with, and how we formally read, an architectonic construct. In direct and simple terms, architectonics is inherently parametric.

The second reason we chose to pair architectonics with parametrics within the book is because parametrics is often neglected in design programs until a student's later years of study. This means that students often do not know of the existence of parametric thinking until well into their academic careers, after their ideas about design process have already evolved and matured. This casts parametrics as an "other", rather than as a foundational way of thinking. What this means is that students' first exposure to parametrics is as an alternative to normative modes of thinking. This places parametric thinking at a distinct disadvantage within most design pedagogy. In addition, this approach creates a missed opportunity to teach parametric modeling while providing a rigorous education in architectonics as an important foundation in the student's architectural education.

The third and final reason we wanted to pair architectonics with parametrics, related tangentially to the above, is that parametric modeling is often solely taught as a way of manipulating complex forms. While parametric modeling handles complex forms very well, there are other, more essential things that it also does well which would benefit young designers. This book solves the above dilemma. By working through the tutorials within this book, you will build a foundation in parametric modeling knowledge while also learning the language of architectonics and how to push the boundaries of its effects.

PARAMETRIC THINKING DIFFICULTIES FOR THE YOUNG DESIGNER

In many design schools, especially in beginning design pedagogy, parametric modeling is seen as foreign to design rather than as a fundamental way we think as designers. It is often intentionally not taught for fear that, by relying on parametric modeling, students won't learn how to draw by hand. It is our contention that it is up to the teacher to promote processes that use both digital and analog methods reciprocally. When parametric modeling is eventually taught, it is often shown as a way of creating and manipulating complex geometries, curvilinear forms, intricate surfaces, etc. rather than a way to manipulate and iterate even the most elementary forms.

Because of this, young designers often don't experiment with parametric tools, learning about and understanding their power, until well into their design education. We have spoken to countless students in the advanced years of their education who are frustrated by and perplexed as to why these tools were not introduced at an earlier time. The fact that parametric tools are introduced late means that students have already learned a specific design process, and as we know, old habits are often hard to break. The combination of being taught the tool late and that it is typically reserved for complex, often curvilinear geometries with convoluted envelopes means that the student has to retrain themselves to use the tool in a new way.

Another danger of being taught parametric tools too late in one's design career is that the parametric interface is often different than any other digital interface students have encountered. If the student had been trained on this interface from the beginning, then it would become second nature to them. Having lived within other digital design interfaces, most of which are strikingly similar to each other but not to parametric interfaces, the parametric interface becomes too different to accept, especially when deadlines and pressures of studio work loom.

This book introduces parametric modeling at its most fundamental. It shows you step by step, how to build a parametric *definition*, which is the name for the underlying algorithm, code, or script that generates the object geometry. The definitions in the book are all linked to basic, elemental, architectonic objects thereby showing you how to make forms which are often a part of your early design education. By working through these definitions, you will construct a foundation of parametric knowledge from which you will be able to self-coach or find more advanced methods from other resources.

Learning parametric modeling can advance your design education in numerous ways. These models allow you to test formal effect and emotive quality more quickly through rapid iteration. In other words, instead of being able to construct one object in a digital environment over the course of an hour, you can create 40 objects in the same amount of time. This will allow you to study a litany of examples, comparing the qualities of one to the next, where you may have only been able to study one or two examples before. This becomes a tremendous education as it allows you to invest in the subtleties of form that a lack of time and patience may have prevented you from examining. This will help build your architectonic intuitions and produce more work than otherwise possible, hopefully refining that work in the process.

In addition, to understand how to create an object by using an underlying algorithm or ruleset, means that you have to have some sense of what you want the parametric definition to do. In other words, to make a clean, effective definition, you have to determine which parts of the object you want to be able to manipulate. This means you have to think more deeply about the object than many of your colleagues who are not using parametric approaches. You will be thinking about the object's underlying character, how it may evolve formally, what those evolutions might deliver in terms of effect, etc. in a way that simply constructing a single object would never afford you. Another way to think about this, by working parametrically you are considering an object as though it were alive, as though it were a thing that evolves and grows. By doing this, you are bringing a fourth dimension to an otherwise three-dimensional object. This is a more advanced way to think about objects; as an active happening rather than as a static phenomenon.

HOW THE BOOK IS STRUCTURED

This book consists of two parts structurally. Part one contains a series of chapters that set up the theoretical background of parametric thinking, how it is defined, its advantages, how it promotes inquiry into comparative emotive effects, how it is currently being used in industry, how it has been used historically, and what types of futures it predicts and projects. Part two is a manual which teaches you had to operate within Rhino/Grasshopper, the primary tool of parametric modeling for designers.

As mentioned, the chapters in part one provide a diverse overview of parametric theory from leaders in academia and industry. In *The Power of Parametric Thinking*, Jeff Quantz introduces and defines parametric thinking at a fundamental level. Geoff Bell explains many of the ways that parametric approaches are used yet hidden from us in our daily experience in his chapter titled *Invisible Parametrics*. In *Architectonics and Parametric Thinking*, I discuss the relationship between architectonic and parametric thinking and how understanding those relationships deeply can make us better designers. In *Customization's Parametric Play*, Marc Manack and I discuss how the design industry is currently undergoing a radical evolution due to the rise of parametric modes of thinking and working. In *Classical Architecture as Parametric Construct*, Francesco Bedeschi presents the argument that parametric approaches are not new and in fact formed the foundation of classical architecture, a tradition upon which all western design disciplines are built. Bedeschi follows this chapter with another titled *Parametric Thinking and Sustainable Design* which focuses on the values that parametric modeling provides to sustainable design approaches. In *Fabricating Parametric Thinking*, Scott Overall discusses parametric modeling's use in concert with fabrication techniques to revolutionize how products are being made and how the relationship between designers and manufacturers is changing. Finally, in *Spatial Computing, Artificial Intelligence, and the Future of Parametric Design* Geoff Bell describes how parametric thinking and modeling is evolving, including its use in augmented reality and its contributions to pursuits in artificial intelligence. These chapters provide a backdrop as to how the means and methods covered in this book become widely used methods in design practice and how they are theorized in academia.

Part two of the book provides a series of chapters that act as a manual of Rhino/Grasshopper operations. This manual shows, using beautiful and clear graphics, procedures for how to build tectonic 3d models and quickly iterate them based on a series of actions. The opening section, titled *Elements*, is about basic maneuvers and begins with the most fundamental Grasshopper definitions, walking readers through the creation of the most fundamental architectonic forms. Even if you have never opened Rhino/Grasshopper before, this section will provide a clear understanding of its interface.

The manual then progresses into a section titled *Constructions*, focused on basic construction methods. In this section you will build tectonic constructs and manipulate them at an elementary level. In addition, you will learn how to create dimensional changes within individual members, create dimensional changes from member to member, offset members, and affect object shape changes through Boolean (and other) operations. This chapter starts with the construction of elementary Frame, Plane, and Solid Elements and teaches you how to aggregate and compose these elements into more complex objects using Rhino/Grasshopper.

In the final section, titled *Morphologies*, the book walks you through morphological operations that allow you to complexify the architectonic objects. In this section you will operate on objects you learned to create in the previous section, submitting them to various morphological transformations. Morphing architectonic objects is one of the best ways to evolve the forms and also to understand their emotive effects and relationships with other forms.

IMPORTANCE OF LEARNING TO THINK PARAMETRICALLY

Though parametric thinking is likely as ancient as abstract thinking itself, this type of explicit thinking and making within the design disciplines using digital computational tools is still relatively new. Human beings are distinction makers, categorizers. For as far back as there are records to prove it, we have thought of things in terms of their internal and external relationships, as having changeable dimensional properties, and as existing within a malleable type. However, it was not until the evolution of computational processing speed that we had digital tools that could effectively handle large amounts of graphic and dimensional information quickly. This suggests that parametricism is a relatively new way of working that carries with it all sorts of opportunities for young designers who pursue it rigorously.

Parametricism alludes to several new approaches to design which are worth briefly touching upon here but that get discussed in more detail in the beginning chapters of the book and whose assets are exhibited within the *Elements*, *Constructions*, and *Morphologies* section of the book. First, this new way of thinking suggests a growth and evolution of rules-based approaches in design. That is, it suggests that we may begin to direct our efforts towards design approaches wherein a set of rules are instantiated, within which numerous formal iterations are played out to find a best fit or premium solution selected by a designer. Rule-based approaches are not new in art and design, but the refinement and increased speed of parametric digital platforms make these approaches more enticing for designers.

Next, the power inherent within a parametric approach and its already proven effectiveness suggests that anything which can be quantified will be. What's more, even that which is qualitative will be brought into a quantitative domain if at all possible. We are already seeing this done in a sophisticated way with tools like Ladybug, Firefly, Kangaroo, etc. which work in concert with, or "plug-into" Rhino/Grasshopper. As an example, Ladybug gives you access to global weather data and allows easily constructable sun path and wind rose diagrams, psychrometric charts, etc. Similarly, Kangeroo contains an embedded physics engine which allows the user to test certain forms and materials under varying stress conditions. The power of these approaches will be too difficult to avoid for designers and their effectiveness and benefits of their outcomes are already being demanded by many clients.

Finally, rule-based approaches, which create forms that are easily manipulated with the click of a button or the pull of a slider, will mean that the traditional nature of design itself will change. Historically, designers have created objects that are mass-producible, or they have created bespoke objects which are not intended to be repeated. Within the domain of parametricism, there emerged a middle ground to this historic phenomenon. Many designers are now creating mass-customizable objects, each different, yet each existing within the same form language. This is an evolution towards a paradigm shift wherein designers construct rule sets which create objects that fit within a language, but never directly, exactly, or intentionally repeat a form.

This new approach will be driven by emerging and evolving digital tools that designers now have easy access to, but also by a lay audience who increasingly expects larger amounts of control over their environment. This lay audience, who already demands more and more agency within their online digital environments, will insist on having more choice within their physical environments as well. To have exactly the same thing as someone else will become a liability, as people who are used to nearly complete manipulation of their digital environment will begin to demand it of their physical environment as well.

All this being said, parametric design approaches will become the primary way that you create and evolve work during the course of your career. It is important to know both the possibilities and limits of these approaches early in your design career and to learn about them in concert with an education in architectural process. Learning the basics of parametric modeling while simultaneously learning the language of architectonics allows them to exist in a fluid partnership, rather than being seen as two disparate entities whose worlds do not connect at all. The underlying language of architectonics is quantitative and parametric by nature. Pairing architectonic with parametric thinking is a natural fit which makes them both easier to learn and less forgettable as foundational design principles.

This book presents the best, most well-rounded current theory with respect to foundational skills in parametricism and architectonics. By reading the theory and working through the exercises in the book, you will build knowledge in how to use these tools most effectively, but more importantly, you will have a sense of how the tools are continuing to change the design disciplines and what this means for your future role as a designer.

ENDNOTES

1 https://www.etymonline.com/search?q=architectonics

THE POWER OF PARAMETRIC THINKING

Jeff Quantz

Your deadline is tomorrow, and the client has just informed you that a crucial input variable - one that you based your entire design on - has changed. Identifying and updating each element affected by the change is a painstaking process that will require many hours of work. Deflated by the daunting task ahead, you think that there must be a way to avoid this situation in the future. What if there was a way to easily link critical inputs with tangible and intangible elements of your design to incorporate modifications, even late in the design process?

Or, maybe you've experienced this scenario: your current project is wrapping up. You've spent countless hours harmonizing the numerous and competing constraints of the project into an elegant design solution tailored specifically to address the project's unique conditions. Moving on to the next project means starting over from scratch. Copying and tweaking the tangible outcome from the previous project to apply to the new project would be straightforward but wouldn't result in a tailored solution specific to the requirements of the new project. What if there were a way to package the hard-earned rules developed during your project into a reusable system that produces bespoke outcomes addressing the specific criteria of unlimited new sites?

Or this one: you received pricing back from the contractors who bid to build your project. The estimate to construct a featured element of your design made from thousands of unique parts is too high. After seeing the high cost, the client wants to eliminate the custom element and replace it with something cheaper. You're demoralized because these custom elements suit the project's requirements better than standard, off-the-shelf products. What if there were a way to design and fabricate unique components as efficiently and economically as identical ones?

Situations like these are becoming increasingly common in design and highlight the shortcomings of traditional design thinking to solve today's challenges. Projects are more complex with lower budgets and shorter schedules. Designers need a new perspective that reframes the design process from the bottom up to address these challenges. Simply digitizing the traditional strategies used by designers for the past several hundred years has proven insufficient. Designers need to think parametrically.

My aim for this chapter is to demonstrate the power of parametric thinking so students and professionals can harness its benefits and incorporate it into their existing design process. This chapter is not intended as a step-by-step guide teaching a specific software or creating stylized outcomes. Instead, I focus on the underlying concepts that usually remain invisible in the tangible outcome. First, I will define several terms, including *parameter*, *parametric modeling*, and *parametric thinking*. Then, I will discuss the importance of organizing your thinking around a reusable system of rules and relationships. Finally, I will highlight the opportunities parametric thinking enables by incorporating it into your design process.

WHAT IS A PARAMETER?

Designers often borrow technical terms from other fields to describe their designs. The term *parametric* originated in mathematics to describe a specific type of equation. In mathematics, *parametric equations* are a "set of equations that express a set of quantities as explicit functions of a number of independent variables, known as 'parameters'.[1] Simply put, a parameter is an independent variable that you have linked to an outcome with an explicit relationship. Let's look at a basic example of a parametric equation (figure 1).

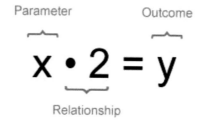

Figure 1: A basic parametric equation (Image by author)

In this example, the outcome of the function is directly related to and dependent on the independent variable x. This link transforms x from an independent variable to a parameter of the outcome y. It is clear what effect changes to the value of x or the relationship linking x with y will have on the outcome. You cannot modify the value of y directly. The value of y is simply a proxy representing the current relationship with the parameter x. To alter the value of y, you must change the value of x or change the relationship between x and y - multiplying by three instead of two, for instance.

Parametric equations become more powerful when you chain them together using the output from one equation as the input for another. Taking the above example one step further, I will define the value of x with a new parametric equation (figure 2) related to a new parameter of x called z.

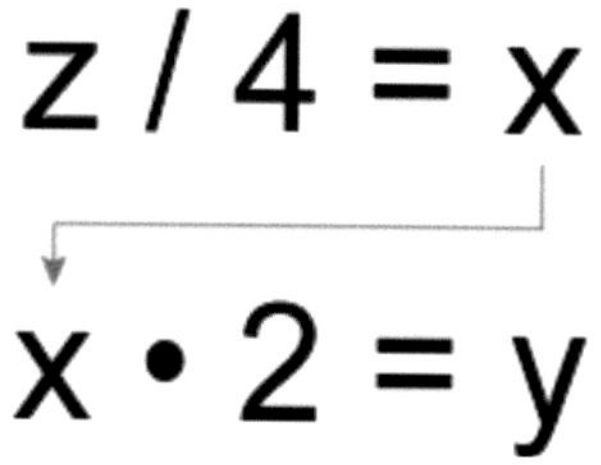

$$z / 4 = x$$

$$x \cdot 2 = y$$

Figure 2: Two parametric equations chained together (Image by author)

Now, the value of y depends on its relationship to x and the relationship between x and z. There is no limit to the number of relationships and parameters that you can link together to express an outcome.

The examples above underscore the concept that "the pivotal part of a parametric equation is not the presence of parameters but rather that these parameters relate to outcomes through explicit functions".[2] This distinction becomes even more important in the context of design. It's because without a direct link tying the parameter to the geometry, any design changes are correlations.[3] Let's look at an example to highlight this.

Suppose you're working on a project which uses a variable for the budget. What happens to the design when the budget is reduced by 30%? Without an explicit relationship between the budget and one or more project elements, you as the designer are free to choose from any number of ways to satisfy the new budget value: reduce the square footage, specify cheaper materials, or eliminate custom elements, to name a few. The explicit link you create between the budget and some tangible or intangible elements of your project clarifies what effect changing the budget will have on the outcome.

WHAT IS PARAMETRIC MODELING?

Parametric modeling takes the concept of expressing outcomes with explicit relationships to parameters from parametric equations and applies it to a geometric model. While there are several definitions of parametric modeling, Daniel Davis provides a simple definition that mirrors the original mathematical definition the closest. According to Davis, a parametric model is "a set of equations that express a geometric model as explicit functions of a number of parameters".[4] Note how similar this definition is to the mathematical one. The only significant difference is substituting "a set of quantities" with "a geometric model". Davis argues that other definitions of parametric modeling "tend to privilege what parametric models do (in terms of model behaviour or stylistic outcomes) but that it is how parametric models come to be (through the construction and maintenance of relationships) that distinguishes parametric modeling from other forms of architectural representation".[5]

Let's look at a basic example of a parametric model and focus on the geometric elements instead of numerical values. Imagine modeling a circle defined by a plane, a center point, and a radius. If I modeled this circle traditionally, I would choose the plane I wanted it to be on - the XY plane, for instance - then either select an existing point in my model or create a new point by typing in its coordinates - I'll assign a value of 8 for the x-coordinate, 3 for the y-coordinate, and 0 for the z-coordinate - to serve as the center point, and finally assign the value of the circle's radius as 1 unit. Modeling this way does not create a persistent link between the circle and its input variables. The circle will be unaffected by any future changes to the values of the variables. To modify the circle, I must transform it directly by scaling, rotating, moving, or deleting it and recreating it with different inputs.

Parametrically modeling the same circle (figure 3) creates a persistent link between parameters and the outcome, which allows you to update the circle after generating it easily. The result is the same: a circle. The difference is how you constructed it. Now, to modify the circle, you simply change the values of the parameters - center point coordinates, radius value, or plane - and the circle automatically updates to reflect the modified parameters.

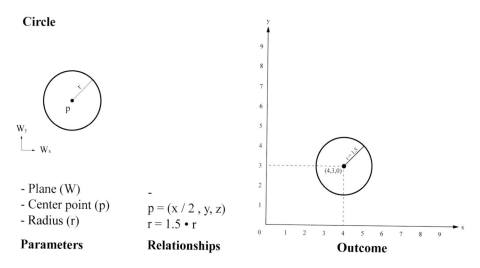

Figure 3: Basic parametric model (Image by author)

The power of this process stems from the fact that each of the circle's parameters (its orienting plane, center point, radius, etc.) are controllable numerically rather than through manual geometric manipulation within the software. I can grow or shrink the circle by quickly changing its numerical inputs. In addition, I can link the circle's size to other attributes of the model (figure 4) such that when they change, the circle's size changes with them.

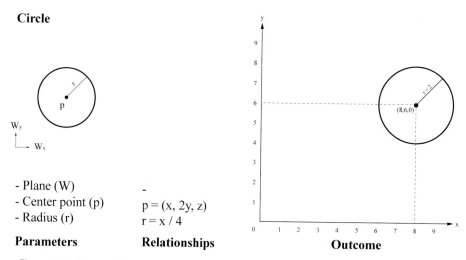

Figure 4: A Parametric model of a circle associating the circle's radius with the x coordinate of the center point (Image by author)

The shift in focus from the creation and refinement of a singular, static outcome to "the construction and maintenance of relationships"[6] highlights the need for a new way of thinking to take advantage of the opportunities provided by this shift. This new way of thinking is called *parametric thinking*.

PARAMETRIC THINKING

In their paper "Parametric Thinking", David Karle and Brian Kelly define parametric thinking as "...a way of relating tangible and intangible systems into a design proposal removed from digital tool specificity and establish relationships between properties within a system".[7] Their definition highlights several characteristics of parametric thinking. First, it echoes Davis' definition of parametric modeling by prioritizing relationships above the creation and iteration of a singular, static object. Second, it reinforces that parametric thinking is independent of any digital tool; parametric thinking could be entirely analog. Most importantly, their definition introduces the concept of a system as the primary means to organize the rules and relationships linking parameters with their corresponding outcomes.

A system is a bottom-up approach to the design process that "asks architects to start with the design parameters and not preconceived or predetermined design solutions".[8] This bottom-up approach ensures that the outcome responds to the project's specific conditions instead of a top-down design approach which forces a preconceived design onto the site. It also "...puts less pressure on the designer to generate the right design and more pressure on them to ask the right questions".[9] Therefore, parametric thinking recasts the designer's role from a designer of individual objects to a designer of systems, each capable of generating many objects.[10]

For a system to be effective, it needs clearly defined inputs and instructions that dictate precisely how the parameters relate to the outcome. The term for this set of instructions is an *algorithm*. An algorithm is simply "a finite sequence of explicit, elementary instructions described in an exact, complete yet general manner".[11] If you've ever followed a recipe to cook with, you're already familiar with the concept of an algorithm. The algorithm creates the outcome based on the instructions you've provided. This allows you to templatize unique methods and transfer key learnings from project to project, so you never have to start from scratch.

The systems-based approach underlying parametric thinking presents the designer with many opportunities, including easily incorporating design modifications, deferring major decisions until late in the process with no impact on the project schedule, outcomes that respond and adapt automatically to local project conditions, and the ability to design, coordinate, and construct unique elements as efficiently as identical ones.

DESIGN MODIFICATIONS

Take a moment to think about your current design process. What are the steps required to make a design modification? Traditionally, modifications require finding each part of your design affected and directly updating it. For simple designs, this targeted process is quick and intuitive. But, as the complexity of the design grows and modifications become more frequent, manually updating individual elements becomes tedious and time-consuming. Each change can take hours or days to incorporate. This stifles creativity and leads to less exploration of potential design solutions. In addition, focusing only on the discrete parts of the design and not thinking holistically can lead to unforeseen consequences that result in poorly coordinated design solutions.

Parametric thinking requires creating a system of interactive relationships that become an integral part of your design process. The links established within your system dictate how it will respond to design changes. Therefore, updating parameters or their relationship with elements of your design updates both the elements and their associations with corresponding elements. "[T]he real benefit of learning to think parametrically," according to Davis, "comes from the cost of design changes."[12] Davis here refers to both economic and time costs associated with making changes during the design process.

Not all modifications, however, can be easily incorporated into your system. Modifications that affect the elements' form, fit, or function are challenging to incorporate. This is why "...it is necessary to define the precise scope of the system"[13] at the onset of the design process. Clarifying the scope of your system at the beginning will clarify which modifications your system can absorb and which modifications require a new system.

For instance, after consulting with your engineer during the early design phase, you select steel as the structural system for your project. With this assumption, you anticipate common modifications of steel structures and design your system to incorporate them easily. These may include structural grid spacing, member profiles, and framing orientation. If halfway through design, the price of steel doubles and the client requests switching to a cast-in-place concrete structure, it would be challenging to adapt your existing system created for a steel structure to address this change. Cast-in-place concrete's form, fit, and function are different enough from steel to warrant a separate system specific to the inherent characteristics of concrete.

No single system can or should incorporate all current and future functionality. Systems that attempt to are slow, difficult to manage, and prone to errors. Systems require constant scrutiny to strike the right balance between being limited and "brittle",[14] which can break during minor modifications, versus being expansive and unmanageable by attempting to foresee and incorporate all possible future changes. Rick Smith, the person responsible for developing and implementing the digital workflow at Gehry Partners to accurately and economically build complex projects, including the Walt Disney Concert Hall and the Guggenheim Museum in Bilbao, remarked that in aviation design, "...parametric models are strictly for much smaller assemblies and subassemblies...there is no concept for parametrically controlling an entire airplane. It simply is not done."[15] Therefore, it is better to split complex systems into several smaller ones which share an interface. Smaller self-contained systems are easier to manage, run faster, and make finding and fixing errors more straightforward. And similar to parametric equations, you can chain systems together using the output from one system as the input for the next.

DELAYED DECISION MAKING

If design modifications are quick and painless to implement, you can delay decisions until later in the design process when more and better information is available. The traditional design process is broken up into phases of work, moving from a vague concept to a high-fidelity design solution required for construction. Each phase adds more detail and specificity to the design and bases its decisions on the outcomes of preceding phases. Therefore, major decisions need to happen in the early phases of the project for the design to progress. Lingering questions can delay the project. Worse still, revising early decisions in the later phases is difficult and expensive because of the amount of rework required due to the increased detail and specificity inherent in the later design phases.

Parametric thinking decouples major decisions from the critical path. The relations created between parameters and corresponding elements enable placeholders to stand in for the exact value until you decide on a solution. Once finalized, you replace the placeholder, and the change will permeate the design automatically and update the affected parts. Decisions can happen at the beginning, middle, or even the end of the design process.

VERSIONING

Associating input parameters with your design elements offers additional benefits beyond painless design modifications and delaying major decisions. Recall the concept from parametric equations that outputs are directly expressed by their relationships with input parameters; changing the inputs changes the outcome. Therefore, a single system can produce vastly different outcomes simply by providing it with different inputs. This ability of your system is called versioning.

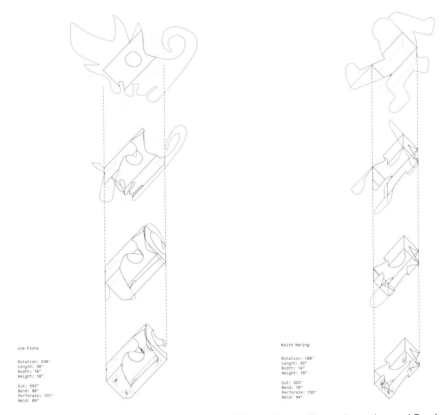

Figure 5: Two versions of the nFold Table using different inputs (Image by author and Frank Jacobus)

Versioning goes beyond any superficial or predetermined aesthetic. "Traditionally, the term implies the copying of a type or original. Yet, in this context, versioning should not be understood as originating from a singular identifiable model, prototype or master form in which all variations or evolutions can be measured by, or traced to, one specific source".[16] In fact, two versions of a single system (figure 5) might look completely different. Each version is the manifestation of the interaction of your system of rules and relationships with specific input constraints and conditions present on each project. So while the versions may appear different, they are each appropriate responses that address local requirements given as inputs.

To achieve this, "[v]ersioning relies on the use of recombinant geometries that allow external influences to affect a system without losing the precision of numerical control or the ability to translate these geometries using available construction technology".[17] The ruleset embedded within your system controls how the "external influences" affect the tangible and intangible elements in a precise way, enabling rigorous control holistically. The versions would remain unrealized without the ability to manufacture the infinite variety made possible by your system efficiently. Pairing parametric thinking with advances in digital fabrication tools allows for the necessary customization to happen on a large scale.

MASS-CUSTOMIZATION

Until recently, your system's capability to produce infinite variety was too inefficient and cost-prohibitive to build. The constraints of mass-production, the predominant manufacturing method for the past century, favor large quantities of standard elements over small quantities of unique elements. Custom elements needed to be standardized to make them cheaper and more efficient to manufacture, resulting in outcomes that were not as specific to the project to address its unique conditions. Parametric thinking, paired with digital fabrication tools, unlocks a new opportunity, called mass-customization, to manufacture custom parts on a large scale economically and efficiently.

Mass-customization depends on the ability to transition from the virtual to the physical seamlessly. Before digital fabrication tools, designs needed to be deconstructed and described prior to manufacturing. This intermediate step often resulted in errors or omissions in the realized form as information was lost or misinterpreted. Now the outcome of your system is captured precisely in a digital file and transferred to a computer-controlled machine capable of producing it exactly as designed. The direct exchange from design to machine eliminates any loss of information and enables accurate results for even the most complex parts.

In addition, you can close the feedback loop between the digital fabrication tool and your system by adding the manufacturing process constraints into your system of rules. Doing so ensures that all outcomes are buildable from the onset of design and won't need to be rationalized in order to be manufactured. Embedding the manufacturing constraints within your system means that "[v]ariety no longer compromises the efficiency and economy of production"[18] and extends the range of design possibilities beyond the limitations imposed by traditional market forces. This enables individual elements to be customized "... to allow for optimal variance in response to differing local conditions...."[19]

CONCLUSION

Designers today face more challenges than ever before. Increased project complexity, tighter budgets, and shorter schedules compress the window designers have to craft tailored solutions that meet the constraints unique to each project. The bulk of the contemporary designer's time is now spent modifying individual elements and tracking down and updating the ramifications throughout the holistic design.

Until recently, this forced designers to make a choice: rely on previously designed elements, proven details, and standard components, limiting the ability to marry the design with the project constraints, or finding a client willing to pay for a bespoke design solution. Parametric thinking offers designers a third choice: a customized design solution with the same speed, precision, and economy provided by a standard, less tailored design. Incorporating parametric thinking into your design process allows you to focus more on what you do best: designing.

ENDNOTES

1 Weisstein, Eric W. CRC Concise Encyclopedia of Mathematics. Boca Raton, FL: Chapman & Hall/CRC, 2003.
2 Davis, Daniel. "Modelled on Software Engineering: Flexible Parametric Models in the Practice of Architecture" PhD diss., RMIT University, 2013.
3 Ibid.
4 Ibid, 31.
5 Ibid, 18.
6 Ibid.
7 Karle, David and Brian Kelly. "Parametric Thinking." Proceedings of Parametricism ACADIA Regional Conference, Lincoln, NE, March 2011, 109–113
8 Ibid, 110.
9 Ibid.
10 Alexander, Christopher. "Systems Generating Systems", Architectural Design, no. 7/6 (London: John Wiley & Sons, December 1968).
11 Menges, Achim, and Sean Ahlquist, eds., *Computational Design Thinking*. Chichester, United Kingdom: John Wiley & Sons, 2011, 11.
12 Davis, Daniel. "Modelled on Software Engineering: Flexible Parametric Models in the Practice of Architecture" PhD diss., RMIT University, 2013.
13 Kolarevic, Branko, and José Pinto Duarte, eds. *Mass Customization and Design Democratization*. Abington: Routledge, 2018.
14 Davis, Daniel. "Modelled on Software Engineering: Flexible Parametric Models in the Practice of Architecture" PhD diss., RMIT University, 2013.
15 Smith, Rick. "Technical Notes From Experiences and Studies in Using Parametric and BIM Architectural Software," (2007): http://www.vbtllc.com/images/VBTTechnicalNotes.pdf
16 SHoP, Sharples, Holden, Pasquarelli, eds. "Versioning: Evolutionary Techniques in Architecture," Architectural Design 72, no. 5. (London: John Wiley & Sons, Sept/Oct 2002).
17 Ibid, 7.
18 Kolarevic, Branko, and José Pinto Duarte, eds. *Mass Customization and Design Democratization*. Abington: Routledge, 2018.
19 Ibid, 3.

INVISIBLE PARAMETRICS

Geoff Bell

There is a certain tendency among architects to make everything a stylistic choice, or to express the parti that drives the design. This has been largely true of parametricism, or at least the brand of parametricism that is often talked about in academic circles or blogs. In the same way that we want to express materiality, structure, and function, many designers have sought to express the parameters and algorithms of a design through the final form and details. The famous "what does a brick want to be" quote from Louis Kahn perfectly expresses the dichotomy of forms that flow out of the internal systems of a material and what it means to deny it, or at least work around its innate order.

You say to a brick, "What do you want, brick?" And brick says to you, "I like an arch", And you say to brick, "Look, I want one, too, but arches are expensive and I can use a concrete lintel." And then you say: "What do you think of that, brick?" Brick says: "I like an arch".[1] Louis Kahn

The same is true of parametric systems - though some may lead a designer to certain forms, at the core, parametric systems are simply a set of rules, with inputs and outputs. A parametric system will have rules that drive its output based on the inputs that are fed into it. All around us are systems and interactions that are governed by this logic of rules with inputs and outputs that determine how things will grow and adapt. Everything from the structure of galaxies to the DNA that drives the development of cells in our bodies has built-in parametric systems that drive their form. The first step to learning how to become a parametric thinker is learning to recognize these systems that are all around us. By learning to understand the parameters that govern a system, whether by nature or by design, we as designers can be empowered to work within those systems or even to create new parametric systems to produce a desired output.

In fact, architecture by its very nature is parametric. Oftentimes in architecture, the word "parametric" is applied to a certain style or approach to form-making, but parametric thinking is an integral part of the design process. Even if a designer is uninterested in algorithms or coding or parametricism as style, understanding the parameters that drive the logics of a design is critical to creating a successful work of architecture. An algorithm is just a series of steps, or a process to find an outcome. The size of a column is an output of a calculation which takes as an input the forces that can be expected to be applied to it. Designers looking to employ natural light in a space might extend an overhang based on the solar angles at certain times of the year. Spaces are sized according to occupancies as defined in building codes, and the overall mass is often governed by rules encoded into zoning laws - Floor Area Ratios, required setbacks, and lot coverage are all rules that determine outputs that a designer can work from.

NATURAL SYSTEMS

Before expanding on this further, it's worth taking a step back and exploring the ways parametric thinking can help us understand the laws that govern the natural world as well, and how that thinking can help inform our own designs. Nature is a master of parametric design, and we are only just beginning to learn how to catch up. In fact, many of the algorithms that might be considered staples of "parametric design" draw their core principles from, or even try to mimic, natural systems. Examples of this include tree branching and L-Systems, fractals and snowflakes, or spirals and Romanesco broccoli; even the phenomenon of fungus searching for food sources can mirror many pathfinding algorithms.

Patterns

Humans are naturally attuned to recognizing patterns. The forms we know as Platonic solids - pyramids, cubes, octahedrons, dodecahedrons, icosahedrons (figure 1) - were described by the Greek philosopher Plato, in his c. 360 BCE dialogue *Timaeus*, as having associations to basic elements, in an attempt to describe the patterns of the universe. Nearly two millennia later, Johannes Kepler again used the platonic solids to describe his understanding of the universe. In *Mysterium Cosmographicum*, Kepler theorized that the relationships between the orbital distance of the (up to then) six recognized planets, could be understood by enclosing the circumscribed forms within each other, all within a sphere.[2] Though mistaken in its conclusions, the model represents humanity's innate desire to recognize patterns in the natural world.

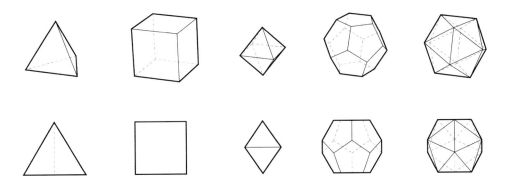

Figure 1: Platonic Solids (Image by author)

Natural Patterns

We don't have to look at such a large scale as the solar system, however, to begin to sense the patterns that form in nature. Patterns occur all around us, and many in fact have been described and repeated mathematically, forming the basis for a number of common "parametric" algorithms still in use in a variety of contexts. We can find patterns in natural symmetries, the branching of trees, spirals, the flocking of birds, meanderings and flows, ocean waves and sand dunes, tessellations and arrays of shapes, bubbles, and the forming of cracks in surfaces. In his book *On Growth and Form*, D'Arcy Wentworth Thompson described similarities in form among biological and mechanical structures, noting for example, the correlations between the internal structure of avian bones and common truss designs. He also described the relationship between the spiral structures found in plants and the Fibonacci sequence.[3]

The Fibonacci sequence is one such "parametric" system that is commonly seen as an example of mathematical influence on form and pattern. The sequence is formed by calculating each number as the sum of the previous two numbers - for example, starting with 0 and 1 as the initial inputs, the sequence emerges as 0, 1, 1, 2, 3, 5, 8, 13, 21, 34, 55, 89, 144, and so on. By applying form to this sequence, a series of square tiles with side lengths corresponding to the numbers in the sequence and drawing circular arcs connecting the corners of these squares, the Fibonnaci spiral emerges (figure 2). The Fibonnaci sequence and spiral can be found in pinecones and pineapples, the horns of bighorn sheep, the shells of molluscs, the arrangement of seeds in sunflowers, and the cross-sections of cabbages. It also forms the basis of computer science algorithms such as the Fibonacci Search Technique.

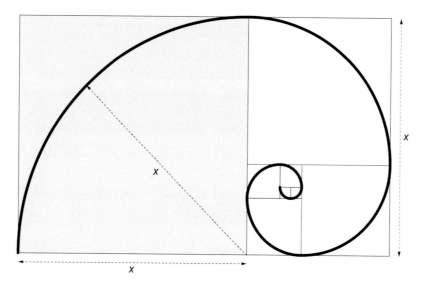

Figure 2: The Fibonacci Spiral, constructed by recursively adding squares with sides equal to the length of the previous two squares (By author)

Self-Organizing Systems

These systems do not have to be so geometrically rigid. Patterns can also emerge from within a system - complexity built up from local, interdependent decisions. A murmuration is a classic example. Murmurations are large groups of starlings that appear to twist and swirl through the sky as a unified organic mass. Though murmurations are perhaps one of the most visually beautiful instances of this "swarming" or "flocking" system (figure 3), it can also be found in vehicular or pedestrian traffic, schools of fish, insects, and even plants. Researcher and programmer Craig Reynolds developed an early system replicating this phenomenon, which he called "Boids," (as a portmanteau of "Birds" and "Droids") which was published at SIGGRAPH in 1987. As a mathematical model, individual elements in swarms generally follow a three-part algorithm:

1. Separation: steer to avoid crowding local flockmates
2. Alignment: steer towards the average heading of local flockmates
3. Cohesion: steer to move toward the average position of local flockmates

Despite the swarm behaving as a whole, an individual bird is only reacting to a relatively small neighborhood of the six or seven closest neighbors. These thousands of individual parameter-based decisions build up to an organized system, seemingly out of chaos. Order from entropy. This is the concept of emergence and allows for highly complex systems to be built from relatively simple rules.

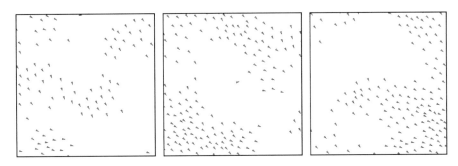

Figure 3: Examples of a swarming algorithm visualized in Processing (Image by Author)

Embedded Logics

Often, the internal logics that define a system do not reveal themselves right away, but are determined over time, or, like flocking, only visible when zooming out to look at the system from a distance. The parameters that inform evolutionary biology, for instance, may not be observable by looking at the shape and size of a beak on a single finch, but by observing variation and change across ecosystems, the patterns of natural selection, and the inputs that enable change, begin to reveal themselves. Or, in the lifecycle of a plant, at a single moment in time, we may not see the effects of transpiration, wilting, decay, gravity and time, but by observing the plant via timelapse, or overlaying multiple moments in time, the forces that shape it become more visible (figure 4). Similarly, in the well-documented chronophoto by Jules Etienne Marey, Joinville Soldier Walking (1883), the soldier's movements are reduced to a series of white lines on a black background, which, when seen overlaid, create a geometrical network that reveal the internal structures of joint rotations, gait, and velocity.

HUMAN-MADE SYSTEMS

Scaling up in size, urban growth also follows many of these same phenomena, and an understanding of these processes can allow one to predict future growth, better plan for eventual urban layouts, and create opportunities for architectural intervention. Some of these systems are more or less organic - people responding to their environment without significant planning - and some are very intentional, pre-determined, and shaped by local or regional authorities.

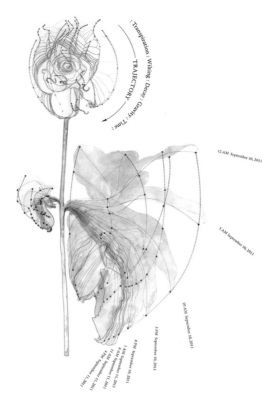

Figure 4: Mapping the decay of a white rose (Image by Author)

Urban Form

The quintessential example of "organic" growth is the medieval city. The streets wind through densely packed corridors in an epigenetic network of spaces that are influenced by, and influence, their neighbors. The scale and density of urban form changes according to a multitude of factors, including topography, climate, water supplies, transportation nodes, and available building materials, in addition to more abstract economic, political, religious, and defensive concepts. Greek cities, for instance, imposed a hierarchy of urban form based on two foci - the Acropolis as the religious center, and the Agora, as the civic center. The rest of the city organized itself around these two points, in a gridded system. Roman cities used the intersecting lines of the cardo (north/south street) and decumanus (east/west street) as a geometrical input of sorts to define the urban development.[4]

In architecture, the primary ways that local authorities govern the built environment are through building codes and zoning. Zoning regulations, especially, perform very much like a parametric system. The idea of Floor-Area Ratios, or FAR (figure 5), is a system of establishing the envelope within which a massing can exist, using as its inputs the area of the site boundary, the footprint of the building, and the number of floors. A zoning district will typically have a predefined FAR, which, when multiplied by the lot size, will output the allowed floor area of a building, which will be further manipulated by the percentage of the site that is built upon, or the number of floors desired. Designers can manipulate these inputs to determine the general forms allowable for their building. Further, in major cities, setback requirements respond to solar angles and the need for natural light in dense areas to define the sectional characteristics of a building. It was the US's first zoning code, the 1916 Zoning Resolution in New York City, that inspired Hugh Ferris's evocative charcoal drawings of imagined buildings. Published in 1929's *The Metropolis of Tomorrow*, these drawings emerged from a systematic interpretation of the parameters put in place by the new zoning law.[5] The constraints put in place by the zoning code allow a framework within which Ferris was able to draw forth expressive forms from as simple an input as a footprint of a site.

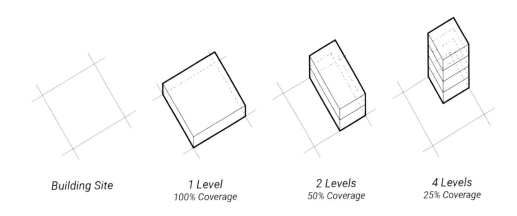

Figure 5: Visualizing permutations of allowable massing with a Floor-Area Ratio of 1:1 (Image by author)

More broadly, zoning is used to govern the overall land use patterns of an area. By defining areas into categories such as residential, commercial, manufacturing, etc., planners define parameters that will cause the patterns of growth in the city to reinforce themselves or evolve. New York City, for instance, uses the three basic categories above, designated (R), (C), and (M), and further modifies them with a number, i.e. R1 - R10, C1 - C8, and M1-M3. In general, a higher number (the input) corresponds to a higher density, or greater intensity of land use (the output).[6]

Industrial Design

Finally, moving back to a smaller scale, we can look to other industries, and how parametric thinking influences the products that we use every day.

In automotive design, for example, the chassis serves as a platform onto which flexible systems can be hosted. A vehicle's "platform" can be defined geometrically as the critical shared dimensions between the centerline of the front axle, the "cowl", between the hood and windshield, and the location of the driver. Within this system, certain dimensions are "fixed", while some are "flexible". The variation of the flexible dimensions, held together by the fixed, creates a parametric system that can be adapted based on the designers' goals. The idea of Platform-Based Design in architecture uses this concept to develop a kit of parts that combines standard interfaces with flexible systems that can adapt to the specific needs of the building, as inputs. Additional inputs might influence the design, such as reduction in wind resistance, which can be tested using wind tunnels or simulated using computational fluid dynamics (CFD) analysis, or safety, for instance the balancing of structural rigidity and deflection in a car's "crumple zone".

We can also look to ergonomics in furniture and industrial design, to see the way inputs, such as the dimensions of the human body, influence the form and location of specific elements, such as the seat height, armrest, backrest, and tilt of an office chair, along with the built-in flexibility to allow the form to adapt to the many different people who might use it. Ergonomics is the process of designing and arranging workspaces, tools, and systems to fit the people that use them, essentially, a parametric system, using the body's dimensions as the input, and, ideally, improved posture and health as an output.

ALGORITHMIC DEPICTIONS

By studying the pattern logic of nature, designers, programmers, and researchers have developed a number of common algorithms that describe and recreate these systems. Flocking is one that we have previously discussed, but others include branching, fractals, and tessellation.

Branching

If you look at a tree, a root system, or even a genealogical record, you can understand the concept of branching. It is one of the simplest examples of recursion. In computer science, recursion is a process in which a function calls itself directly. In this case, the branching algorithm performs the branching function on itself, infinitely, or at least until told to stop. A tree, for instance, will grow and branch until it can no longer support itself, whether structurally, nutritionally, or spatially. The rules of branching are as follows:

1. Take an element and split it into two or more sub-elements
2. Do this again for each sub-element until some rule is satisfied

A good example of a branching algorithm is a Lindenmayer, or "L-System," (figure 6) described by Aristid Lindenmayer in 1968 to describe the growth processes of plants and behavior of plant cells. An L-System is defined as a parallel string rewriting system. An initial string (text) is the input to a set of rules that specify how the elements of the strings are overwritten by new strings. A simple L-System might start with the string "X" and a set of two rules: 1. X=XY and 2. Y=YX. Each time the rules are applied, every time the system sees "X" it will be replaced with "XY" and each time the system sees "Y" it will be replaced by "YX."

Iteration 0: X
Iteration 1: XY
Iteration 2: XYYX
Iteration 3: XYYXYXXY

And so forth.

Since Lindenmayer's introduction, L-Systems have been used many times to generate realistic models of algae, trees, and other plants.

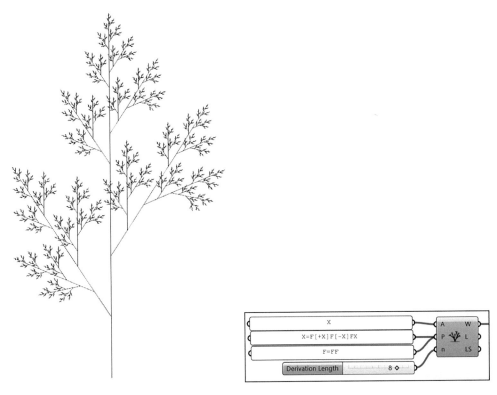

Figure 6: An example of an L-System, generated using the RABBIT plug-in for Grasshopper (Image by author)

Fractals

L-Systems belong to another broad category called fractals. Benoit Mandelbrot first coined the term *fractals* (from the Latin adjective *fractus* meaning *broken* or *fractured*) in 1975, and later expanded on the concept in his 1982 book *The Fractal Geometry of Nature*. In it, Mandelbrot describes a fractal as "a rough or fragmented geometric shape that can be split into parts, each of which is (at least approximately) a reduced-size copy of the whole".[7] Fractals help to define geometry that is too irregular to be described in simple Euclidean terms, which includes many natural systems, like clouds, coastlines, romanesco broccoli, lightning bolts, and snowflakes. In addition to the description above, fractals also by definition feature a fine structure at multiple scales, a self-similar nature, and a simple and recursive definition.[8]

One of the earliest fractals to be described is the Koch Snowflake, by Helge von Koch.[9] This system is built up over multiple iterations, starting with an equilateral triangle and adding new triangles to each edge, recursively. Using the triangular input, the instructions for the algorithm cause the system to become infinitely more complex, and the perimeter infinitely long (figure 7).

1. Divide the line segment into three segments of equal length.
2. Draw an equilateral triangle that uses the middle line segment as its base, pointing out.
3. Remove the line segment from the base of the triangle.

Figure 7: Iterations of a Koch Snowflake (Image by author)

Cellular Automata

The final systems discussed here are cellular automata, developed by Stanisław Ulam and John von Neumann, researchers at Los Alamos National Laboratory in the 1940s, building on Ulam's studies into the growth of crystals, and von Neumann's concepts for self-replicating robots.[10] In his book *A New Kind of Science*, mathematician Stephen Wolfram describes the relevance of cellular automata to biology, chemistry, physics, essentially all branches of science.[11] The nature of a cellular automaton includes three factors: a grid of cells, each cell having a state (on/off, true/false, etc.), and each cell having a relationship with its neighbors in a cluster. With each iteration of the system, each cell will change its state according to the input rule and its neighbors' states.

A well-known example of this is the "Game of Life" developed by British mathematician John Horton Conway in 1970. The evolution of this system relies entirely on the initial input of cells,

Figure 8: An example of a cellular automaton, based on Conway's Game of Life, generated using the RABBIT plug-in for Grasshopper (Image by author)

and the outcome is determined over multiple iterations by the set of rules:
1. A live cell with two or three live neighbors will survive.
2. A dead cell with three live neighbors comes to life.
3. Otherwise, the cell dies (or stays dead).[12]

Though taking place in two dimensions, the system can be visualized spatially by overlaying each iteration vertically (figure 8).

If there is one take-away from this chapter, it should be that parametricism need not be expressed according to any preconceived style or form, but in fact, parametric systems are all around us. Parametric thinking, then, begins by training your mind to recognize these systems, and to understand how inputs to the systems influence the outputs, creating infinite variation.

Parametric design is not limited to form-finding and theoretical exercises but is a powerful tool to respond to and shape the environment around us. Though there can also be great joy in the unexpected "emergent" results that sometimes come from parametric design (and natural systems), parametric thinking is all about designing the system that will properly get you from input to desired output.

ENDNOTES

1 Lesser, Wendy. 2017. *You say to Brick: The Life of Louis Kahn*. Farrar, Straus and Giroux.
2 Bartusiak, Marci. *Archives of the Universe: 100 Discoveries That Transformed Our Understanding of the Cosmos*. 2006. Vintage Books.
3 Thompson, D'Arcy Wentworth. *On Growth and Form*. 1992. Cambridge University Press.
4 Trachtenberg and Hyman. *Architecture: From Prehistory to Postmodernity*. Second Edition. 2003. Prentice-Hall.
5 Ferriss, Hugh. *The Metropolis of Tomorrow.* Dover Edition. 2005. New York: Dover Publications, Inc.
6 The City of New York. 2021. Zoning Resolution. Article 1. General Provisions.
7 Mandelbrot, B.B. 1982. *The Fractal Geometry of Nature*. San Francisco, CA: W.H. Freeman and Company.
8 Kenneth Falconer, 2003, *Fractal Geometry: Mathematical Foundations and Applications*. Chichester, UK: John Wiley & Sons, Ltd.
9 von Koch, Helge (1904). "Sur une courbe continue sans tangente, obtenue par une construction géométrique élémentaire". Arkiv för matematik, astronomi och fysik (in French). 1: 681–704.
10 Shiffman, Daniel. 2012. *The Nature of Code: Simulating Natural Systems with Processing*.
11 Wolfram, Stephen. 2002. *A New Kind of Science*. Champaign, IL: Wolfram Media, Inc.
12 Shiffman, Daniel. 2012. *The Nature of Code: Simulating Natural Systems with Processing*.

ARCHITECTONICS AND PARAMETRIC THINKING

Frank Jacobus

Architectonic thinking embodies parametric considerations. Our perception of architectonic elements and objects, as defined throughout this book, is entirely based their parameters. For instance, a frame member in a building is perceived as such due to its dimensional properties , which are some of its parameters. A significant enough change in these dimensional properties might make us perceive the frame as a planar or solid figure. As young design students, we learn about architectonics and this way of thinking becomes foundational to our design strategies moving forward. We also learn, classically and rightly, that the most successful path to good design is via energetic iteration. We evolve these characteristics as a way of imagining, discovering, and intuiting how specific forms map most successfully in the given context of programs, in the largest sense of the term. Unfortunately, what we discuss less often is that the iteration of architectonic assemblies, and the fundamental difference in the emotive qualities of these assemblies, is rooted in the evolution of their parametric characteristics.

Parametric thinking is not discussed in earnest in most design programs until a student's second year at the earliest and third or fourth year most typically. This means that the chance to effectively pair the notions of architectonic and parametric thinking is lost, which ultimately results in them being thought of as entirely separate entities. Another significant negative result of this compartmentalization in design education is that parametric thinking is assumed to refer to a type of design which is entirely *other*, not aligned at all with the foundational notions of architectonic thinking and the types of forms that usually promotes. This makes parametric thinking foreign and frightening for many young designers who have been trained with a false notion of difference between these ways of thinking. In fact, this partitioning of architectonic and parametric thinking often makes the word parametric itself a frightening way of working for young, and even seasoned, designers.

We hope to break down this hard distinction between parametric and architectonic thinking and ease the nervousness designers may feel about diving head-first into parametric thinking. This chapter defines both parametric and architectonic thinking in fundamental terms and shows how they are directly related. The chapter also discusses the advantages of iterating architectonic work parametrically and gives examples of how young designers can use this as an effective working process.

DEFINING PARAMETRIC THINKING AND MODELING

As you have read in the previous chapters and will read again later, parametric thinking is not a new phenomenon and is as important to the history of the built environment as architectonic thinking. One of the chapters in this book discusses how parametric thinking was used in the ancient classical world to determine size and proportional relationships between all parts of a building. Parametric thinking is used at all scales, from regional planning to urban design, all the way down to the smallest elements being fit for fabrication.

Parametric thinking is simply defined as thinking in terms of the quantifiable characteristics (parameters) of any object or phenomenon. All parts of an object that can be measured constitute its parameters. We do not need digital tools to think parametrically, but we now have digital tools that afford rapid morphological iteration through the use of parametric logics. Parametric software has translated a way that human beings have thought and constructed for thousands of years into tools that automate what we once had to achieve manually. In this way, these tools have made it faster and easier to work and think as designers. The only caveat to this is that one must learn the software in order to receive the benefits that it promises.

Not too long ago our digital tools had no capacity to automate parametric thinking and modeling. They were not object oriented and parameter based as most of them are now. If a designer drew a building elevation with one-hundred windows and the window size changed, they had to redraw the window and copy/paste it across the façade. There was no automated tracking of base points, spacing, centering, etc., so this was a thankless manual process that took much longer to execute than it does today. The basic promise of parametric modeling tools is that they allow the designer to spend a greater amount of time assessing the object itself, and less time manually drawing and copying individual lines.

DEFINING ARCHITECTONICS

Parametric thinking and modeling maps perfectly with architectonic logics. Similar to the word *parametric*, the word *architectonic* can confuse or frighten even seasoned designers. This book simplifies the discussion of parametric thought and architectonics in order to make it more approachable to all design audiences. Architectonics is often discussed in early design education but rarely systematically defined. This causes many designers to know the term but be relatively unclear about its operative definition. Below we provide basic definitions of the components that constitute the architectonic object.

Our use of the term *architectonics*, or *tectonics* as a common abbreviation within the discpline of architecture, represents the visual syntax that is specific to all design disciplines and is generally related to all of the visual arts. Architectonics is the syntax of architectural form. It includes an object's elemental constitution as well as the often-nuanced relationship between its parts. If we think about form as a language, we can understand architectonics as a vocabulary of elements, aggregated and ordered into a system of communication.[1]

Architectonics is the essential framework from which meaning making in architecture is made possible.[2] In this way, architectonics establishes the underlying basis for formal aesthetics in the design disciplines. The architectonic object is an assembly which includes an aggregation of individual elements communicating through an ordered relationship. Every architectonic object is a quickly discernible whole which contains elements, attributes, and orders; the unique combinations of which help create a specific identity and endow these objects with emotive effects. In this way, architectonics constitutes the beginning organization of feeling within architectural objects.

Of course, the rich complexities found in the built environment are not ultimately reducible to architectonics alone. We make this reduction here so that students gain knowledge of the often-invisible framework which binds architecture's multifarious attributes. The complex content of architecture (program, materiality, structure, history, symbol etc.) can both beautifully obscure or enhance its underlying organization. Where it obscures, it limits our capacity to understand its roots. Our innate emotive response to form is born predominantly from the panoply of elements, specifically sized, proportioned, and ordered, that constitute any object. Our constructive impulse relies on this elemental order as a framework upon which we can build the layered complexity which is inherent in any piece of architecture. As architects and designers, it is our responsibility to understand the nature of this elemental order, to be expert in its ingredients, to know how each is distributed and to what effect. What follows is a dissection of the elements, attributes, and orders that exist within any designed architectonic object.[3]

Architectonic objects are constructed of elements that are perceived as either Planes, Frames, or Solids, or some combination therein. What these elements are called specifically may differ slightly depending on the culture of the setting where their characteristics are being taught. Planes might be referred to as sheets, frames as sticks, solids as masses or volumes, etc. Even so, the general nature of these architectonic elements remains the same. Each of these elements has a parametric relationship to the other. For example, as one enlarges a parameter (width) of a Frame Element, they begin to create a Planar Element. Similarly, as one enlarges one parameter of a Planar Element (depth), they begin to create a Solid Element. Each of these elements is frozen in a parametric process of becoming[4] (figure 1).

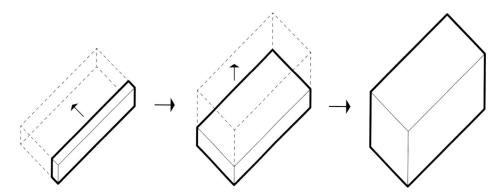

Figure 1: Frame Element Becoming Planar and Solid Element (Image by Author)

Elements that are perceived as Solid are typically volumetrically similar in all directions. If one dimension of a Solid becomes two or three times longer or shorter than any other dimension, then the element typical reads as Frame or Plane. It is important to note that the description of an element as Solid does not imply that it is physically solid, just that is perceptually so. The internal composition of Planes, Frames, and Solids, and of architectural objects in general is not at issue here; it is the perception of those elements that truly matters and the fact that the changing nature of the element depends on the evolution of its dimensional parameters.[5]

When an element is perceived as a Frame it is typically a similar dimension in two directions but at least three or four times longer in one of its directions. The closer the long dimension is in length to the shorter dimensions, the more the frame element looks squat and compressed. The greater the length in the longest direction, and more dissimilar it is from the two shorter dimensions, a feeling of tenuousness and brittleness is the result. Again, major perceptual changes all as the result of seemingly minor dimensional adjustments[6] (figure 2).

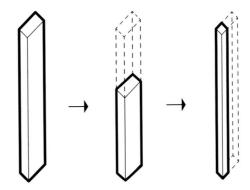

Figure 2: Standard Frame, Squat Frame, Brittle Frame (Image by Author)

An element that presents as Plane typically has one shortened dimension and two others that are elongated but not necessarily similar. As the shortened dimension lengthens, and to the extent that it lengthens, to that same extent will the element begin to be perceived as solid. If one of the lengthened directions shortens and not the other, then the planar element begins to appear as a frame. Through these simple exercises we see that basic architectonic elements exist along a spectrum and their taxonomic positioning depends upon often subtle changes to their dimensional parameters, easily controllable within parametric software.

When we reflect on the elements described above, we notice that the perceived category of each element is determined by the same parametric criteria, height/length/width. For a moment, consider the profound perceptual difference between an extremely thin frame and a robust solid. While the thin frame likely appears fragile and the solid likely appears stable, it was a relatively minor dimensional difference that caused these major effectual changes. One of the powerful things about parametric thinking is that it helps us understand that each of these tectonic elements exists on a spectrum and even subtle changes in the dimensional parameters of an object can have a major impact on how an object or space feels. Parametric software affords the ability to quickly iterate these changes, thereby helping the designer rapidly grasp the perceptual effects that the changes will create.

Planar, Frame, and Solid Objects are primary architectonic categories meant to describe the nature of an architectonic assembly as a whole. In other words, a grouping of Planar Elements would constitute a Planar Object. Planar, Frame, and Solid Objects can be reduced further into three subcategories, those composed of straight extrusions, those composed of formed (bent) extrusions, and those composed of both straight and formed extrusions[7] (figure 3).

Figure 3: Planar, Frame, Solid Object (with Straight Extrusions and Formed Extrusions) from The Making of Things: Modeling Processes and Effects in Architecture (Image by Authors)

As architects and designers, we aggregate and compose elements into an ordered whole to form larger, more complex assemblies. To arrange once independent elements into a cohesive ordered whole is to create a perceptible system that can be counted on, putting viewers and inhabitants at ease as to what might be coming next. To order is to create distinctive relationships between things, it is an infrastructural proposition. When one perceives an object, they are perceiving the spaces between things as much as they are perceiving the things themselves. The relationships formed by the ordered arrangement of architectonic elements is a field condition.[8] The field condition itself is a parametric phenomenon wherein the dimensional spacing between elements can have an enormous impact on the nature of the object or system.

There are common ordering systems such as linear, grid, pinwheel, centric, etc. that represent the common ways designers create order within a coherent architectonic system. All of these ordering systems can be reduced to three primary types, Centers, Lines, and Networks.[9] Because each of these ordering types, along with their subtypes, can be mathematically defined, they are another piece of the parametric definition of any object. Any architectonic object that is composed of an aggregation of these elements has an order, whether clearly discernible or not, that fits into one of the three categories mentioned above.

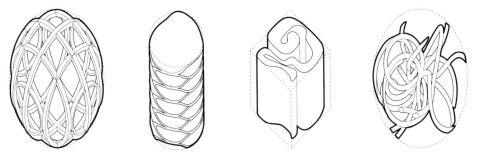

Figure 4: Regularity and Irregularity in each Ordering Type from The Making of Things: Modeling Processes and Effects in Architecture (Image by Authors)

One characteristic of an ordered whole, whether we are discussing a Planar, Frame, or Solid Object, is whether the elements are arranged regularly or irregularly within Centric, Linear, or Network ordering systems. For instance, an object can be ordered linearly but the elements within that object can be arranged irregularly. Similarly, an object can have an order that is Centric, but the elements that are arranged within that order can appear irregularly placed with respect to one another. Conversely, an object can have an order that is a Network, and the elements can fit regularly in relation to one another within that Network.[10]

Figure 5: Densification of Frame Creates the Perception of Solid from The Making of Things: Modeling Processes and Effects in Architecture

For this reason, in addition to their order, architectonic objects can be defined as Regular or Irregular based on the dimensional relationship of the spacing between the elements along their ordered paths. An object falls into the *Regular* category when its elements have a relatively consistent ordering of elements. *Regular* objects have a generally discernible, uninterrupted pattern created by their elements and potentially by the voids between the elements. All spacing does not need to be equal within objects that fit in the *Regular* category as long as one perceives constancy in the arrangement that exists.[11]

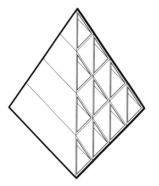 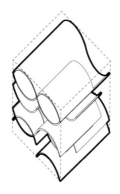 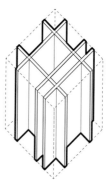

Figure 6: Planar Objects Whose Nature Radically Changes Per the Viewer's Perspective from The Making of Things: Modeling Processes and Effects in Architecture

An object falls into the *Irregular* category when there is not a consistent rhythm and/or order with respect to its constituent elements. When one cannot rationally or intuitively detect an order then an object is considered *Irregular*. This might come about due to a unique array of disparate parts of which an object is composed, varied orientation of those parts, or inconsistent spacing therein. An object being perceived as *Regular* or *Irregular* is also a direct result of the parametric characteristics embedded within.[12]

All architectonic objects are composed of an ordered aggregation of the elements above. By combining these elements into ordered arrangements, we make objects that have a unique identity that can also be classified into the categories of Plane, Frame, and Solid. But density of spacing, whether Regular or Irregular, directly affects the object's reading. For instance, if we compose a series of Frame Elements which are positioned relatively sparsely, then we have an object which reads as a Frame. However, if we have an object made of Frame elements and those elements are tightly packed together, leaving little to no space between the individual Frames, then we have an object that feels more like a Solid.[13]

   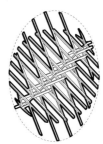

Figure 7: Bounded versus Unbounded Objects from The Making of Things: Modeling Processes and Effects in Architecture

To provide another example, a series of aggregated Plane elements, sparsely placed in relation to each other along a linear axis, would easily be perceived as a Planar object. Whereas a series of aggregated Planes densely packed would be perceived as more closely identified to a Solid object. The proximity and density of an object's elements in relation to each other is also a parametric phenomenon that deals directly with the number and spacing of elements.

Another characteristic of objects that is indirectly related to attributes of sparsity and density is the perception as to whether an object is *Bounded* or *Unbounded*. Objects are considered *Bounded* when their primary geometry is clearly discernible, and they have the characteristic of spatial containment. Objects are considered *Unbounded* when it is difficult to discern the nature of the primary geometry and it seems as though space leaks easily from the object's edges. The Bounded or Unbounded nature of an object is also a parametric quality as it deals with numerical qualities (like density of elements), geometrical qualities (such as the framing of a bounding geometry with individual elements), and similar aspects of element spacing discussed previously.

ATTRIBUTES AND EFFECTS

All architectonic objects are composed of a limited number of formal attributes: balance, scale, proportion, symmetry, light, space, shape, line, color, material, rhythm, and texture. All of these can be affected parametrically. The attributes listed above are what give individual forms their unique character. Below is a list of these object attributes with an indication of how parametric tools can help a designer quickly iterate their qualities. Our hope is that, while you work through the exercises in the book, you consider how the transformation of these attributes parametrically can help you manage the overall qualities of the objects you are designing.

Balance

Balance is a condition in which two forces that oppose one another are brought into equilibrium. This does not mean that the two forces are visually identical, it simply means that the visual weight perceived in one part of an object is relatively equal to the visual weight perceived in another. Within a parametric model, individual elements and/or groupings of elements, can be separately scaled and proportioned to affect the relative balance within an object.

Scale

Scale is an issue of size. It is the relation of the size of one object to another, or the relative size of an object to our bodies. Within a parametric model the scale of individual elements or the entire object can be easily adjusted and readjusted with a slider tool. This allows quick views of the effect of different element scale in relation to one another.

Proportion

Proportion also refers to size but differs from Scale in that it is a relationship of parts to a whole within a given object rather than between separate elements. Within a parametric model one can define each element as a unique member so that its size and location can be changed without changing the size and location of other members. Using this method one can easily affect the proportional relationships within any given model.

Symmetry

Hard Symmetry is the exact correspondence between two sides of an object along a central axis. Soft Symmetry allows for subtle distinctions between the sides but maintains the majority of the equivalence. Within a parametric model there are numerous methods for experimenting with various types of symmetry. As already mentioned, one can create a parametric script that affords the control of individual members of any given object. One can also create a script that reflects elements along a given axis such that there can be effortless axial change with elements who are bound to the constructed axis.

Space

Space is the primary raison d'etre of making architecture and it cannot exist without form. Space is created by varying levels of enclosure born of the ordered arrangement of physical forms.[14] This being said, spatial change occurs within a parametric model through the scaling, moving, adding, subtracting, carving, etc., of individual elements.

Shape

Shape is closed outline, or the perception of closure with regard to a contour. One can define a range of shape change within a parametric model at the scale of the individual element or at the scale of the whole object, or both. This process requires that one thinks of any given shape as existing within a spectrum of shapes and the controls in the parametric model then exist within that spectrum. Often this is done by defining the geometry manually rather than through the script itself.

Line

Lines are the connection between two points. Within a parametric model one can determine whether they desire to manipulate the model at the scale of the point, the line, the individual element, or as a grouping of elements. Within this book, due to its introductory nature and the scale of the objects we are proposing, we primary manipulate the parametric script at the level of the individual element or as a grouping of elements.

Rhythm

Rhythm is created by a patterned interplay of all formal attributes. This most typically is affected by element spacing but could also include more nuanced properties of element width and height. As described earlier, the parametric model allows straightforward management of element size and spacing and therefore is an effective way of experimenting with object rhythm.

The above are many of the attributes of architectonic elements and objects as aggregated ordered assemblies. Architectonics forms the basis for the architectural object as a construct. It is important to understand architectonics as a language in order to gain mastery of form making and its effects. By understanding architectonics, we can more aptly read formal interrelationships, quickly understand new possibilities within any given form as it is affected by outside forces and become more skillful at realizing the origins of emotive effects within architecture. Our intention here is to pair architectonic language with parametric thinking so that, as students learn parametric modeling, they are simultaneously engrossed in the underlying effects of varying architectonic arrangements.

There is a natural fit between architectonics and parametric thinking. The qualitative feelings and effects that architectonics engenders primarily arrive through quantitative means. Learning parametric modeling alongside a study of architectonics allows you to create variations of architectural constructs, whether radical or nuanced, more quickly. Using this process properly, you can spend your time examining the different options, considering the causality of each design decision, etc. rather than drawing and redrawing individual lines. This ultimately allows you to become a better judge of what a final best result would be, having the confidence of someone who has seen and considered a vast array of options.

As already mentioned, parametric modeling is not limited to architectonic issues. Anything that contains a quantifiable character or attributes can be managed using these tools. Even qualitative phenomenon can be assigned quantitative properties in order to examine them parametrically. The capacity of the creative human mind is perhaps the only limitation in this regard. The environmental problems we currently face will be managed using parametric modeling tools. Issues of building construction costs, materiality, programming, site development, etc., all will be managed using parametric modeling tools. The individual and often minute components used to fabricate architectural works will be modeled parametrically.

It will become increasingly important that design students learn to master parametric modeling tools. This will not only allow them to interrogate and evolve their designs more effectively, but it will also allow them to provide the kind of valuable feedback that our clients will expect moving forward. Parametric and architectonic thinking constitute the past, present, and future of form inquiry. While architectonics is the syntax of architectural form, parameters represent its underlying mathematics. The natural interconnections between parametric and architectonic thinking is an important starting point for designers learning parametric modeling.

Learning parametric modeling through an architectural lens creates a more memorable experience for you as a designer. It also affords you a powerful instrument of inquiry which allows rapid iteration and therefore a quicker feedback loop. Since the advent of parametric modeling software, an unfortunate cultural disconnect has been created that sees parametric modeling and early design education as necessarily separate concerns. This disconnect has become a major problem in design education. This book recombines parametric and architectonic thinking, expanding your agency and advancing your knowledge of parametric and architectonic modeling simultaneously.

ENDNOTES

1 Hall, E.T. *The Hidden Dimension*. New York, NY: Anchor Books Doubleday, 1966, 81.
2 Johnson, Mark. *The Meaning of the Body: Aesthetics of Human Understanding*. London and Chicago, IL: University of Chicago Press, 2007, pxi.
3 Jacobus, Frank, Angela Carpenter, Rachel Smith-Loerts, Justin Tucker, and Randal Dickinson. *The Making of Things: Modeling Processes and Effects in Architecture*. New York, NY: Taylor and Francis, 2022.
4 Ibid
5 Ibid
6 Ibid
7 Ibid.
8 Allen, Stan. *Points and Lines: Diagrams and Projects for the City*. New York, NY: Princeton Architectural Press, 1999.
9 Jacobus, Frank, Angela Carpenter, Rachel Smith-Loerts, Justin Tucker, and Randal Dickinson. *The Making of Things: Modeling Processes and Effects in Architecture*. New York, NY: Taylor and Francis, 2022.
10 Ibid.
11 Ibid.
12 Ibid.
13 Ibid.
14 Arnheim, Rudolf. *The Dynamics of Architectural Form*. Berkeley and Los Angeles, CA: University of California Press, 1977.

Much of the description of what constitutes the architectonic objects, its elements and attributes, comes from our previous book titled *The Making of Things: Modeling Processes and Effects in Architecture*. *The Making of Things* sets up a taxonomy of architectonic objects and is a great reference for those interested in inquiries involving formal type, especially with regard to emotive effect.

CUSTOMIZATION'S PARAMETRIC PLAY

Frank Jacobus and Marc Manack

The power of technology is its capacity to amplify human capabilities. Much of the technological space we inhabit in the 21st century is data driven, responsive, interactive, and social. Online commercial and retail vendors all now use data mining, recommender algorithms, and social networking as tools for generating a shopping space that responds to individual desires. In the design disciplines many obstacles to diversity and individuation of space have been overcome in recent years due to mass-customization processes that use parametric digital coding to allow variety in object formation without adding significant increased expenses in production. Architecture is now evolving to meet the demands of this new type of space.

In this chapter we will define and discuss the rise of metadesign and mass-customization in the design disciplines. Using multiple project examples, we will show how parametric modeling is the foundation for these processes and is a large part of the reason that these new ways of making have emerged. As an approach that maintains a deeper connection to the type of digital, fluid, connective space that most human beings now inhabit, these projects represent design and production approaches that enable lay people to take a greater amount of control over their designed spaces. The shapes of designed objects have been relatively fixed historically because of the constraints and economic implications of mass-production. The complexities of the production process have also helped reinforce a division between "designer" and "consumer". This new type of design thinking trades fixity for flexibility in the designed object. The distinct line separating designer and consumer blurs as a result of new parametric processes. In lieu of designing unchanging objects, a designer's role evolves to be one who provides a parameterized formal language and its rules, setting these criteria adrift into the social realm to begin their litany of formal morphologies.

METADESIGN AND NEW MODES OF SPACE MAKING

There has been an explosion of social and user-generated media on the internet over the past twenty years.[1] During these years we have begun moving away from forms of media wherein users are passive receptors of delivered content, towards a paradigm that favors interactivity and user creativity. Software abounds that allows users increasing control over their delivered content. Spotify, Google Play, SoundCloud, Pandora, Last FM, among others, are music listening spaces wherein users have exceptional levels of control over the content being delivered to them, especially relative to recently historic examples. The applications mentioned above collect information about the user's listening preferences in order to suggest new content. Users are becoming accustomed to having high levels of control over content, as well as being habituated to existing in spaces that continually learn about their preferences and then alter themselves towards the user's desires. For designers this should suggest questions and ideas about architectural space-making as it alludes to new design processes. One label for this new design process is *metadesign*, which reflects the new types of protean spaces we are becoming accustomed to online.

Metadesign can be defined as a "mode of integrating systems and setting actions in order to create environments in which people may cultivate creative conversations and take control of their cultural and aesthetic production".[2] Metadesign focuses on the "design of general structures and processes, rather than on fixed objects".[3] This approach allows lay people access to tools that can be used to evolve spatial solutions within a framework provided by a designer. The effect of this is formal variety and continual evolution in product outcome. When translated into an architectural design realm this approach has specific implications for the role of the architect or designer. In lieu of designing objects or spaces, the architect now provides working tools to lay people. Parametric thinking is a way to connect architecture to this emerging digital realm. Parametric properties will be established by design professionals to provide the framework and constraints for individual objects or spaces. Once these parameters are established the design space becomes morphologically diverse but still has boundaries or limits which ensure its manufacturability.

MASS-CUSTOMIZATION AND 21st CENTURY MANUFACTURING PROCESSES

Industrial production techniques have evolved considerably over the past two decades. In *Flexible Manufacturing System for Mass Customization Manufacturing*, the authors define three types of manufacturing concepts. The first type, known as a Standardized Product, has predefined attributes, giving the consumer no choice except whether or not to purchase the product. The second type, known as a Configured Product, allows customers to choose from limited options which the manufacturer has specified. The Configured Product indicates a trend toward mass-customization but limits the extent of that customization for cost purposes. The third type is called a Parameterized Product. This product is built using parametric modeling and as such allows the consumer to significantly modify its features. The Parameterized Product is mass-customizable.[4] Joseph Pine defines mass-customization as a "strategy that [seeks] to exploit the need to support greater product variety and individualization".[5] The goal of this manufacturing strategy is to give the consumer more choice while maintaining the cost advantage of mass-producing the same object.[6]

Over the past decade a number of major corporations have experimented with allowing users to have greater control over product outcome. This signals an evolution from configured to parameterized products. Toyota's Scion cars, for instance, were based on the idea of considerable user customization. A number of large shoe companies have experimented with allowing users to drastically affect the material and pattern choices of the shoes they were buying as well.[7] Similarly, The Lego Group has created software that allows you to design your own objects digitally and have the pieces shipped to you so you can build the physical construction at home. In an article titled *Variety is Free: Manufacturing in the Twenty-First Century*, Joel D. Goldhar and David Lei cite examples of companies providing increasing user choice through digital manufacturing processes. In one example Levi Strauss offers "made to order" blue jeans that are built by entering a customer's measurements into a computer, after which a pattern is sent via phone lines and cut by a robot.[8] Digital tools in this case allow highly personalized information to be translated into a constructed product. In another case Vought Corporation, an aerospace manufacturer, can produce 600 different designs using the same equipment.[9] In this case, understanding the manufacturing parameters and ensuring that each newly designed piece falls within those parameters is essential to Vought's business. These are examples of metadesign practices already in place that are evolving from a configured to a parameterized process wherein individual users are given more opportunity to make decisions about a final product.

In a TED talk titled *A Primer on 3d Printing*, Lisa Harouni describes Additive Manufacturing, as a process whereby lay users manipulate parameterized digital data to arrive at unique products that meet their specific needs and desires. This differs from the variant production process described earlier in that there is an allowable formal morphology within given manufacturing constraints as opposed to a simple exchange of specific product attributes.[10] In another TED talk Paola Antonelli describes furniture that users will be able to customize from their homes and print at a local manufacturing station.[11]

There are numerous software strategies being developed and used that are helping manufacturing processes evolve from the standardized product approach, wherein success is determined by uncovering specific user needs, to a parameterized approach that invests less in specific user needs and more in tools that users are given to arrive at a product that is desirable. One such approach, described by Eric von Hippel and Ralph Katz, is that of "Toolkits for User Innovation".[12] Toolkits for User Innovation are "design tools that enable users to develop new product innovations for themselves".[13] These Toolkits allow users to "create a preliminary design, simulate or prototype it, evaluate its functioning in their own use environment, and then iteratively improve it until satisfied".[14] The application of Toolkits or their equivalent in the architectural realm represents a transitioning from an object centered design approach to an approach that favors the generation of operational structures that allow individual lay users to transform the design space, within a set of manufacturing constraints, to arrive at a desired customized product.

EXPERIMENTING WITH PARAMETERIZED PRODUCTION

To experiment with parametrized production processes, I worked with a group of students from the University of Idaho on a lamp construction project we titled *Drift*. The title originated from the idea that, once a parametric definition is cast out in the social realm, the formal variants become a type of drift, as one sees a litany of variants evolving, many of which were unexpected and many others unwanted by designers who typically seek high levels of control. The intent of our work was to construct the parametric definition for a lamp whose form could easily be manipulated by lay users. This meant that "rules" had to be established within each lamp's parametric definition that would restrict lay users from choosing a formal variant that falls outside the object's manufacturing and use constraints. The intent of this process is to allow lay users the ability to change the formal nature of the object to fit their needs and desires while not changing the inherent method or process of manufacturing. What it suggests for future design processes, as already mentioned, is that the designed object will evolve from the making of a static object, and a fixation on that object's form, to a process that is seen as the creation of a formal language and the establishment of rules for that language. In this scenario designers remain vital in creating form and order in a broad sense and lay users become instrumental in iterating the language to suit their specific needs and desires (figure 1).

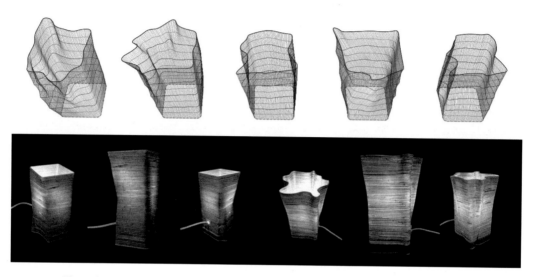

Figure 1: Drift Lamp Shape Morphology, Frank Jacobus (Image by Frank Jacobus)

The underlying nature of this metadesign process was fascinating as it presented a number of new design considerations to contend with. First, we had to design a lamp whose parametric definition was meaningful. In other words, we considered how significant it would be for any lay user to change an object parameter. If the parameter was simply about the length or size of a member, then it probably wasn't significant enough. Second, we had to ensure that the object could be built within a specific amount of time to ensure relatively rapid iteration. Without this constraint it was clear that we were not creating a mass-producible, mass-customizable object. The ultimate goal of the project was to create a user-friendly parametric definition and interface through which lay users could manipulate the lamp's formal qualities into a shape they desired.

Physically constructing the object helped us create an affective definition and set of parametric constraints. By laser cutting parts, for instance, we discovered the constraints of the laser cutter bed, the restrictions of the chosen materials and manufacturing processes, and the effect of assembling the specific material. In addition, knowing the exact function and use of the object, such as whether it was a wall, desk, or ceiling lamp, and what it was attempting to cast light on, etc., helped generate particular object parameters. Determining, for instance, the type of bulb one wanted to use forced us to think of functional constraints such as the ability to reach one's hand in the lamp to loosen or tighten a bulb. These functional considerations became the constraints of the parametric definition and the part of the built-in "rules" that lay users would have to abide by. Figure 1 shows an example of one of the lamps. The original form of this lamp is an extruded rectangle. Height, width, and shape were transformable to a specified extent within the object definition itself. Within this figure the lamp shown on the left-hand part of the image is an example of minor changes made to the original form by a lay user, while the lamp on the right side indicates major changes to the original form.

Another important factor that helped determine object constraints was a desire (by the designer) for lay users to adhere to an object language. For instance, if while building the parametric definition the designer allows too much flexibility within the rules, then certain iterations of the object could become distorted beyond the limits of the object language. In extreme cases the object would no longer seem as though it belonged within the same formal language, in which case its relation to its typological family would be destroyed.

These are the types of discussions that have emerged and will continue to emerge with the rise of parametricism and metadesign. Much of the designer's process is invisible to the lay public. Some of the designer's process is even invisible to the designers themselves. Parametricism and its importance in metadesign will mean that much of what has been implicit in the design process will need to become explicit. The rules that all designers contend with while designing objects will need to be formalized so that the parametric definitions they build provide appropriate boundaries for the lay user.

PARAMETERIZED PRODUCTION MEETS 3D PRINTING

The processes already discussed suggest that an architect's role is evolving away from the development of singular fixed objects and into the conceptualization of objects whose form changes based on the inputs and desires of a lay audience. Future objects will contain, as part of their primary ethos, the capacity for individual responsiveness. Difference, not sameness, will typify the years ahead for spatial production; a world not of forms as individual static objects, but rather of form languages within which individual formal variants are being continually explored.

In *The Alphabet and the Algorithm*, Mario Carpo outlines how the cultural expectation and recognition of objects emerges from the way the object is produced. According to his argument, the pre-industrial process of constructing numerous hand-crafted copies of objects left each one slightly visually different from the next. This meant that visual "similarity", rather than "sameness", was a primary way that people intuitively understood objects. The industrial age transformed this paradigm, allowing us to build as many identical copies as we desired. This evolved our visual expectations from that of "similarity" to that of "sameness". Contemporary digital tools such as CNC machines and 3D printers, in conjunction with parametric software, begin to force another paradigm shift characterized by visual difference from one object to the next, while perhaps maintainging a typological language. The parametric software is virtually a machine of difference within given sets of parameters, and the CNC machines and 3D printers are not particularly punitive when the thing printed or cut changes from one object to the next. If the promise of parameterized production is that objects become individualized to the people who desire them, one can imagine the implications of such a change in design thinking, production methods, and the economics of the made object.[15]

There is currently incredible work being done in the realm of full-scale 3D printing. Ronald Rael and Virginia San Fratello, in their book *Printing Architecture*, provide recipes for printing with numerous materials and reveal some of the sensuous formal resultants.[16] Neri Oxman and her colleagues at the MIT Media Lab have been developing 3d printing strategies with new materials and techniques that are transforming the way objects are made.[17] Similarly, figures such as Achim Menges are invested in questions about new materiality in relation to emerging fabrication types. These are just a few of the now countless examples of experiments in this domain.

Carpo's argument, alongside the groundbreaking work of the figures discussed earlier, establishes a theoretical benchmark off of which we can begin a discussion of the effects and implications of full-scale 3D printing in relation to parametricism. For instance, how is design transformed when parametric thinking into full-scale 3D printing meets normative economic constraints? How do we discuss the litany of formal transformations within the objects themselves; does this revive typological questions and instantiate topological ones? Does the fact or promise of difference achieved through these processes transform the architect's role?

A project that we created called the Type Chair was specifically designed to delve into the questions posed above. The chair was constructed of three-dimensional letters, all randomly oriented into a nest, from which a relatively simple chair shape was carved. Within this project there were a few key questions that acted as design generators. First, how do we create objects that would be difficult if not impossible to produce with methods other than 3D printing? Second, how can we evaluate economic constraints and test the implications of aggressively moving in the direction of general affordability in this regard? Finally, how do we create a system that allows lay users vast formal choice varieties with respect to the final object outcomes (figure 2)?

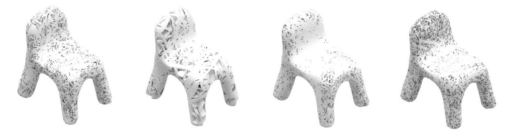

Figure 2: Four Garamond Variants of the Type Chair (Image by Frank Jacobus and Jeff Quantz)

The parametric definition of the Type Chair allowed users to enter any letter, or set of letters that they chose, to choose from a long list of fonts, and to choose a relative size and density of text. Once these choices were made, the parametric tool delivered the formal outcome. The tool worked in real time such that, with additional user input, new formal outcomes would arise virtually automatically. In addition, the script was written in a way that allowed users to see how long the chair would take to print and at what expense.

What the users didn't see, and didn't need to see, was the underlying complexity within the given script. For instance, we divided the chair into six parts, each having their own programmatic requirements. The six divisions are Legs, Joints, Seat Bottom, Seat Top, Chair Back Face, and Chair Back Rear. This allows the parametric definition to specifically define element densities (and potentially sizes) based on specific needs without having to manually perform these operations. At potentially tenuous areas, such as the Joints, where the Legs meet the Seat Bottom, more structural capacity is required and therefore more assurance of letter density was needed. At the Seat Top and Chair Back Front more density was also required for comfort but potentially needed to be a different density level than at the Joints; the allowance for this density creates a smoother, less striated surface. The Legs, Seat Bottom, and Chair Back Rear don't require density for comfort or structure so could each employ different levels of sparsity if desired to save in overall material cost (figure 3). The Chair Back Rear, the Seat Bottom, and the Legs afford a greater allowance for formal liberty than other parts of the chair. Because of this, these areas have an increased capacity to deliver user-desired form, but also have a slightly increased ability to affect overall cost. These are all rule-based details within the script itself which control the users' choices and allow constructability and affordability. Users do not want to be burdened with nuanced construction, material, and economic issues and so, as designers, we need to manage these things behind the scenes.

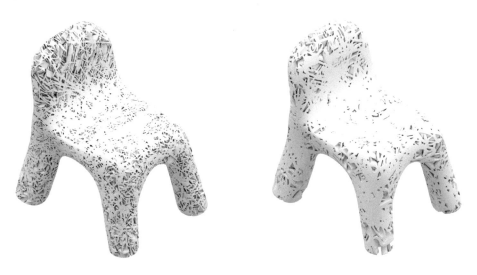

Figure 3: *Type Chair Formal Variants Cost Comparison (Image by Frank Jacobus and Jeff Quantz)*

The Type Chair provides an example of an embedded rule set that limits the potential formal free-for-all that might occur if lay users are given carte blanche. While being given free design reign may seem like a benefit for the lay user, in reality it is not what they're looking for at all. The lay user wants to have just enough choice, and they want the result to be something that works, is buildable, and accounts for time and cost considerations. The Type Chair optimization algorithm embraces rule-based thinking that delivers designed objects for a changing cultural environment which demands more interaction and control.

Development of the Type Chair, and the algorithm used to produce its unique variants, was a foundational full-scale 3D printing experiment situated at the intersection of economics and form. This project considered how underlying, often hidden programmatic considerations for individual objects, must be addressed in relation to economic effects as we move toward parametrized models of object production wherein lay users directly impact formal outcomes.

Though the discourse of 3D printing often centers on the democratization of design by lay users, the reality is that these consumers don't want to assume the responsibility for the conception of these objects, nor do they want to bear the burden of the time it takes to invent, draw, and make them. What it does imply, however, is that they will expect uniqueness in their object environment; a world in which methods of customization will become commonplace, and the inability to customize will be unacceptable. Parametric thinking is vital in this type of design space. Future designers will be creators of form languages and their foundational rules, and they will do so using parametric methods (figure 4).

Parametric designers have an enormously important role to play in this emerging world. As this new way of making evolves, architects will not only have to design objects, but we will also have to understand their DNA and what that means for the object's potential variants. To design in a world of parameterized objects means to go beyond fixed, immobile form and instead design the rules that affect real-time object transformation.

Figure 4: Final Printed Type Chair (Image by Frank Jacobus and Jeff Quantz)

PARAMETERIZED PLAYFUL ELEGANCE

The last of the three projects to be discussed in this chapter is called the nFold Table. It is a playful use of parametric modeling to fold recognizable two-dimensional shapes into an infinite variety of three-dimensional forms. In our case, we used two-dimensional examples extracted from the work of artists such as Ezra Jack Keats, Keith Haring, Jim Flora and others (figure 5).

The basic premise of the nFold Table's parametric definition is that the tool will take any closed curve, scale the curve to a preset size, and then fold it into one of three volume options that are sized to a standard coffee table. On the surface this seems like a relatively simple task, but there are nuances to the definition which are worth discussing. For instance, the definition allows the lay user to quickly alter the orientation of the existing shape. It also rejects shapes that do not meet built-in folding requirements, which account for things such as mounting space for castors, structural stability, etc., and does so without the user knowing that the orientation was rejected. In other words, the tool simply moves to the next orientation and folds the shape from there. Two-dimensional shapes with interior linework can also be uploaded and folded by the script. This allows some visual depth and detail to be included in the final coffee table.

Ultimately, the parametric definition allows lay users to upload any shape they want, it runs through the litany of all possible orientations to select only those that work within the rules we

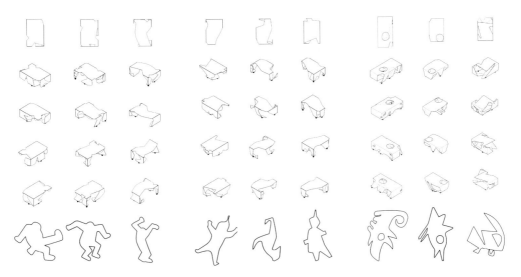

Figure 5: N-Fold Table Variants after Vetting in the Grasshopper Script (Image by Frank Jacobus and Jeff Quantz)

as the designers had established, and it delivers usually between 30 and 40 formal options for users to choose from. Within the script there is even a mechanism that measures weld seam length so that users also have relative cost options presented to them.

Our goal with this project, besides making as interesting and beautiful a coffee table as possible, was to make the lay user's interaction with the tool smooth, allowing them to focus purely on the formal outcomes as they arrive. As projects like the nFold table become the norm, it will be incumbent upon designers to understand the possible hazards for cost, manufacturability, material use, etc., and embed strategies that deal directly with these constraints within the parametric script. The promise of this type of work and thinking is relatively infinite individuation of the designed object.

CONCLUSION

The space of digitally designed environments, both interactive and evolutionary, alludes to new patterns of making in architecture and product manufacturing that favor flexibility and engage new audiences in the design process. The Drift Lamp, the Type Chair, and the nFold Table are examples of new types of design strategies that relinquish some of the controls over individual spaces or objects that the designer once held and allow lay people a greater capability of transforming the designed space. For this to happen, designers' roles must evolve to include a larger focus on the construction of manufacturing frameworks and the establishment of object languages, instead of merely being purveyors of fixed objects and spaces. This design method suggests that designers will learn about an individual problem in order to understand its necessary constraints, and then design the parameterized rules and formal language around those limitations. This process accentuates design as a social activity and aligns with many of the digital spatial types we interact with today.

In the mid-20th century Michel Tapie, Reyner Banham and others became proponents of *un art autre*, a movement which strived for a "dynamic and persuasive alternative to the conventional thinking and operational lores", that in Banham's view, "blighted most contemporary architecture and design".[18] During this time Banham also predicted a "triumph of interactive software that would have the flexibility and rhetorical force of futurism without the baggage of style".[19] The early 21st century design environment seems ripe to take on this challenge. The potential of parameterized design as a social activity affords a new vibrancy in architecture that breaks with conventional thinking about design and the architect's role. When this potential is reached, the outcomes of design will become more fluid, dynamic, and evolutionary.

ENDNOTES

1 Metadesign as an Emergent Design Culture. Elisa Giaccardi. *Leonardo*, Vol. 38, No. 4, (2005), pp. 342-349, 300

2 Ibid

3 Ibid.

4 *Flexible Manufacturing System for Mass Customization Manufacturing*. Guixiu Qiao, Roberto Lu, and Charles McLeon.

5 Pine, Joseph (1993): Mass-Customization: The New Frontier in Business Competition, McGraw-Hill, 1993

6 Ibid.

7 The Practice of Everyday (Media) Life: From Mass Consumption to Mass Cultural Production?. Lev Manovich. *Critical Inquiry*, Vol. 35, No. 2 (Winter 2009), pp. 319-331

8 Variety Is Free: Manufacturing in the Twenty-First Century. Joel D. Goldhar and David Lei. *The Academy of Management Executive* (1993-2005), Vol. 9, No. 4 (Nov., 1995), pp. 73-86

9 Ibid.

10 Harouni, Lisa. "A Primer on 3d Printing". http://blog.ted.com/2012/01/23/a-primer-on-3d-printing-lisa-harouni-on-ted-com/

11 Antonelli,Paola."Design and the Elastic Mind". http://www.ted.com/talks/lang/en/paola_Antonelli_previews_design_and_the_elastic_mind.html

12 Shifting Innovation to Users via Toolkits. Eric von Hippel and Ralph Katz. **Management Science**, Vol. 48, No. 7 (July, 2002), pp. 821-833

13 Ibid.

14 Ibid.

15 Carpo, Mario. *The Alphabet and the Algorithm*. Cambridge, MA: The MIT Press, 2011.

16 Rael, Ronald, and San Fratello, Virginia. *Printing Architecture*. New York, N.Y.: Princeton Architectural Press, 2018

17 Last modified September 24, 2018. Accessed October 3, 2018. https://en.wikipedia.org/wiki/Neri_Oxman

18 Banham and 'Otherness': Reyner Banham (1922-1988) and His Quest for an Architecture Autre. Nigel Whiteley. *Architectural History*, Vol. 33, (1990), pp. 188-221

19 Ibid.

Much of this writing came from two previous published papers by Frank Jacobus, Marc Manack, and Jeff Quantz. The first paper is titled *Beyond Control: Parametrics and Metadesign as a Model for Mass-Customization* and the second paper is titled *The Type Chair: Formal and Economic Optimization in Full-Scale 3d Printing*.

Reviewed but not Cited
Ferre, Albert, and Sakamoto, Tomoko. 2008. *From Control to Design: Parametric/Algorithmic Architecture*. New York: Actar
Borden, Gail Peter, and Michael Meredith. 2012. *Matter: Material Processes in Architectural Production*. New York: Routledge.
The Ontology of Mass Art. Noël Carroll. *The Journal of Aesthetics and Art Criticism*, Vol. 55, No. 2, Perspectives on the Arts and Technology (Spring, 1997), pp. 187-199

CLASSICAL ARCHITECTURE AS PARAMETRIC CONSTRUCT

Francesco Bedeschi

Over the past 30 years, the discipline of architectural design has experienced an increasingly strong transition towards the use of digital tools for drawing and composition. It began towards the end of the 80s with the advent of CAD - Computer-Aided Design - which represented a deep revolution both methodological and conceptual, speeding up the production of two-dimensional drawings and introducing the concept of 3D modeling previously limited to the construction of physical models.

Quickly, there has been a proliferation of ever faster and more powerful tools, equipped with advanced modeling and representation functions that have allowed architects to produce new shapes and geometries controlled by mathematical functions or generated in an automated manner by the software itself.

One of the most interesting examples of this is the work of Frank Gehry who, in the early 2000s, designed memorable buildings such as the Guggenheim, Bilbao and the Walt Disney Concert Hall in Las Vegas, using CATIA™, a software derived from the aerospace industry, and subsequently developing its own 3D digital design platform called "Digital Project".[1]

More or less in the same years, we witness the birth and subsequent development of another computerized design tool, Building Information Modeling (BIM), a term used for the first time in 2002 by Jerry Laiserin,[2] and which has now become a standard spread all over the world and characterized by the ability of the software to manage multiple dimensions of the design and construction process, instead of just replicating the ability of hand drafting within a digital platform. In fact, the projects carried out in BIM include the analysis of duration and times (4D), cost analysis (5D), the management phase of the work (6D), and finally the assessment of sustainability (7D)[3].

Parallel to the two previous examples, towards the end of the 2000s, we witnessed the birth and subsequent rapid development of another approach to architectural design based on the use of so-called "parametric" or "algorithmic design" tools. The main interpreter of this philosophy is Patrik Schumacher, a long-time collaborator of Zaha Hadid and, since 2016, director of the Zaha Hadid Architects studio after the death of the founder. In 2008, Schumacher was the first to coin the new term *parametricism* in one of his famous writings: "Contemporary avant-garde architecture is addressing the demand for an increased level of articulated complexity by means of retooling its methods on the basis of parametric design systems. The contemporary architectural style that has achieved pervasive hegemony within the contemporary architectural avant-garde can be best understood as a research programme based upon the parametric paradigm. We propose to call this style: Parametricism."

Parametricism is the great new style after modernism. Postmodernism and Deconstructivism have been transitional episodes that ushered in this new, long wave of research and innovation."[4] Schumacher clearly speaks of "innovation" and there is no doubt that these tools have exponentially expanded the creative capacity of modern designers, paving the way for completely new forms of design especially if we think of the integration that these tools allow, for example, with the emerging 3D printing techniques of both architectural components and even entire buildings.

I have always followed the evolution of these tools since their origin, and in 2013 I had the opportunity to deepen the study and application of parametric design techniques as part of a post-professional Master of Architecture at the CASE - Center of Architecture Science and Ecology of the Rensselaer Polytechnic Institute of NY.[5]

It was a very significant experience that allowed me to fully understand the operating logic of these tools and their applicability in various areas of architectural design. At the same time, I was able to reflect on the similarity between this type of so-called innovative design and the construction methods of classical architecture codified for the first time by Marco Vitruvio Pollio in the first century BC in the famous treatise "De Architettura", a work rediscovered and translated in the Renaissance, which formed the foundation of western architecture until the end of the 19th century.

As is well known, classical architecture is based on the use of architectural orders both from a constructive point and architectural language point of view, especially in ancient Rome, when we witness a fusion between the trilithic system of Greek derivation, and the vaulted arch system introduced by the Roman builders.

If we analyze in depth the great monuments of Imperial Rome such as the Colosseum, built in Rome in the 1st century BC, one can understand how the proportions of the building, as well as all the details of the various construction elements, are strictly controlled by the four overlapping classical orders: the Doric order on the ground floor, the Ionic order on the first floor, the Corinthian at the next level and finally a further undefined order, called Composite and in fact used only in the Colosseum. The historian of architecture John Summerson in the book "The Classical Language of Architecture",[6] offers us an introduction to the stylistic elements of classical architecture and traces their use and variations in different eras: in particular in Chapter 2, dedicated to the grammar of antiquity, the author describes in great detail the geometrical and proportional relationships that exist between the various components of a bay of the Colosseum and which are intimately linked to the different architectural orders used.

If we pause to reflect on the fundamental rule that determines the composition of an architectural order, that is the diameter of the column, we can easily derive the concept of "parameter" as the dominant module of the compositional process. A process, which in the classical era, was guided by the search for harmony between the parts, obtained through the control of proportions, or as Summerson himself says, "by ensuring that the ratios in a building are simple arithmetical functions and that the ratios of all parts of the building are either those same ratios or related to them in a direct way".

It is therefore clear that, long before the advent of modern parametric design tools governed precisely by the definition of mathematical algorithms, the architects of the past used the same methodological approach although declined in various articulations.

It is important to remember how, from the second half of the 1400s and for the following four centuries, the great masters of architecture gave life to a series of personal interpretations of the classical rules indicated by Vitruvius. Leon Battista Alberti was the first to describe the classical orders partly referring to Vitruvius and partly on the basis of his own direct observations of classical monuments. Sebastiano Serlio, almost a century later with his work "The Seven Books of Architecture"[7] wrote the first architectural treatise whose purpose is more practical than theoretical and is the first to codify the five architectural orders of the modern era, helping to spread the classicist language and the new Mannerist trends throughout Europe.

Even illustrious masters such as Vignola in 1562, Palladio in 1570, and Scamozzi in 1615 published their studies on classical architecture and the use of the architectural order, generating their own interpretative theories and establishing each, on their own, the mathematical and proportional rules at the base both of their own theoretical speculations and by applying them in their realized buildings.

In light of such a variety of interpretations, it is interesting to quote Summerson again when he says, "so it is a mistake ever to think of the 'five orders' as a sort of child's box of bricks which architects have used to save themselves the trouble of inventing. It is much better to think of them as a grammatical expression imposing a formidable discipline but a discipline within which personal sensibility always has a certain play - a discipline, moreover, which can sometimes be burst asunder by a flight of poetic genius."

The poetic genius of which Summerson speaks is certainly found in the work of another great master of the past, Francesco Borromini (1599-1667), a true genius of architecture, capable of pushing the architectural composition to a level never seen in precedence. In his most daring works such as the famous Roman churches of San'Ivo alla Sapienza and San Carlino alle Quattro Fontane, it is possible to clearly read Borromini's interest in irrational numbers, i.e. those numbers that express the relationship between the circumference and its diameter, between the side and the diagonal of the square, between the smaller side and the diagonal of a rectangle that has a ratio of 1: 2 between the sides.

Also, in this case we are faced with an "algorithmic" approach in which it is possible to establish numerical and proportional relationships between all parts of the building which is therefore happily balanced and harmonious.

Together with Borromini, it is necessary to mention another great interpreter of the relationship between mathematics and architecture: Guarino Guarini (1624-1683).

The architect and mathematician, in addition to having left us absolute masterpieces such as the Chapel of the Holy Shroud in Turin, wrote an important treatise on mathematics and geometry in which there are various architectural references such as, for example, the XVIII treatise concerning the problem of the measurement of the circle and of particular curves such as the spiral, the square, the ellipse, the shell, the cycloid, taken up by the Greeks and analyzed by many mathematicians and scientists of the time; the XXIV treatise, which concerns the conic sections, of fundamental importance both for their applications in the astronomical field and for the development of Desargues' projective geometry, and the XXXII treatise, which concerns the development on a plane of curved lines and three-dimensional surfaces and interpreted by some critics as a theoretical illustration of the results obtained in the construction of the vaults.[8]

Therefore, it is evident that since ancient times, passing through the Renaissance and the Baroque, there is a clear relationship between the architectural composition and the rules of mathematics and geometry. This relationship has governed the work of the great masters of the past who, within these rules and relationships, have been able to generate forms and spaces of great complexity and harmony.

In the 20th century we meet another great architect who was the first to define the concept of "parametric architecture", anticipating Patrik Shumacher's formulation on "Parametricism" by about 60 years. Luigi Moretti (1907-1973) one of the greatest interpreters of the Italian rationalist movement and author of great masterpieces of modern architecture, including the Casa delle Armi at the Foro Mussolini in Rome, the Casa del Girasole in the Parioli district of Rome and the Casa GIL in the Trastevere district of Rome.

Moretti between 1950 and 1954 was also the director of "Spazio" a magazine of art and architecture and in 1951 in the Spazio 6 issue he published an essay entitled "Structure as form" where he defined the terms *form* and *structure* and introduced the term *parametric architecture*. Alicia Imperiale, in her article entitled: "An 'Other' Aesthetic: Moretti's Parametric Architecture" published in Log, Fall 2018, No. 44 (Fall 2018), pp. 71-82[9] offers us an in-depth reading of Moretti's thought with respect to the theme of parametric architecture when she writes: "Moretti's notion of the parametric initially defines his parameters. Translating those parameters into a measurable quantity, he used them to analyze and make logical comparisons between different elements, devising a *parametric* architecture in which the mathematical relationships among all parts of a building are designated at the outset. At its core, this approach reflected his embrace of scientific method as a design principle and as an expanded idea of function in architecture. The careful selection of parameters would provide an objective balance between form and function."

Moretti also elaborates a series of studies for the construction of a stadium based on the principles of equivalence in the vision of the field by the spectators seated in the stands. He introduces the concept of "performance" as a starting point for the design of the space, linking it to the needs and desires of the occupants and for this reason he is applauded by Bruno Zevi, one of his greatest critics.

It is also worth remembering that Moretti, in his studies for the parametric design of stadiums, uses the first electronic computers to manage the large amount of data in an automated manner.

AN EDUCATIONAL EXPERIENCE

I would now like to illustrate an educational experience that I conducted in the architectural design courses at the University of Arkansas Rome Program in the academic years 2017/2018 and 2018/2019 in which I worked with my students to define a construction process of parametric models of classic buildings using the Rhino5/Grasshopper™ software.

The idea was born from the desire to combine innovation and tradition in educational processes: there is no doubt that architecture students entering the world of work in the 21st century must have basic skills in the use of parametric modeling software; at the same time the study experience in Rome offers them the opportunity to interact directly with the great masterpieces of the past made by masters of the caliber of Donato Bramante, Michelangelo Buonarroti, Gian Lorenzo Bernini, or Francesco Borromini.

The objective of the exercise was to teach the use of parametric modeling software by decoding the compositional rules adopted by the great architects of the past by means of the direct analysis of some buildings in Rome. The module of the architectural design course called "investigations on parametric orders" was divided into three phases.

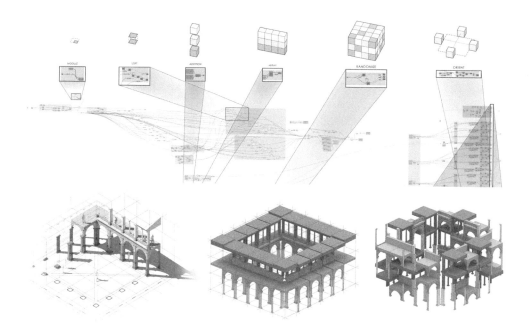

Figure 1: Student Analysis of Classical Architectural Form 1, University of Arkansas Rome Center

The first phase was the survey and analysis of the proposed building; in this phase the students had to measure, both with direct survey techniques and using basic photogrammetry techniques, the portion of the building assigned to them. Once the elevation or section had been drawn, the students conducted a series of geometrical and proportional analyzes using the comparison of the classical orders as a reference. A useful text for this phase of the work was Robert Chitham's "The Classical Order of Architecture",[10] a publication that presents a modern interpretation of the Classical Orders. The new edition of this successful title includes the proportions in both metric and imperial measurements to make the orders more accessible and to provide a valuable reference for designers.

The analysis phase was of fundamental importance to decode the compositional rules and establish the best parametric modeling strategy.

The students had to identify the main module adopted by the designer and all related sub-modules, as well as decompose into primary elements or the "typical" bay in the case of courtyards or the main facade in the case of buildings or churches. This first phase is the most important as it allows you to fully understand the compositional "grammar" and the relationships existing between the various parts and sets the conditions for correct parametric modeling as the algorithm is based precisely on the relationships between the various components.

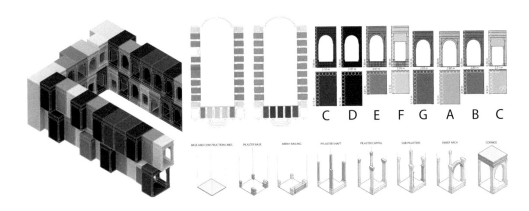

Figure 2: Student Analysis of Classical Architectural Form 2, University of Arkansas Rome Center

In the second phase, students were asked to create a parametric model of the building assignedto them using GrasshopperTM and to optimize the basic algorithm through the fewest possible number of components used. The goal was not to recreate the building in a "faithful" way, inserting all the details as would have been done in the case of a model intended for photorealistic representation, but rather to understand the operating logic of the software by recreating the geometrical and proportional relationships decoded in the analysis phase.

As already mentioned, the classical order is in effect a parametric system based on precise dimensional modules related to each other according to rules defined in various ways by the treatise writers of the past. Clearly, the experience of direct measurement and the individual analysis conducted by the students allowed them to confirm these rules rather than to find new and original ones.

In the process of building the parametric model, the students had to identify the various steps in a clear and progressive way; this allowed them to create a definition in Grasshopper that could be subsequently altered to generate new forms and new spatialities.

In fact, once the parametric model was reconstructed, the students were offered a third step: creative interpretation and the generation of new configurations by experimenting with the possibilities offered by the parametric modeling software. The idea behind this third phase is based on the concept of "variation on the theme", which is very common in the musical field: variation is that compositional procedure by virtue of which a basic thematic element is transformed into something else which maintains a very close relationship with the model.

In this phase we wanted to test students' understanding of the workflow while introducing one or more variables related to individual creativity. The variables were things such as the introduction of randomizing functions that allowed the spatial reconfiguration of the building, to the creation of scripts linked to the rhythm of the constituent elements capable of deforming the basic module within predetermined limits and then adding a new element to the achievement of a new proportional order.

In other cases, the original spatial configuration was changed by keeping the size of the single module fixed and applying it to new generators in such a way as to produce completely new spaces.

ENDNOTES

1 https://web.archive.org/web/20070206222853/http://www.gehrytechnologies.com/products-designer.html
2 https://www.cadalyst.com/cadalyst-author/jerry-laiserin-95
3 https://www.united-bim.com/what-are-bim-dimensions-3d-4d-5d-6d-7d-bim-explained-definition-benefits/
4 https://www.patrikschumacher.com/Texts/Parametricism%20-%20A%20New%20Global%20Style%20for%20Architecture%20and%20Urban%20Design.html
5 https://www.case.rpi.edu/
6 https://mitpress.mit.edu/books/classical-language-architecture
7 https://library.columbia.edu/libraries/avery/digitalserlio/manuscripts.html
8 https://matematica.unibocconi.it/articoli/guarino-guarini-architetto-e-matematico
9 https://www.jstor.org/stable/10.2307/26588508
10 https://books.google.it/books?id=VKNGxKTmjSwC&printsec=frontcover&source=gbs_ge_summary_r&redir_esc=y#v=onepage&q&f=false

PARAMETRIC THINKING AND SUSTAINABLE DESIGN

Francesco Bedeschi

As discussed in the previous chapter, the introduction of parametric design tools in the field of architecture represents one of the major innovations of the last 15 years. We have also seen that this approach is not completely new, as it finds cultural and methodological references in the historical evolution of our discipline. However, if we analyze the way in which these tools are used today, we discover that they find application in a variety of fields: from the general design of a building to the verification and analysis of structures; from environmental impact studies of entire urban settlements to the detailed analysis and design of building components. A particularly important area that is benefiting more and more concretely from these tools is that of Sustainability, which has now become an imperative for every architect who is designing a building and whose goals are to minimize the energy and environmental impact of the project.

As we will see later, the market of parametric design software offers a wealth of solutions to meet this specific need, but before diving into the discussion of the main characteristics of these solutions, it is important to understand where this need comes from.

The 21st century presents us with a great challenge: how to mitigate the impact of the built environment on our planet and thus contribute to the achievement of the objectives set by the United Nations in the 2030 Agenda for Sustainable Development.[1]

Published in 2015, the agenda addresses the increasingly serious problem of climate change and the impact of human action on the resources available on our planet. Within the document are the 17 Sustainable Development Goals (SDGs), which are an urgent call for action by all countries - developed and developing - in a global partnership. They recognize that ending poverty and other deprivations must go hand-in-hand with strategies that improve health and education, reduce inequality, and spur economic growth while tackling climate change and preserving our oceans and forests.[2]

There is no doubt that architecture and urban planning can play a fundamental role in this challenge. The importance of designing low environmental impact buildings has been discussed for many years and it is useful to mention the work of the architect Edward Mazria, founder of the Architecture2030.org program,[3] who in the October 2003 issue of Metropolis magazine[4] published the famous article entitled "It's the Architecture, stupid!".[5] In his work, Mazria, in addition to demonstrating the enormous impact of buildings with respect to greenhouse gas emissions, clearly identifies the way forward to reverse the trend when he writes: "Achieving these reductions in the Architecture sector will require nothing short of a revolution in the architectural design community. The challenge is that the architecture inherited from our predecessors is no longer valid today. The global problems we now face provide the basis for a new architecture and a dialogue with nature that will give this new architecture its uniqueness."

The concept of "new architecture" Mazria talks about is fundamental but cannot be truly defined as "new". The issue of the impact of human action on the planet and in particular that linked to the built environment has been addressed since the early 1970s; it is useful to mention the Club of Rome, founded at the beginning of the 70's by the Italian entrepreneur Aurelio Peccei and Alexander King, the Scottish Head of Science at the OECD.[6] In 1972, the Club's first major Report, The Limits to Growth, was published. It sold millions of copies worldwide, creating media controversy and also impetus for the global sustainability movement. This call for objective, scientific assessment of the impact of humanity's behavior and use of resources, still defines the Club of Rome today. While Limits to Growth had many messages, it fundamentally confronted the unchallenged paradigm of continuous material growth and the pursuit of endless economic expansion. Fifty years later, there is no doubt that humanity's ecological footprint substantially exceeds its natural limits every year. The concerns of the Club of Rome have not lost their relevance.

For more than 50 years the scientific community has questioned the real sustainability of our growth and there is no doubt that buildings and large cities play a key role in this regard.

Returning to Mazria's work, it is interesting to mention another passage that brings us back to the center of the theme addressed in this chapter: he talks about the importance of energy simulation tools that must be increasingly integrated into the design processes, simplifying the use and making them easily accessible from the early stages of the project. In particular, Mazria writes: "The adoption of these performance standards should be linked to an intensive federal program to refine and transform complex and cumbersome building performance simulation programs so they are user-friendly, graphic in format and seamlessly integrated with the Computer-Aided Design and Drafting (CADD) programs currently used by architecture firms. This will ensure that architecture firms will have the appropriate tools necessary to comply with the new standards."

This is a topic that today, after 20 years, has not yet been completely resolved; however, a series of new tools are constantly being developed that tend exactly in that direction: integrating environmental and meteorological data into parametric modeling software allowing us to understand and visualize in real time the behavior and performance of the designed buildings.

One of the most significant projects that somehow paved the way for the development of this methodology is certainly ECOTECT, a software developed in the early 2000s by architect and university researcher Andrew Marsh.[7] ECOTECT[8] was one of the first complete building design and environmental analysis tools to cover the full range of simulation and analysis functions required to understand how a new project will operate and perform. It allowed designers to work efficiently in three dimensions and apply all the tools necessary for a sustainable and energy-efficient project. Created to be used from the earliest stages of design, ECOTECT shows results in three dimensions within the actual context of the design. Designers can interact with data, usually in real-time and with immediate visual feedback, whether surface-mapped information, spatial volumetric renderings, or simple shadow animations. ECOTECT was written and developed by architects with its application in architecture and the design process firmly in mind.

Finally, the software was equipped with advanced scripting functions that provided customization of the analysis based on specific project needs.

In part because of the success and validity of this tool Autodesk, a leading company in the design software sector, acquired it, starting the development of a series of other products, such as Vasari[9] which was subsequently merged into the inside the BIM-Revit package. The legacy of ECOTECT has also been influential to other protagonists of the world of parametric modeling, especially thanks to the advent of Grasshopper, the native plug-in of Rhinoceros 3D.[10] Grasshopper today represents the most widespread tool among architects with regards to parametric modeling. Its use and rapid diffusion is progressively transforming the way in which buildings are designed, giving substance to theoretical concepts developed by leading professionals like Patrik Schumacher, long-time collaborator of Zaha Hadid and director of the Zaha Hadid Architects studio after the death of the founder in 2016. In the previous chapter I have already spoken of the concept of "parametricism" coined by Schumacher; here I am interested in addressing the issue of developing open-source plug-ins designed to conduct energy and environmental analysis based on various programming languages such as Python, C# or VisualBasic which are integrated into the Rhino/Grasshopper work environment. In an interview published on AECMagazine in 2009, Bob McNeel, the founder of the company that created Rhino3D says: "Grasshopper is a way for designers to look at design problems as a set of sophisticated relationships and to map those relationships graphically and programmatically into a system that allows them to interactively play with alternatives. Grasshopper began as a simple tool but has increased in complexity due to its open-source nature including the ability of expert users to extend the system with C# and Visual Basic components."[11]

Thanks to these features, a multitude of specific applications have been created in recent years that have integrated many of the ECOTECT functions into the Rhino/Grasshopper work environment. One of the most interesting examples is certainly the Ladybug Tools package[12] developed since 2012 by Mostapha Sadeghipour Roudsari and Chris Mackey, and whose features were first presented at the 13th International conference of Building Performance Simulation Association in Chambery, France, Aug 25-28, 2013.[13]

Ladybug Tools is one of the best examples of the attempt to create an interface between the world of energy-environmental simulation based on complex and unintuitive calculation engines such as EnergyPlus, eQuest, Radiance or OpenStudio and the most common work environments for architects such as Rhino3D or Revit. The idea is to create the conditions for an integrated workflow that does not require too much specific knowledge and that allows understanding and verification of performance from the early stages of the project. It is in these phases, in fact, that the most important decisions of a project are made, such as orientation, definition of geometry, form factor and the relationship between opaque and transparent surfaces. These are actions that fall entirely within the architect's domain and that can contribute to a significant reduction in the building's energy consumption as well as increasing the well-being and quality of life of the occupants.

It is therefore evident that having tools capable of reading the environmental data of a given location and translating them into precise analysis of quantitative phenomena such as solar radiation represent the ideal working method to keep the expected performance of the project under control. The parametric tool offers the possibility of real-time verification with respect to the various design hypotheses and the use of additional plug-ins, equipped with automated verification and control functions. These tools greatly amplify the scope of design process optimization allowing designers to make decisions based on objective data and not just on personal intuition. As I wrote in the previous chapter, my personal experience with respect to the world of parametric design was mainly formed during the post-professional Master of Architecture at the CASE - Center for Architecture Science and Ecology of the Rensselaer Polytechnic Institute which I attended in 2013- 2014.[14] The program I followed was called "Environmental Parametrics" and was entirely based on the use of parametric design tools applied to the performance of buildings. As part of this program, I was able to deepen different working methods using various tools which I subsequently followed the development of, applying them in my architectural design courses at the University of Arkansas Rome Program.

It was in the context of the Master that I started using the Ladybug Tools plug-ins already mentioned, and I had the opportunity to test other working methods based on different tools such as, for example, DIVA developed by Solemma and subsequently integrated into the within the current Climate Studio software package.[15] All these software are able to integrate within Grasshopper's parametric workflow and more recently have also begun to communicate with the BIM world through the connection with Dynamo,[16] a visual programming plugin for Revit, developed by Autodesk. There are also many so-called "stand alone" tools or completely autonomous software that can import generic 3D models made with the most common software such as Autocad or SketchUp and perform analyzes and simulations internally such as Sefaira[17] or IES VE Gaia.[18] All these tools have a common basis: to offer quick and not excessively complex solutions to be used in the early stages of the project, made accessible to professionals who do not have programming skills to guide design choices with low environmental impact.

However, the working methodology based on parametric design also offers much more advanced opportunities that can be used in the subsequent phases of the project, especially in the context of the optimization of construction processes.

One of the most interesting parametric design tools is based on "multi-objective optimization". This approach allows the user to input many goals which the tool works through simultaneously, producing a range of optimized trade-off solutions between the extremes of each goal. This methodology is the basis of some plug-ins such as Galapagos developed by David Rutten, the developer of Grasshopper, or Octopus[19] which introduces the Pareto-Principle for Multiple Goals. These tools, based on Evolutionary Solvers or Genetic Algorithms, make the most of the potential and characteristics of the parametric instrument. As David Rutten writes: "They are very flexible and able to tackle a wide variety of problems. Moreover, because the run-time process of the evolutionary solvers is progressive, intermediate answers can be harvested at practically any time so even a pre-maturely aborted run will yield something which could be called a result. Finally, Evolutionary Solvers allow for a high degree of interaction with the user. The run-time process is highly transparent and browsable, and there exists a lot of opportunity for a dialogue between algorithm and human."[20]

As an example of the working process of this tool, I optimized the geometry of a prefabricated building facade module to maximize solar radiation on the photovoltaic panels yet simultaneously increase the amount of natural light for the parts of the facade not directly exposed to sunlight. These two objectives were at odds with one another but thanks to the use of the Pareto-Principle for Multiple Goals method of the Galapagos plug-in, I was able to identify the best geometric configurations of the prefabricated module to be installed in the different areas of the facades according to their orientation and solar radiation. This example indicates how parametric design tools can be exploited to increase the performance of the project and, therefore, its energy-environmental sustainability. This working methodology also finds applicability in other areas of sustainable design, such as Life Cycle Assessment (LCA) of buildings and materials. LCA is a fundamental aspect of the building design principles in the circular economy context, recently published by the European Community.[21] It involves analyzing the impact of the life cycle of building materials, components, and building as a whole, concerning some environmental parameters while minimizing the use of high-impact materials in favor of those that are more sustainable and durable. Also, in this area, software solutions interact with the parametric design tools and allow users to make a series of very accurate assessments of the materials used in the project. Among the many software available it is worth mentioning OneClick LCA, one of the most widespread globally and which includes an integration module with Grasshopper.[22]

It is also important to mention other tools created to address particular building characteristics, such as Computational Fluid Dynamics (CFD) analytics, which are very useful for understanding the behavior of natural ventilation inside or outside buildings and, therefore, improving occupants' well-being by limiting the consumption of energy for mechanical ventilation or air conditioning. In this case, the Ladybug Tools package includes a specific solution, Butterfly, which uses the OpenFOAM[23] CFD calculation engine, a widely used open-source application. Butterfly is built to quickly export geometry to OpenFOAM and run several common types of airflow simulations that are useful to building design. This includes outdoor simulations to model urban wind patterns, indoor buoyancy-driven simulations to model thermal comfort and ventilation effectiveness, etc.

AN EDUCATIONAL EXPERIENCE

As in the previous chapter, here too I would like to share some elements of the work done with the students at the University of Arkansas Rome Program as part of an elective course titled "Environmental Parametrics "held in Spring 2021. The aim of the course is to teach students the use of the Rhino3d/Grasshopper parametric design software and specific plug-ins regarding sustainable design through a series of exercises to be applied to some credits derived from the energy certification protocol LEED environmental.[24] In fact, the protocol provides for a series of simulations and specific calculations in various areas including energy, water management, materials, site management and the well-being of the occupants. The credits were selected from those that best lend themselves to the creation of specific definitions in Grasshopper and the students were guided in the construction of the algorithms by Antonello Di Nunzio, one of the Ladybug Tools developers who collaborated on the course.

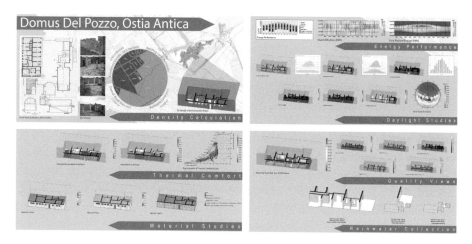

Figure 1: Student Analysis in Environmental Parametrics Class Taught at the University of Arkansas Rome Center

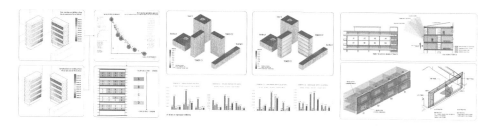

Figure 2: Professor Analysis Example in Environmental Parametrics Class, University of Arkansas Rome Center

Once the individual exercises phase was completed, the students were asked to apply the methodologies they learned by conducting environmental analysis on some Roman Domus of the Republican period located in the archaeological area of Ostia Antica. The intent of the final exercise was, on the one hand, to verify the skills learned and, on the other, to demonstrate to the students that some characteristics of sustainability were very clear and already present in the time of the ancient Romans. This helped provide evidence for the students that good practices of the past are still extremely relevant.

ENDNOTES

1 htttps://sdgs.un.org/2030agenda
2 https://sdgs.un.org/goals
3 https://architecture2030.org/
4 https://metropolismag.com/viewpoints/architects-pollute-sustainability/
5 http://www.mazria.com/ItsTheArchitectureStupid.pdf
6 https://www.clubofrome.org/history/
7 http://andrewmarsh.com/about/
8 https://web.archive.org/web/20080724093511/http://squ1.com/products/ecotect
9 https://www.ntnu.no/wiki/display/digilab/Autodesk+Vasari
10 https://www.grasshopper3d.com/

11 https://aecmag.com/news/rhino-grasshopper/
12 https://www.ladybug.tools/about.html
13 https://www.ibpsa.org/proceedings/bs2013/p_2499.pdf
14 https://www.case.rpi.edu/
15 https://www.solemma.com/climatestudio
16 https://dynamobim.org/
17 https://www.sketchup.com/products/sefaira
18 https://www.iesve.com/software/gaia
19 https://www.food4rhino.com/en/app/octopus
20 https://www.grasshopper3d.com/profiles/blogs/evolutionary-principles
21 https://ec.europa.eu/docsroom/documents/39984
22 https://oneclicklca.zendesk.com/hc/en-us/articles/360019399220-Grasshopper-Integration
23 https://www.openfoam.com/
24 https://www.usgbc.org/leed

FABRICATING PARAMETRIC THINKING

Scott Overall

With the development of computing technology in the 1960s, the aerospace and automotive industries were developing a new form of manufacturing to leverage digital technology. Numerical control machining, while already existent as punch-card systems, was not yet considered more efficient or accurate than previous methods due to the time needed to create punch card inputs and accommodate for the potential for user error in their creation. Researchers within industry and academia were looking to a new form of machining, computer numerical control (CNC), to solve existing systems' inefficiencies.[1] Simultaneously, the creation of computer-aided drafting (CAD) and computer-aided manufacturing (CAM) software, credited to Pierre Bézier for his development of UNISURF and mathematical descriptions of surfaces in the automotive industry[2] and Ivan Sutherland for his development of SKETCHPAD at MIT as the first CAD software with a graphical user interface,[3] began to open new possibilities for interacting with the early CNC machines at the time. With evidence that the newly developed CNC, CAD, and CAM technologies could improve efficiency in manufacturing, it was not until the 1970s when the cost of computers began to fall for their adoption to spread beyond just the most well-funded institutions. These technologies spread throughout manufacturing industries, significantly improving productivity and capabilities that continued to advance as software and hardware developed over time.[4]

The first CAD software packages embedded concepts of parametricism from the beginning, with SKETCHPAD using parametric formulas Ivan Sutherland called "atomic constraints", but they fell away when AutoCAD rose to dominate the industry by utilizing an explicit drafting process at the start of the 1980s. In 1988 parametric CAD modeling entered the mainstream with the release of Pro/ENGINEER, which allowed engineers to model in a parametric manner to allow for changes in design even late into the design-engineering process, allowing detailed models to adapt quickly to slight changes without significant manual re-modeling. Architects were slow to adopt these parametric processes to solve fabrication challenges, primarily sticking with traditional drafting processes until the 2000s. However, pioneering architects such as Frank Gehry had begun to show the possibilities of the technique utilizing the parametric CAD software CATIA to solve complex geometric challenges in Gehry's work in the 1990s.[5]

With the rise of parametric CAD software in architecture in the 2000s, like Digital Project and Grasshopper for Rhino, architects could produce more complex designs that were not previously feasible to model in detail, utilizing existing CNC and CAM technologies to fabricate such designs efficiently. Designs still needed to be conceived within the constraints of available fabrication techniques, requiring the designer to have a more intimate understanding of the limits of different CNC tooling processes and develop new methods of communication of design intent to bring a design from concept to construction. In projects such as SHoP Architect's Barclays Center, Botswana Innovation Hub, and Syracuse University National Veterans Resource Center, fabricating parametric projects even necessitated the designer to assume responsibilities not typical to an architecture practice. In these projects, SHoP worked directly with fabricators to develop and model systems to work within the limitations of the available tooling to deliver complex designs efficiently.

Parametric fabrication in the present can deliver exciting designs that take new and novel forms to create unique experiences, find efficiencies in modular construction, enable detailed three-dimensional coordination between trades, and facilitate precise quality control and tracking. Systems made of large quantities of highly variable parts to create a more complex whole, often called mass-customization, are now possible in ways not seen in the past. With mass-customization, new challenges arise that require designers to design and think parametrically. Manually modeling mass-customized parts is no longer an option and the scripting of parametric models is now an essential tool for architects looking to achieve such designs. Managing and communicating the complexity of a design also becomes a process that benefits automation, allowing the tracking and sorting of parts in ways that follow their properties. Lastly, ensuring that a model is capable of manufacture presents sets of micro-scale challenges that the designer must think of in a parametric manner to ensure that material tolerances, thicknesses, and connections are all considered. Fortunately, an architect versed in parametric thinking combined with traditional skills of communicating and coordinating building systems is well suited to address these new mass-customization challenges.

EVERYTHING IS PARAMETRIC

For a designer not trained in parametric thinking, one may believe that parametric fabrication only applies to formally organic architecture with complex surface geometry; however, this is not the case. The formally complex architecture emphasizes mass-customization and parametric design, but one can consider everything parametrically. Systems rarely repeat without any variation, even in more typical-looking projects. For example, a façade unit might need to change width and height to divide evenly along many walls of a building that do not have consistent dimensions or floor-to-floor heights, even if the designer does not intend them to appear different. It may not be necessary to build parametric modeling systems to represent this level of variation but conceptualizing the system as a parametric fabrication can be beneficial in understanding the range of variation a system can handle.

Modular housing construction is another example of a system that benefits when conceptualized as a parametric fabrication though formally appearing indistinguishable from more typical stick-built buildings. Modular units may need to stretch to adapt to changes in a building's mass and have varying boundary conditions that the designer needs to accommodate. Due to the complexity of an extensive modular system, even a slight change from one unit to the next has a tremendous impact on the number of parts that need to adapt to the change, making explicit modeling of a system particularly demanding to maintain. For SHoP's modular residential building B2 in Brooklyn, New York, SHoP built parametric fabrication models in CATIA to capture the range of variation in the units and used them to coordinate with their off-site fabrication. As a result, nearly the entirety of B2 was encoded as a parametric fabrication model though it is not immediately apparent through its form (figure 1, 2).

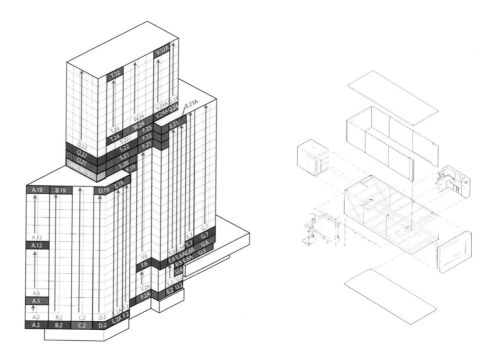

Figure 1: B2 modular massing diagram   Figure 2: B2 modular unit exploded axon diagram

MATERIALS AND TOOLING

CNC machining has made mass-customization more attainable, but every material and process has limits. When designing for parametric fabrication, the designer must consider the boundaries of a material type and the limits of a tooling process to control what parts of a system can be variable. One can conceptually organize materials into categories with standard tooling processes and constraints. Common material types include but are not limited to sheet, cast, extruded, monolithic, and additive materials. For each of these material types, a fabricator can tool them in ways that facilitate the desired degree of variability and mass-customization a design requires.

Sheet materials typically include sheet metals such as aluminum, steel, copper, brass, or zinc. They come in various thicknesses, which can be water jet or laser cut, bent, rolled, or stamped. Cutting and bending of sheet materials are typically done on CNC machines and can easily facilitate variability without losing efficiency. Sheet materials are among the most used materials in parametric fabrication and act as critical parametric rain screen elements in SHoP's Barclays Center and Botswana Innovation Hub (figure 3, 4).

Figure 3: Barclays Center rain screen wireframe model

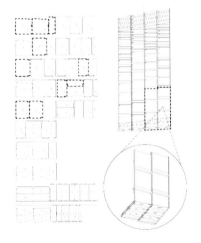

Figure 4: Barclays Center mega panel drawings showing unfolded sheet metal and corresponding folded assembly

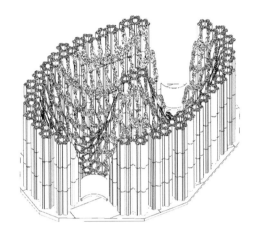

Figure 5: WAVE/CAVE pavilion fabrication model

Extruded materials are typically aluminum extrusions, though other materials such as terracotta can also be extruded. One example of terracotta extrusion is SHoP's WAVE/CAVE in Milan, Italy[6] (figure 5, 6). CNC cutting extrusions to length is typical and can easily facilitate variability. Extruded materials, particularly metals, also are CNC machined after cutting to create holes and other features in the extrusion. Fabricators can also roll metal extrusions to create curves, though more limitations may exist on curve types and how variable they may be. The need to develop unique dies for any change in an extrusion's cross-section limits the amount of variability an extrusion can achieve. However, the dies are typically CNC machined. It would be unwise to use unique dies, but varying dies can be used within reason if there is enough repetition of profiles.

Cast materials such as cast terracotta, concrete, glass fiber reinforced concrete (GFRC), or glass fiber reinforced polymer (GFRP) are poured into a mold of any type. Cast materials allow for a large amount of freedom to shape the geometry within the mold with complicated shapes and curvatures as molds are often CNC machined. Still, molds limit variability from unit to unit as they are more efficient when used multiple times. A fabricator can only cast a limited number of times into a mold before needing to re-create it and may efficiently achieve some variability at large scales if there is some repetition. If molds are not created as one-offs and have some amount of repetition, a designer can create a variable, parametric system efficiently. A fabricator can also use other techniques to manage unique conditions, such as blocking off molds for holes punched into a unit to prevent the creation of entirely individual molds. One-off molds can be used for highly bespoke systems, though at an additional cost.

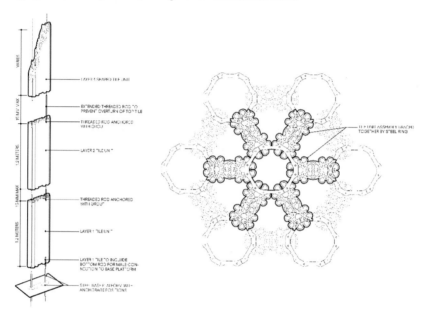

Figure 6: WAVE/CAVE extruded terracotta tile assembly

Monolithic materials such as timber, stone, and sometimes polymers are large solid substances that can be milled and cut with CNC machines to create wide varieties of shapes and complex surfaces or reliefs at an architectural scale. The materials are typically constrained by their uncut size and require varying efforts to cut and mill. Soft materials like timber can be CNC cut and milled quickly, facilitating large variability. However, complex tool paths to create complicated surface relief may still require long tooling times that could slow their execution at large scales. For example, SHoP's Syracuse University National Veterans Resource Center shows the speed and flexibility of CNC milling timber to create a form with no repetition of elements with minor loss in fabrication efficiency (figure 7, 8). Harder materials such as stone can be cut and milled in similar ways. However, long cut times that require supervision may result in inefficiencies, and it may be better to cut the materials to size with saws that have few degrees of freedom but quicker cut times.

Additive materials represent the most cutting-edge material fabrication, representing 3D printing technologies and all materials that 3D printing can utilize. From traditional plastic printing to concrete and metal printing, additive materials have relatively unbound constraints in creating complex geometries with less waste associated with subtractive techniques like milling. Despite the advantages, additive materials still have restrictions that a designer needs to consider. Print volumes are limited in size, and large units' print times are often prohibitive. Many additive materials also still require additional finishes to provide the material with weather or fire protection it might require which can be challenging to apply after the material is printed. Additive manufacturing has only begun to be used in architectural scales in projects such as SHoP's Flotsam & Jetsam in Miami, Florida, as they continue to solve their efficiency challenges.

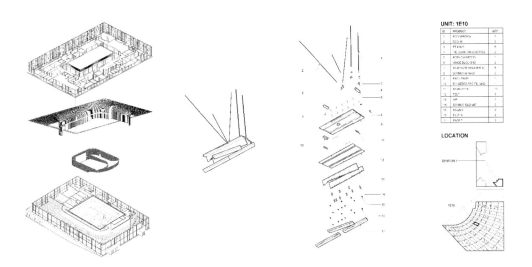

Figure 7: Syracuse university National Veterans Resource Center exploded axon showing extents of interior timber feature wall systems

Figure 8: Syracuse University National Veterans Resource Center CNC milled timber unit drawing

The previous outline of material types and their tooling processes is only a rough guide for what fabrication processes are available to a designer. Specific materials may differ in their available tooling processes, and tooling can vary from fabricator to fabricator. A broad understanding of available fabrication processes can aid preliminary material selection, system design, and the design of the assembly of systems and their form. Collaboration with a fabricator to better understand their limitations and capabilities will allow the designer to refine the system to a constructible parametric design.

System Design

When designing for fabrication, once the designer has chosen a prospective material assembly, it is essential to define the parts of construction in terms of their allowed variability or parameter space. "System Design" in Architecture typically refers to developing a construction system, often with a subcontractor or party responsible for the system's fabrication. In a traditional process, the designer and fabricator may create these through drawings of the most typical unit of a system and separate drawings of any exceptions to that specific unit. For example, in a unitized curtain wall, the party responsible for documentation will only draw the most common unit and separate drawings for units that accommodate corners, parapets, soffits, or other exceptions to the typical unit. When designing parametrically, system design takes on a new meaning. A parametric system must be able to adapt and handle situations which have no standard units. The designer can define the same unitized curtain wall as parametric extrusion profiles that vary in length and angle to accommodate assorted sizes, shapes, and boundary conditions. Even if units repeat, it only means that their parameters are the same, not that they are any less parametric.

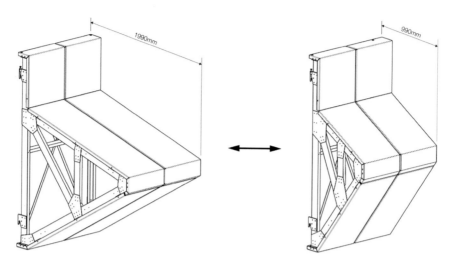

Figure 9: Botswana Innovation Hub variation within a rain screen panel system.

Variations of a unit that a single system design can accommodate are a change-in-kind. In contrast, a variation that a system design cannot facilitate would be a change-in-type and would require an additional system design or exception to the original system design to fabricate the entire assembly. A successful parametric system can adapt to most conditions with few exceptions to the base system design, requiring only changes-in-kind to meet the requirements of all units. To ensure the bounds of a system are appropriately defined, a system design needs to describe both the parameters and the parameter space in which the system remains valid. (figure 9)

Micro-scale considerations become critical in creating a system design that one can successfully fabricate. Material thicknesses and tolerances that might not be visible in concept images significantly impact its overall constructability. Joints between parts of a system become of particular concern. Imagining a joint in which three or more members connect, the designer must consider how each member might modify themselves relative to one another to allow the connection to meet the system's needs while remaining efficient in fabrication and construction. One must ask, do parts offset to avoid clashes? Are they trimmed back? Are parts always oriented to a consistent plane in space, or do they need to rotate freely in all axes? (figure 10) By conceptualizing these joints parametrically and building parametric systems to model them, the designer can quickly iterate through ideas and test them on a range of conditions to ensure they remain valid over the range of variation required.

While conceptualizing a parametric system design does not inherently require a parametric 3D model, it is of such immense benefit that it is unwise not to pursue it. A parametric 3D model can serve many valuable functions early in a design when the system needs to be validated to work for its intended range of variation, visual appearance, and constructability. As a design advances, the 3D model can provide detailed quantity take-offs to ensure that only the materials needed are purchased; this also aids in factory floor planning. As the design enters the construction phase, the model can be used for fabrication directly, as most CAM software can read the 3D modeled parts to create the G-code that CNC machines use to encode toolpaths. The 3D model can also serve as a quality control check against the final fabricated unit to verify that it meets the original intent. Lastly, the model carries value as a means of risk management. From experience, if the fabricator has a proper 3D fabrication model that matches the system design and accounts for proper construction tolerances, a model without clashes is ultimately constructible and has very few unknown variables.

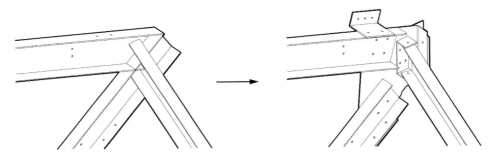

Figure 10: Botswana Innovation Hub resolution of a parametric joint.

ARCHITECTS ARE NOT (USUALLY) FABRICATORS

While parametric design for fabrication carries immense value, how exactly it fits into the architectural design process is much less clear. In a world free of liability, the architect and fabricator could coordinate from architectural intent to fabrication model to constructed system together through a single coordinated 3D model.[7] This ideal process is not easy to do in practice as the architect does not hold liability as a fabricator, and the fabricator does not hold liability as an architect. There typically must be a separation between the two.

Typically, an architect would document a design intent through drawings and basic parametric models. The architect then shares those documents with a general contractor responsible for coordinating with each subcontractor that interfaces with the design; one of whom would be the subcontractor responsible for fabricating the system. The fabricator subcontractor then produces their own set of drawings and models for the system based on the architect's design. A back and forth of communication occurs while the architect and fabricator continually try to reconcile their separate models as the fabricator develops the system design with input from the architect. This process can be inefficient as it requires a duplication of complex modeling work and delays in coordination with other trades that might be waiting for the models to reconcile so they know how to interface their work with the system. Despite the inefficiencies, this process traditionally separates the liability. It would not be problematic for simple systems that do not have complex models where it is quick to complete the model reconciliation process, though this is not always the case.

Alternative delivery processes do exist. The architect could spin off a team to work on the model coordination process as a subcontractor rather than a design architect. However, it requires the modeling team to work separately from the architect and assume separate liabilities. The only benefits are that the modeling team may have a pre-existing knowledge of the intended parametric system. Once the architect has spun off a model team, they must coordinate through the same channels as a subcontractor and suffer many of the same inefficiencies of model reconciliation to prevent conflicts of interest. A design-build firm may circumvent these issues if the fabrication capabilities are in-house, though this is uncommon.

Alternatively, an architect may undertake detailed modeling work to ensure the project meets design intent as part of their architectural due diligence if the project team agrees to it as part of the architect's scope. In SHoP Architect's Syracuse National Veterans Resource Center, SHoP delivered the primary wooden feature wall in what was informally referred to as an "elevated design intent model" to capture a level of detail beyond conventional design intent to include the fabricator's shop drawings in 3D (figure 11). The fabricator could use the model for reference in this delivery method. However, they would be responsible for re-modeling to reconcile their model with the design intent model as in the traditional process described above. Because of the level of detail in the original model, the fabricator constructed the wall system from a model that was nearly a one-to-one conversion of the design intent model.

These alternative delivery models are still unconventional, and the ones listed here are not the only ways to engage in the process. Further examples and specifics of each way of engaging in parametric fabrication in practice are beyond this chapter's scope. Finding the best way for an architect to engage in the parametric fabrication process is an open question that does not have a universally agreed-upon solution but is also a realm with potential for positive evolution that helps streamline these processes.

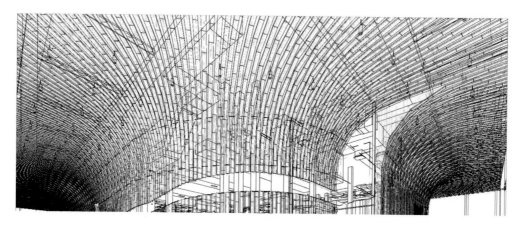

Figure 11: Syracuse University National Veterans Resource Center model x-ray view

POSSIBILITIES OF PARAMETRIC FABRICATION IN THE PRESENT AND FUTURE

Parametric thinking in fabrication has opened up new possibilities of form, experience, and efficiency, enabling the construction of many of the world's most sophisticated designs. With the ability to think parametrically about fabrication, architects can empower themselves to conceptualize new forms and experiences that were not possible in the past. With this skill set, those new forms and experiences can then be realized into something constructible, allowing the building concepts to go beyond paper to the real world.

Formally complex buildings may deploy some of the most visually apparent uses of parametric fabrication, but as noted, projects of many types can benefit from a parametric approach. The construction industry remains one of the least digitized industry sectors[8] and has suffered from low rates of productivity gains year-after-year compared to the larger economy.[9] The growth of parametric fabrication thinking in architecture and construction will be an essential step in elevating the industry to the efficiency levels of broader manufacturing to tackle the immense complexity and variation seen in our built environment, even in buildings without the formally appearing parametric.

In the future, the spread of parametric thinking in fabrication and the associated digital and mechanical tools can improve efficiency to make quality spaces more affordable and environmentally friendly with less waste through more efficient 3D modeling and pre-construction planning when preparing for fabrication. An increase in off-site modular fabrication will see efficiency gains associated with the precision enabled by parametric fabrication. New material technologies will be continually developed and enabled by parametric thinking, with additive materials maturing towards more widespread adoption, enabling flexible building systems not previously seen at scale. The construction industry will also develop new tooling and assembly processes such as robotic assembly systems to enable new parametric systems at scale. Architects and fabricators are actively developing these technologies, and developing one's skill set in parametric thinking is essential to participating in the future of these technologies effectively.

ENDNOTES

1 Ross, Douglas T. 1957. "Development of a Research Effort in the Automatic Programming of Numerically Controlled Machine Tools." Association for Computing Machinery Session of the Indianapolis Meeting of the American Association for the Advancement of Science. Indianapolis: Association for Computing Machinery.
2 Bézier, Pierre. 1971. "Example of an Existing System in the Motor Industry: The Unisurf System." Proceedings of the Royal Society of London. London: Royal Society. 207-218.
3 Sutherland, Ivan. 1963. Sketchpad: A Man-Machine Graphical Communication System. PhD dissertation, Cambridge: Massachusetts Institute of Technology.
4 Noble, David F. 1984. *Forces of Production: A Societal History of Industrial Automation*. New York: Knoff.
5 Davis, Daniel. 2013. "A History of Parametric." Daniel Davis. August 6. Accessed May 13, 2022. http://www.danieldavis.com/a-history-of-parametric.
6 Overall, Scott, John Paul Rysavy, Clinton Miller, William Sharples, Christopher Sharples, Sameer Kumar, Andrea Vittadini, and Victoire Saby. 2018. "Made-to-Measure: Automated Drawing and Material Craft." Technology | Architecture + Design (Taylor & Francis) 2 (2): 172-185.
7 SHoP Architects. 2002. "Eroding the Barriers." Edited by SHoP Architects. Versioning: Evolutionary Techniques in Architecture (Wiley-Academy) 90-100.
8 McKinsey Global Institute. 2015. Digital America: A Tale of the Haves and Have-Mores. Industry Report, McKinsey & Company.
9 McKinsey Global Institute. 2017. Reinvinting Construction: A Route to Higher Productivity. Industry Report, McKinsey & Company.

SPATIAL COMPUTING, ARTIFICIAL INTELLIGENCE, AND THE FUTURE OF PARAMETRIC DESIGN

Geoff Bell

The rapid pace of technological change makes it impossible to write about in a way that won't immediately be outdated at the time of publishing. For that reason, more important than any specific technology is the way of thinking that allows designers to interface with and make the most of technology even as it evolves. This chapter will snapshot and frame a portion of our current trajectory to spark some initial ideas about how "parametric thinkers" can approach design and its relationship to technology.

I remember seeing an elaborate and complicated automatic washing machine for automobiles that did a beautiful job of washing them. But it could do only that, and everything else that got into its clutches was treated as if it were an automobile to be washed. I suppose it is tempting, if the only tool you have is a hammer, to treat everything as if it were a nail.[1] Abraham Maslow

There is a danger within the insular nature of architectural culture to think of parametric or computational design as somehow separate from the broader technological development. The coupling of architectural theory and computation has led to a great deal of obfuscation around the technology and the role it plays in design. Technology need not be thought of as some scary "other" world, but as a tool, like a contemporary extension of the slide rule, French curve, or T-square. The goal of this chapter is not to exhaustively explain any specific technology, or to view it fully through the lens of architectonics, but to suggest potential paths forward, and to point towards other areas of research that intersect with, but also expand far beyond typical notions of architectural design. Ultimately, technology should be judged not by its complexity and learning curve, but in its ability to make a designer's work easier rather than more cumbersome. We simply tend not to notice when algorithms do their job well. To paraphrase Maslow's Hammer: "To a carpenter with only a hammer, every problem starts to look like a nail." The advantage of parametric thinking is that it allows us to start with the problem, understand its properties, and design a custom "hammer" to fit the need.

SPEAK MACHINE

To address the growing need for greater productivity in design, engineering, and construction, the process of design is steadily shifting from manual activities to automated algorithms.

As discussed in previous chapters, an algorithm is nothing more than a series of steps for a computer to follow, like a recipe. Meanwhile, as architects, what we typically deliver is the recipe for a building, not the building itself. Knowing this, the way designers can best respond to automation and technological advancement is by being parametric thinkers; by learning to "speak machine", in the words of design technologist John Maeda.[2] Learning how to communicate with machines is an important aspect to engaging with the future of technology, and integral to making use of parametric thinking in computational design. One way that we communicate with machines is through programming languages, like C++, C#, Python, or Java. These are human-readable ways of writing instructions, that can then be compiled into machine language, and eventually, 1's and 0's. Despite the rapid pace of technological change, this fundamental way of communicating with machines has not.

Over time, more user-friendly ways of doing this have been developed, making it possible to communicate machine logic without learning complicated programming rules or syntax. This has been especially helpful for designers, who tend to be much more visual thinkers, less easily engaged by the abstractions of coding. Visual scripting is an example of this, including common applications built into design software, such as Grasshopper for Rhino, Dynamo for Revit, Blueprints in Unreal Engine, and xGenerative Designer in Dassault's 3DExperience Platform. It's not unreasonable to think that as these programs become more embedded into typical workflows, that the methods for communicating with machines might become even more human-relatable, either through AI-enhanced natural language processing, spatial computing, or deep learning applications that predict intent in real-time. Even so, understanding the process behind the way that programs take this input and translate it into machine logic is vital to critical engagement with the design process.

FINGERPRINTS

The second major theme to identify in current technological development is the increasing ability of technology to respond to the human "fingerprint" and craft. A complaint you'll often hear if you spend any amount of time around architectural institutions is that the process of design has lost its connection to the hand (and by extension, some would say, "the heart"). There's an inherent value, it's supposed, to the physical act of making a thing, through the connection of the body to creation - in drawing, sketching, or model-making. This idea has been and continues to be argued about since the inception of Computer-Aided Design (CAD) and with every change in technology since. Up to now, the innovations in design technology have, to some degree, layered abstractions onto the design process. The keyboard and mouse, for example, forced many designers to, at some point in the design process, abandon the physical tools of pencil and paper or sketch modeling, and engage with the design model via a two-dimensional backlit screen. Computational design, next, provided yet another layer of abstraction, turning the visual-graphic drawings and models into text instructions, scripts, and code.

Recent developments, however, such as consumer-grade virtual and augmented reality devices, have begun to swing the pendulum of abstraction in the opposite way, enabling designers the opportunity to engage with computer graphics physically once again, via 6 degree of freedom motion controllers and headsets, and the early stages of human hand tracking. Design authorship in VR and AR has the potential to combine the iterative speed, precision and efficiency of CAD tools with the experiential qualities of handcraft, radically reshaping the way we design.

To better understand, at least at a snapshot level, the current and upcoming trends in parametric technology, this chapter will explore in more detail several broad categories of technology that are currently reshaping design. These are:

1. Spatial Computing
2. Computer Vision
3. Deep Learning and AI

Figure 1: A virtual reality "sketch" on a digitized site (Image by author)

SPATIAL COMPUTING

For the purposes of this chapter, we can define spatial computing as human-machine interaction in which the computer takes in and gives out data relative to real objects and spaces. More simply put, this includes technology such as virtual and augmented reality. How does this relate to parametric design? As you can see in the definition, with its inputs and outputs, spatial computing is essentially a parametric system! In some cases, like using reality capture for augmented reality, the spatial environment is the input. In others, virtual reality, for instance, the position of your hand or head becomes an input (or taking it a step further, in the current terminology of the "metaverse", YOU are the parameter).

Currently, virtual reality Head-Mounted Displays (HMDs) like the Oculus (Meta) Quest and HTC VIVE enable low barrier-to-entry consumer-forward interaction with virtual reality and hand-tracking through motion controllers. Design authorship tools quickly began to exploit this interaction through three-dimensional "painting", modeling, and sculpting applications. Handheld devices from Apple and Android now come with AR software built in, making the technology accessible to anyone with a smartphone. AR devices like Microsoft's Hololens allow users to look directly through the display and use gesture recognition to interact directly with the environment. Virtual collaboration tools are becoming more accepted and widespread, with greater adoption driven by remote or hybrid work arrangements.

For new designers, or people outside the profession, these tools have the potential to make design significantly more approachable, especially as the technology matures and adoption becomes more widespread. By de-abstracting the tools to a more humanistic level, users can experience the design in a way that more closely mimics reality. Ultimately, however, these tools are simply ways of accessing data, and as always, more important than the tool itself is the way that it is used.

The concept of spatial computing is crucial for architects, who tend to think and work in three dimensions, but typically must communicate in two-dimensional drawing sets and imagery. By further engaging the "computing" aspect of spatial computing, parametric thinkers can, rather than simply taking AR and VR applications at face value, begin to exploit the technology in an integrated, data rich design process. For instance, by combining a parametric system with a curve drawn in VR, a designer can access all the benefits of computational design alongside handcraft and quick sketching, in real time applying surface, structure, or additional design elements hosted on that curve. A massing model laid out in a collaborative virtual space could be connected to a parametric toolkit that automates the laying out of slabs, columns, and facade details, allowing immediate design feedback on a flexible model. Or one might imagine using AR to design a building directly on a physical site, taking into account inputs like adjacent buildings, solar position, and access points in real time.

Another concept related to spatial computing is reality capture, also called 3D scanning or digitization. This is technology that translates physical space to virtual space to enable machine interaction. Reality capture is a rapidly improving technology, to the point that LiDAR (Light Detection and Ranging) systems, which used to require prohibitively expensive and heavy equipment on a tripod, is now a standard part of iPhone cameras. Autonomous vehicles also often rely on real-time LiDAR sensors to build a map of their constantly changing surroundings, extracting elements as inputs, and outputting the correct path forward. Because spatial computing relies on these environmental inputs, reality capture is an essential element in spatial computing processes.

COMPUTER VISION

Like spatial computing, computer vision uses the environment as an input, through object recognition in video or images. Computer vision is a field of Artificial Intelligence (AI), which allows algorithms to extract meaningful information from images or videos. The benefit of computer vision is in the ability to process data much more rapidly, and some might say more objectively, than the human eye. If you've ever been asked by a website to prove you aren't a robot by identifying cars, or traffic lights, or street signs, you've contributed to computer vision models. As the technology matures, the applications for building design and construction are becoming increasingly clear.

Broadly, computer vision allows machines to identify and respond to elements that it "sees". In building design, these could include things like safety issues on a construction site, building code violations in a model, out of tolerance deviations from design during construction, or potential life safety concerns in a building plan. The many redundancies and inefficiencies in the design process have long been used by design teams as a "check" of sorts to flag errors and omissions, but these sorts of automated quality control checks are likely to become increasingly critical as more aspects of design are generatively or parametrically produced, and as the ever-growing demands for greater and greater efficiencies are addressed by authoring platforms.

Computer vision can also be used for real-time human-machine interaction. A camera attached to a robot, for instance, can allow it to adapt to a changing environment, identifying key elements for it to respond to and freeing human designers to work more intuitively alongside their digital fabrication tools. Automation tools should be thought of as assistants in this way, rather than as algorithms taking over the design process.

DEEP LEARNING

Deep learning expands on the AI applications of computer vision using the concept of training data and neural networks.[3] Before moving forward, this section will require learning a few definitions:

Artificial Intelligence - Any technology which enables computers to mimic human behavior.

Machine Learning - AI techniques that give computers the ability to learn without being explicitly programmed to do so.

Deep Learning - A field of machine learning in which neural networks enable progressive learning to gradually improve outcomes by performing a task repeatedly.

Neural Network - An algorithm or set of algorithms that identify relationships in a set of data in a way that mimics the human brain (figure 2).

Convolutional Neural Network (CNN or ConvNet) - A type of neural network that is commonly applied to visual imagery.

Generative Adversarial Network (GAN) - A method of training generative models by testing them against real examples.

When the human brain receives information, whether it be through sight, sound, touch, taste, or smell, it processes that data and gives you an output - pleasure or pain, happiness or sadness. This is essentially the same concept as a parametric system - an input is processed to generate an output. AI algorithms are parametric in the same way. A neural network approaches the complexity of the human brain using interconnected pathways, weights, biases, and thresholds.

As "parametric design" continues to be more and more integrated into architectural workflows, the scale and complexity of projects also continues to increase, integrating a wide array of new technologies and specialties. Methods for managing and organizing this complexity will therefore become more and more important parts of an architect's toolkit. There is still a long way to go before these algorithms will be able to accurately mimic human intelligence, but even in the short term there is great potential for the technology to assist designers, whether through ideation, by processing large data sets for design options, or by accurately predicting designers' needs and "taking care of the boring parts" of building design.

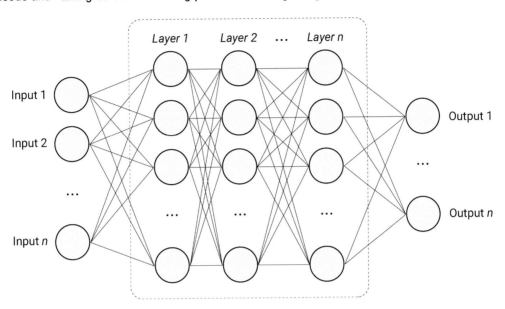

Figure 2: Diagram of a neural network (Image by author)

Further, deep learning algorithms have the ability to analyze designs in real time, providing valuable feedback to enrich decision making. For instance, a program might recognize a programmatic layout as it's being produced, populate schedules, bills of material, and specifications automatically, allowing cost, timeline, and procurement data to be reported back immediately, providing a fine grain level of detail from the earliest stages of design. Or, as a plan is being laid out, qualitative feedback might be made available - how satisfied have people been with similar spaces in the past? Are people likely to use the space in the way that it is intended, or are they likely to find their own way, despite the designed use? The complexities of human nature make these divergences a common occurrence, but something that deep learning has the potential to predict.

With the rapid proliferation of deep learning algorithms now being deployed, it can be anticipated that the field will have a significant impact on architecture and the way we think about parametric systems in the future. In fact, even in the early stages of trying to come to grips with the technology, deep learning is already beginning to be implemented in design processes.

Data is the engine that drives these systems. Many established architects have decades of built and unbuilt work that rarely has a life beyond individual projects, except perhaps in designers' minds. Deep learning algorithms present an unprecedented opportunity to parameterize that data, to learn from it, and deploy it on future projects. The handoff of construction documents to

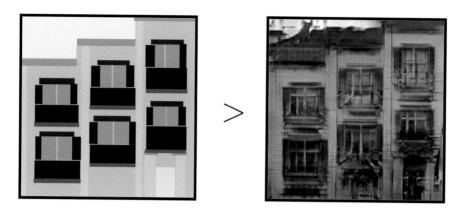

Figure 3: Facade image generation using interactive image translation with pix2pix-tensorflow algorithm by Phillip Isola, Jun-Yan Zhu, Tinghui Zhou, Alexei A. Efros (Image by author)

contractors in the typical project delivery process has trained architects to think of each project as unique, one-off problems, but deep learning will empower designers to make use of these hard-won solutions without simply recycling ideas.

On the other hand, deep learning has the potential to recognize and deploy overused stylistic expressions - if a designer often uses a specific curve, angle, or design element - leading to self-referential tropes. Think of how often you can look at a building and clearly see that it was designed in Revit. Optimistically, it could be said that this might push designers to think more broadly, freeing up time to explore more, and more varied, design solutions. That outcome is not guaranteed but will require designers to think critically (and parametrically) to take control over the algorithms, rather than being controlled by them.

For many designers (and a great deal many other professionals) the development of deep learning and AI brings with it a great deal of anxiety about the future of their work. Will we be automated out of a job? Will machines take over? The history of technological innovation has always brought with it changes to industry and work, and while not always for the greater good, the best way to adapt to these changes is not necessarily to be an expert in any single technology, but to train your mind to think parametrically. This way of thinking empowers designers to be able to understand and influence technological development, to think critically and recognize the value or lack of value in a new "innovation"; to not simply be a user of technology but to more deeply understand the inputs that the systems rely on and how to achieve the best outcome.

CONCEPT/REALITY

Wolfgang Amadeus Mozart was famous for his ability to "compose on the spot", improvising entire pieces directly from the mind to the pianoforte. One of the greatest challenges we have in architectural design is the process of bringing ideas to life, the disconnect between thought and practice. For a concept to reach reality, it goes through endless rounds of sketches, iterations of models, the disconnected phases of schematic design, design development, construction documents, back and forth emails, calls, and mountains of paper. By making strides toward approaching users (humans) on their level; spatial computing by accessing human experience;

and AI by learning from human thought; we are at the precipice of a revolution in the way we bring concepts to reality. By connecting virtual modeling to the human hand, reducing the barriers to iteration, eliminating the time spent on rote tasks, and unlocking data in the design process, we increasingly have the ability to make technology work for us, rather than the other way around.

ENDNOTES

1 Maslow, Abraham H. (1966). *The Psychology of Science: A Reconnaissance*. 1966. Gateway. p. 15.
2 Maeda, John. *How to Speak Machine: Computational Thinking for the Rest of Us*. 2019. Portfolio/Penguin.
3 Readers interested in greater engagement with AI and deep learning are encouraged to research TensorFlow or PyTorch, and the tutorials provided by those platforms.

2 ELEMENTS

In the **ELEMENTS** section of the book you will learn the basic maneuvers in Rhino/Grasshopper through the lens of architectonics. At their most elemental, all built forms can be thought of as a relationship of points. Perhaps the most fundamental lesson in Rhino/Grasshopper is to learn how to create a point or an array of points and control their locations. From this you can build all sorts of complex geometries. In the lessons within the **ELEMENTS** section you will start with point, change its coordinates, generate a line, move the line, create a surface using the line, learn to work with axial vectors, learn to extrude, learn about boundary representations, create a linear array, learn to offset, rotate geometries, and place a number of other indispensable tools in your toolkit.

E1   Point Line Plane Solid
E2   Surface Line Plane Solid
E3   Base Element
E3A   Array
E3B   Array 1D Scale Reduce
E3C   Array Rotate
E3D   Array Toggle 3D Scale Split
E4   Populate Point Curve
E5   Surface Subdivide
E6   Element Populate Orient
E7   Element Curve Divide Orient

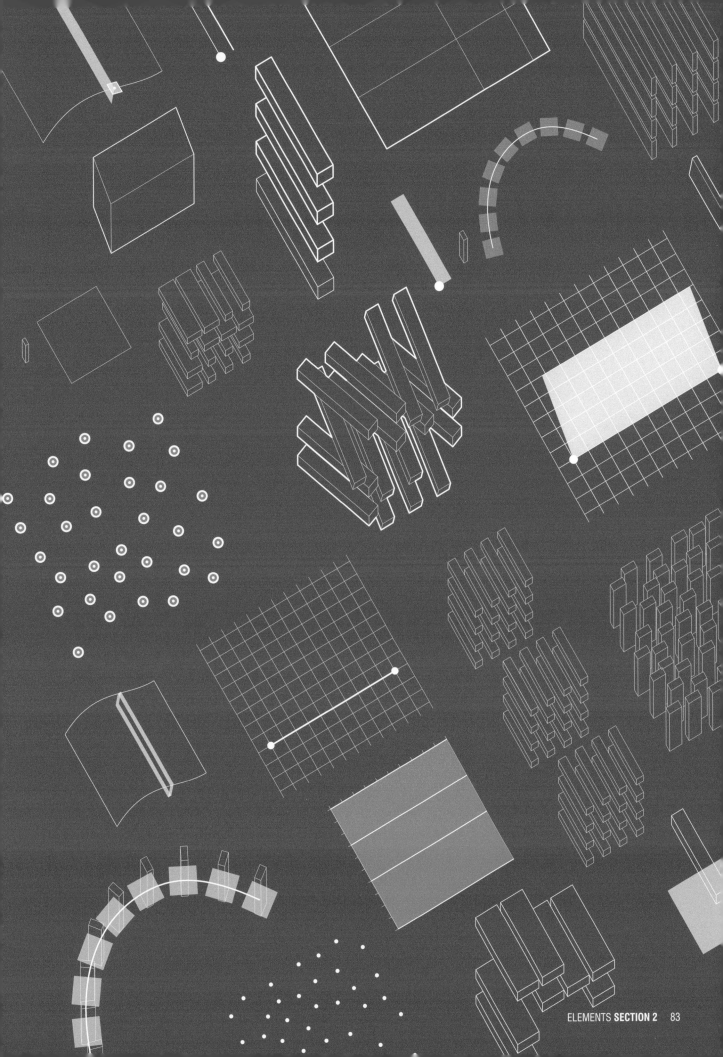

E0 GLOSSARY

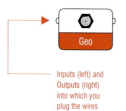

Inputs (left) and Outputs (right) into which you plug the wires

BUTTON
One of the things that makes Rhino/Grasshopper so user friendly once you get used to it, is that its underlying algorithms have been made into buttons which one can intuitively select based on what they are trying to accomplish. Within this book, by typing in the text shown in the red bar, the correct button will appear on the Grasshopper canvas.

In this particular case, if you wanted to assign a pre-existing Rhino geometry to a button, you could right-click and select *Set One Geometry*. Once you do this you will see that the Grasshopper button turns green.

MULTIPLE INPUTS
One thing that may confuse a new user to Rhino/Grasshopper is that there can be multiple buttons that seemingly do the same things. The best way to overcome this is to experiment with each button to understand how it is nuanced from the next.

Likewise, there often are multiple inputs in a single button. Inputs are the knobs and letters/names that you see on the left side of the button. By hovering your mouse over the letter/name beside the knob you will see what information it is looking for.

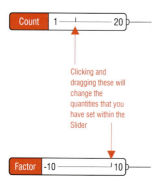

Clicking and dragging these will change the quantities that you have set within the Slider

SLIDER
Enables parametric manipulation. One of the most important devices within Rhino/Grasshopper to manipulate and iterate form.

By double-clicking on the Grasshopper canvas a keyword window will appear. To create a slider, type in a number range using the less than sign as follows: 1<20, this will create a slider enabling dimensional or element adjustments between 1 and 20.

It is good practice to change the name of the slider to reflect the geometric manipulations it controls. To do so, double-click the word *slider*. This will open a dialogue box that allows multiple types of geometry and name adjustments.

MD SLIDER
The MD Slider (Multi-Dimensional Slider) adds dimensionality to a typical slider, allowing users to easily move objects along the x and y axis.

Add this tool to the Grasshopper canvas by double-clicking on the canvas and typing *MD Slider*.

Double-click within the MD Slider to change its parameters.

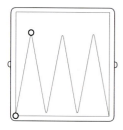

GRAPH MAPPER
The Graph Mapper allows you to control the coordinates of individual points. This affords a greater amount of control than a typical slider. By right-clicking on the Graph Mapper you can select from a number of graph types. Once you have selected a graph type you can double click on the Graph Mapper to open the graph editor.

Manage data here

MANAGING DATA
As your expertise in Rhino/Grasshopper grows, you will begin to manage data within the buttons wisely. By right-clicking on the input names (left side of button) you will open a dialogue box that allows you to flatten, reverse, graft, and simplify data.

PANEL

The Panel tool can be used a number of ways within Rhino/Grasshopper. To insert the Panel tool double-click the Rhino/Grasshopper canvas and type *Panel*. It can be used to manipulate geometric or dimensional parameters. By connecting to another button with a wire, it can also be used to explore what type of information is running through the button. Experimenting with Panels is an excellent way of discovering more about what is going on behind the scenes parametrically within Rhino/Grasshopper.

PANEL (BRANCH AND LIST)

To make a Branch or List Item Index one would use the panel tool which can be accessed as described above. Anything input into the Panel tool in Brace Brackets like these {} will create a Branch Index. Anything input into the panel tool within Box Brackets like these [] will create a List Index.

As you become more spphisticated in your use of Rhino/Grasshopper you will begin to manipulate Data Trees, which include different types of indexing. This book introduces you to these items in a very rudimentary way.

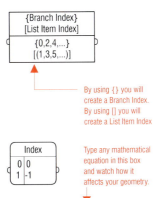

PANEL (MULTILINE DATA)

Another Panel tool attribute is the ability to make Multiline Lists. Multiline lists are used to separate data into different lines in a list.

EXPRESSION

To create an expression in Rhino/Grasshopper double-click the canvas and type *Expression*. An expression allows you to manipulate data using any mathematical equation that you type in.

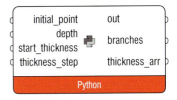

SCRIPTING

One of the most amazing attributes of Rhino/Grasshopper is its ability to allow users to write scripts to create their own buttons. The sky is the limit with respect to what you can create in this way. To do this, double-click on the Rhino/Grasshopper canvas and type *Python,* this will open the *GHPython Script* button. Double-clicking this button will open a window into which you can directly write in Python code.

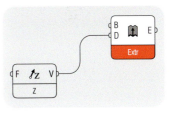

GROUPING

Rhino/Grasshopper definitions can become extremely visually complex, so it is important to organize them as you go. One way to do this is to group buttons which you consider to be a team performing a larger function.

To group buttons, highlight the buttons by dragging your mouse from top left to bottom right over the buttons, then right-click within the highlighted area (not on the buttons themselves) and choose the *Group* option. You can then name the group by right-clicking and typing in a name in the empty area at the top of the dialogue box.

TOGGLE

Within a definition you may want to toggle a binary expression such as 'on/off' or 'true/false' which will make the defintion active in the 'on' or 'true' positions but inactive in the other positions. To do this you will use the Toggle tool.

PREVIEW

The preview button allows you to preview geometries with various material and color inputs. It is a great way to quickly test the eventual visual outcomes of what you are working on.

SWATCH

Swatches allow you to select any color you want and is typically used with the Preview option.

E1 POINT LINE PLANE SOLID

1. Make two dynamic points
   Move points by changing coordinates
2. Connect two points. Generate a line
3. Move line using a vector transformation
4. Generate a 2D surface using two curves
5. Extrude surface

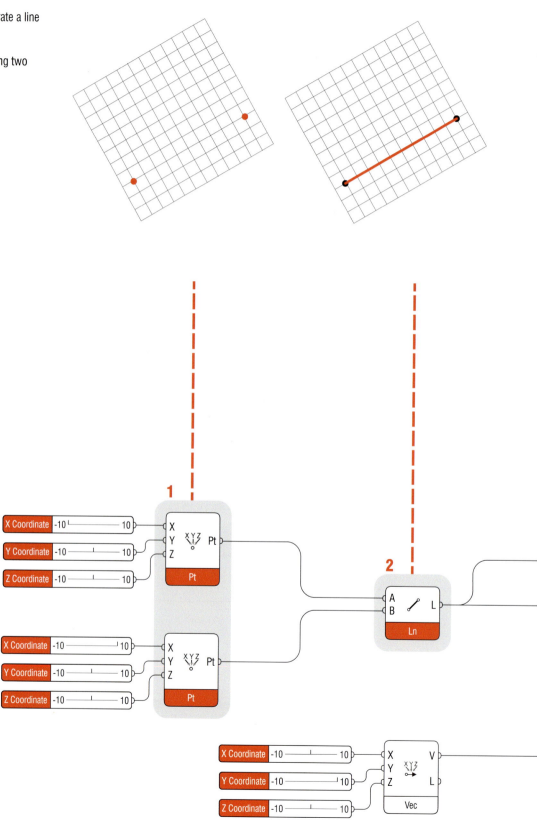

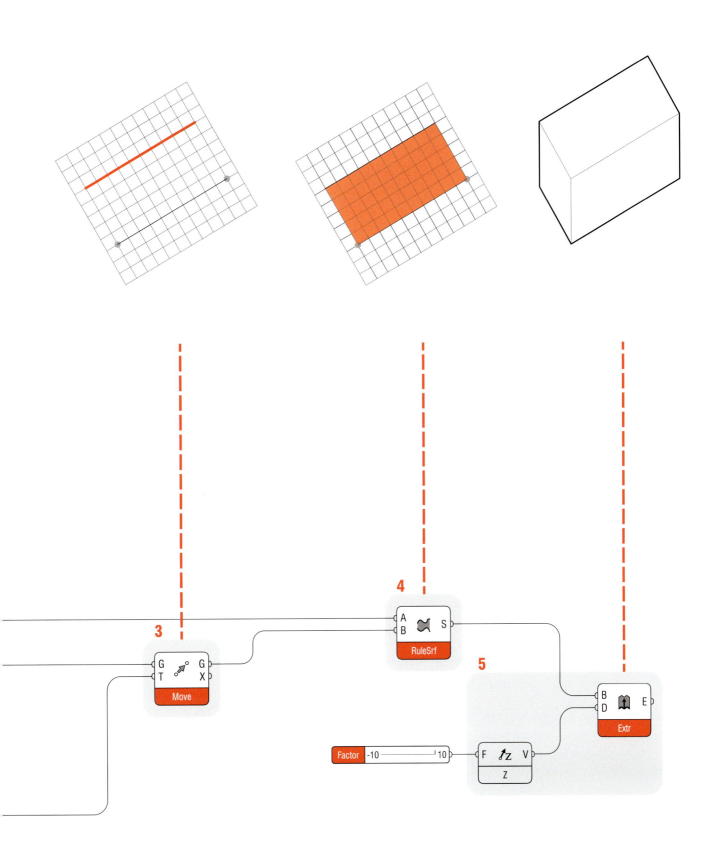

E2 SURFACE LINE PLANE SOLID

1. Create a surface in rhino. Set one surface
2. Evaluate surface, get two points and create a line. Points can be moved using UV coordinates with MD Slider
3. Offset line a distance and create surface between two lines
4. Offset surface
5. Connect surfaces to create extrusion
6. Create a solid

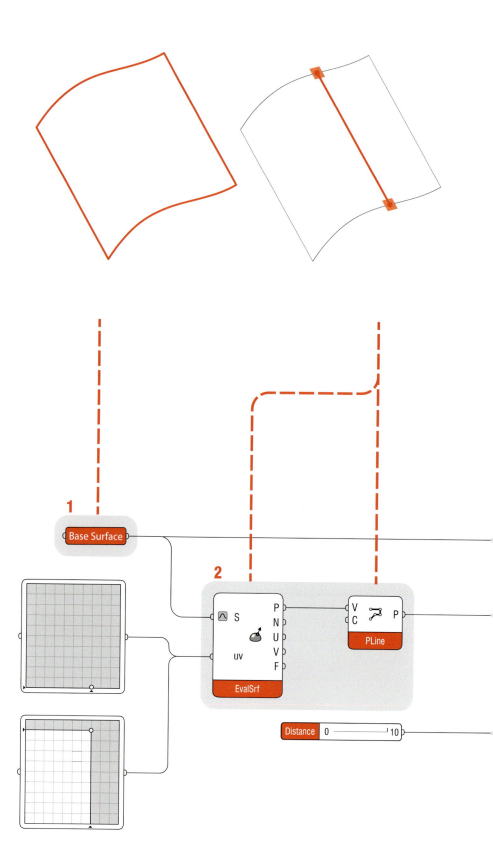

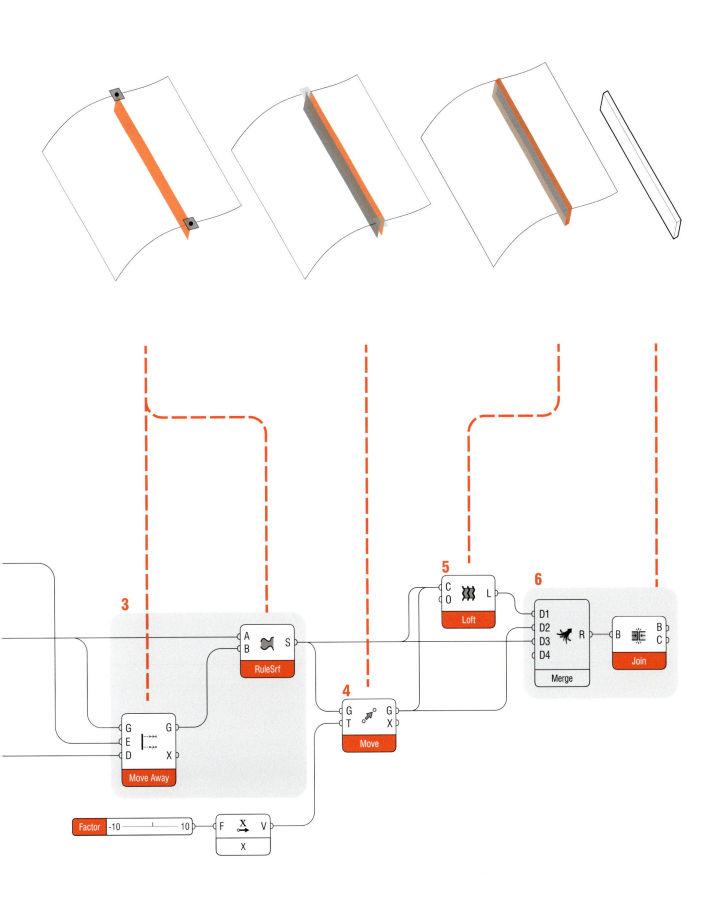

E3 BASE ELEMENT

1. Construct a base point and line. Control coordinates using XYZ slider
2. Offset line a certain distance using dim X slider
3. Create planer surface
4. Extrude and make the element into a frame dimension of XYZ size

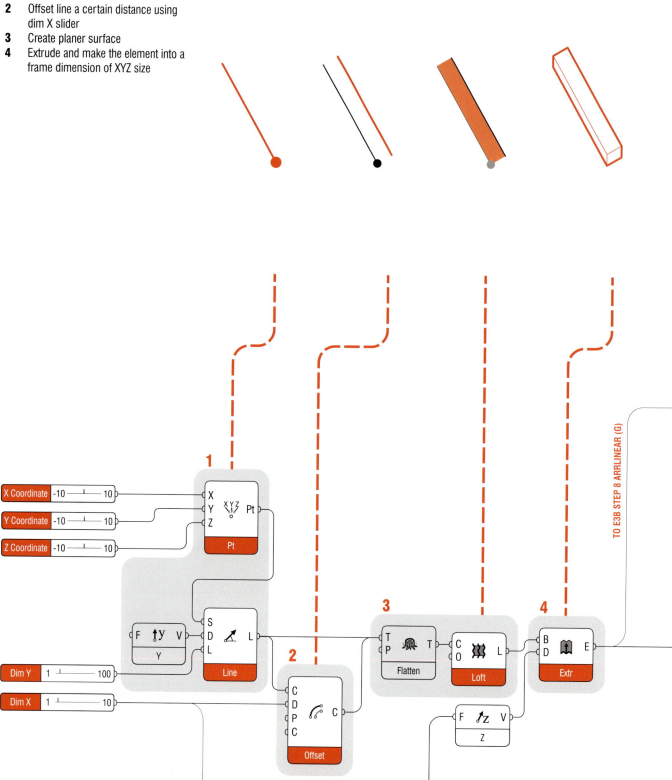

E3A ARRAY

5 Deconstruct box
5A Define a plane
6 Create a box defined by a base plane
7 Offset and copy the element vertically. Offset the multiplied elements horizontally. Control the spacing of the offset

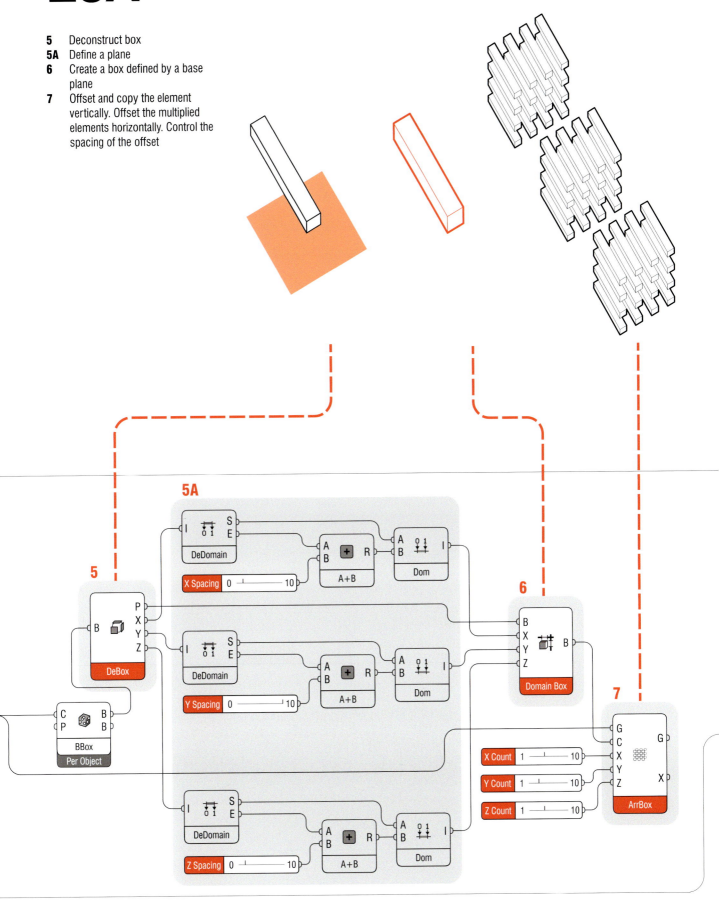

E3B ARRAY 1D SCALE REDUCE

8 Mix array element in the vertical direction
9 Move element horizontally, controlling spacing and count
9A Mix and divide the list
10 Resize a certain distance
11 Merge
12 Reduce the list by a percentage

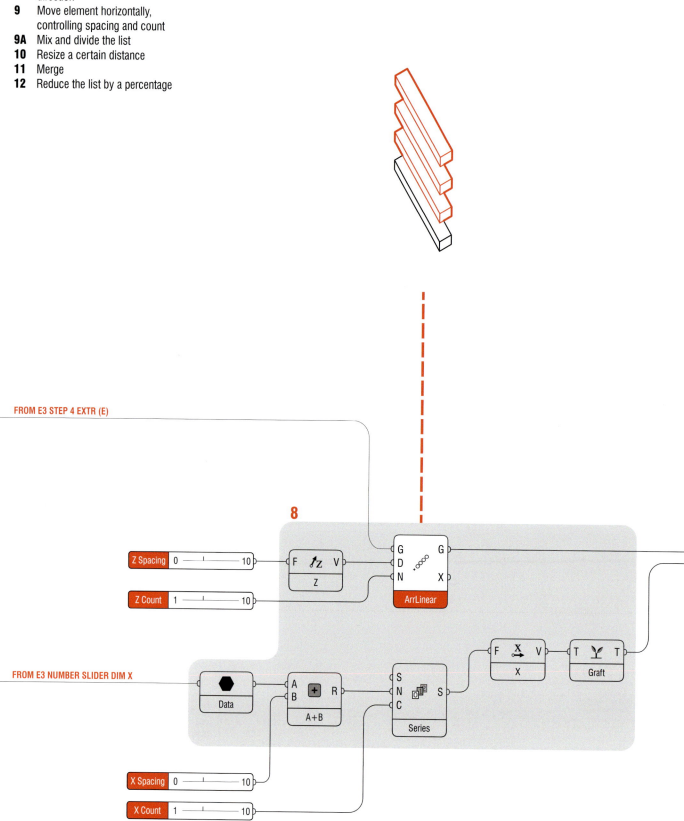

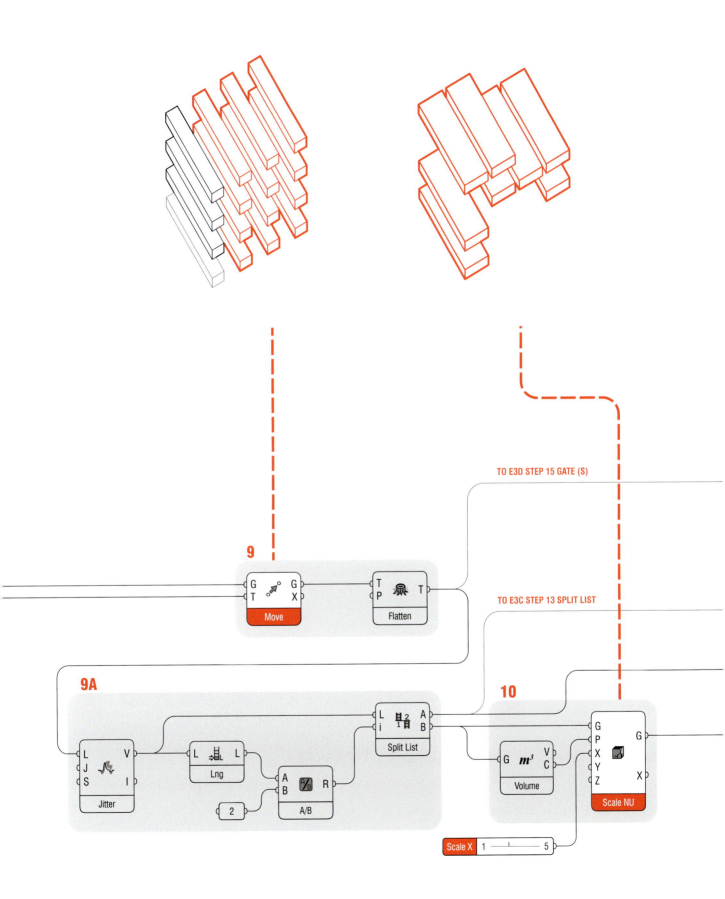

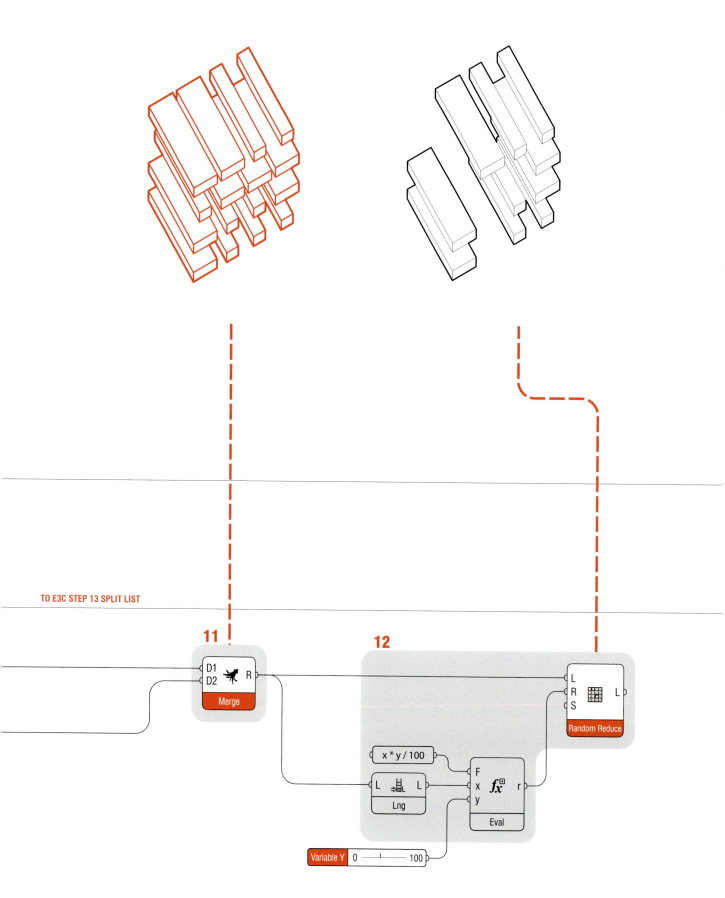

94　**2 E3B ARRAY 1D SCALE REDUCE**

E3C ARRAY ROTATE

13 Continued from E3B Step 9A Split List. Divide the list
14 Rotate elements horizontally and vertically by adjusting angle

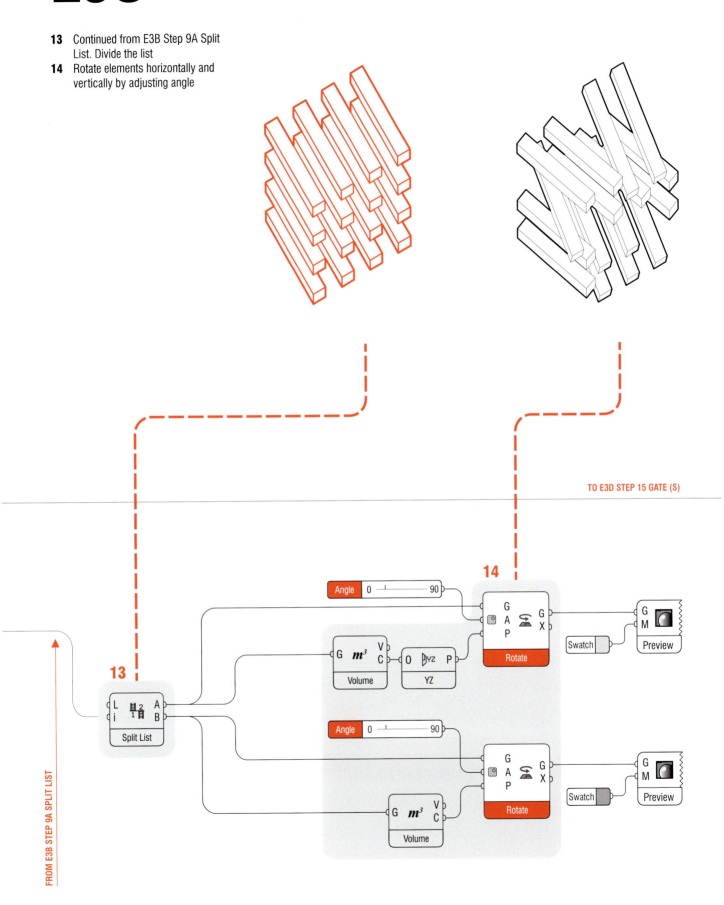

E3D ARRAY TOGGLE 3D SCALE SPLIT

15 Gate with toggle, True = Scale all, False = Scale some
16 Scale all of the elements simultaneously
17 Mix the list and divide
18 Scale some elements in the XYZ dimension

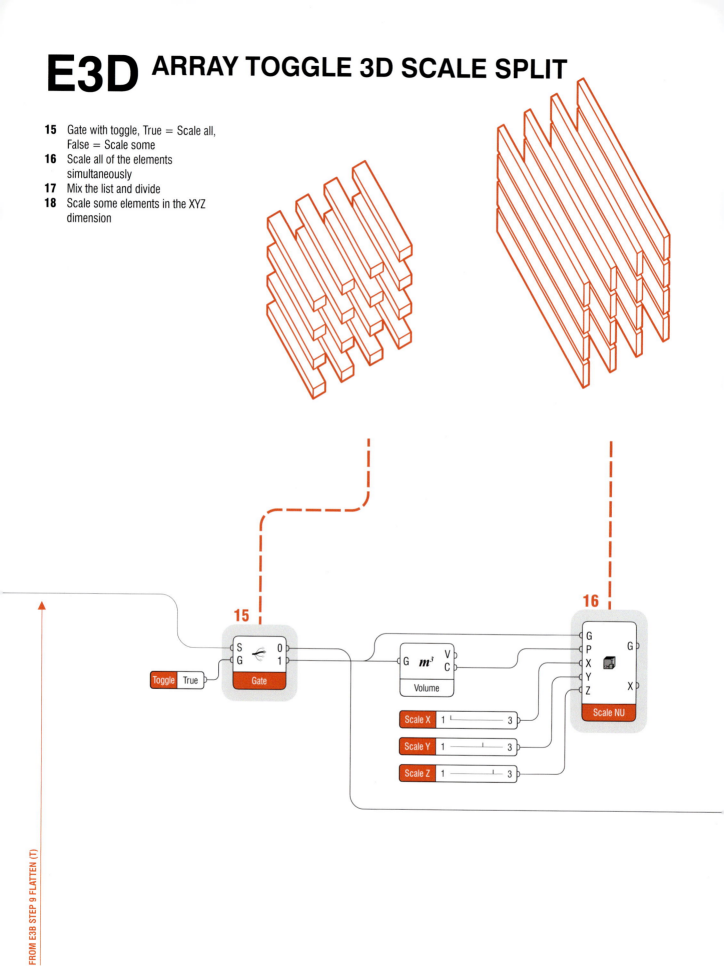

96 2 E3D **ARRAY TOGGLE 3D SCALE SPLIT**

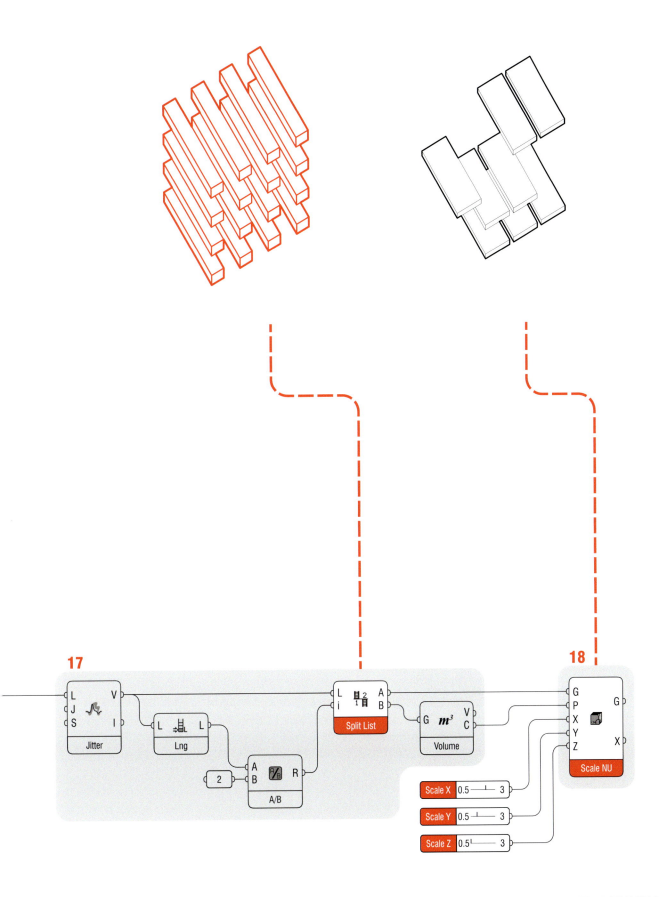

E4 POPULATE POINT CURVE

1. Create base rectangle
1A. Move slider to increase number of points
2. Connect two points. Generate a line
3. Modulus Operator
   0=False, 1=True
4. Create circles or rectangles
5. Conditional statement with the stream filter component. If slider number is even it gives rectangles, else circles

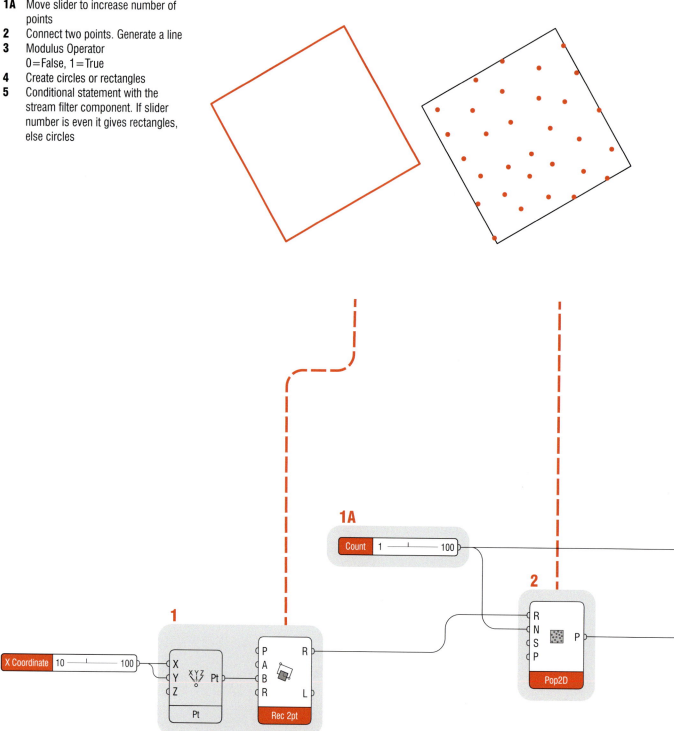

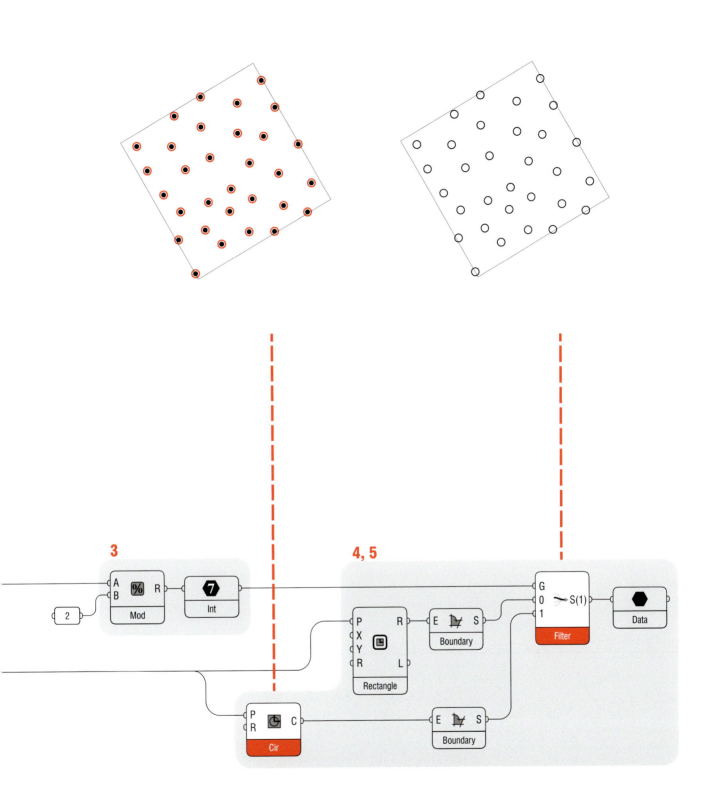

POPULATE POINT CURVE E4 **2** 99

E5 SURFACE SUBDIVIDE

1 Create a surface
2 Prepare V divisions
3 Prepare U divisions
3A Get UV domain
3B Remap domain divisions and create sub-domains
4 Create the domain mask using sub-domains and split surface

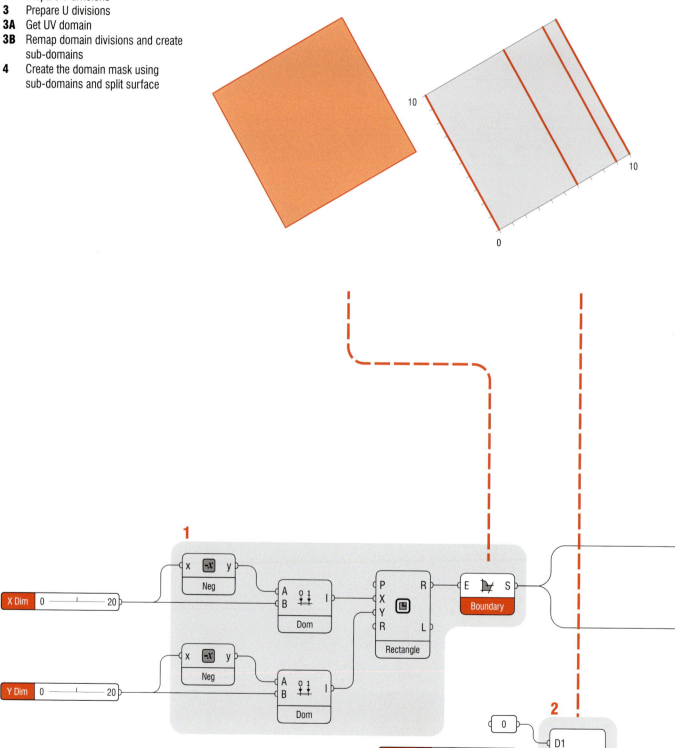

100 2 E5 SURFACE SUBDIVIDE

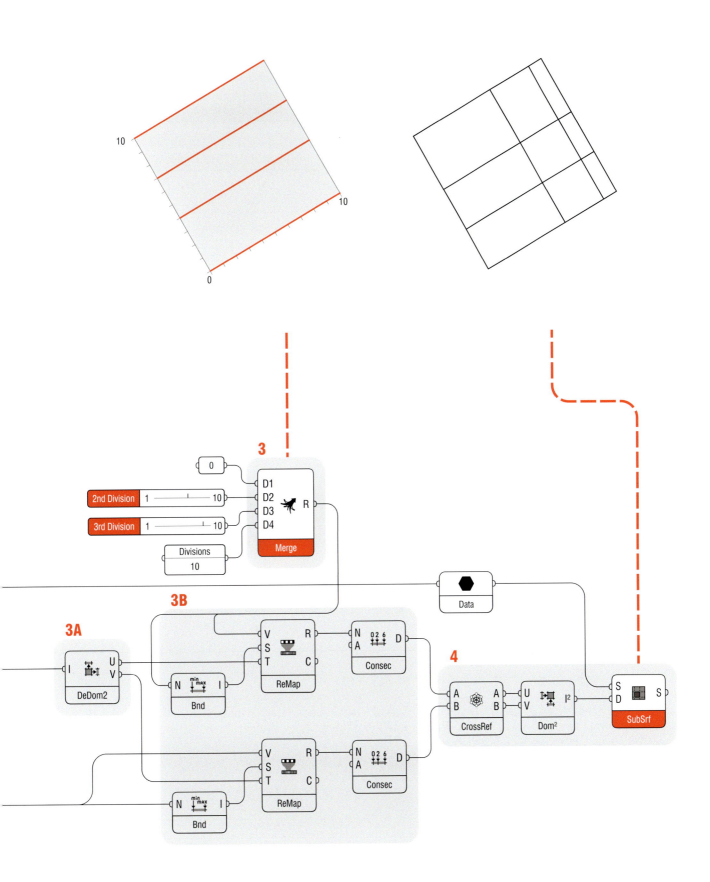

E6 ELEMENT POPULATE ORIENT

1. Create a box
2. Create a rectangle
3. Get random points inside the rectangle
4. Orient box from X direction to Y direction, inside rectangle
5. Orient box in same X direction, inside rectangle

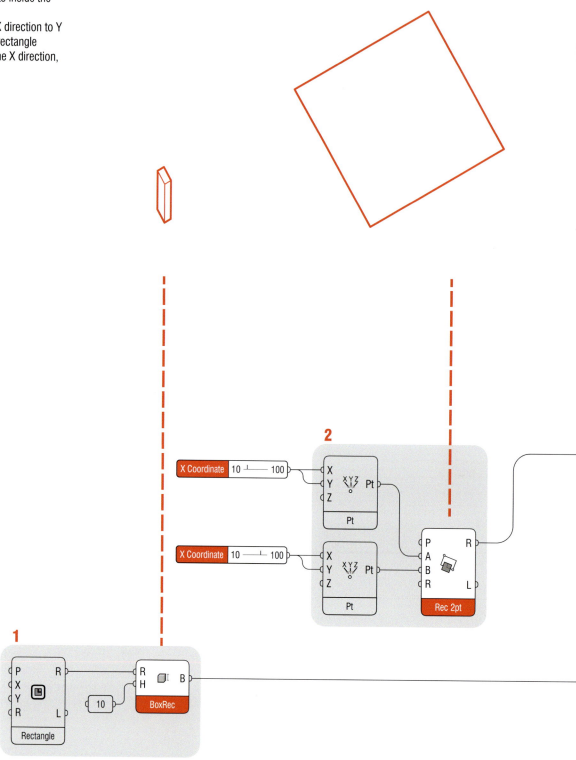

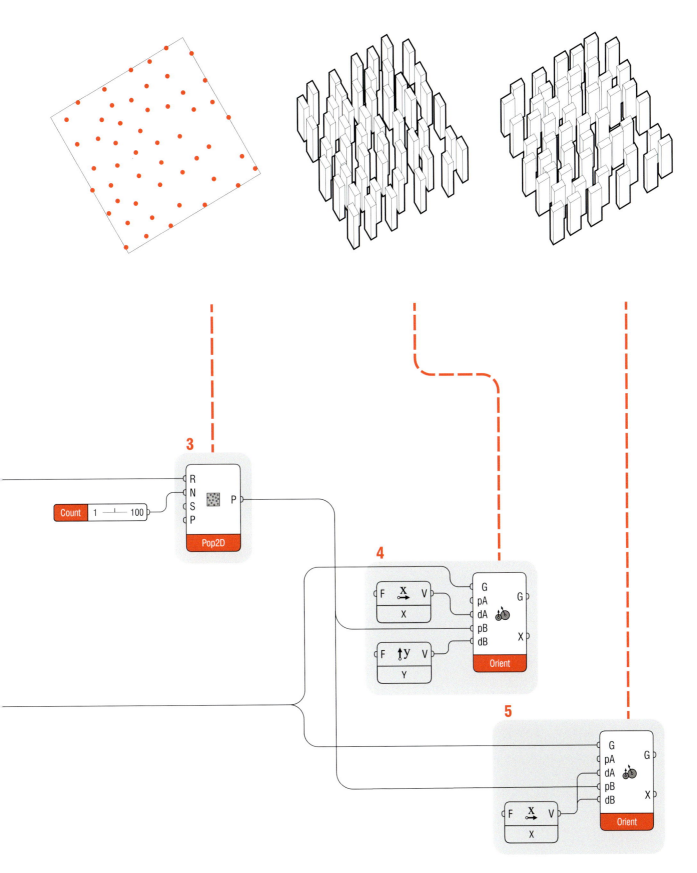

ELEMENT POPULATE ORIENT E6 **2** 103

E7 ELEMENT CURVE DIVIDE ORIENT

1. Create a box
2. Create curve in Rhino and set one curve, generate equally spaced planes along curve
3. Orient box to follow curve
4. Orient box to follow curve at a 90 degree angle

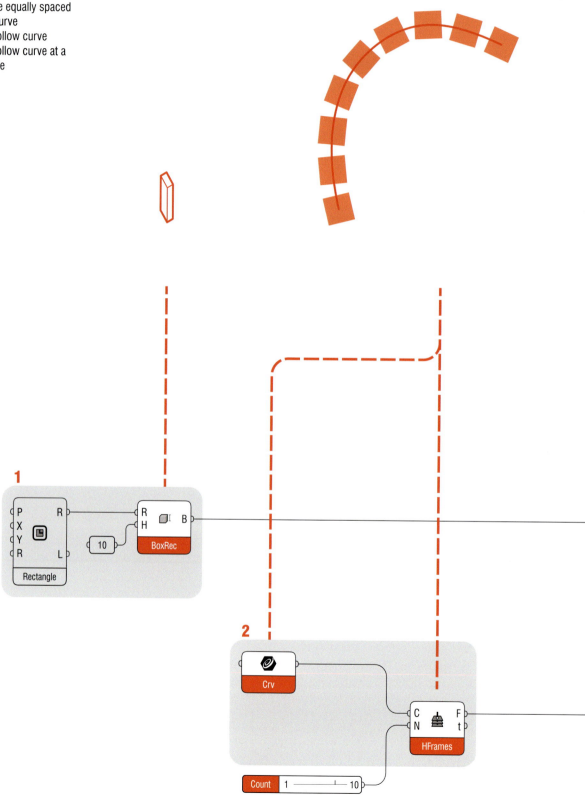

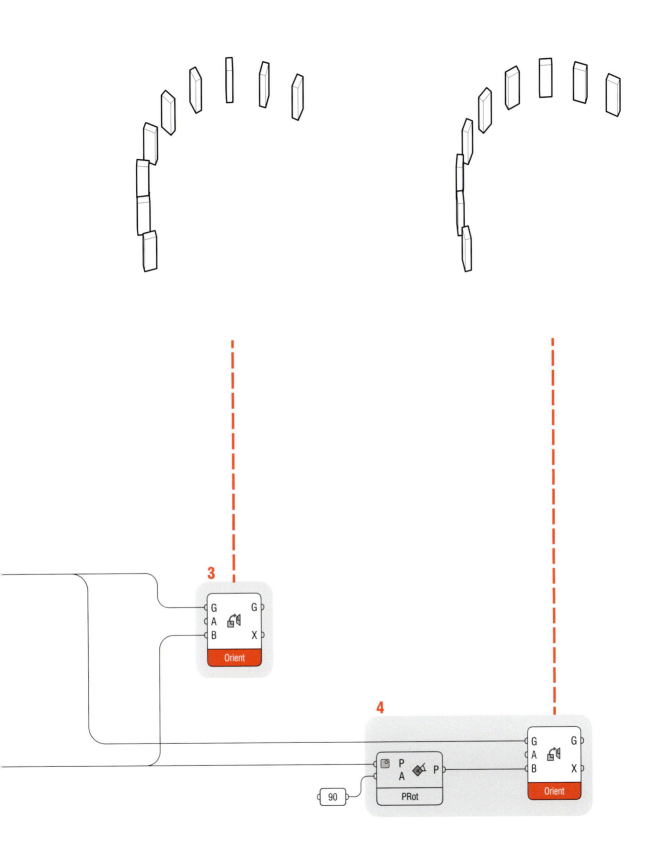

3 CONSTRUCTIONS

In the **CONSTRUCTIONS** section of the book, you will learn how to build tectonic constructs and manipulate their parameters using Rhino/Grasshopper. Through this process you will build complete, functioning parametric definitions that create tectonic objects from scratch and allow users to iterate dimensional changes within the individual and collective members of a given object, affecting overall object shape and character through a variety of operations. The **CONSTRUCTIONS** section is broken into four object types, *frames*, *planes*, *solids*, and *hybrids*, which collectively form the general basis of architectonic typologies. By working through this section, you will learn how to create multiple variations of each of these types. Though there are many ways to construct any given object within Rhino/Grasshopper, the definitions in this book have been refined to provide you a window into the most expedient, cleanest ways of doing so. A series of verbs will be employed for each object and shown in the top left corner of every Definitions page. These verbs are related to how designers think though constructive practice and will be used as parametric drivers within each definition.

Intentional minor redundancy is included within the definitions of each object to provide you with additional practice and so as not to overwhelm you with continually new content. This redundancy will also aid in your ability to find out how to accomplish tasks you may have missed early in the book without the lack of that knowledge stopping your overall progress. In working through these definitions, use the sliders to create as many variants of each object as possible. This is a great way to learn deeply what each parameter does and gives you ideas as to what kind of objects you might build on your own in the future. We include our own variants of the chosen objects at the end of each chapter to inspire you as to all the beautiful alternatives that can be born from a single parametric definition. The ability to examine a multitude of options is a powerful aspect of parametric modeling.

3.1   **Frame Objects**
3.2   **Plane Objects**
3.3   **Solid Objects**
3.4   **Hybrid Objects**

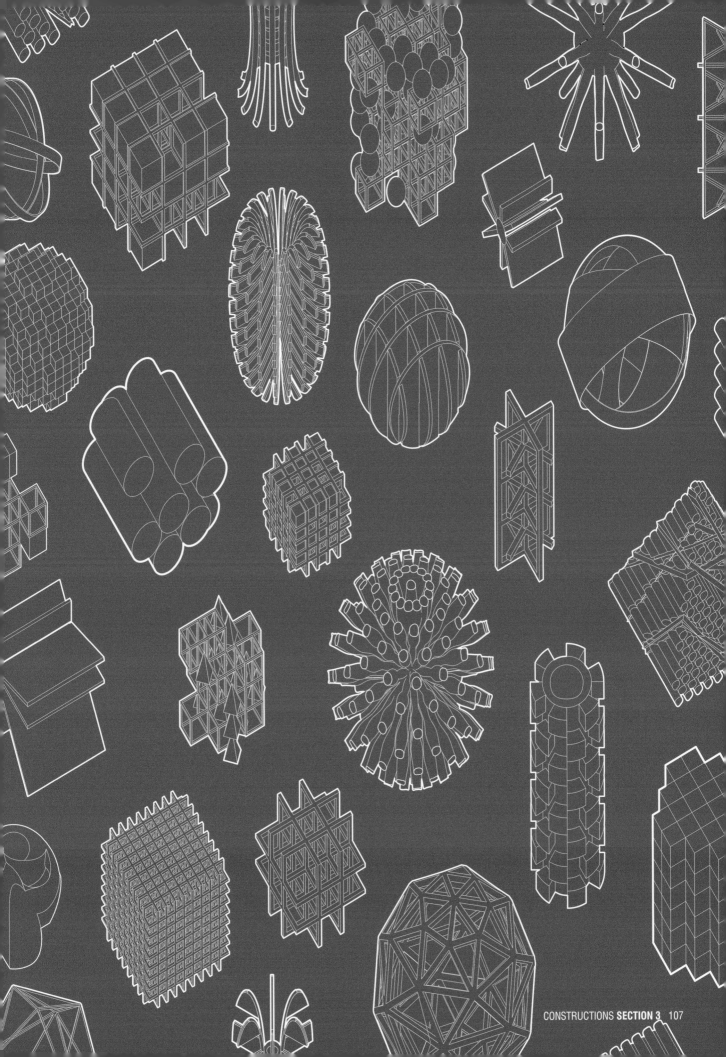

3.1 FRAME OBJECTS

In this book we make a distinction between objects that are composed exclusively of Frame Elements and those that are composed of Planar and Solid Elements. We also make a distinction between a Frame Element and a Frame Object. A Frame Element is a single member within any object that is dimensioned in a way that is proportionally perceived as a frame, as opposed to being perceived as a plane or a solid. A Frame Object, on the other hand, is an aggregation of exclusively Frame Elements in an ordered arrangement. Our previous book, *The Making of Things*, deconstructs this architectonic language thoroughly. Though in-depth definitions of these phenomena fall outside the scope of this work, we have included the architectonic taxonomic map from *The Making of Things* to help you conceptualize the relationships between the object types discussed above.

In this chapter you will learn how to construct four basic Frame Objects, evolving each using a series of verbs which are tied directly to parametric operations in Rhino/Grasshopper. As you build these definitions, experiment with changing elemental profile shapes, sizes, quantities, spacing, etc. for each object. Look carefully at how these individual changes substantively affect each object's visual character and its emotive affect. For instance, thickening Frame Elements gives them a sense of robustness and begins to make the Frame Object appear more like a Solid Object. On the other hand, thinning the Frame Elements can make them, and the Frame Object as a whole, appear tenuous and brittle. Play with the definitions you are building, test different approaches, look long enough to consider how each arrangement resonates emotively in a new way. Additionally, as you work on these definitions and iterate different variations, be sure look at as many other buildings as possible and notice which are similar to the objects you are creating; designers refer to this similarity as a shared "language".

F1   **Division of Boundary**
F2   **Tessellation**
F3   **Revolve**
F4   **Axial Array**

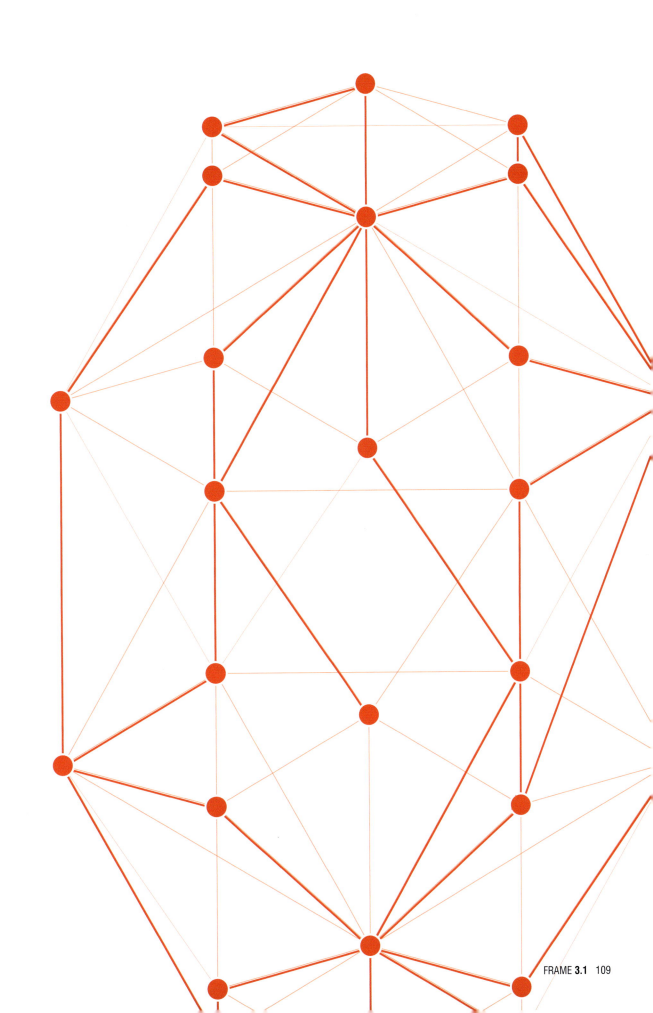

F1 DIVISION OF BOUNDARY

1. Create cube
2. Get 3 edges of cube on X Y Z
3. Divide X Y Z edges with planes
4. Cull first and last plane
5. Get border curves
5A. Clean and explode into X Y Z branches
5B. Get intersections
6. Explode initial intersection curves and create a unique flat tree with all curves
7. Extend curves
8. Get first and last plane of each curve
9. Create frame profile curve
10. Create frames

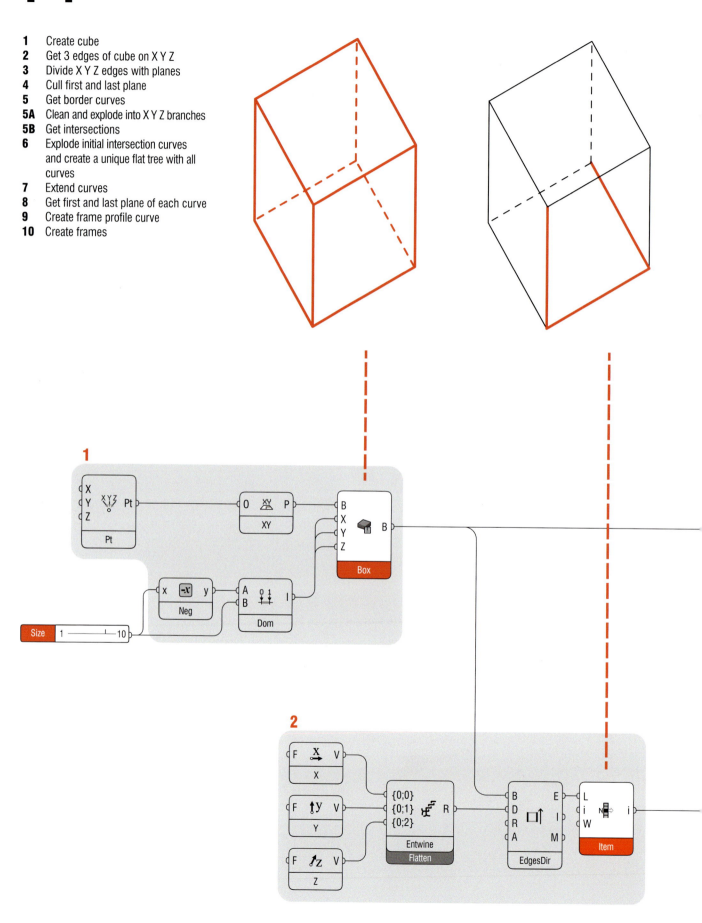

3.1 FRAME F1 **DIVISION OF BOUNDARY**

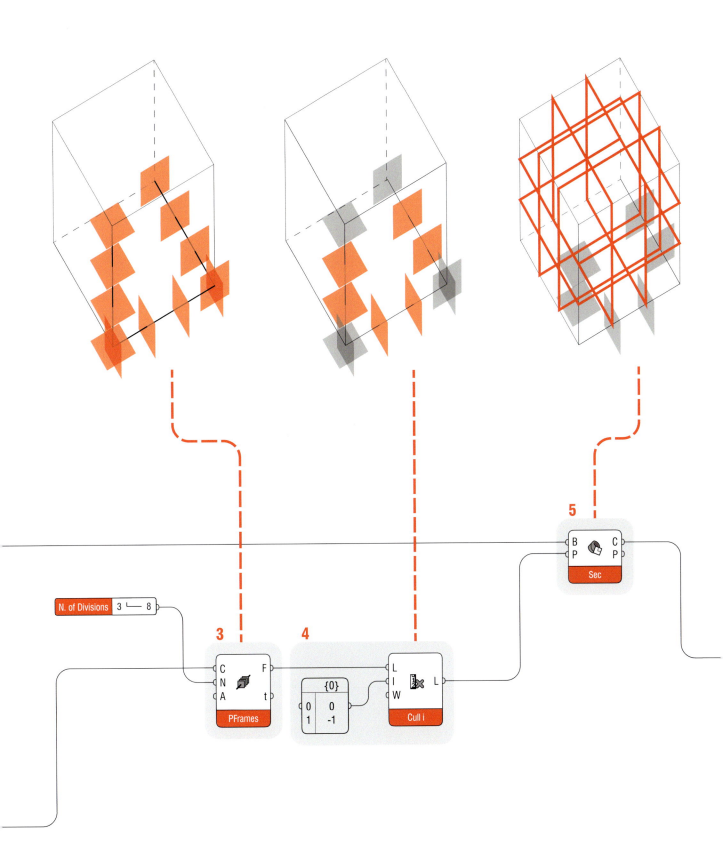

DIVISION OF BOUNDARY FRAME F1 **3.1** 111

F1

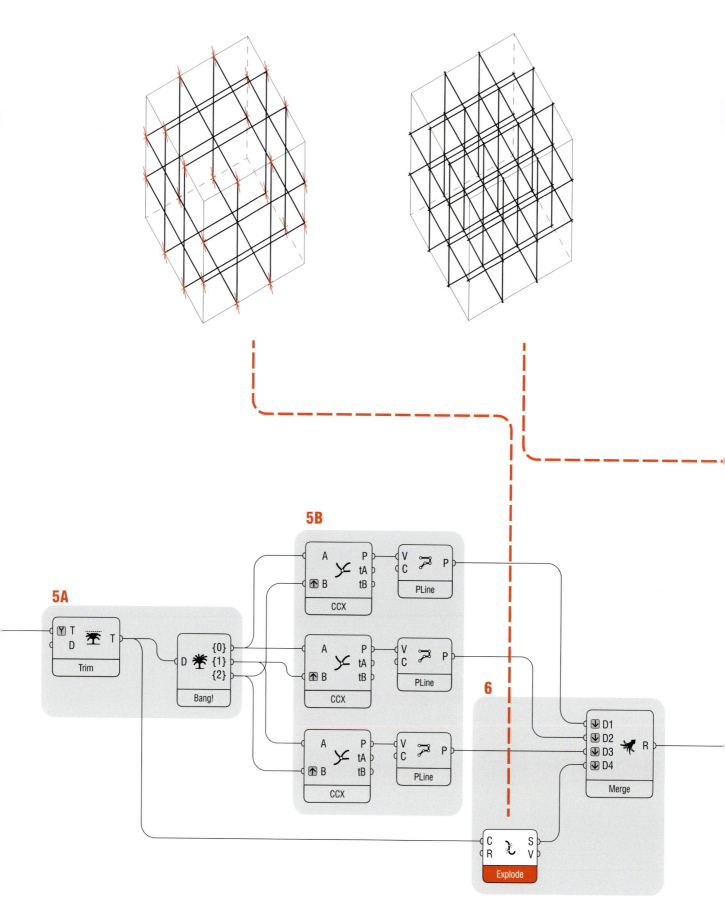

3.1 FRAME F1 **DIVISION OF BOUNDARY**

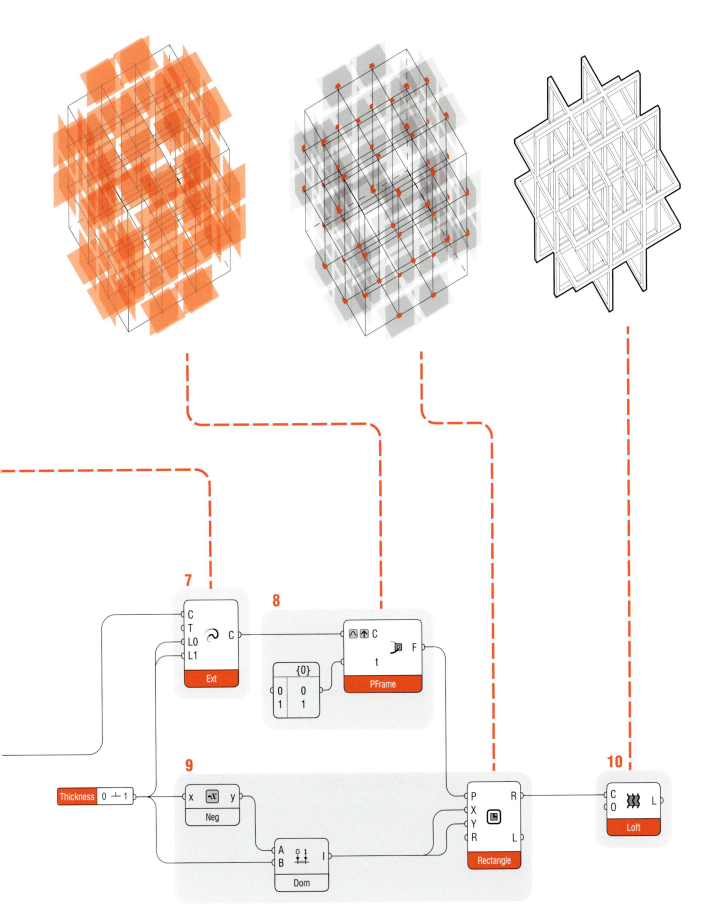

DIVISION OF BOUNDARY FRAME F1 **3.1**

THICKNESS ▼

DIVISIONS ▼

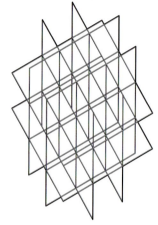
CU . ST . SM . LD

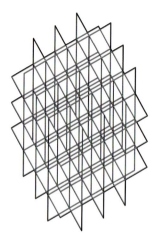
CU . ST . SM . MD

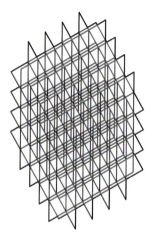
CU . ST . SM . HD

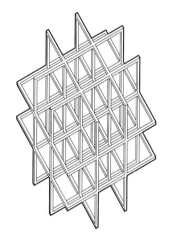
CU . ST . ME . LD

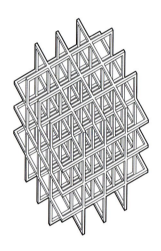
CU . ST . ME . MD

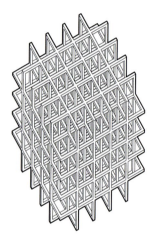
CU . ST . ME . HD

CU . ST . LA . MD

CU . ST . LA . HD

CU . ST . LA . HD

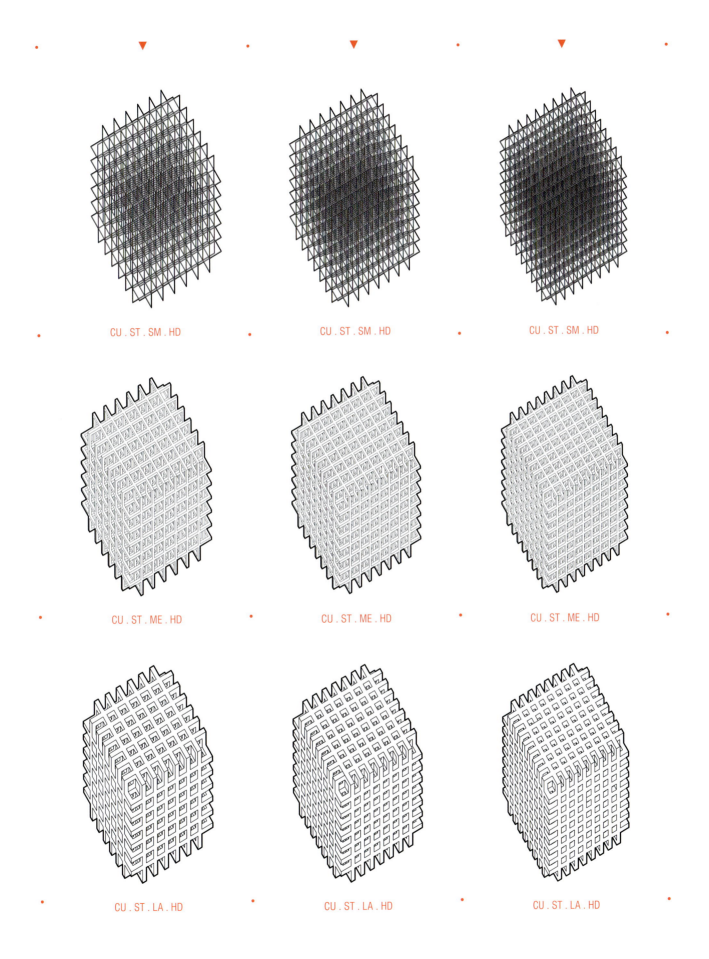

F2 TESSELLATION

1. Create sphere
2. Create regular point matrix grid on sphere
3. Flip point matrix. Split the data into two branches with a pattern
4. Join even and odd items and remove null branches
4A. Join even and odd items and remove null branches
5. Flip branches and create series of vertical polyline curves
6. Flip branches and create series of vertical polyline curves
6A. Remove first and last branches that contain points of degeneration
6B. Remove first and last item, Flatten Entwine and remove input
7. Create closed horizontal polyline curves, Remove small segments, Divide polyline into segments
8. Create clean tree with two branches, Remove last item on each branch, Divide polyline into segments, Create clean tree with three branches by polyline, Graft Entwine and remove input
9. Shift index by -1, Get first and last perpendicular frame
10. Align frames to sphere center
11. Create rectangle
12. Create frame elements

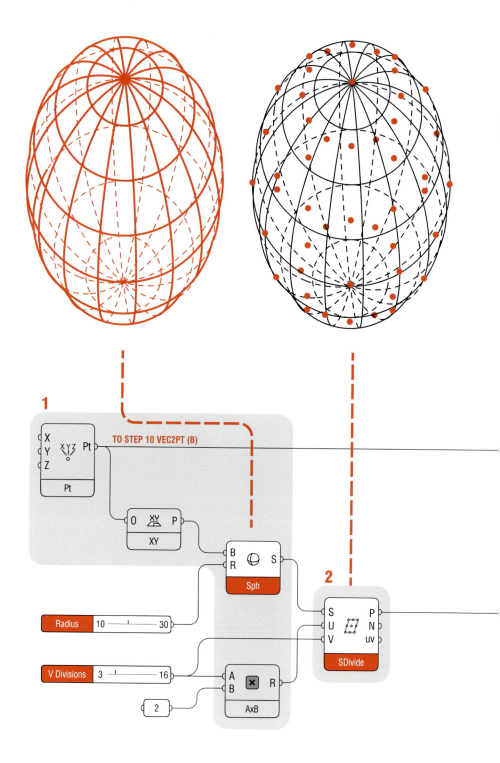

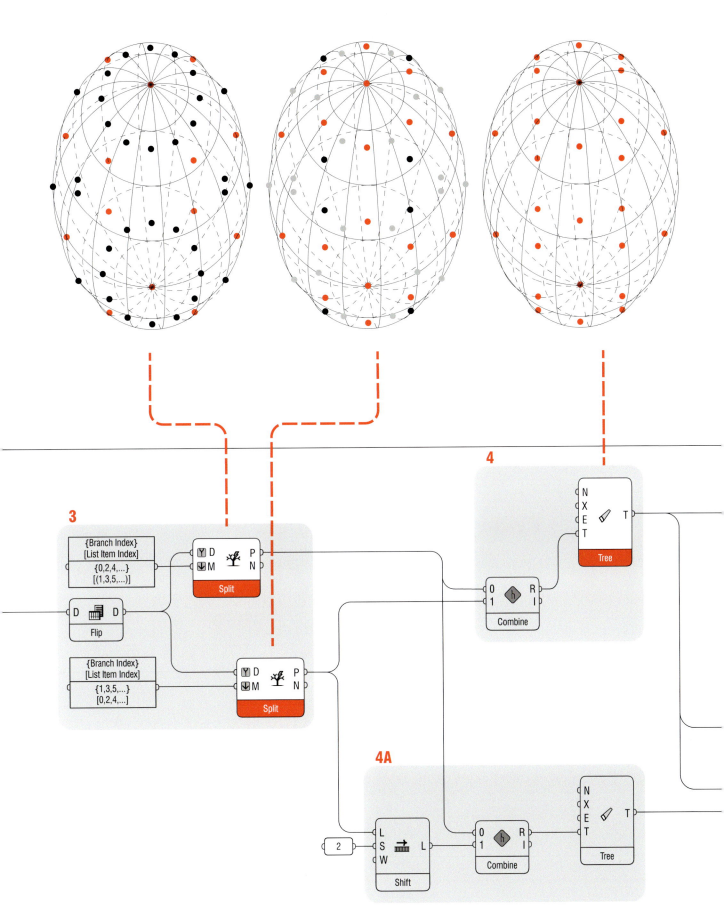

TESSELLATION FRAME F2 **3.1** 117

F2

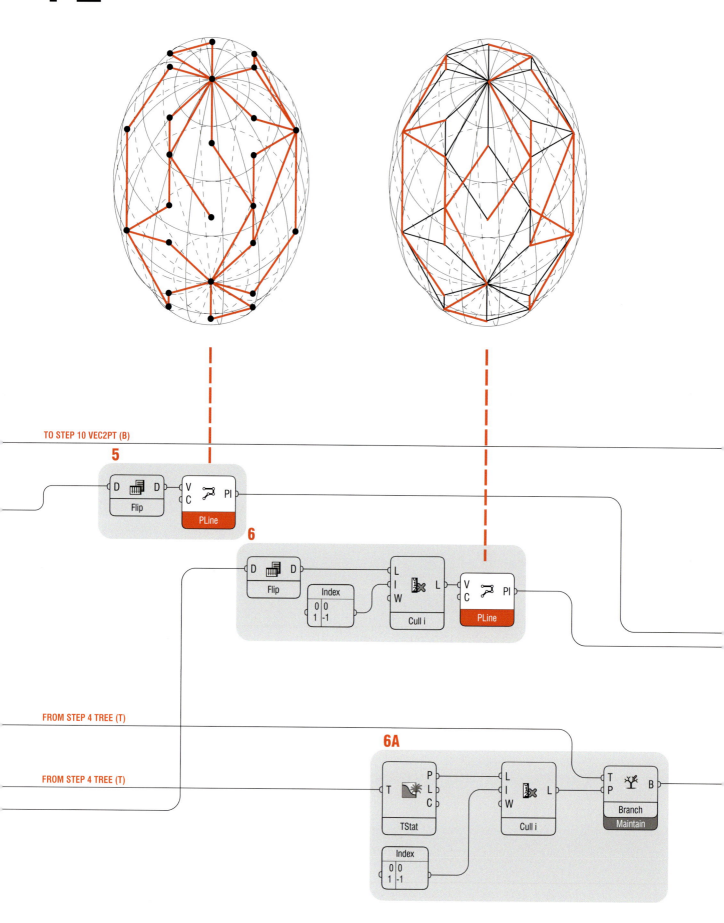

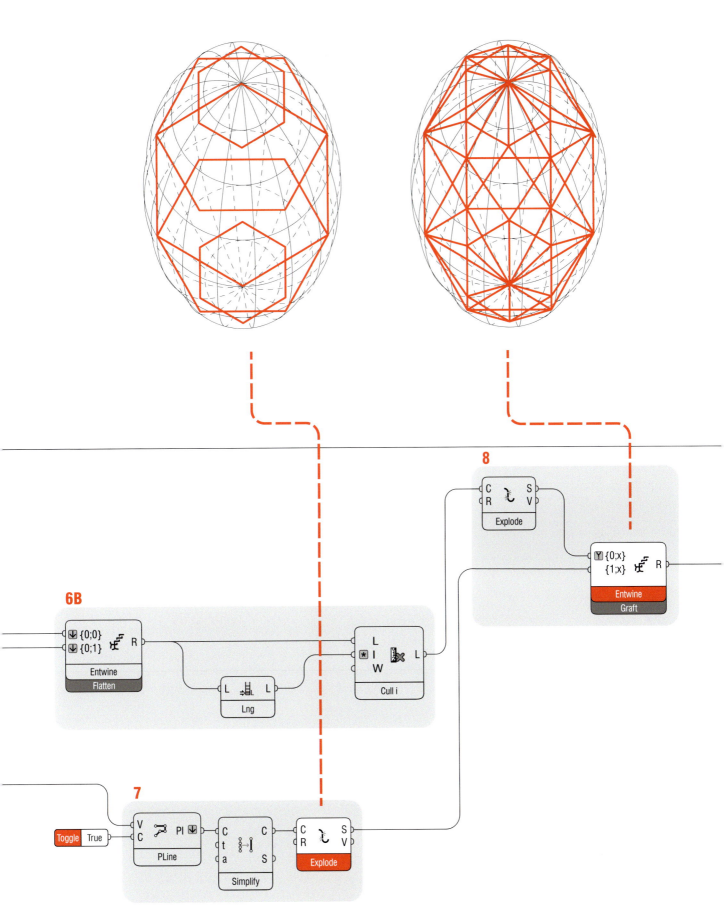

TESSELLATION FRAME F2 **3.1**

F2

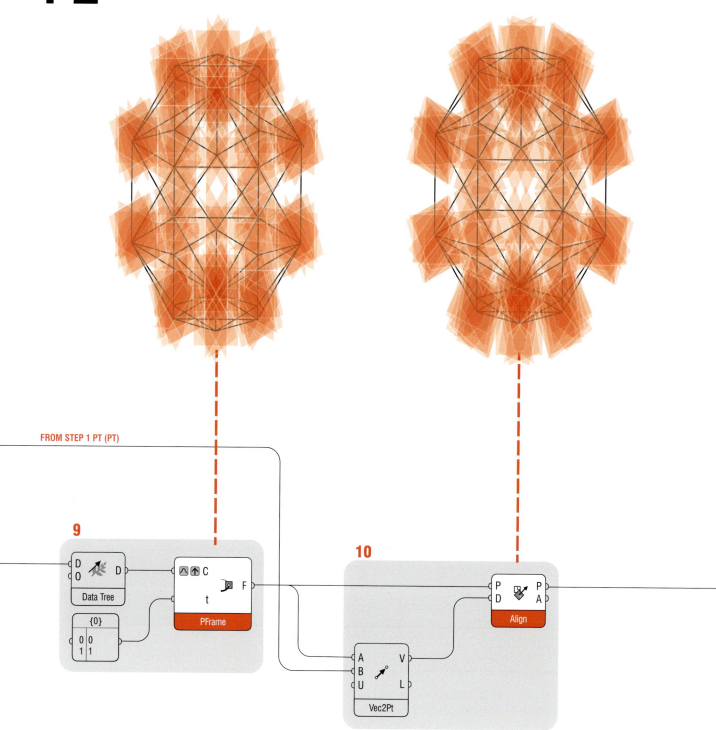

3.1 FRAME F2 **TESSELLATION**

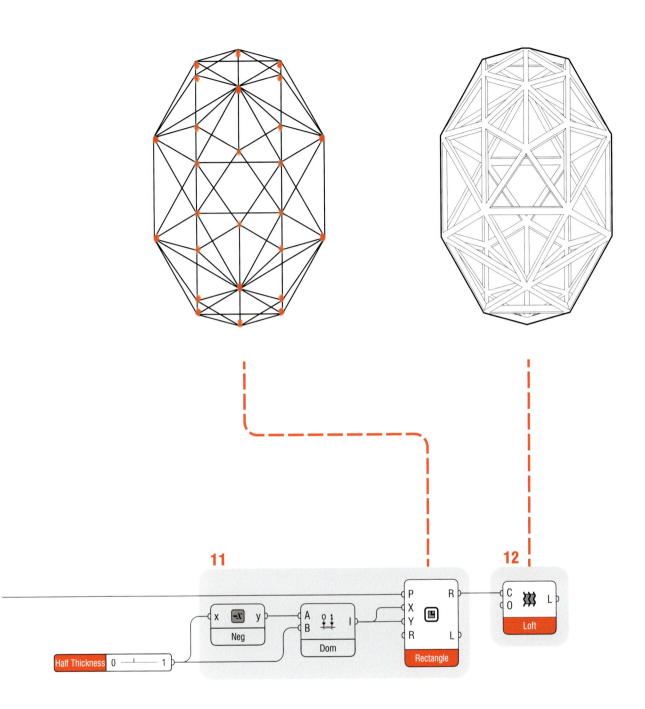

THICKNESS ▼

DIVISIONS ▼

SP . ST . SM . LD	SP . ST . SM . LD	SP . ST . SM . LD
SP . ST . ME . LD	SP . ST . ME . LD	SP . ST . ME . LD
SP . ST . LA . MD	SP . ST . LA . MD	SP . ST . LA . MD

3.1 FRAME F2 TESSELLATION **VARIATIONS**

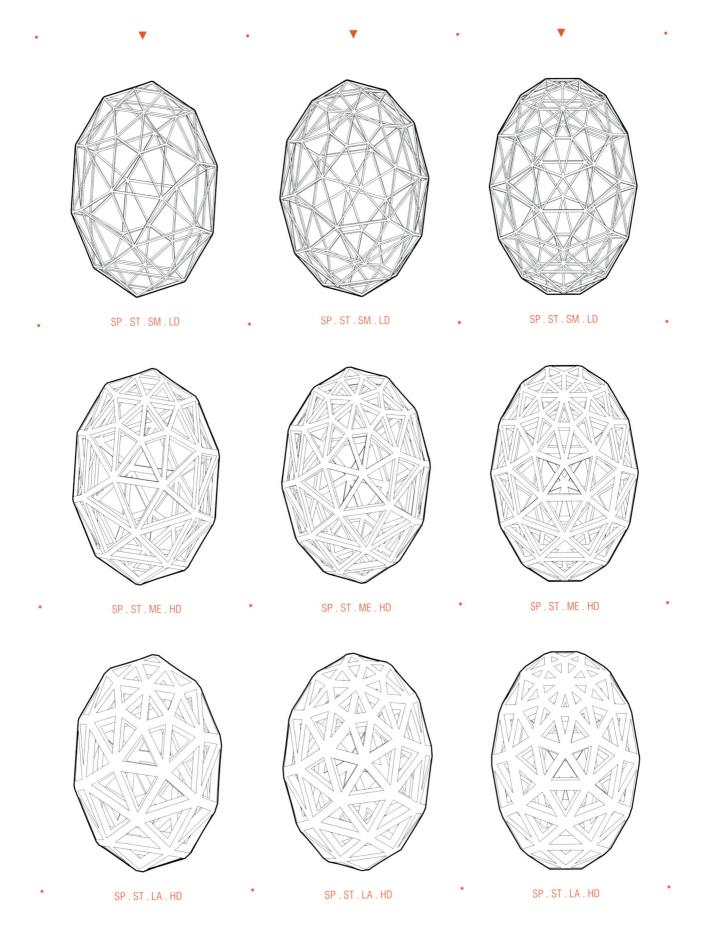

VARIATIONS TESSELLATION FRAME F2 **3.1**

F3 REVOLVE

1 Create cylinder
2 Create center vertical axis
2A Get cylinder seam
3 Translate vertical axis
4 Create curve
5 Divide vertical axis into 3 parts
6 Take center division curve
7 Create pipe around curve from Step 4
8 Divide center division curve in Step 6 with perpendicular planes
9 Get points on curve, find closest point on curve from Step 4
9A Calculate radius of curve and circle
10 Create circles
11 Create frame elements
12 Polar array frame elements
13 Cap ends and union

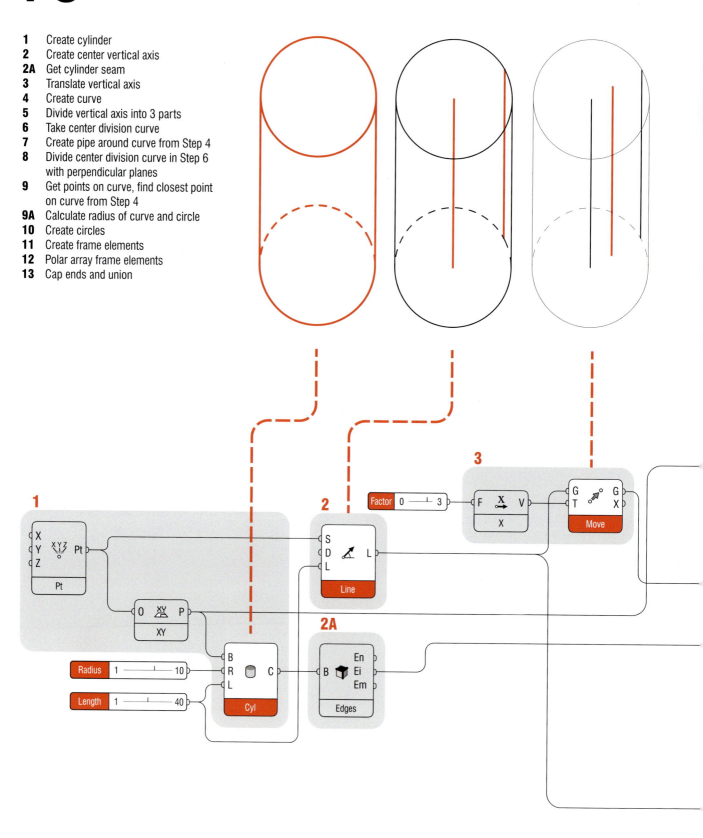

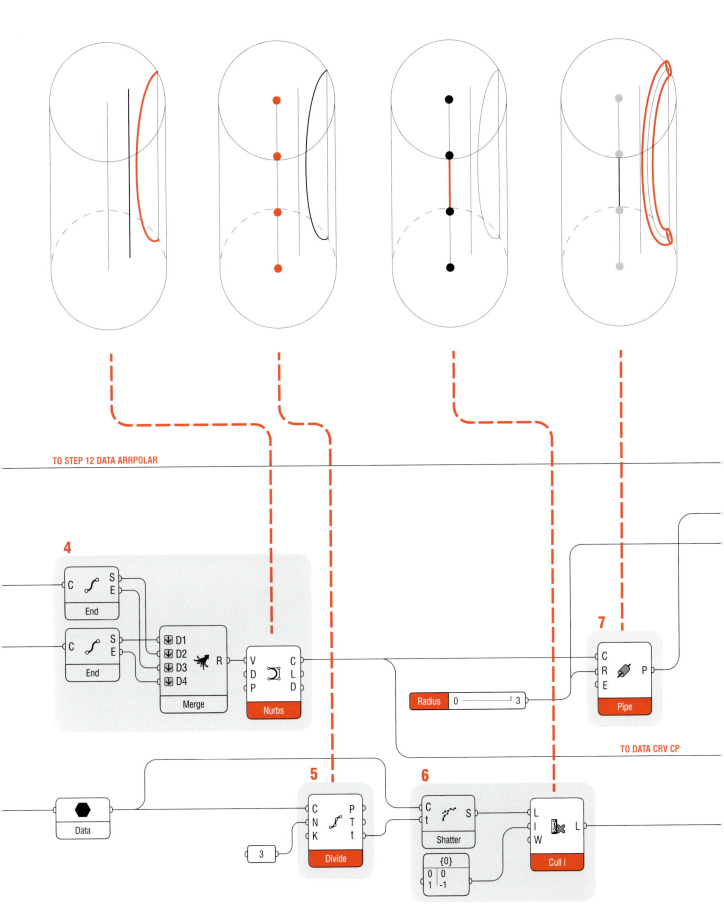

F3

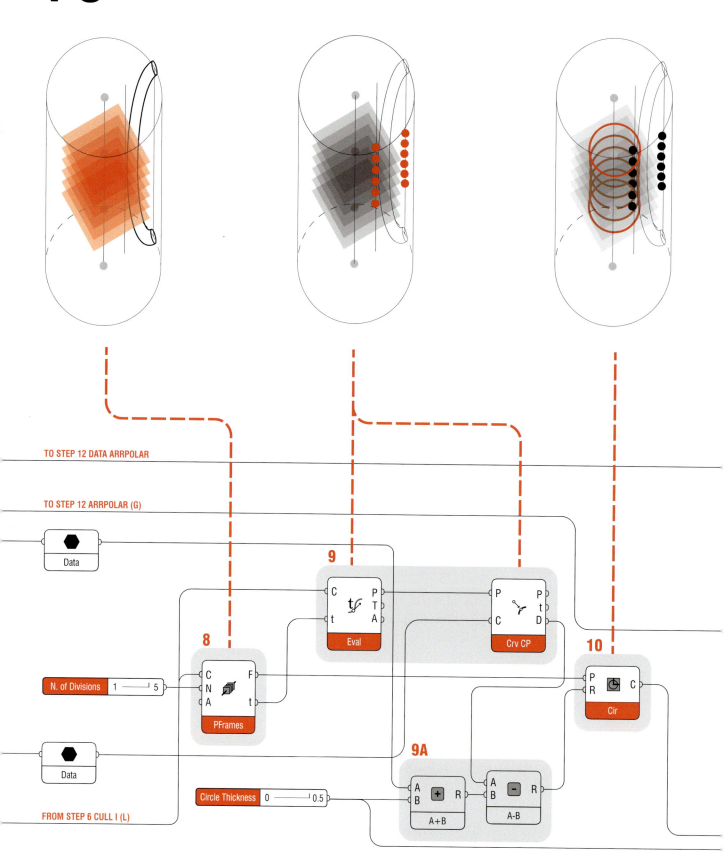

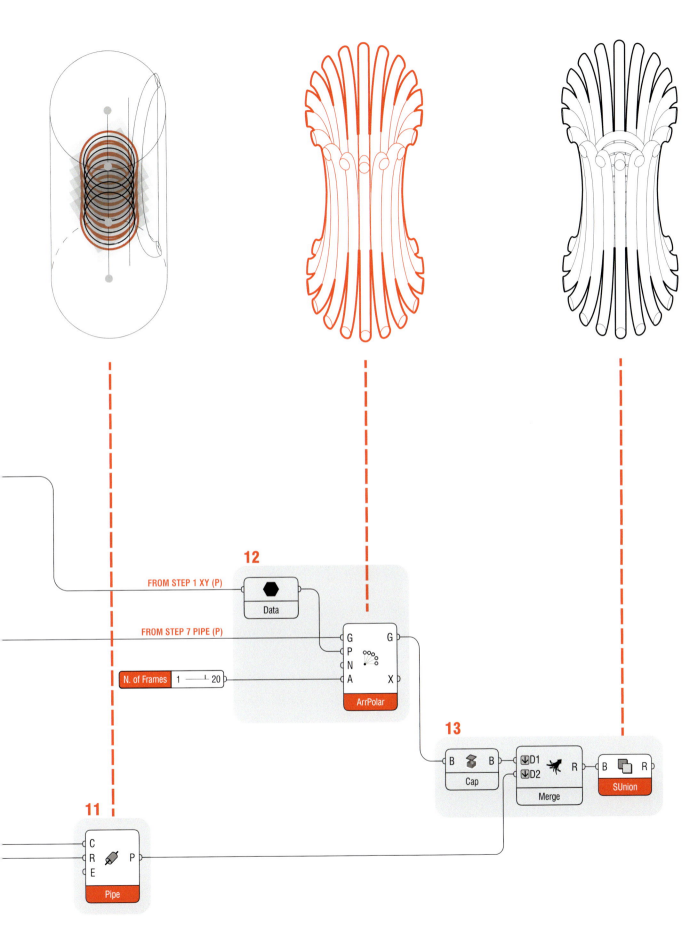

DIVISIONS ▼

THICKNESS ▼

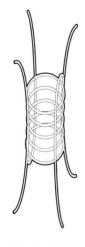
CY . FO . SM . LD

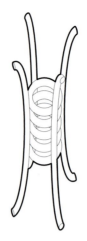
CY . FO . ME . MD

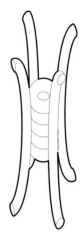
CY . FO . LA . HD

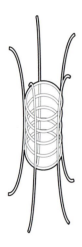
CY . FO . SM . LD

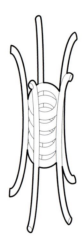
CY . FO . ME . MD

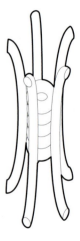
CY . FO . LA . HD

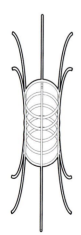
CY . FO . SM . LD

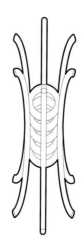
CY . FO . ME . MD

CY . FO . LA . HD

128   **3.1** FRAME F3 REVOLVE **VARIATIONS**

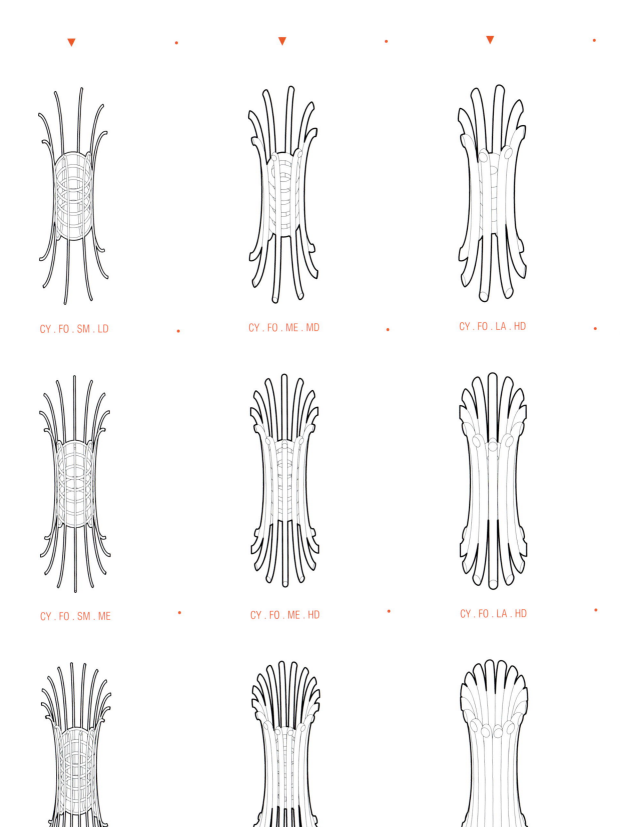

F4 AXIAL ARRAY

1. Create cylinder
2. Create vertical axis
3. Divide vertical axis
4. Get even divisions
5. Get odd divisions
6. Create curves at first set of points
7. Get end points
8. Connect points with line
9. Create curves with rotation at second set of points
10. Flatten and combine all curve sets
11. Extend curves
12. Get perpendicular plane at first and last point of each curve
13. Create rectangle at each plane
14. Create frame elements
15. Array about axis

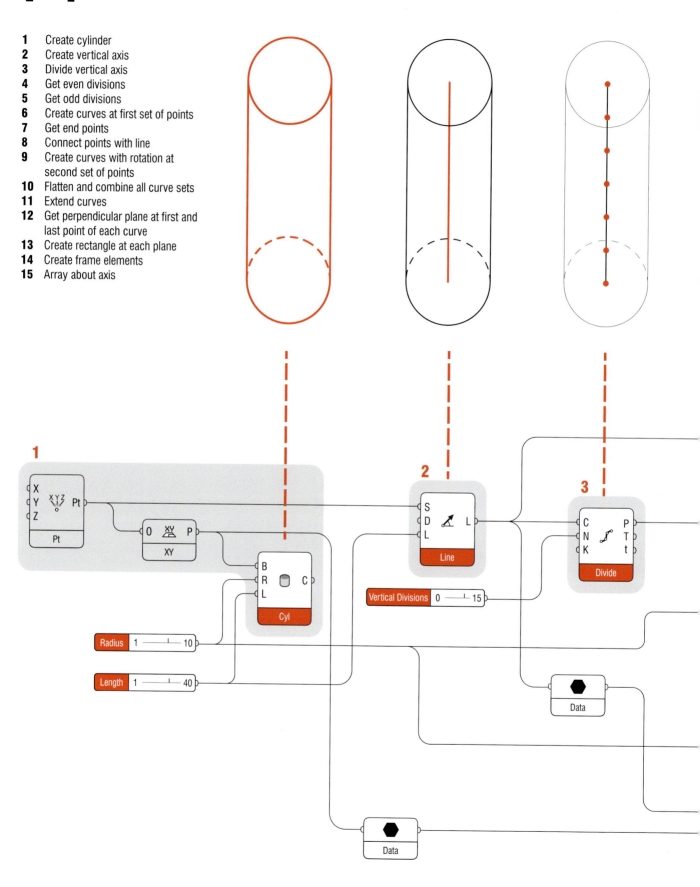

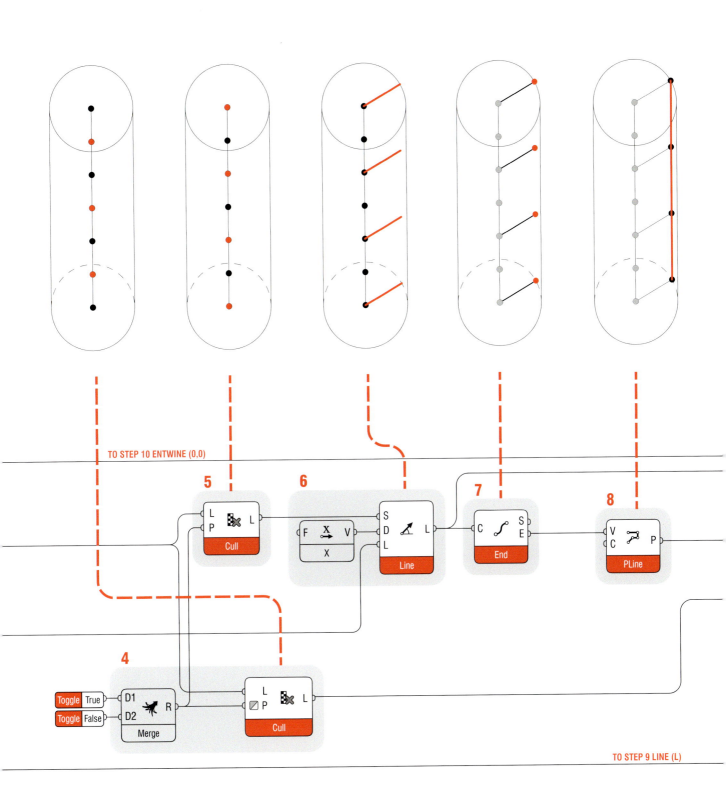

F4

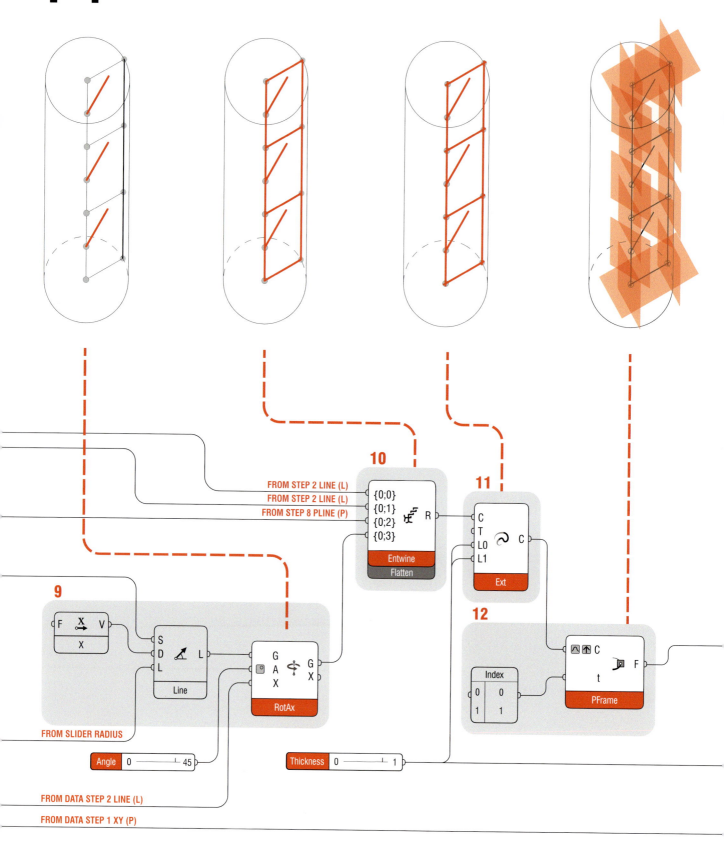

132   3.1 FRAME F4 **AXIAL ARRAY**

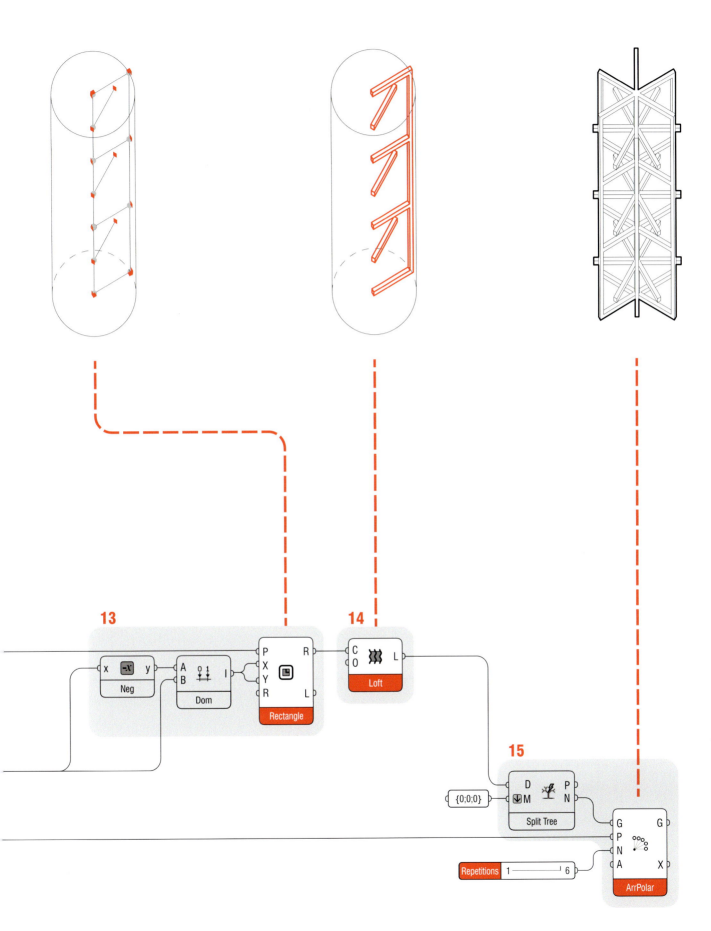

THICKNESS ▼ ▼ ▼

DIVISIONS ▶

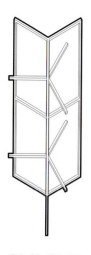
CY . ST . SM . LD

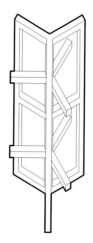
CY . ST . ME . LD

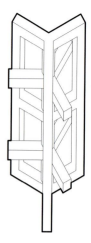
CY . ST . LA . LD

▶
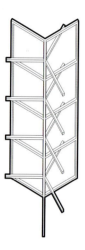
CY . ST . SM . LD

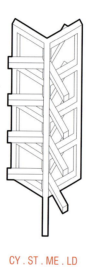
CY . ST . ME . LD

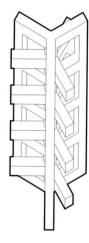
CY . ST . LA . MD

▶
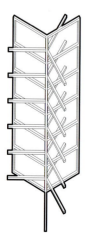
CY . ST . SM . LD

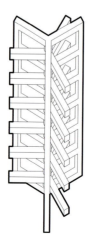
CY . ST . ME . MD

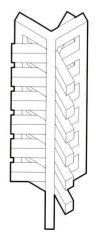
CY . ST . LA . MD

134   3.1 FRAME F4 AXIAL ARRAY **VARIATIONS**

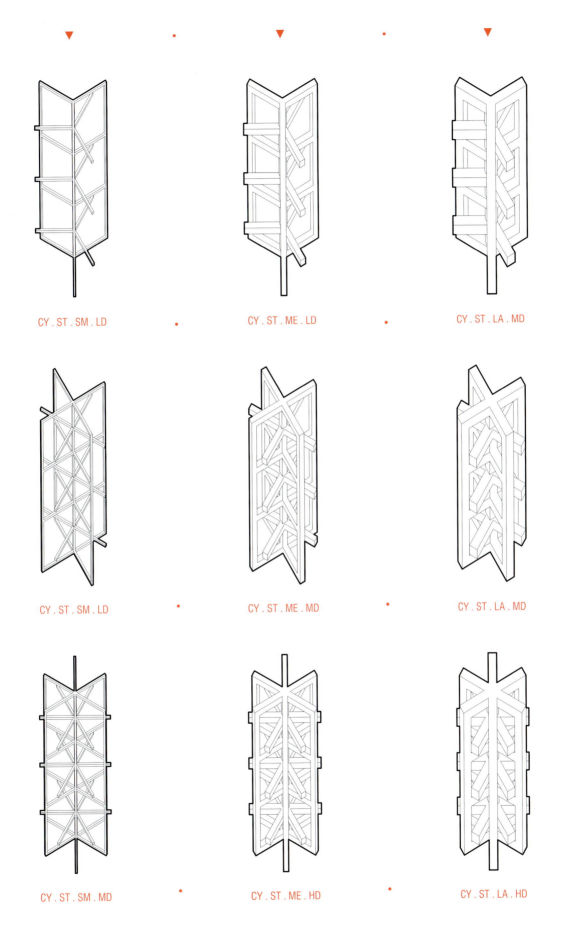

3.2 PLANE OBJECTS

In this book we make a distinction between objects that are composed exclusively of Planar Elements and those that are composed of Frame and Solid Elements. We also make a distinction between a Planar Element and a Planar Object. A Planar Element is a single member within any object that is dimensioned in a way that is proportionally perceived as a plane, as opposed to being perceived as a frame or a solid. A Planar Object, on the other hand, is an aggregation of exclusively Planar Elements in an ordered arrangement. Our previous book, *The Making of Things*, deconstructs this architectonic language thoroughly. Though in-depth definitions of these phenomena fall outside the scope of this work, we have included the architectonic taxonomic map from *The Making of Things* to help you conceptualize the relationships between the object types discussed above.

In this chapter you will learn how to construct four basic Planar Objects, evolving each using a series of verbs which are tied directly to parametric operations in Rhino/Grasshopper. As you build these definitions, experiment with changing elemental profile shapes, sizes, quantities, spacing, etc. for each object. Look carefully at how these individual changes substantively affect each object's visual character and its emotive affect. For instance, bending Planar Elements gives them a sense of elasticity and tension as they are perceived as desiring to spring back into a straight position. Densifying Planar Elements, even when each is thin, will make a Planar Object appear more like a solid, becoming more susceptible to maneuvers like carving acting as a space creator. Play with the definitions you are building, test different approaches, look long enough to consider how each arrangement resonates emotively in a new way. Additionally, as you work on these definitions and iterate different variations, be sure look at as many other buildings as possible and notice which are similar to the objects you are creating; designers refer to this similarity as a shared "language".

P1   **Waffle**
P2   **Centric Intersection**
P3   **Modular Growth**
P4   **Wrap**

PLANE **3.2** 137

P1 WAFFLE

1 Create cube
2 Create sphere
2A Select cube or sphere
3 Get edges on X and Y, Flatten Entwine and remove input
4 Create perpendicular plane divisions
5 Remove first and last from list
6 Get curves of object from Step 2
7 Create surfaces
7A Get vectors normal to surfaces
7B Move surface to one side of plane
7C Define direction and distance of plane extrusion
8 Get curves at intersection
8A Extend curves past intersections
8B Get half the plane thickness
8C Set a boolean tolerance
9 Get half the length of curve at intersection
9A Create vector of positive direction and vector of negative direction
9B Create base rectangles for boolean subtractive elements
10 Create rectangular element for boolean difference at top half
11 Create rectangular element for boolean difference at bottom half
12 Extrude surfaces from Step 7, split items into two groups
13 Boolean difference top half
14 Boolean difference bottom half

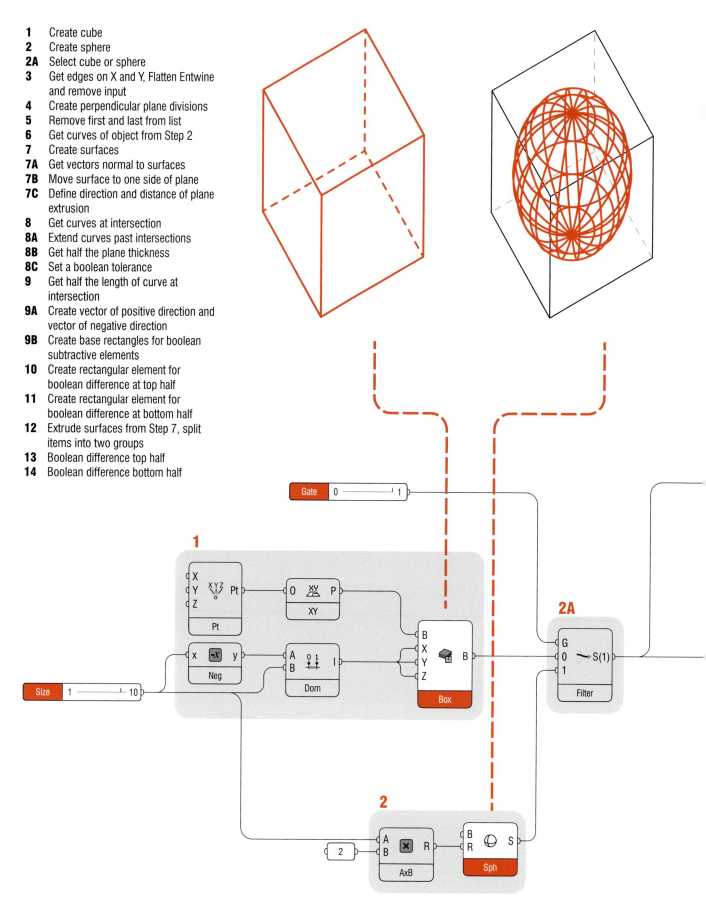

138 3.2 PLANE P1 **WAFFLE**

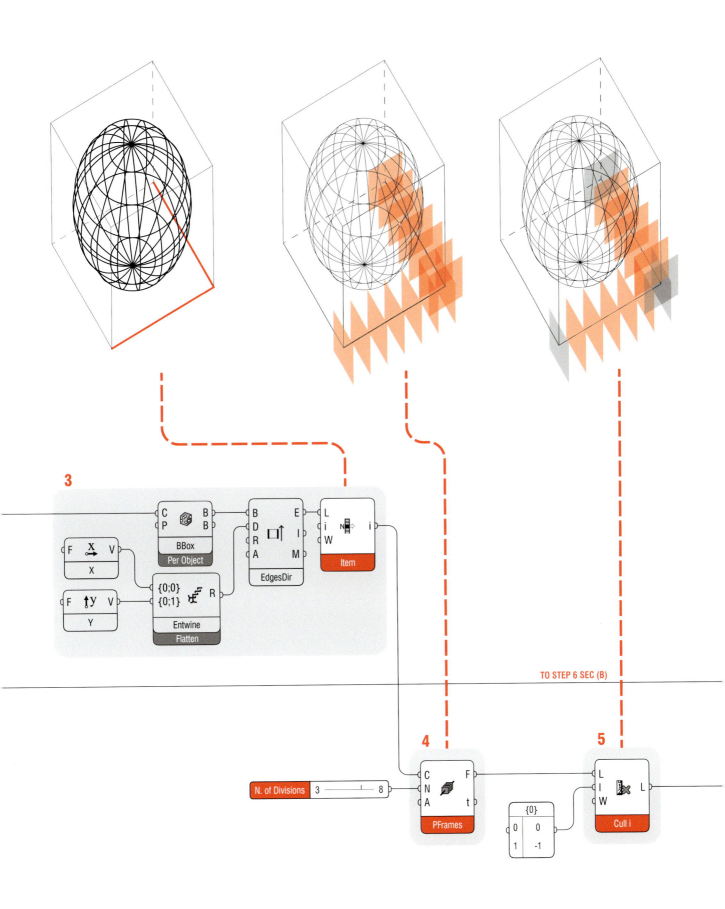

WAFFLE PLANE P1 **3.2**

P1

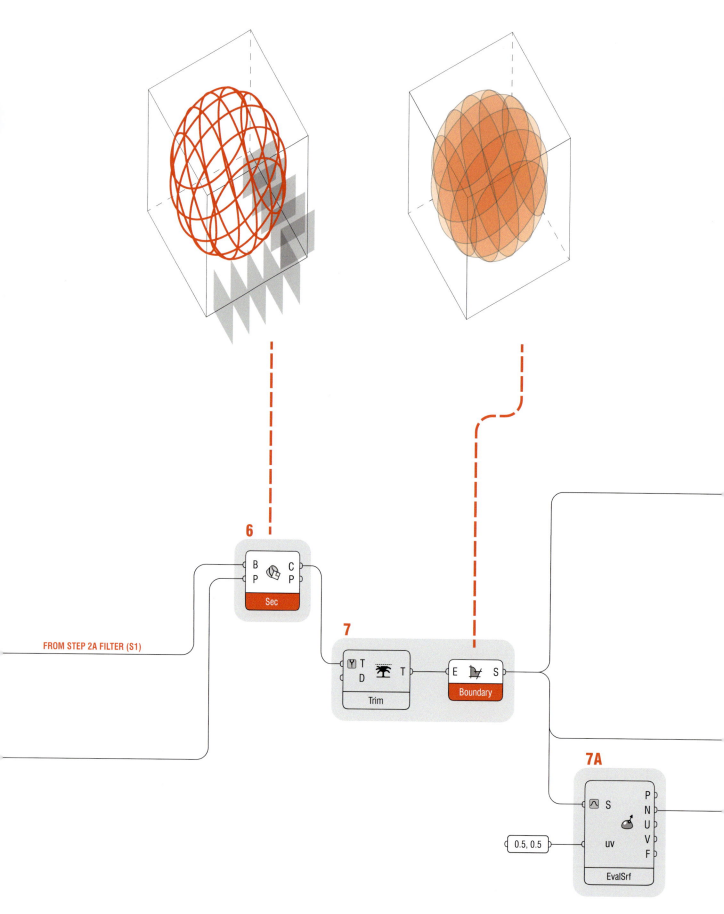

140 **3.2** PLANE P1 **WAFFLE**

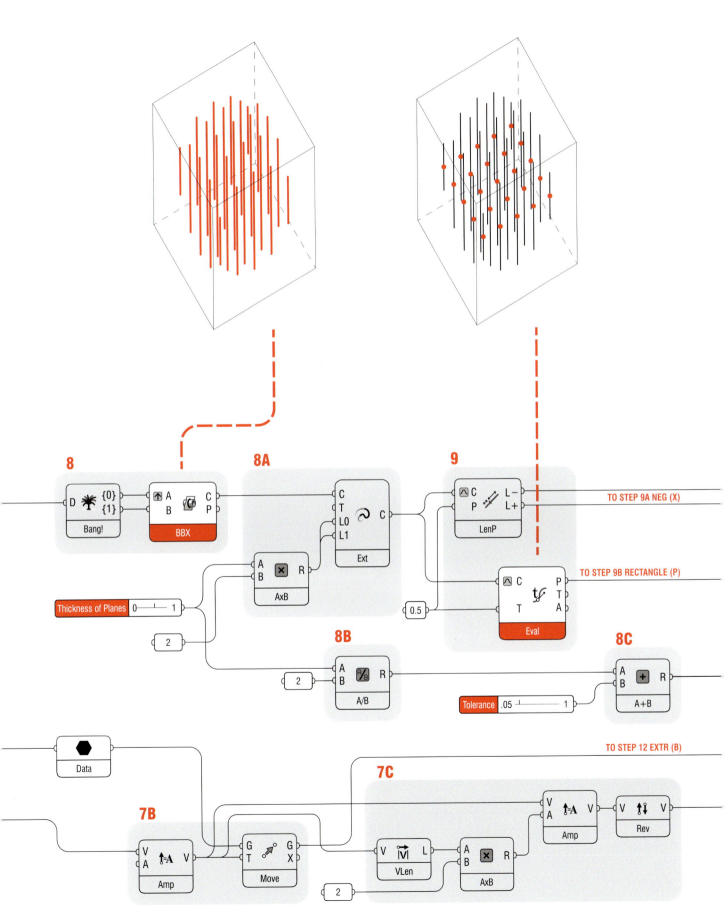

P1

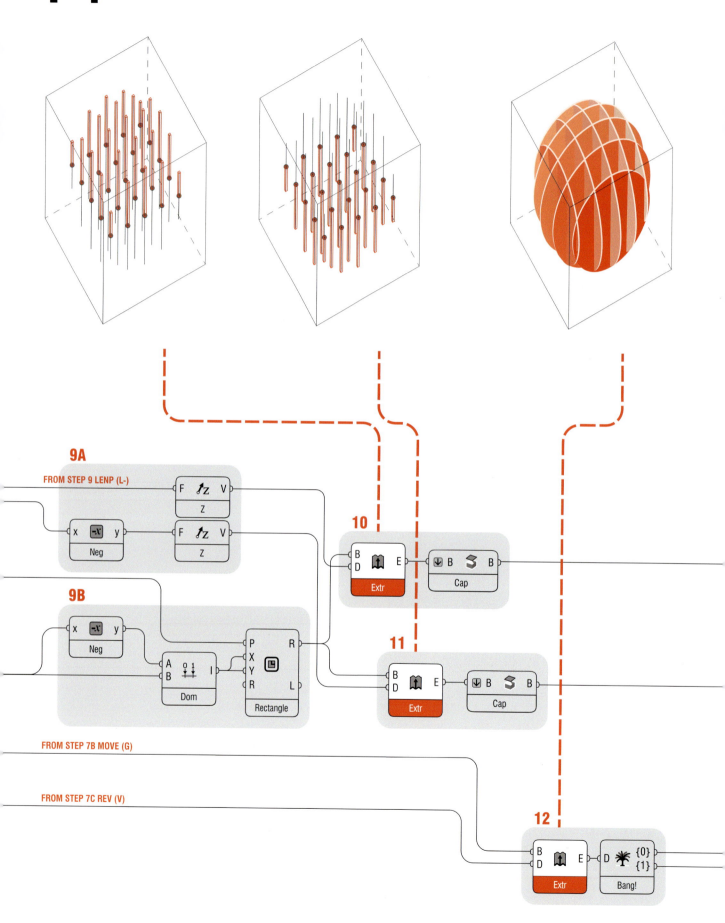

142   3.2 PLANE P1 **WAFFLE**

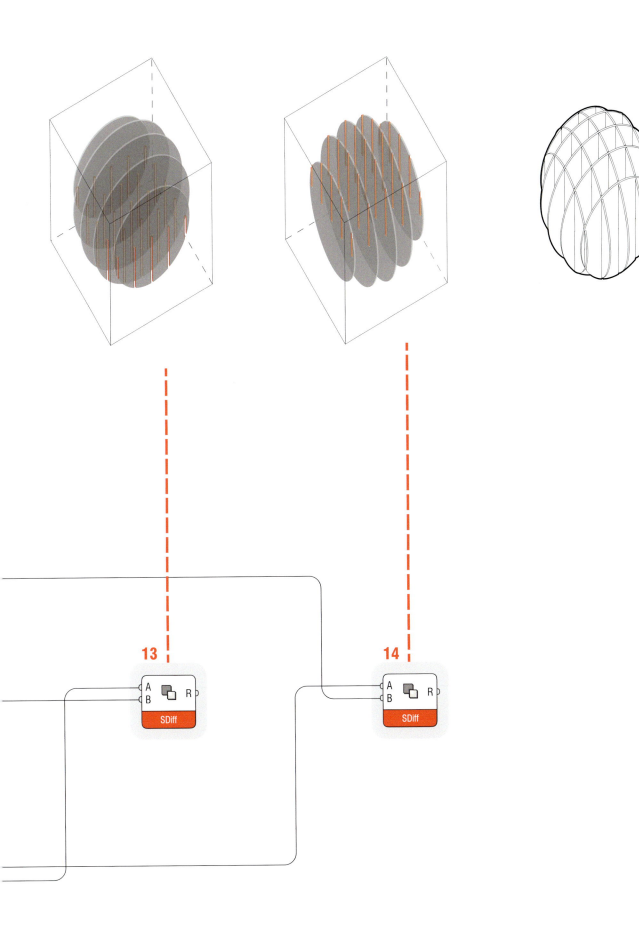

WAFFLE PLANE P1 **3.2** 143

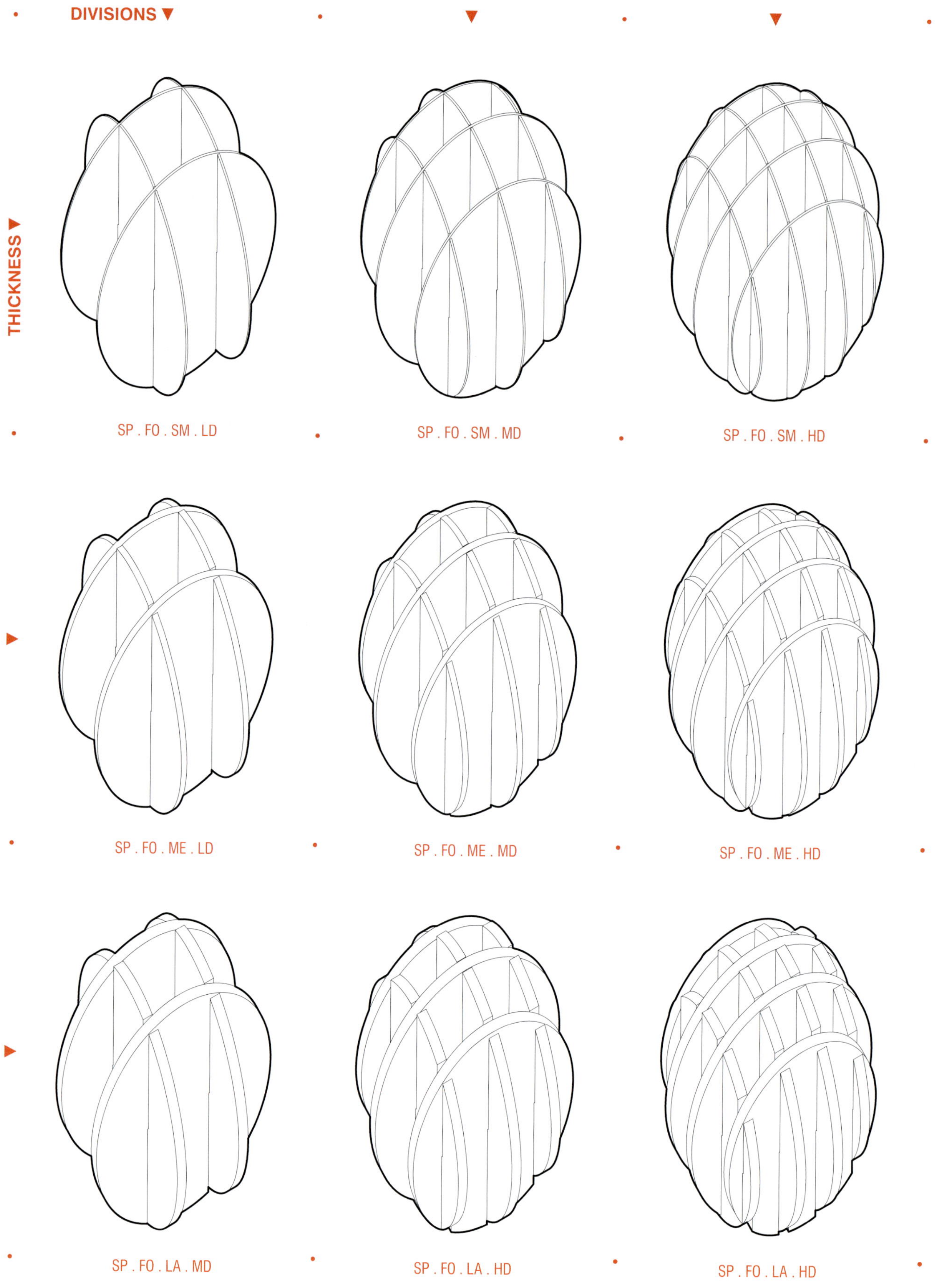

DIVISIONS ▼

THICKNESS ▼

SP . FO . SM . LD

SP . FO . SM . MD

SP . FO . SM . HD

SP . FO . ME . LD

SP . FO . ME . MD

SP . FO . ME . HD

SP . FO . LA . MD

SP . FO . LA . HD

SP . FO . LA . HD

144   **3.2** PLANE P1 WAFFLE **VARIATIONS**

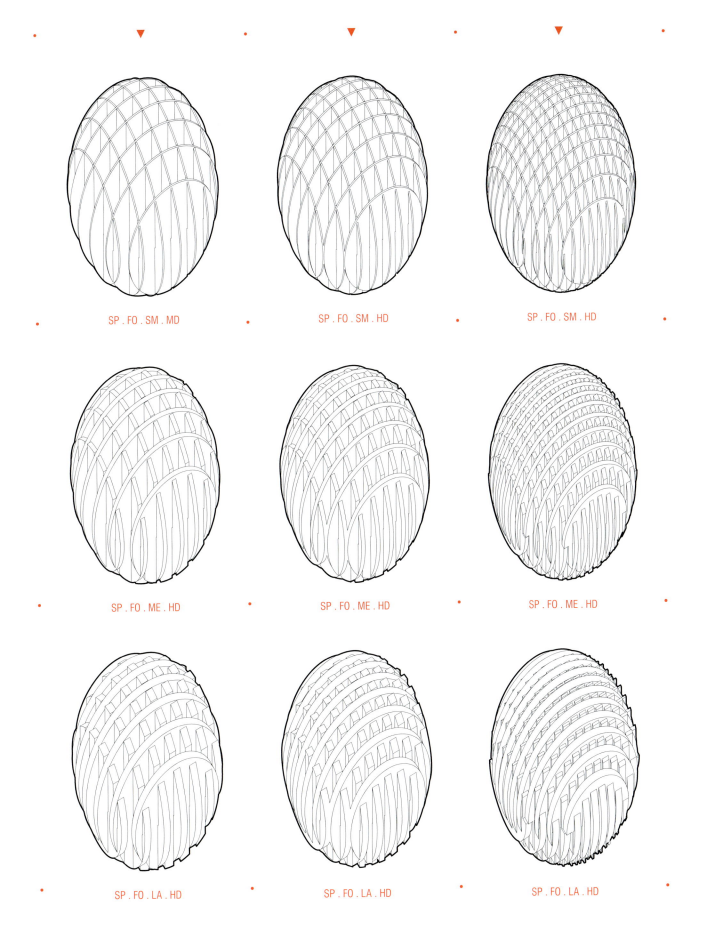

P2 CENTRIC INTERSECTION

1 Create cube
2 Deconstruct cube
3 Get the center point of cube faces
4 Get the first face
5 Get the second face
6 Establish control point on face
6A Get edges of the face
7 Project control points to edges
7A Get start and end points of edges
8 Create curves between points in three sets: orthogonal, diagonal 1, and diagonal 2
9 Project curves to opposite face
10 Create planar surface between curves
11 Get surface normals
11A Get half the plane thickness
11B Move surfaces by half the plane thickness
11C Define direction and distance of plane extrusion from Step 15
12 Create circle curve at base point on cube face
13 Project curve to other cube face
14 Create solid
15 Extrude surfaces from Step 11C
16 Subtract intersecting geometry

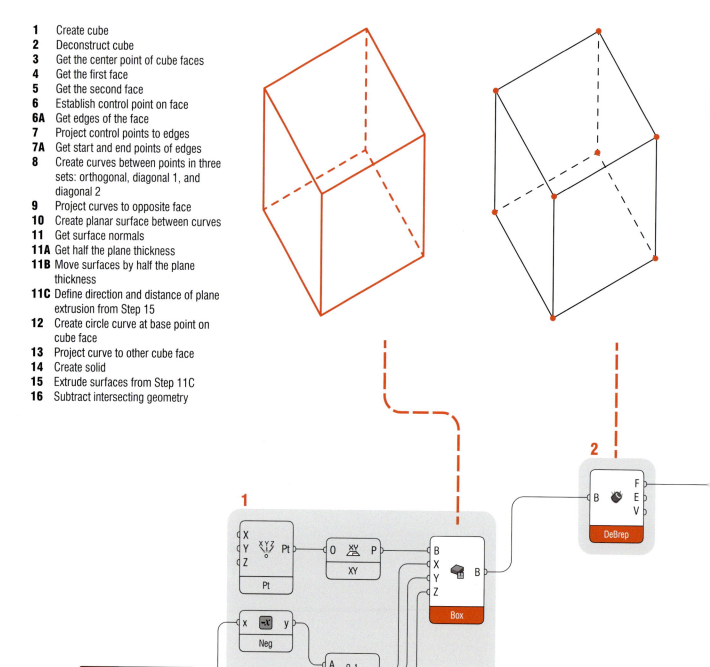

3.2 PLANE P2 CENTRIC INTERSECTION

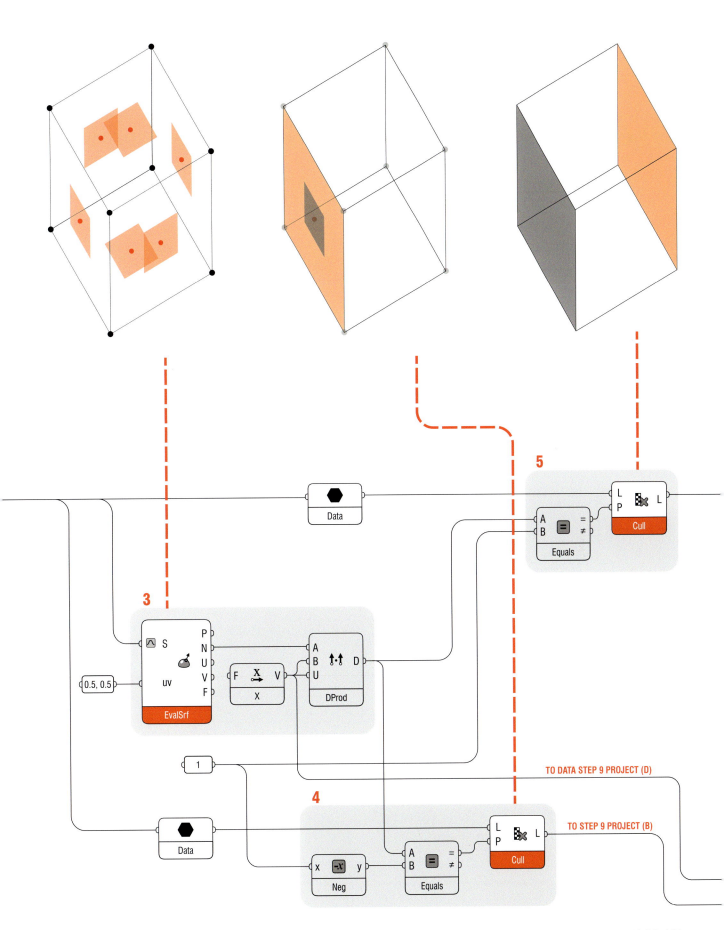

CENTRIC INTERSECTION PLANE P2 **3.2**

P2

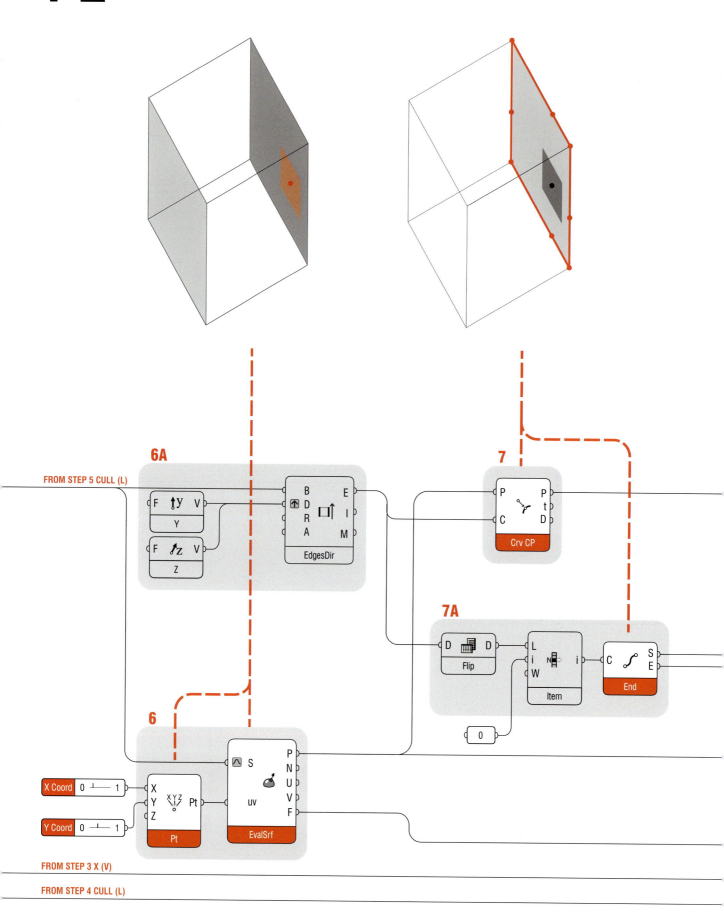

148   3.2 PLANE P2 **CENTRIC INTERSECTION**

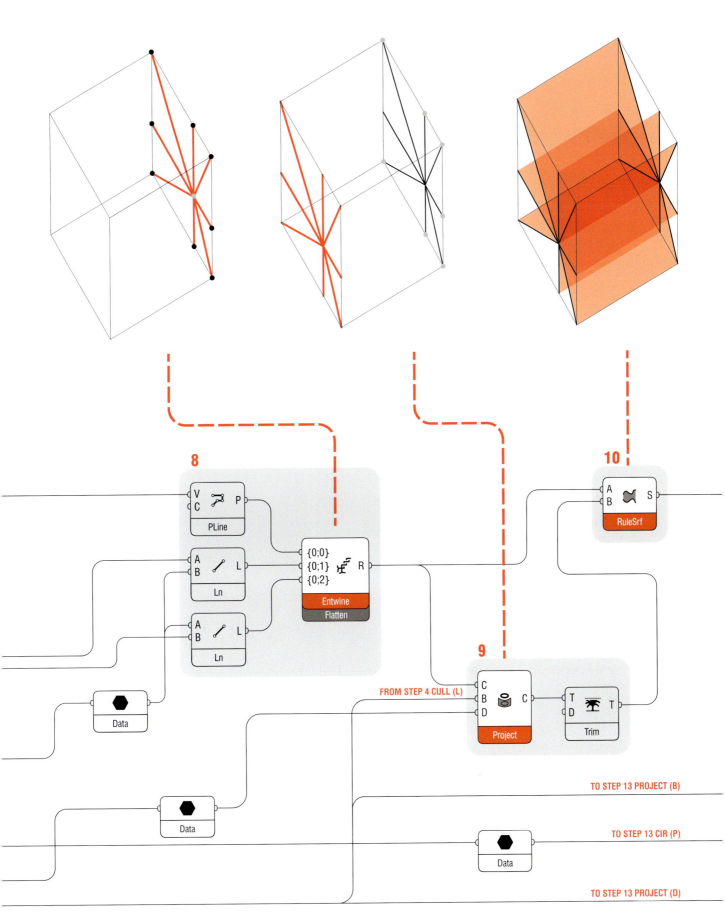

CENTRIC INTERSECTION PLANE P2 **3.2**

P2

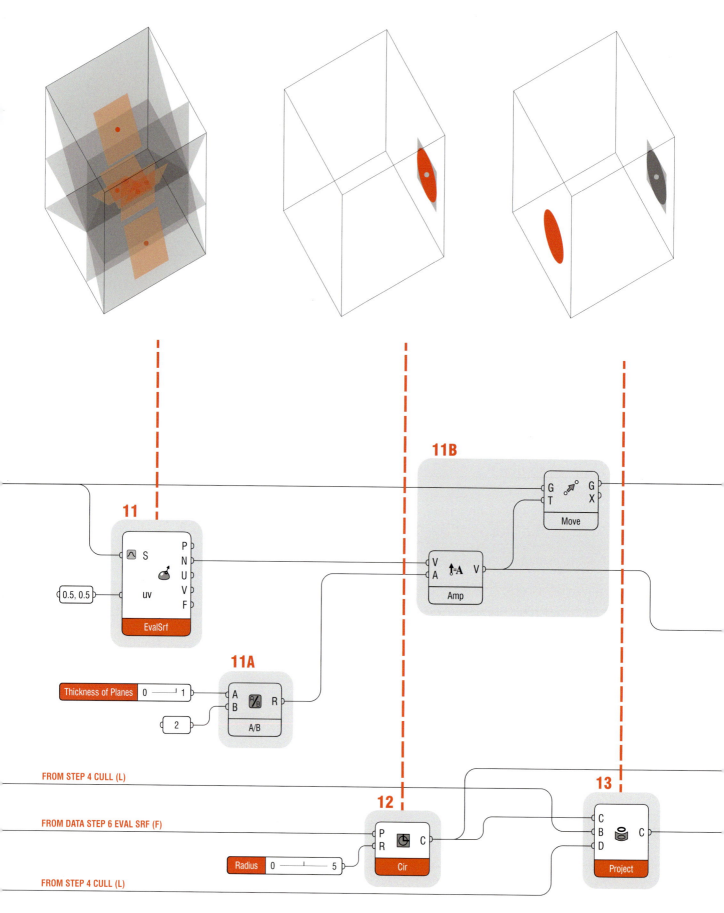

150 3.2 PLANE P2 **CENTRIC INTERSECTION**

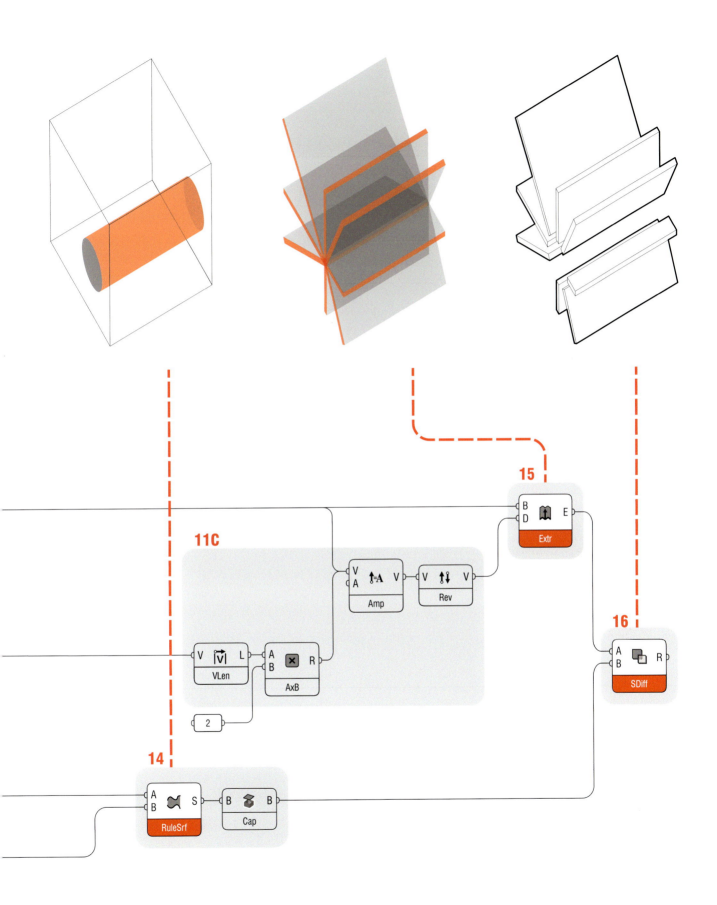

CENTRIC INTERSECTION PLANE P2 **3.2**

RADIUS ▼

THICKNESS ▼

CU . ST/FO . SM . LD 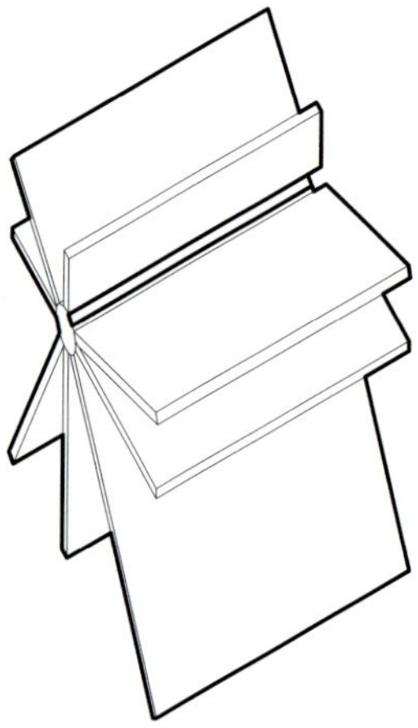   CU . ST/FO . SM . LD 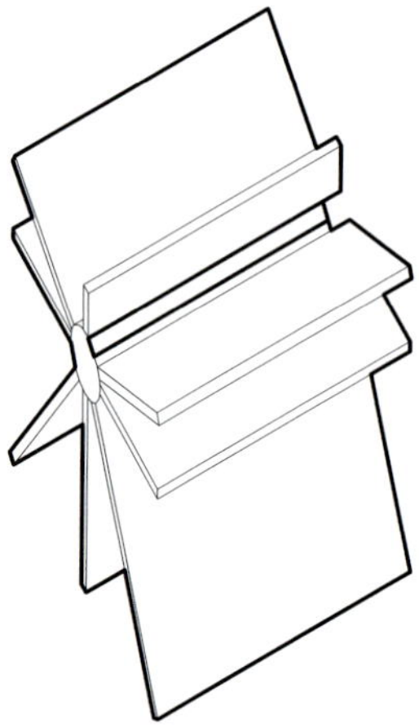   CU . ST/FO . SM/ME . LD

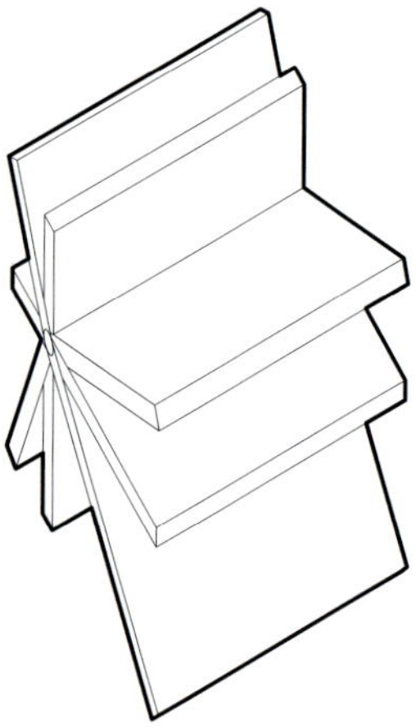

CU . ST/FO . ME/SM . MD 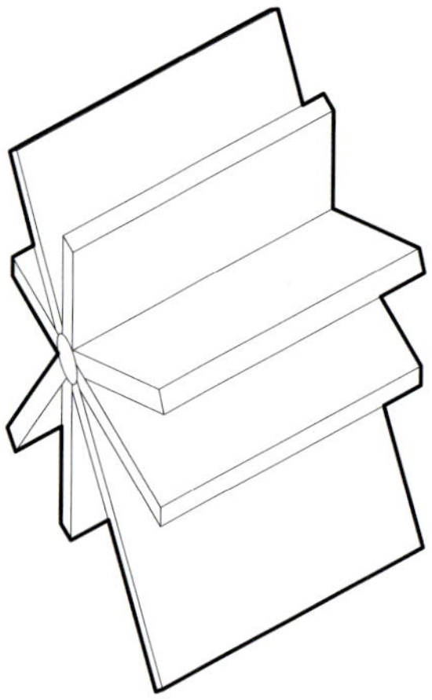   CU . ST/FO . ME/ME . MD 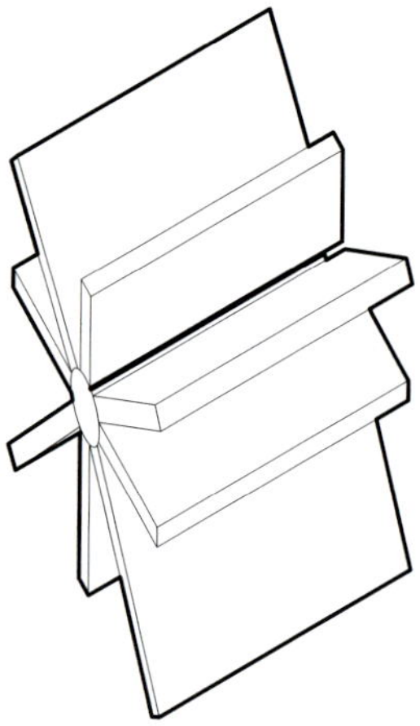   CU . ST/FO . ME/ME . MD

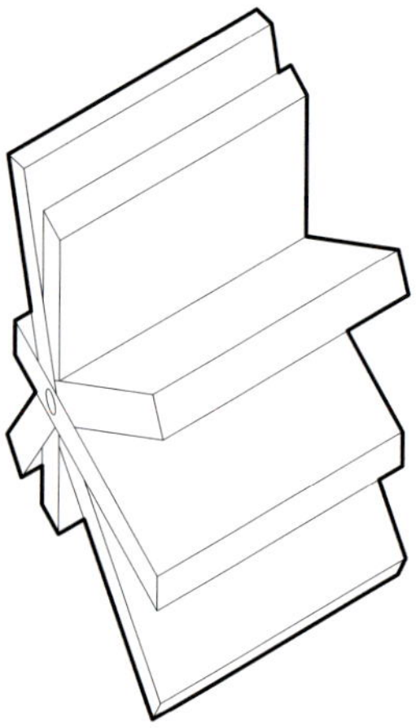

CU . ST/FO . LA/SM . MD 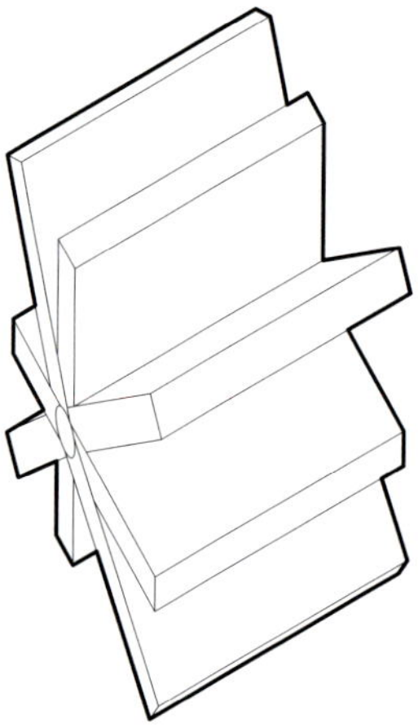   CU . ST/FO . LA/ME . MD 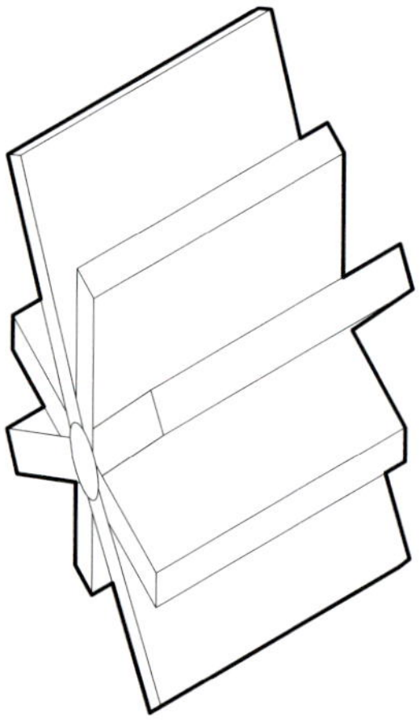   CU . ST/FO . LA/LA . MD

152   **3.2** PLANE P2 CENTRIC INTERSECTION **VARIATIONS**

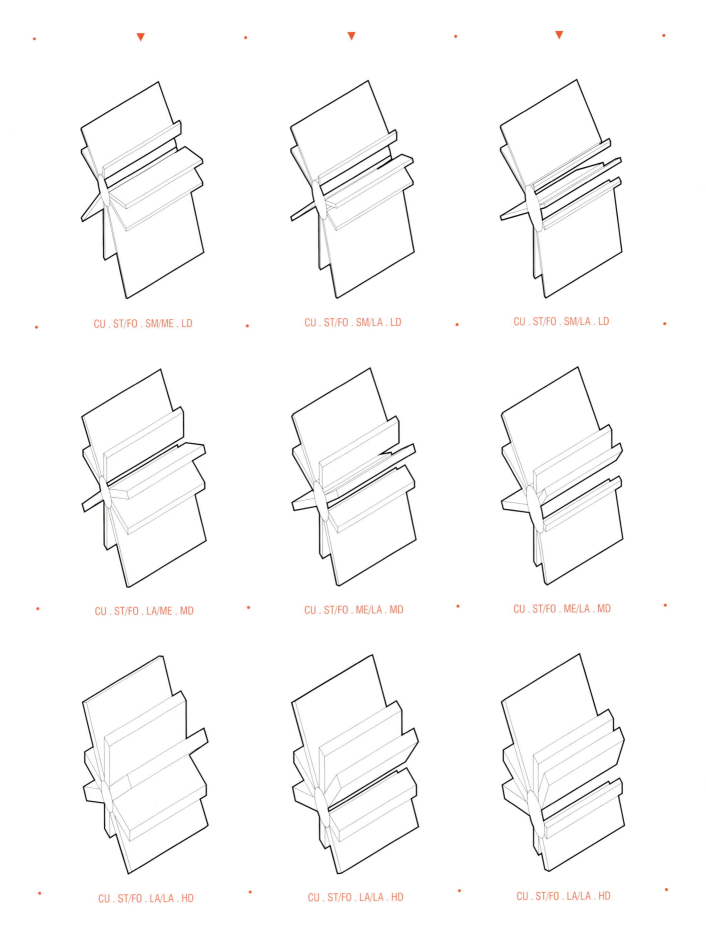

P3 MODULAR GROWTH

1   Create base curves
2   Get inner curve
2A Create the cylinder surface
3   Divide inner and outer curves
4   Extrude inner cylinder
4A Display outer curves
5   Create surfaces between inner and outer curves with alternating pattern
6   Create surfaces between inner and outer curves with alternating pattern
6A Create list of vectors to use for vertical division pattern
7   Extrude first set of surfaces
8   Extrude second set of surfaces
9   Repeat both sets vertically

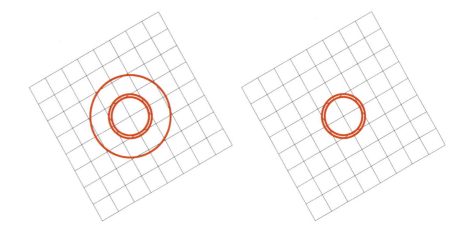

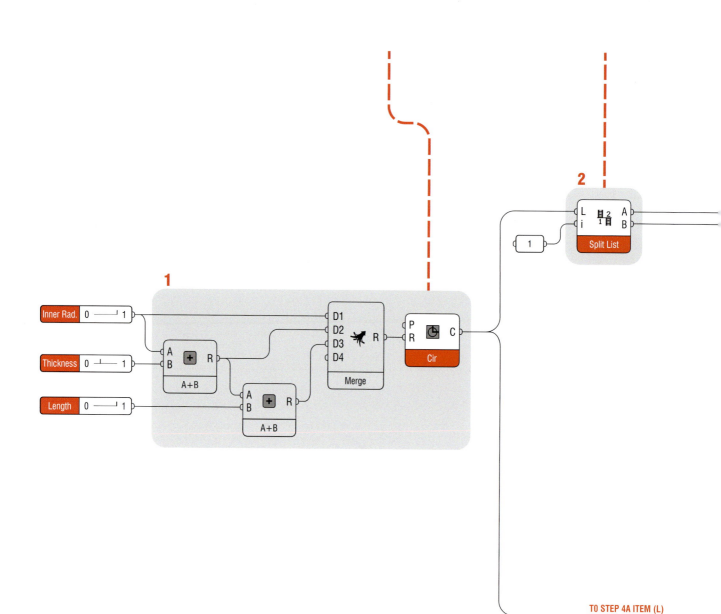

TO STEP 4A ITEM (L)

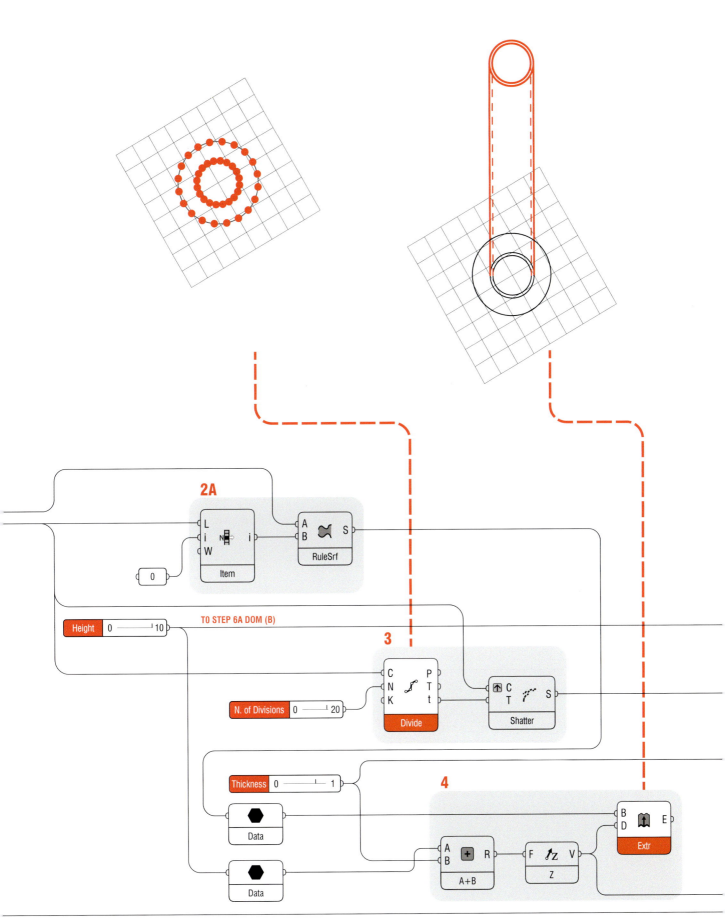

MODULAR GROWTH PLANE P3 **3.2**

P3

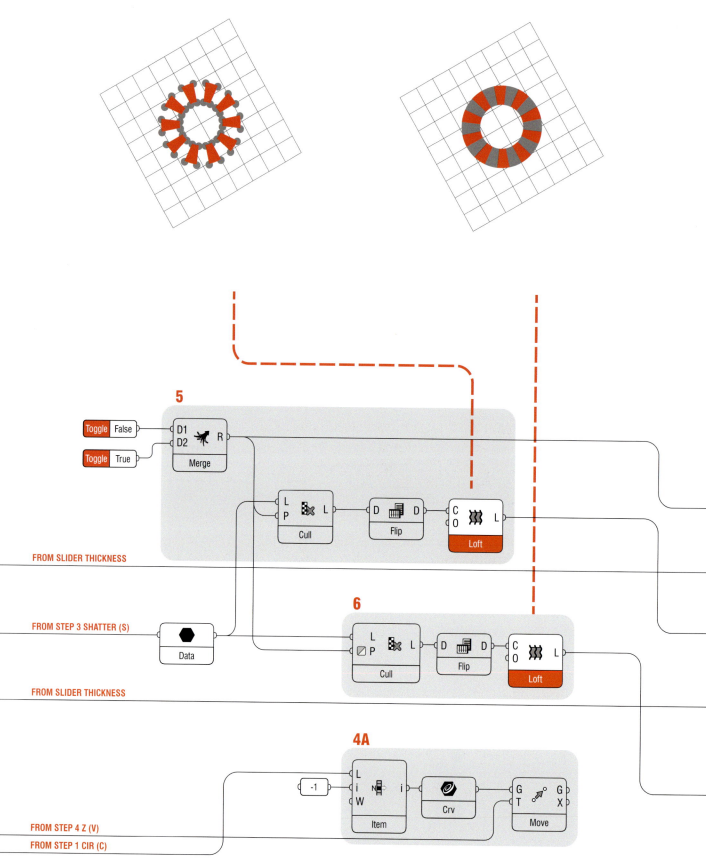

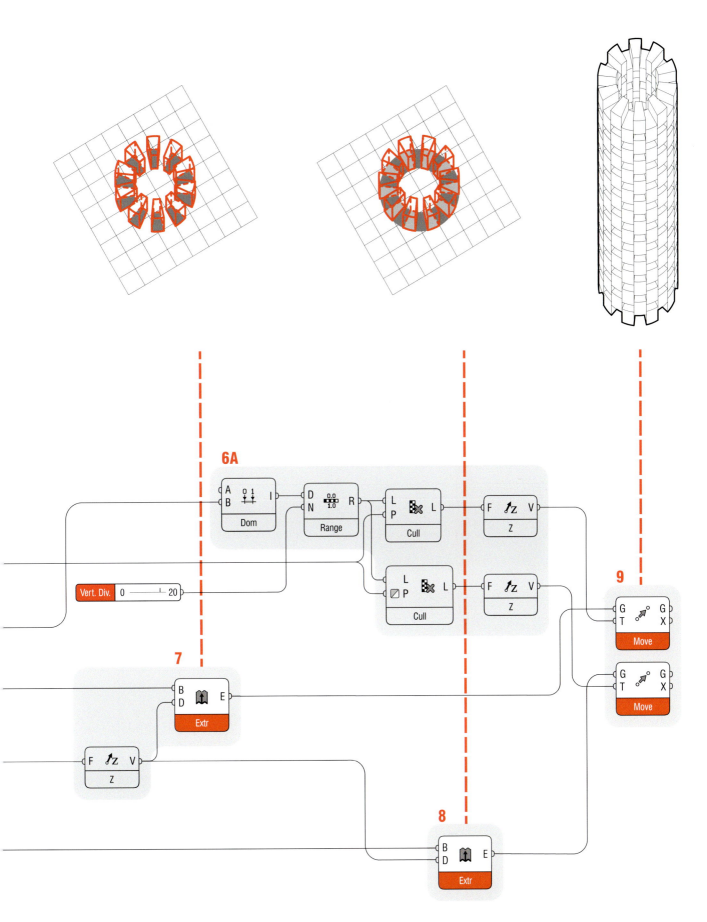

MODULAR GROWTH PLANE P3 **3.2**

DIVISIONS ▼

THICKNESS ▼

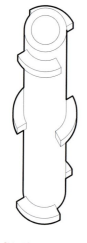
CY . FO . ME/ME . LD

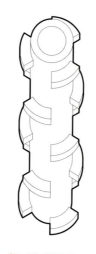
CY . FO . ME/ME . LD

CY . FO . ME/ME . LD

▶

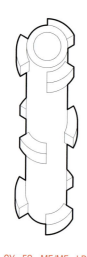
CY . FO . ME/ME . LD

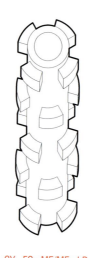
CY . FO . ME/ME . LD

CY . FO . ME/ME . MD

▶

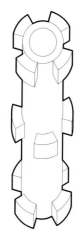
CY . FO . ME/ME . LD

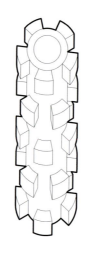
CY . FO . ME/ME . MD

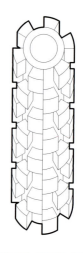
CY . FO . ME/ME . HD

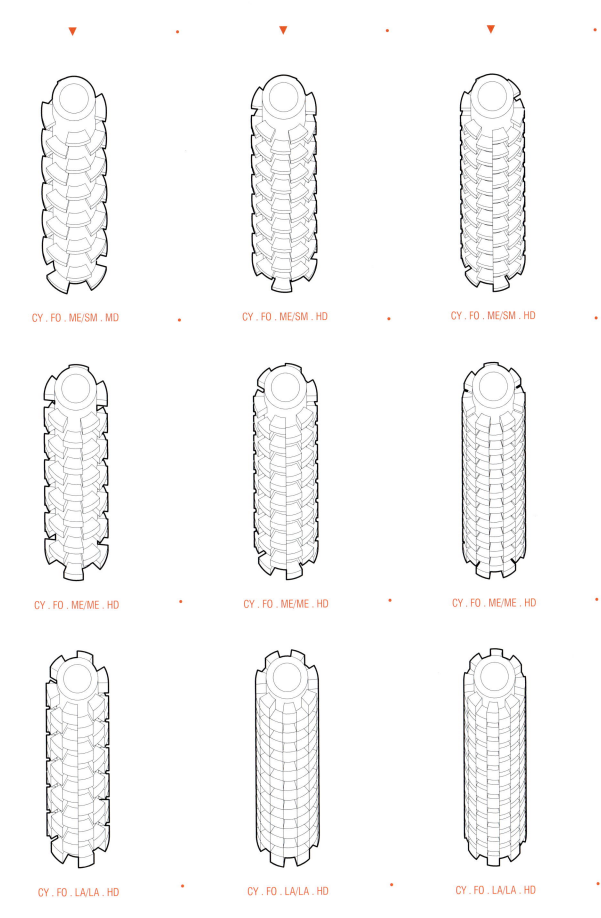

VARIATIONS MODULAR GROWTH PLANE P3 **3.2**

P4 WRAP

1 Create sphere with defined radius using an expression
To create expression, right click on the input x and change to lowercase L (l), then double click on component and replace the default expression text to read as shown, select ok
1A Create base plane at center of sphere
1B Create cube primitive
2 Get base curve at center of sphere
2A Create series of numbers for offset
2B Create random normal vectors
3 Create offset circles
4 Change orientation of circles, set vectors to move circles for width
4A Set the vector to move circles
5 Set thickness
5A Create surfaces between the thickness vectors
6 Extrude thickness along the width

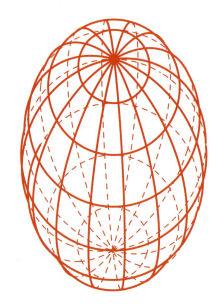

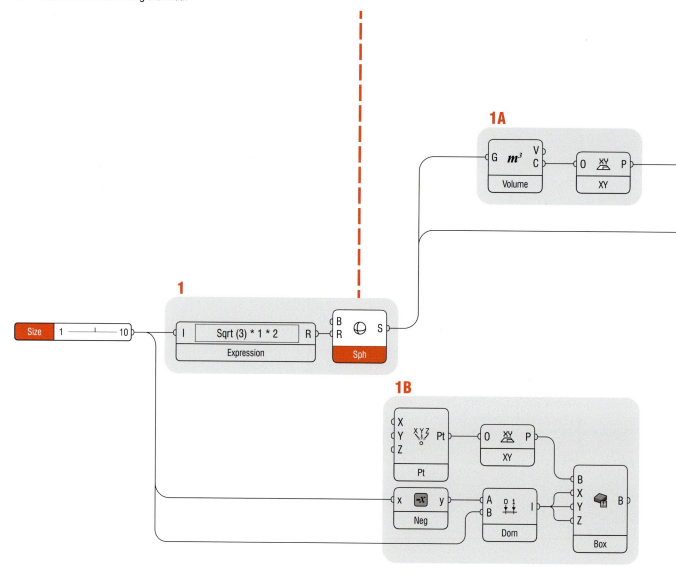

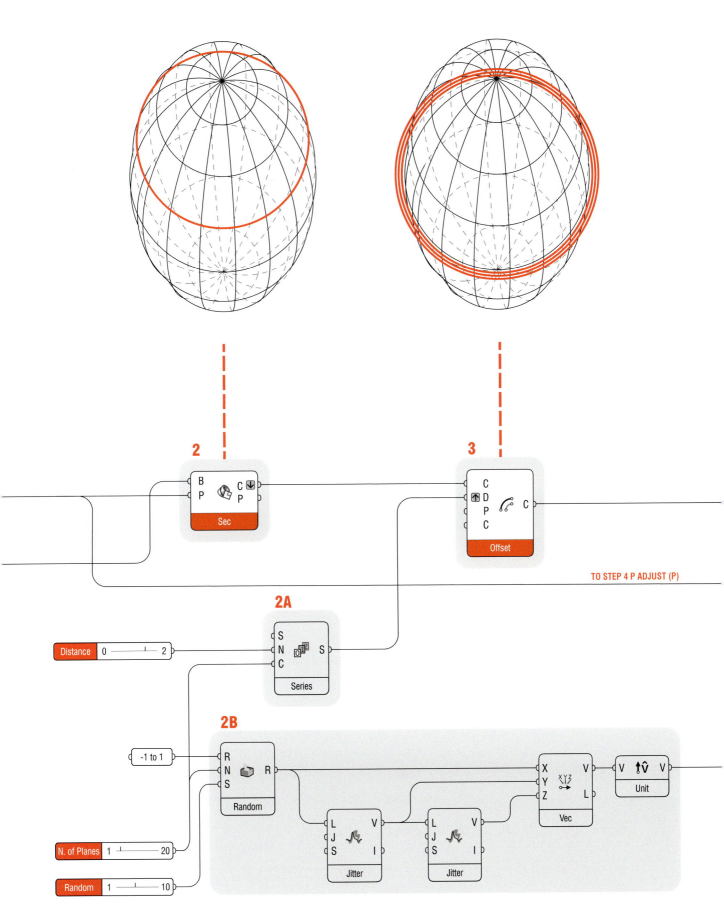

P4

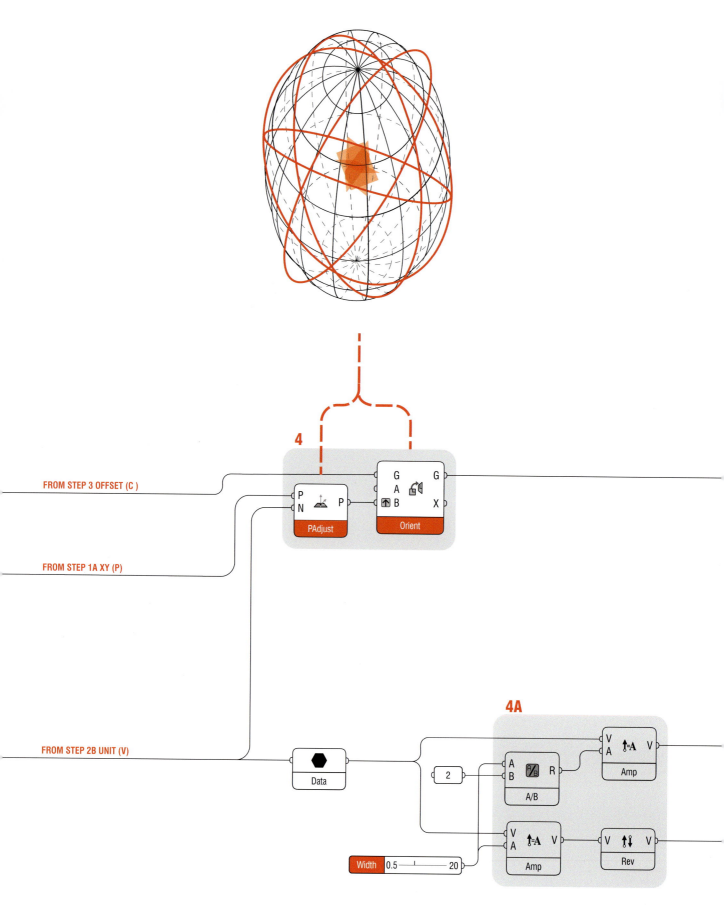

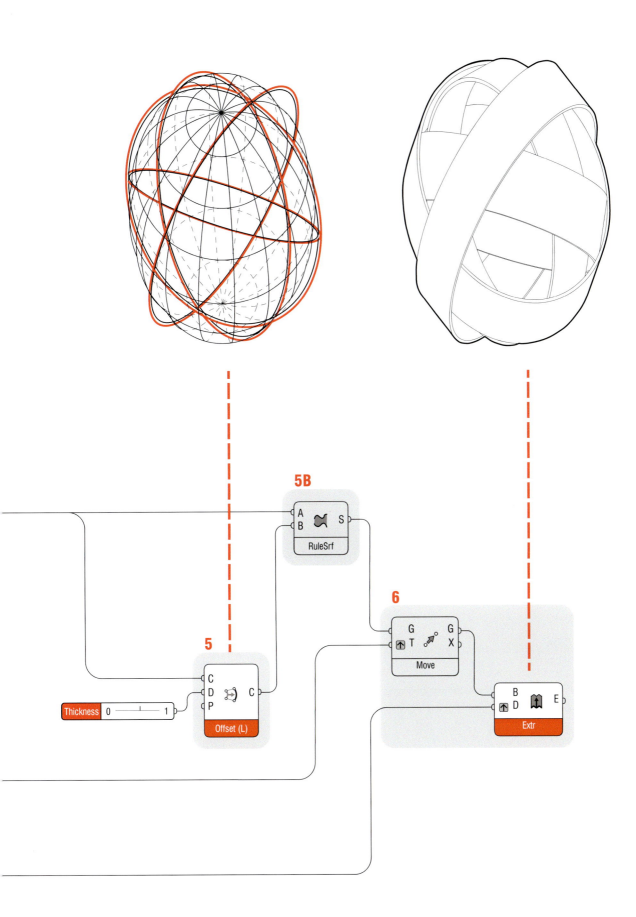

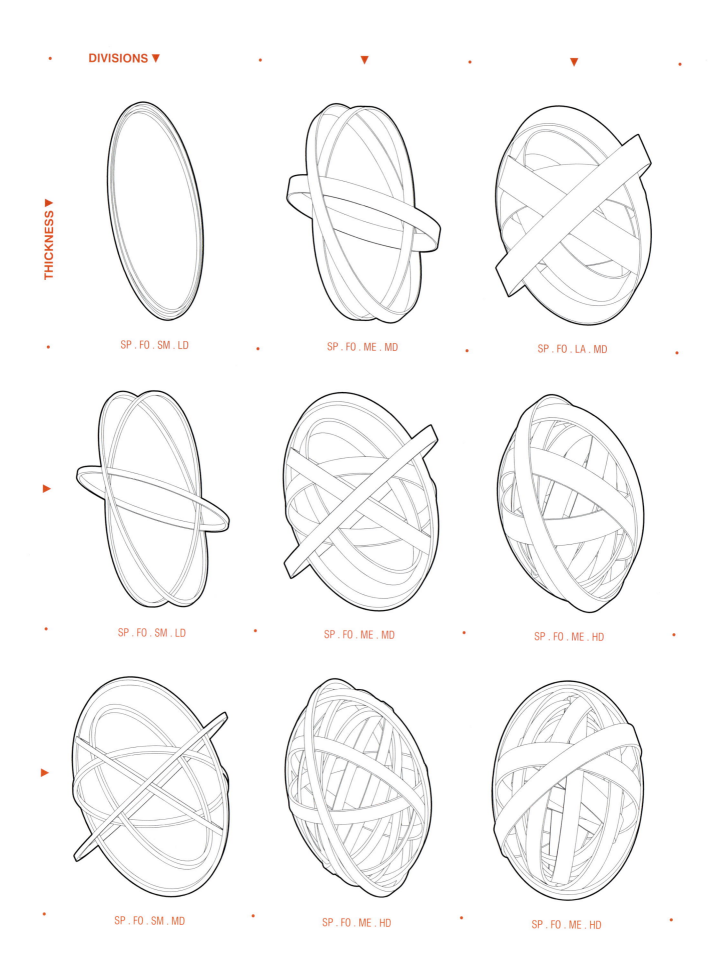

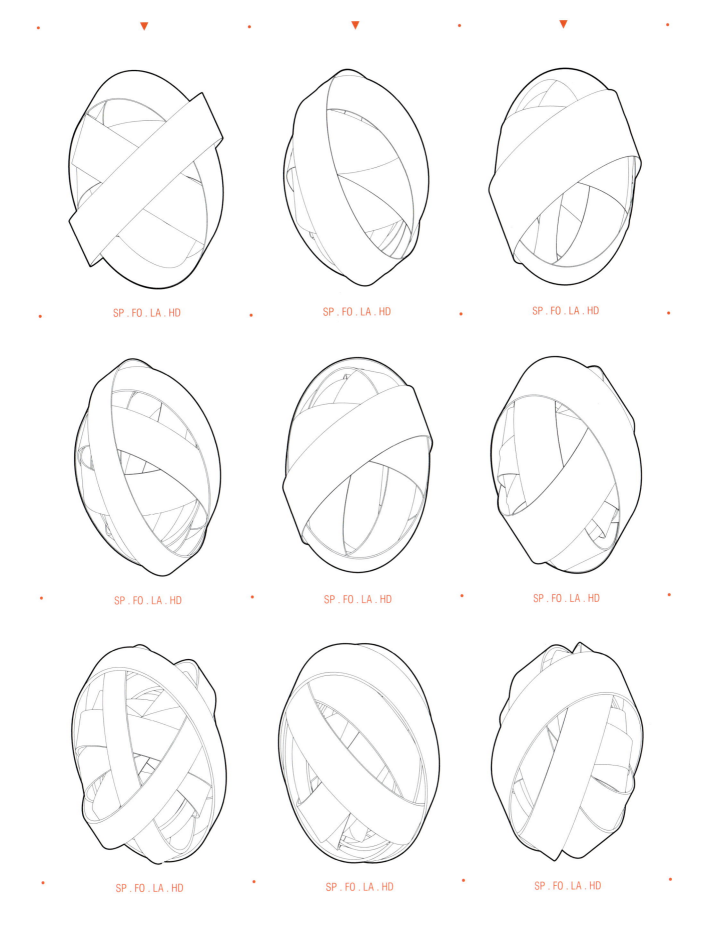

3.3 SOLID OBJECTS

In this book we make a distinction between objects that are composed exclusively of Solid Elements and those that are composed of Planar and Frame Elements. We also make a distinction between a Solid Element and a Solid Object. A Solid Element is a single member within any object that is dimensioned in a way that is proportionally perceived as a solid (mass), as opposed to being perceived as a plane or a frame. A Solid Object, on the other hand, is an aggregation of exclusively Solid Elements in an ordered arrangement. Our previous book, *The Making of Things*, deconstructs this architectonic language thoroughly. Though in-depth definitions of these phenomena fall outside the scope of this work, we have included the architectonic taxonomic map from *The Making of Things* to help you conceptualize the relationships between the object types discussed above.

In this chapter you will learn how to construct four basic Solid Objects, evolving each using a series of verbs which are tied directly to parametric operations in Rhino/Grasshopper. As you build these definitions, experiment with changing sizes, quantities, spacing, edge profiles, etc. for each object. Look carefully at how these individual changes substantively affect each object's visual character and its emotive affect. For instance, using vertically oriented Solid Elements will generally make the Solid Object appear taller. The location and orientation of elements within a Solid Object also suggests things about its nature. For instance, a horizontal aggregation of elements might signify lateral movement of people within this space. Play with the definitions you are building, test different approaches, look long enough to consider how each arrangement resonates emotively in a new way. Additionally, as you work on these definitions and iterate different variations, be sure look at as many other buildings as possible and notice which are similar to the objects you are creating; designers refer to this similarity as a shared "language".

S1	**Voxel**
S2	**Density**
S3	**Boolean**
S4	**Bundled**

S1 VOXEL

1 Create then select closed brep
2 Get bounding box
3 Divide domain of X, Y, and Z
3A Dimension voxels X, Y, and Z
4 Create 3D grid
5 Create boxes about each point
5A Convert boxes to meshes
6 Get vertices of meshes
7 Get clean voxels
7A Remove boxes outside of brep
8 Preview final voxels

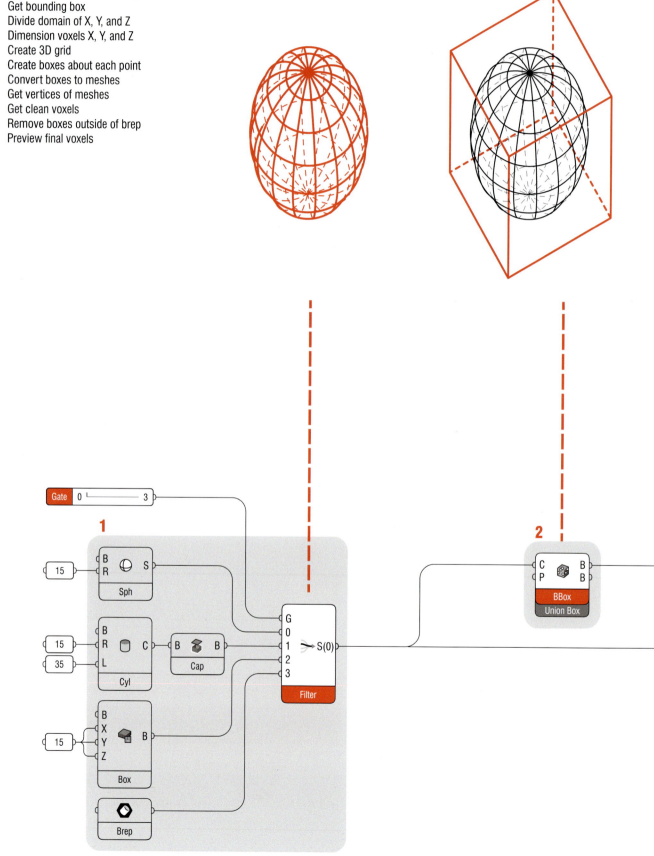

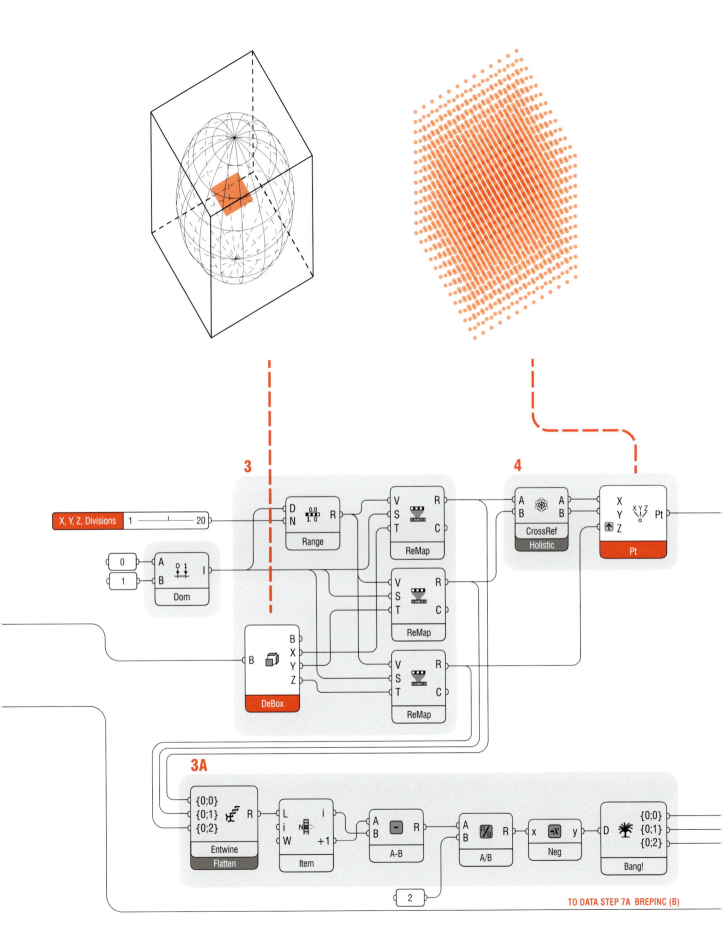

S1

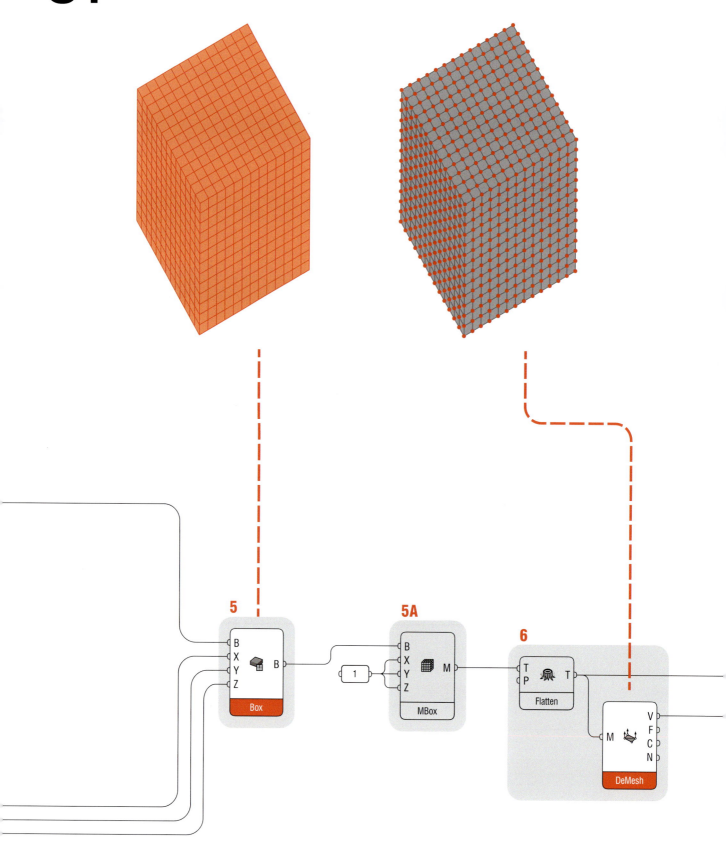

FROM STEP 1 FILTER S(0)

3.3 SOLID S1 **VOXEL**

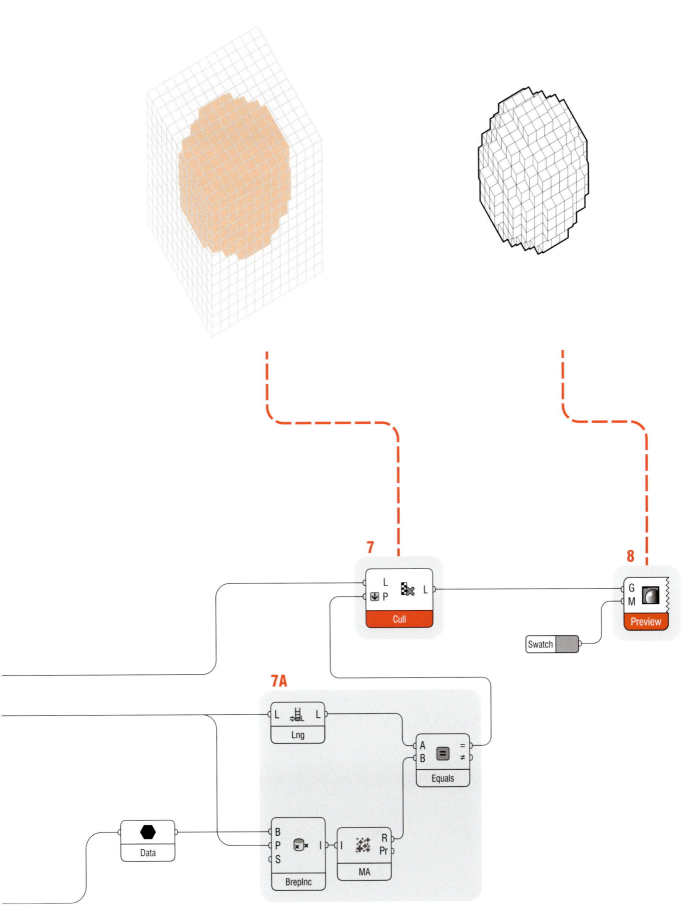

VOXEL SOLID S1 **3.3** 171

DIVISIONS ▼

PRIMITIVE SHAPE ▼

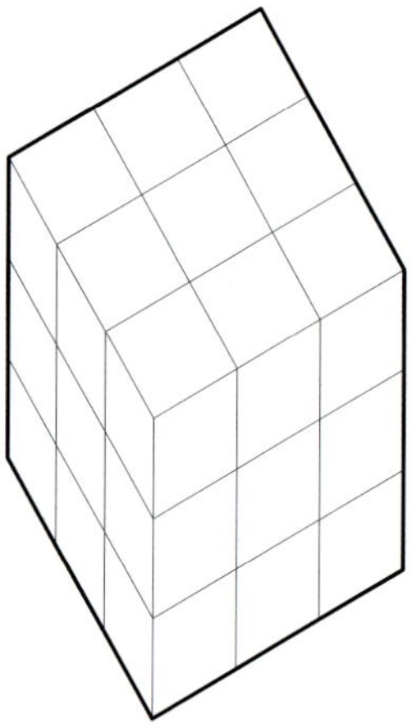

CU . ST . LA . HD

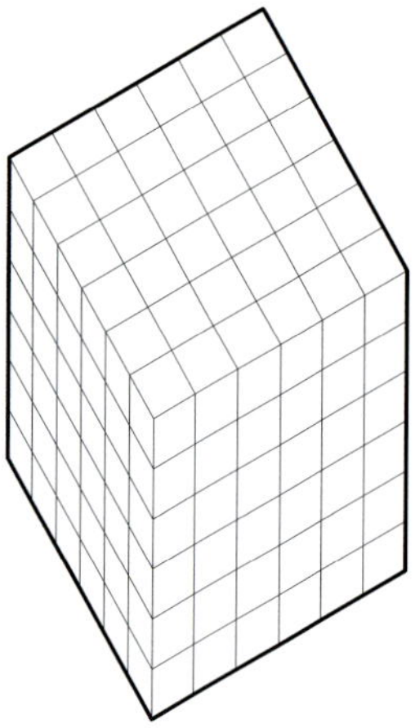

CU . ST . ME . HD

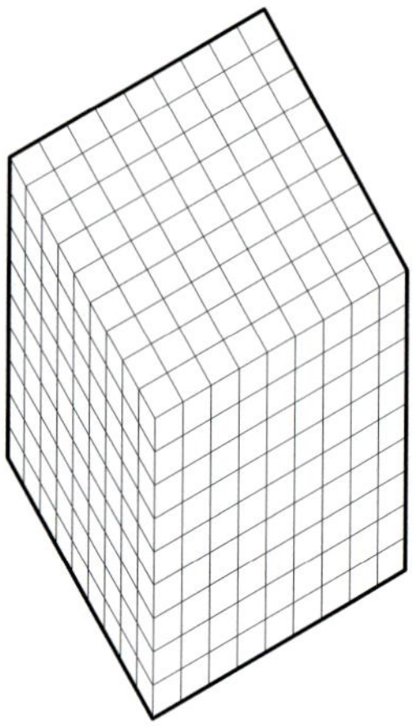

CU . ST . SM . HD

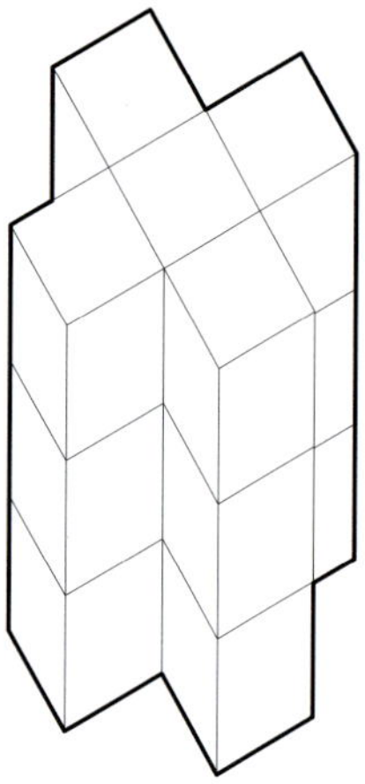

CU . ST . LA . MD

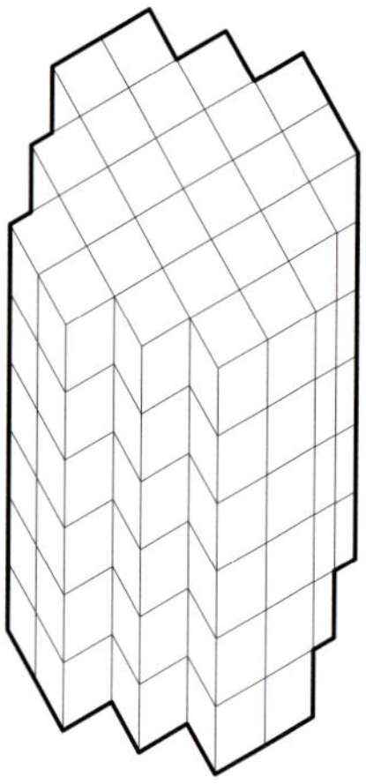

CU . ST . ME . MD

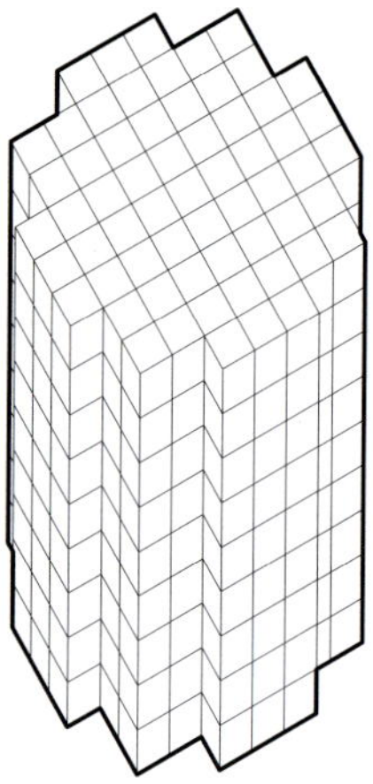

CU . ST . SM . MD

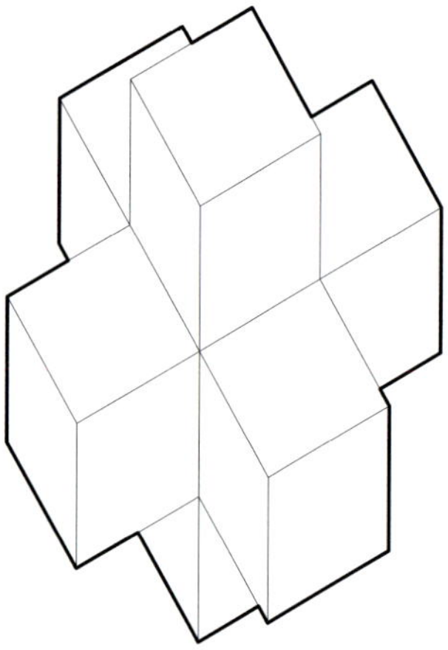

CU . ST . LA . LD

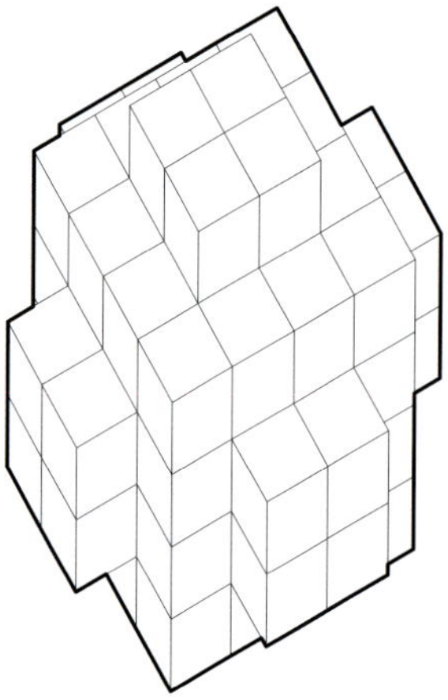

CU . ST . ME . MD

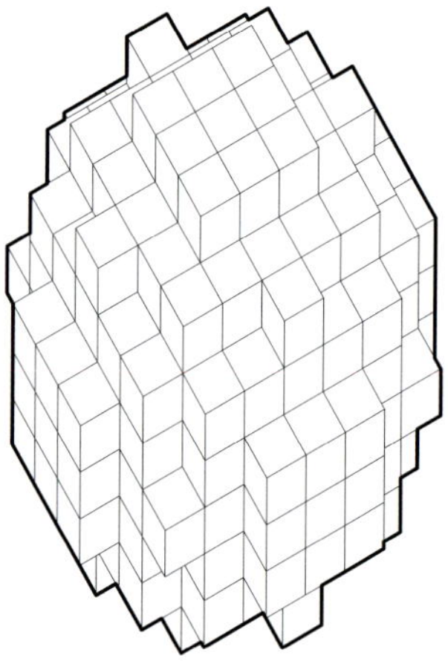

CU . ST . SM . HD

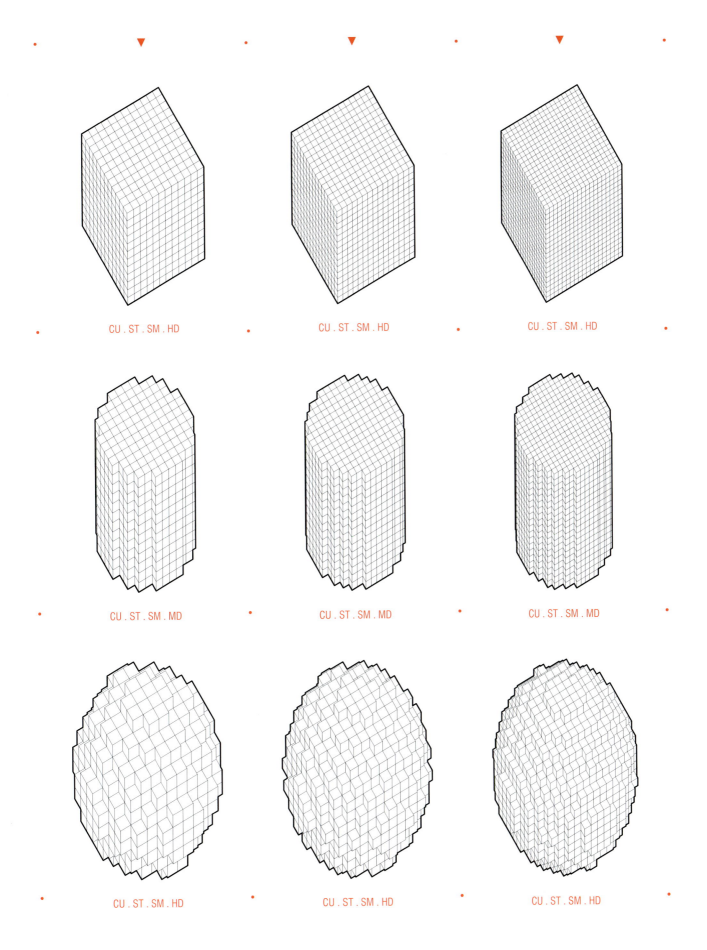

S2 DENSITY

1. Create sphere
2. Get domain of sphere and establish a pattern on sphere boundary
3. Flip the data, split data into first set
4. Split the data into second set
4A. Clean up duplicate points
5. Project points to sphere boundary, create line from center to points
6. Create center core for optional cutting of pipe elements
7. Create variables for pipe elements
7A. Create pipe
8. Close pipes to make solid
9. Preview final geometry

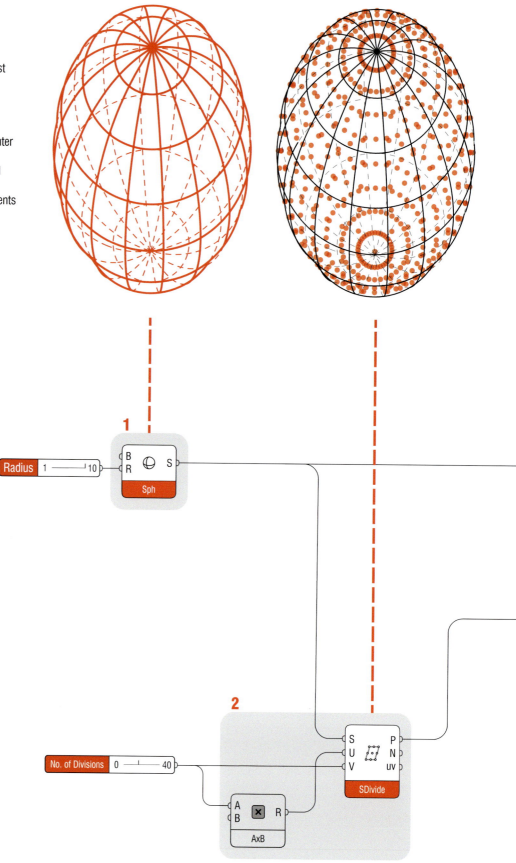

174   3.3 SOLID S2 **DENSITY**

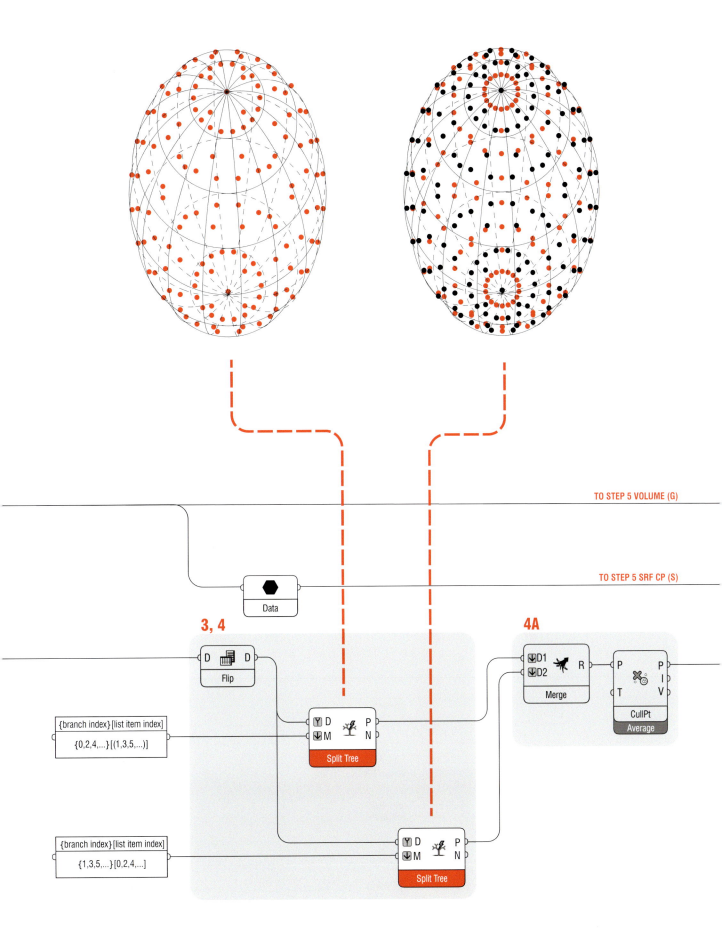

S2

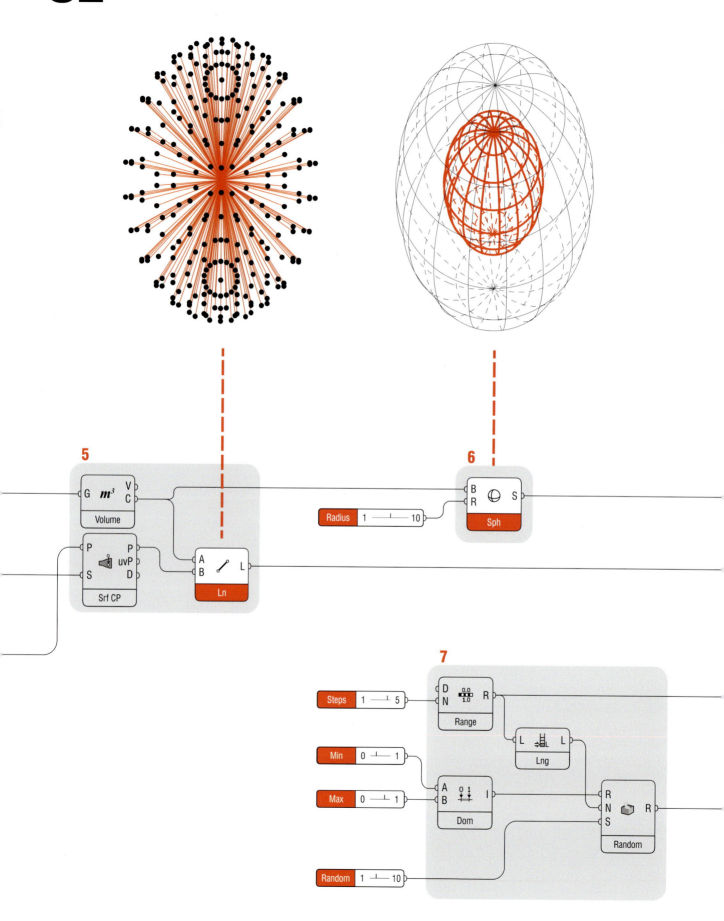

176 3.3 SOLID S2 **DENSITY**

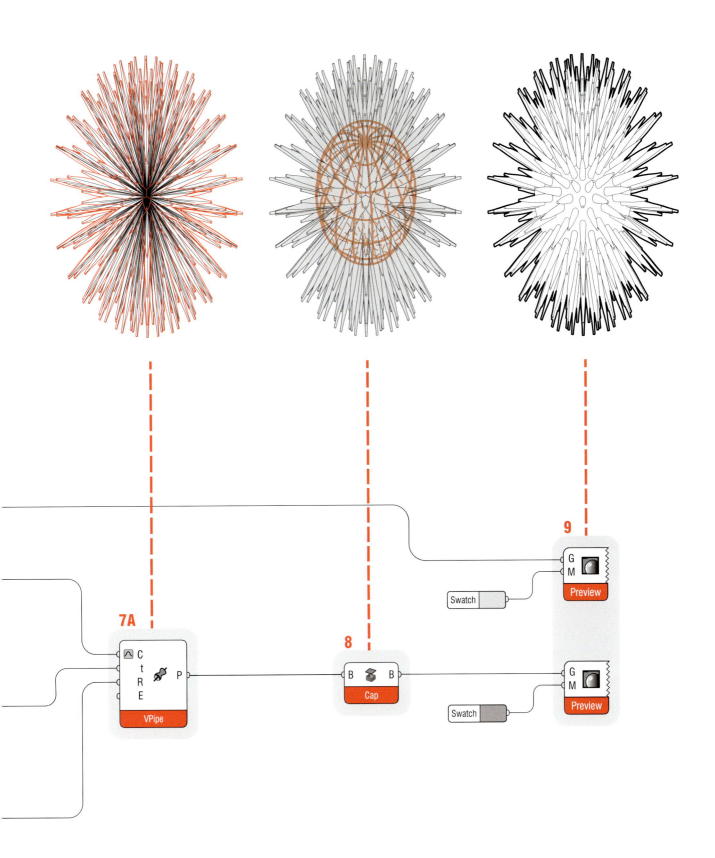

THICKNESS ▼

DENSITY ▼

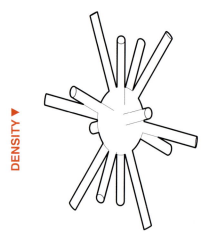
SP . FO . ME . LD

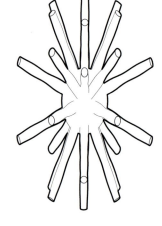
SP . FO . ME . LD

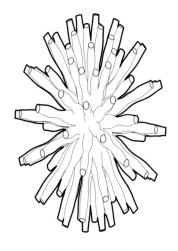
SP . FO . ME . MD

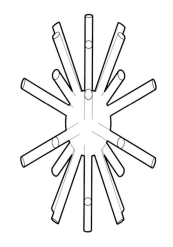
SP . FO . ME . LD

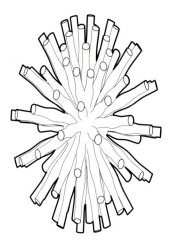
SP . FO . ME . MD

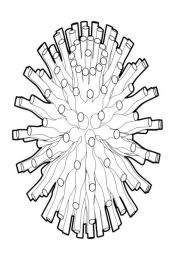
SP . FO . ME . HD

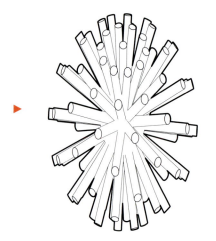
SP . FO . ME . MD

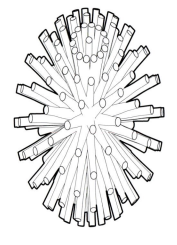
SP . FO . ME . HD

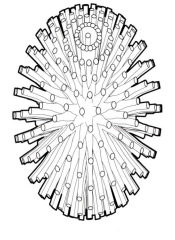
SP . FO . SM . HD

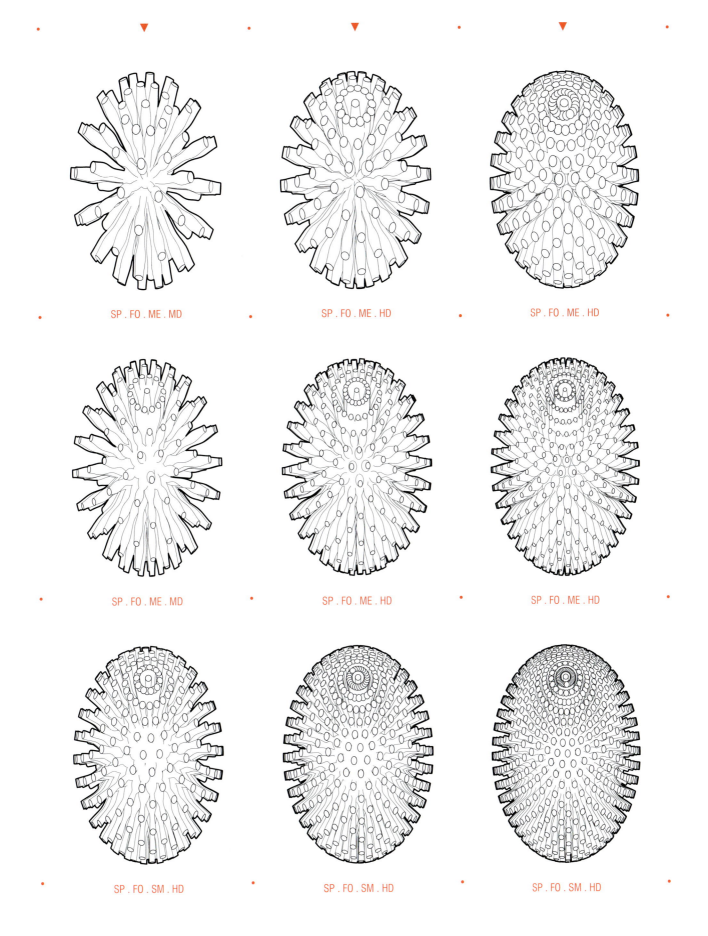

S3 BOOLEAN

1 Create base geometry
2 Input base geometry from a model
3 Boolean with solid intersection
4 Boolean with solid difference
5 Preview solid intersection
6 Preview solid difference

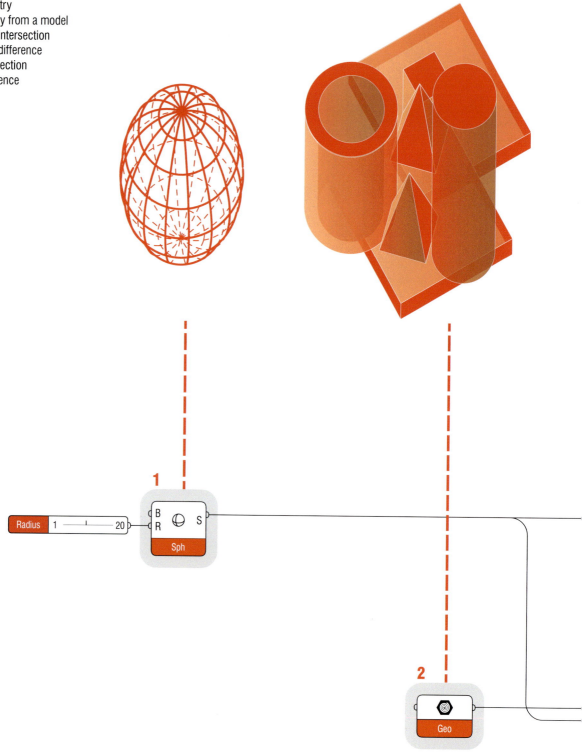

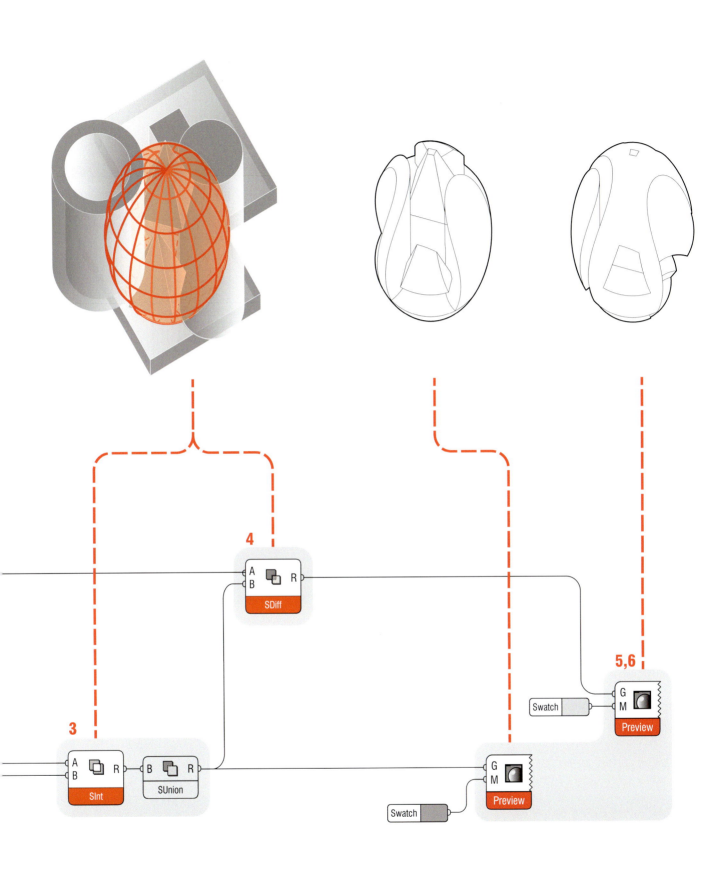

BOOLEAN SOLID S3 **3.3**

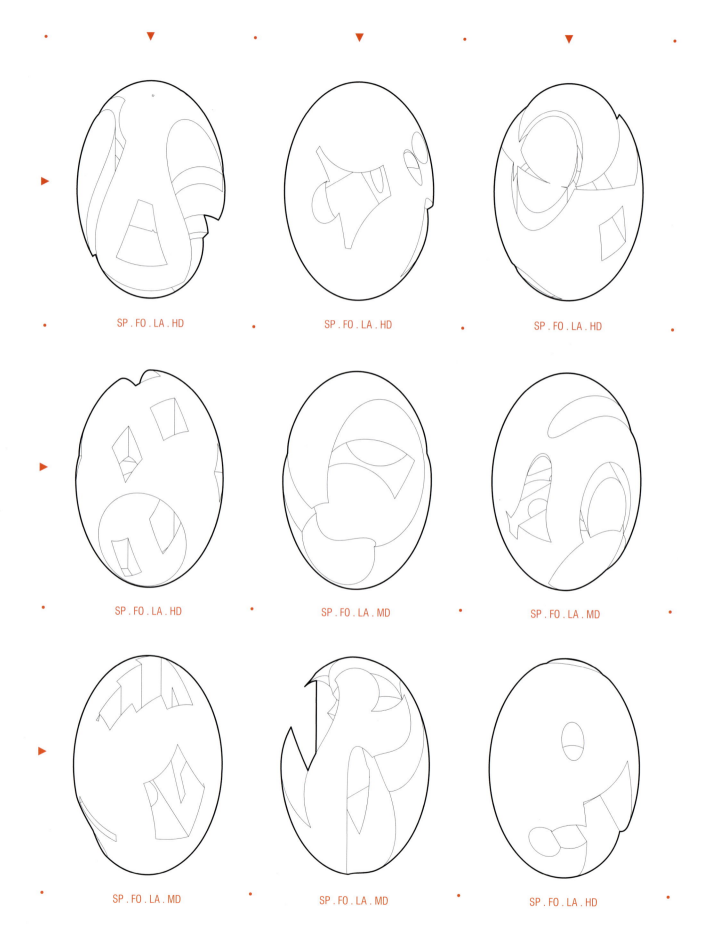

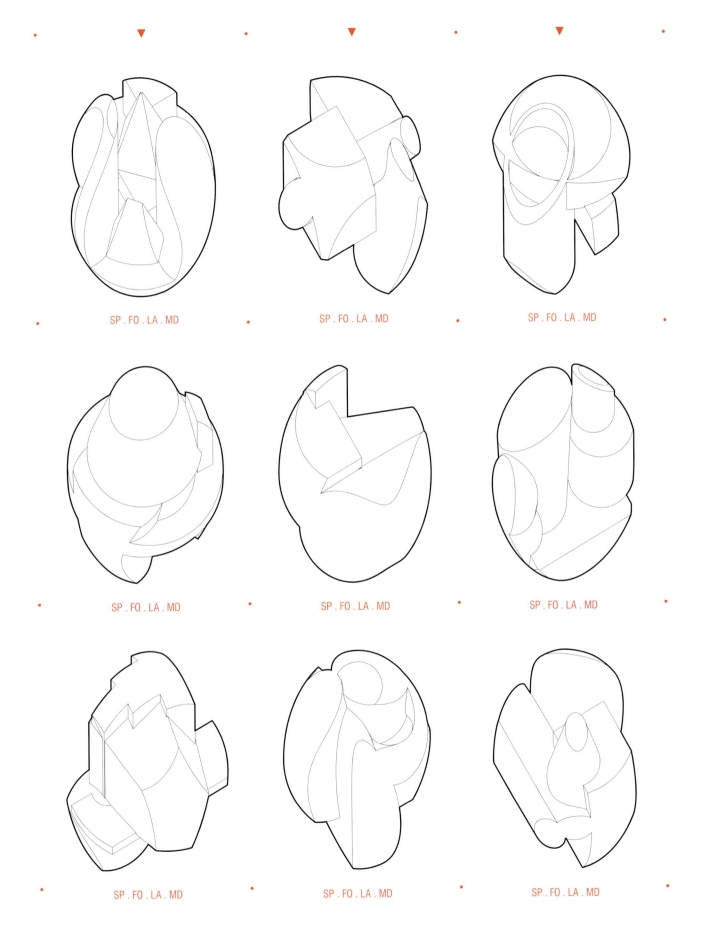

S4 BUNDLED

1. Select a closed brep
2. Get the bounding box
   - **2A** Define domain
   - **2B** Divide domain XYZ
   - **2C** Calculate line length
   - **2D** Calculate the radius and proximity of the pipes
3. Get the base point of the grid
4. Create the bundled pattern
5. Create lines at the points
6. Trim with the selected close brep
7. Create solid pipes

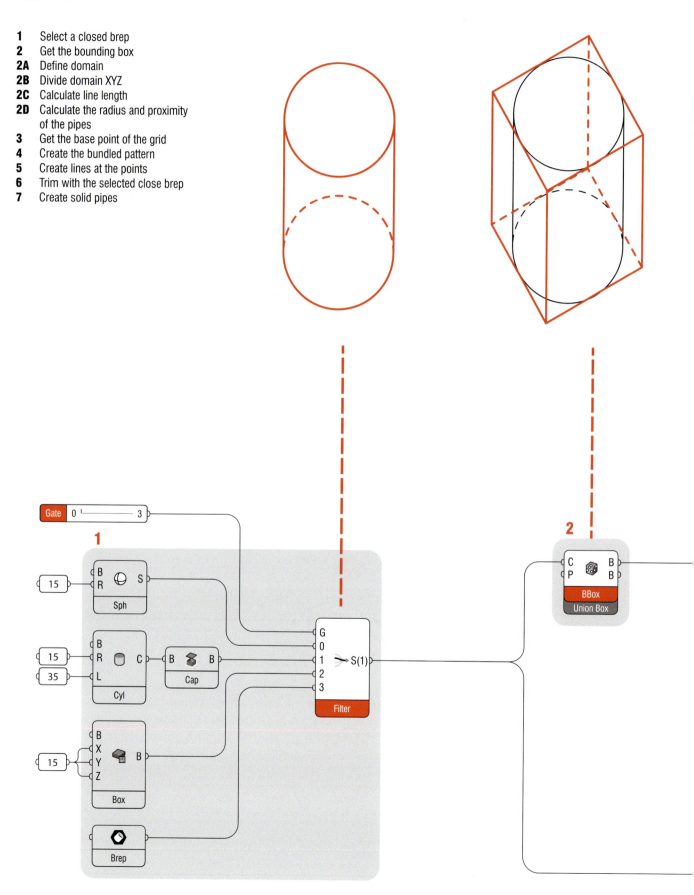

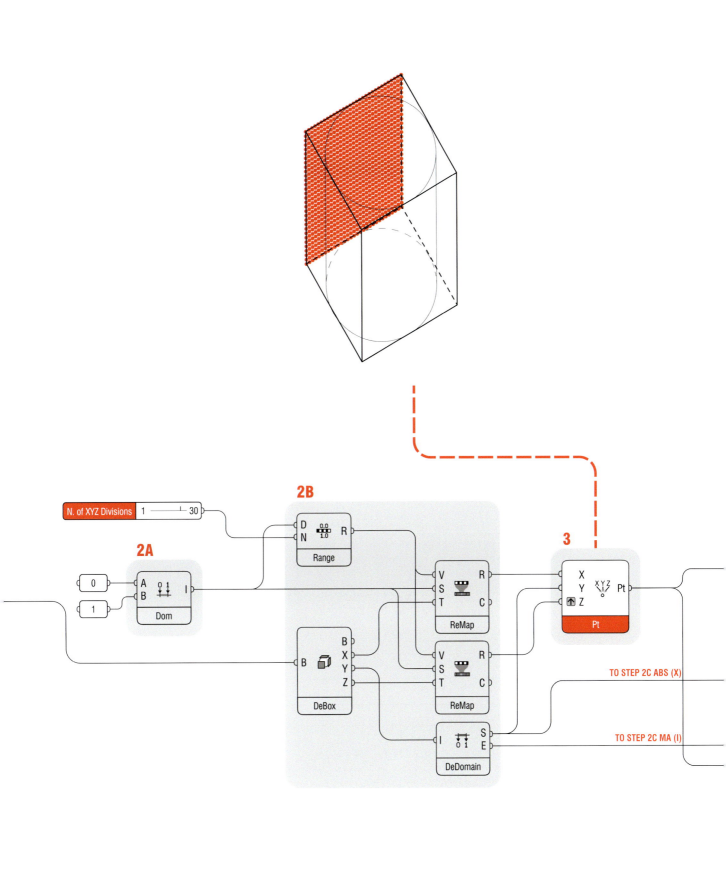

S4

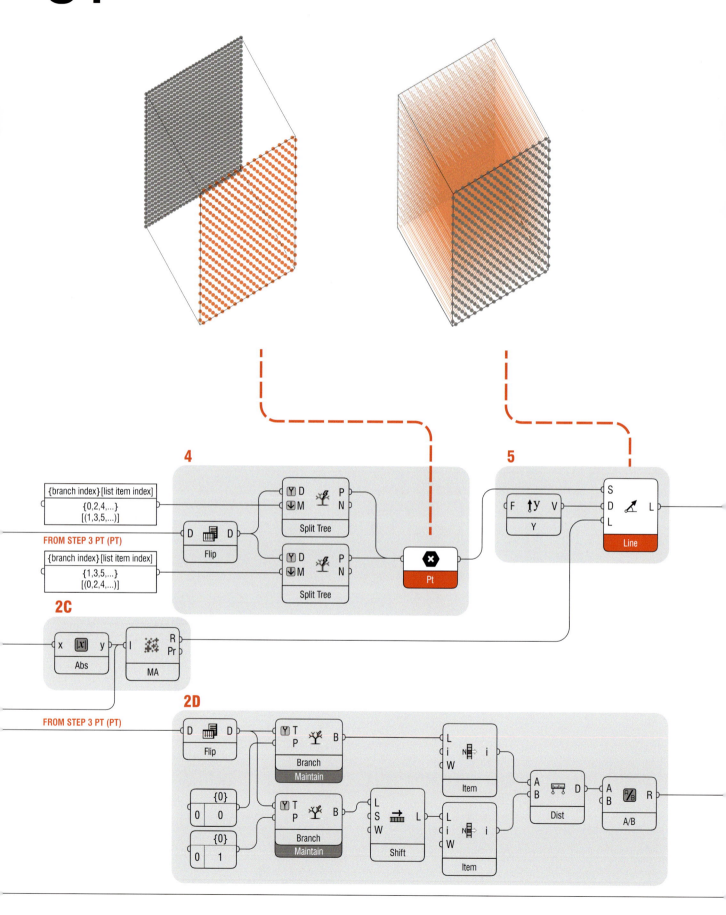

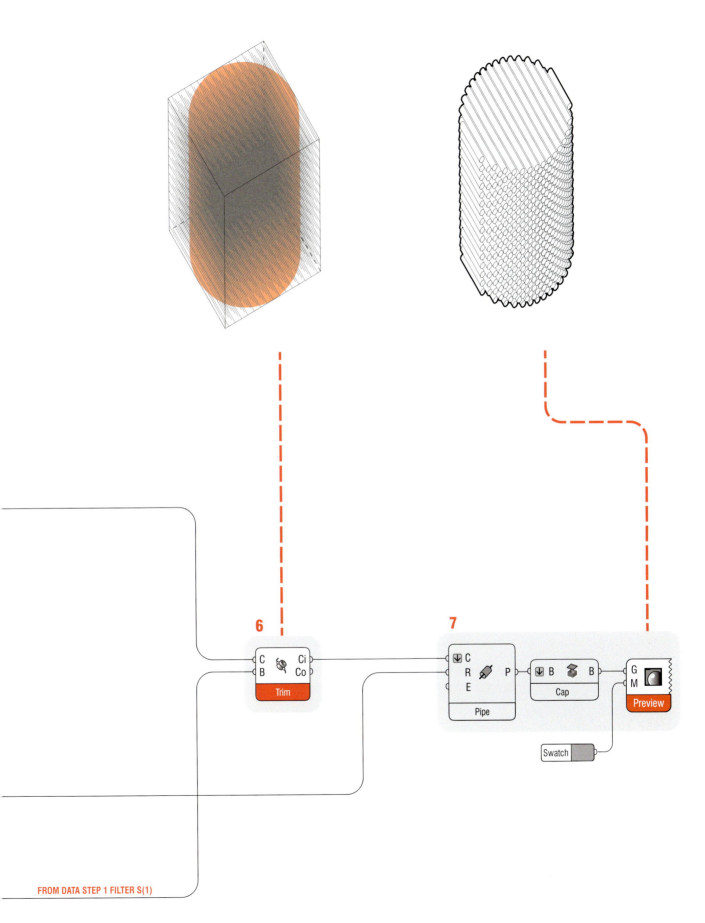

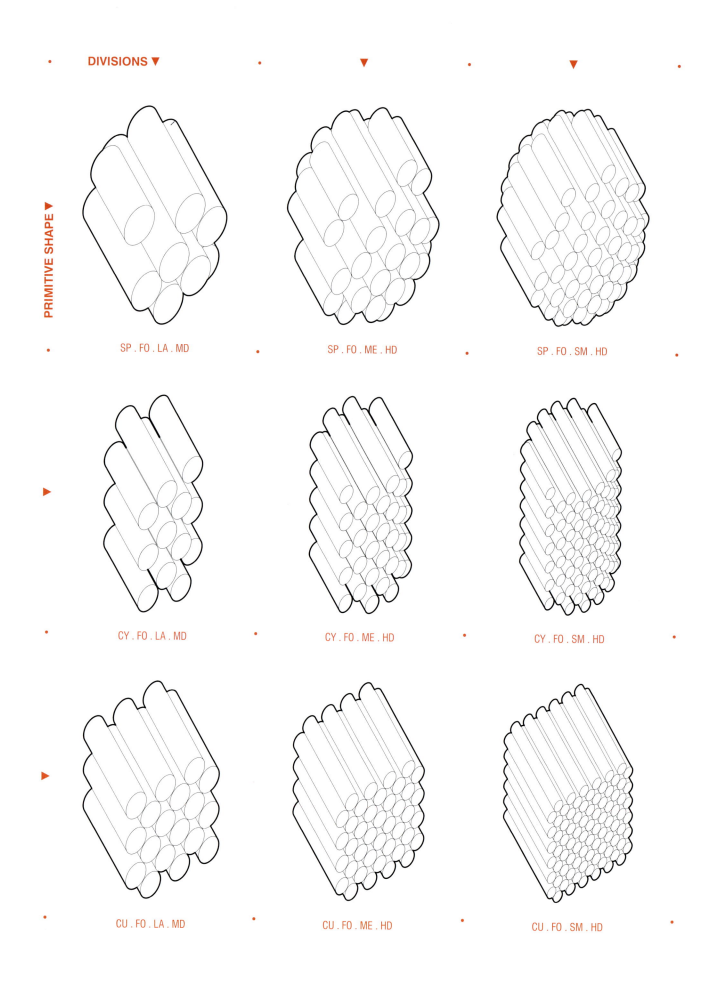

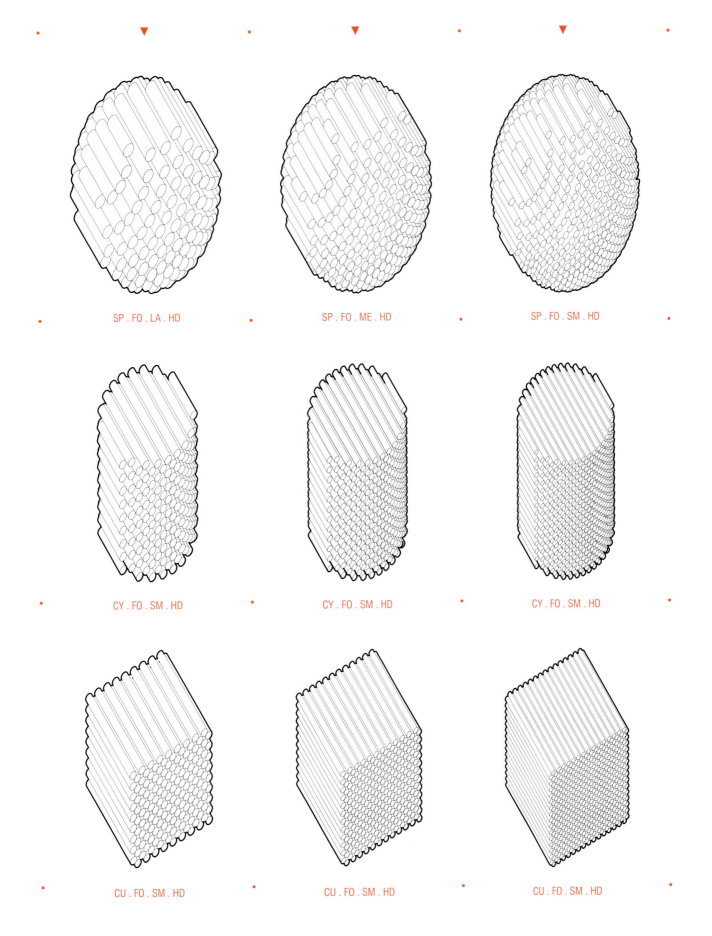

3.4 HYBRID OBJECTS

In this book we make a distinction between objects that are composed exclusively of Frame Elements and those that are composed of Planar and Solid Elements. We also make a distinction between objects which are exclusively composed of either Frame, Plane, or Solid Elements, and those that are composed of a combination of these, which we refer to as Hybrid Objects. A Hybrid Object is defined as an ordered aggregation of two or more primary elemental types. Our previous book, *The Making of Things*, deconstructs this architectonic language thoroughly. Though in-depth definitions of these phenomena fall outside the scope of this work, we have included the architectonic taxonomic map from *The Making of Things* to help you conceptualize the relationships between the object types discussed above.

In this chapter you will learn how to construct four basic Hybrid Objects, evolving each using a series of verbs which are tied directly to parametric operations in Rhino/Grasshopper. As you build these definitions, experiment with changing elemental profile shapes, sizes, quantities, spacing, etc. for each object. Look carefully at how these individual changes substantively affect each object's visual character and its emotive affect. For instance, thickening Frame Elements gives them a sense of robustness and begins to make the Frame Object appear more like a Solid Object. On the other hand, thinning the Frame Elements and using them to support a thickened Solid Element can make the Frame Elements appear tenuous but can also make the Solid Element look as though it floats. In another scenario, when Frame Elements penetrate Planar Elements within a Hybrid Object, the visual effect of slippage and mobility is created. Play with the definitions you are building, test different approaches, look long enough to consider how each arrangement resonates emotively in a new way. Additionally, as you work on these definitions and iterate different variations, be sure look at as many other buildings as possible and notice which are similar to the objects you are creating; designers refer to this similarity as a shared "language".

H1	**Solid Plane**
H2	**Frame Solid**
H3	**Frame Plane**
H4	**Solid Frame**

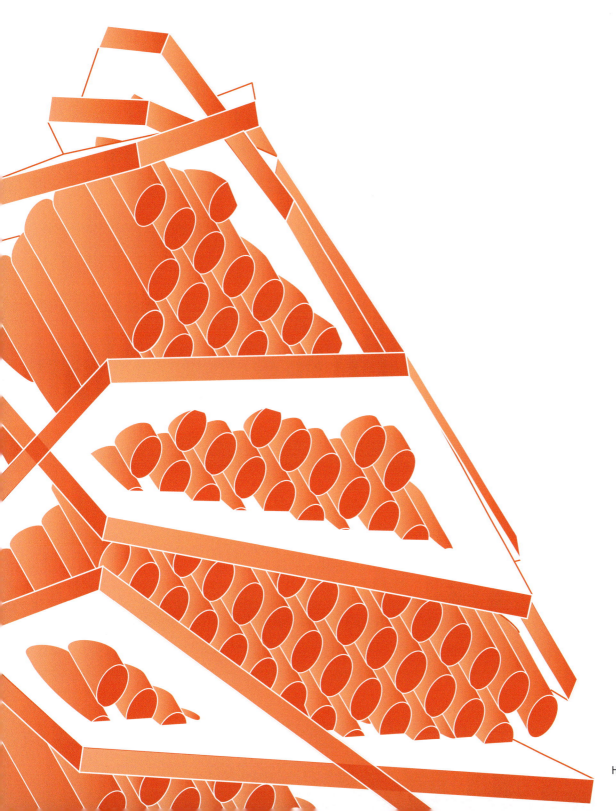

H1 SOLID PLANE

1. Select closed brep
2. Get bounding box
3. Get points inside the bounding box
3A. Create a random vector for step 5 and step 11
4. Divide XYZ domains
4A. Create base point grid
4B. Calculate line length
5. Create planes
6. Cut base solid, Flatten data tree to remove invalid intersections for step 11
7. Create a pattern of points
8. Create lines at the points
9. Trim lines to base solid
9A. Calculate pipe radius
10. Create solid pipes
11. Increase size of the cutting shapes and set thickness of cutting planes from step 6
12. Extrude planes and create a single solid
13. Extrude planes
14. Trim pipes with cutting planes
15. Preview geometry

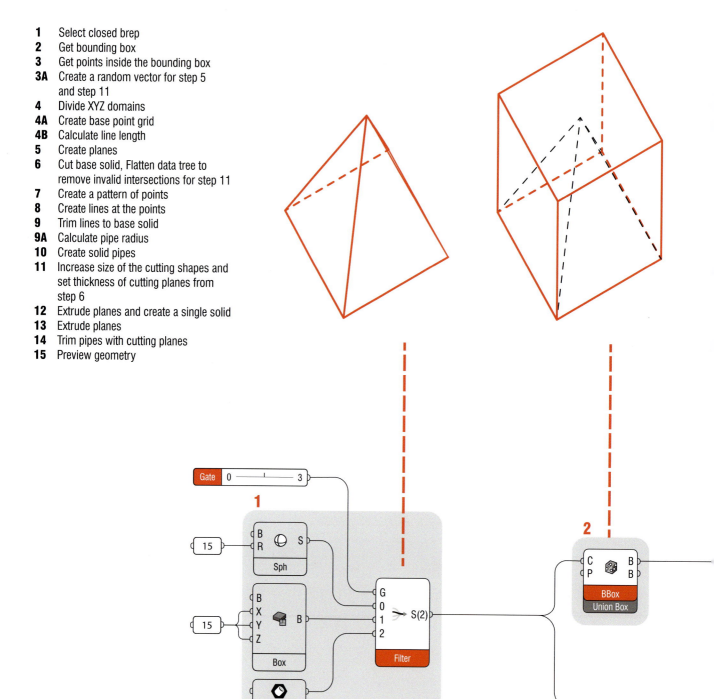

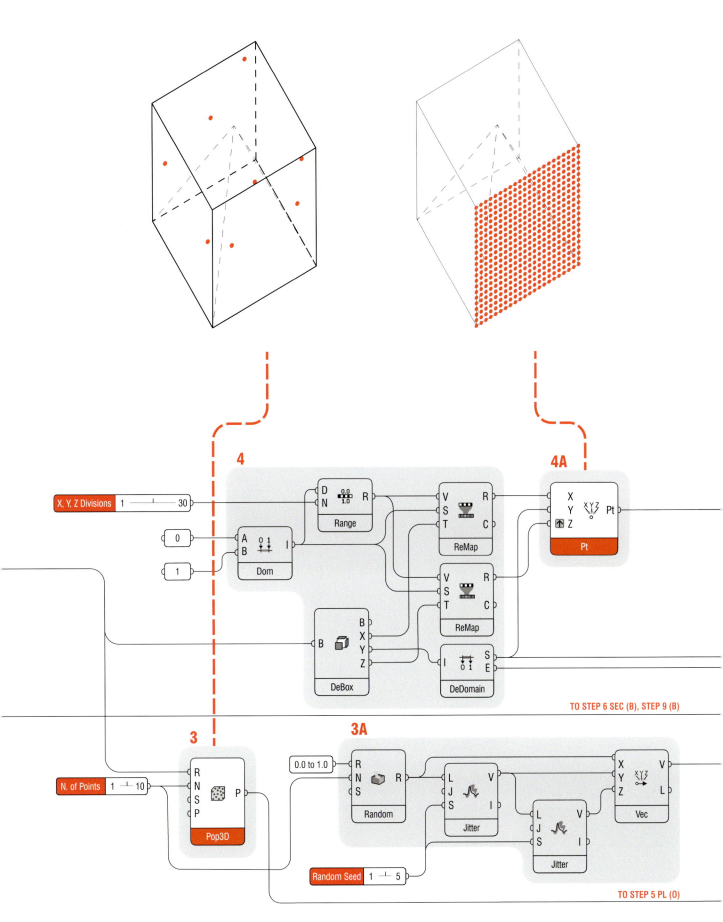

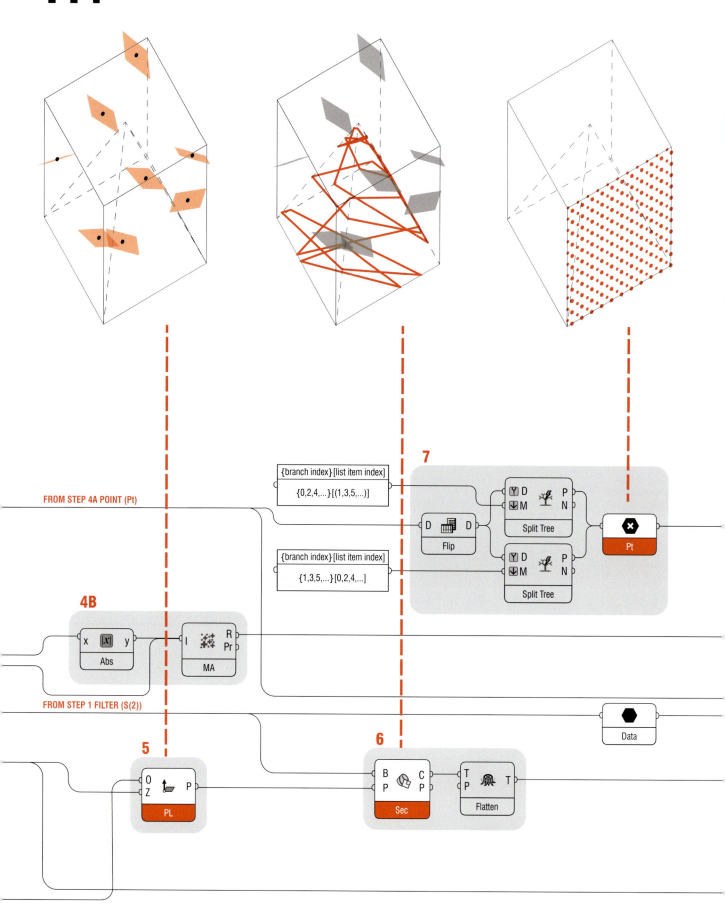

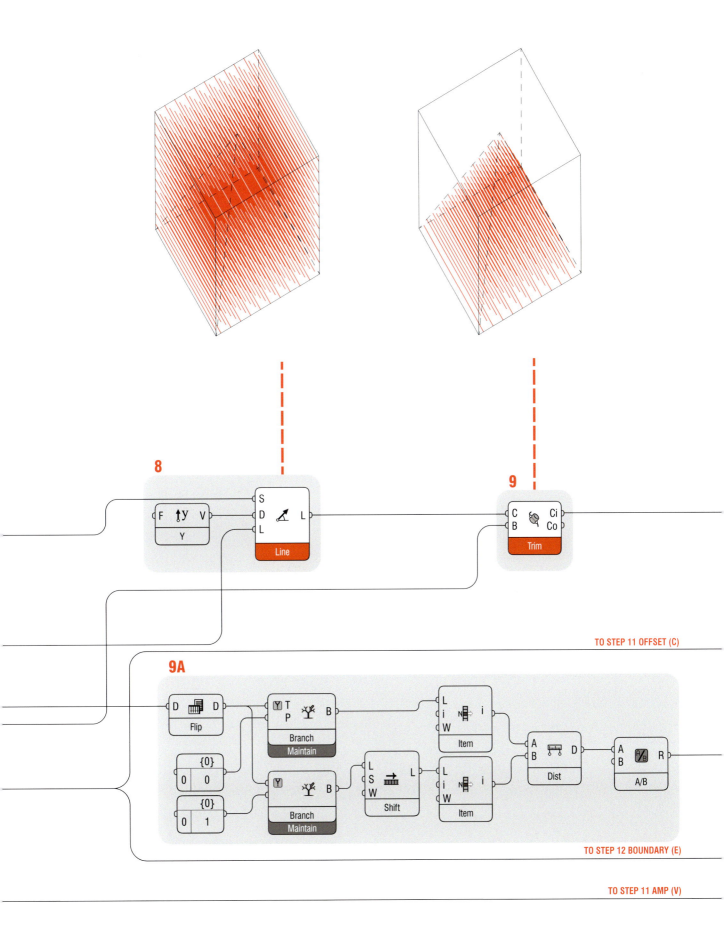

TO STEP 11 OFFSET (C)

TO STEP 12 BOUNDARY (E)

TO STEP 11 AMP (V)

SOLID PLANE HYBRID H1 **3.4**

H1

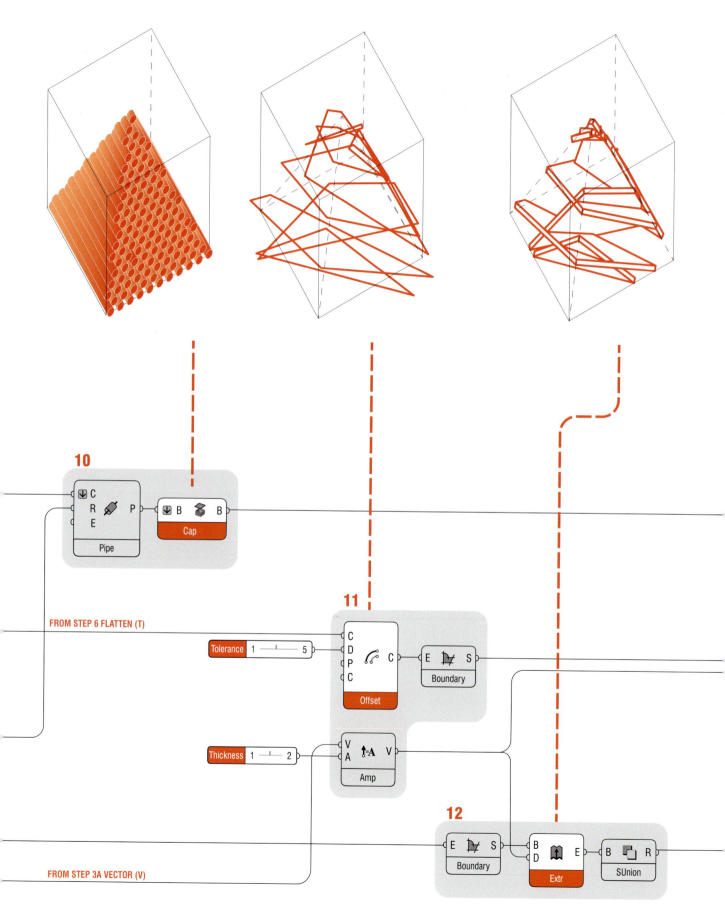

196 3.4 HYBRID H1 **SOLID PLANE**

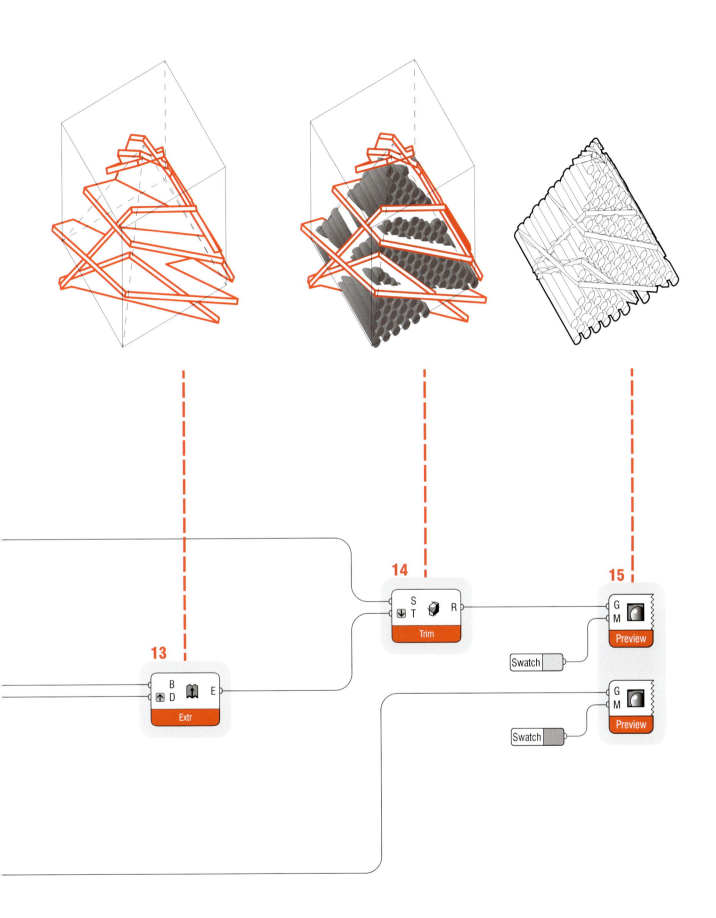

DIVISIONS ▼ ▼ ▼

THICKNESS ▼

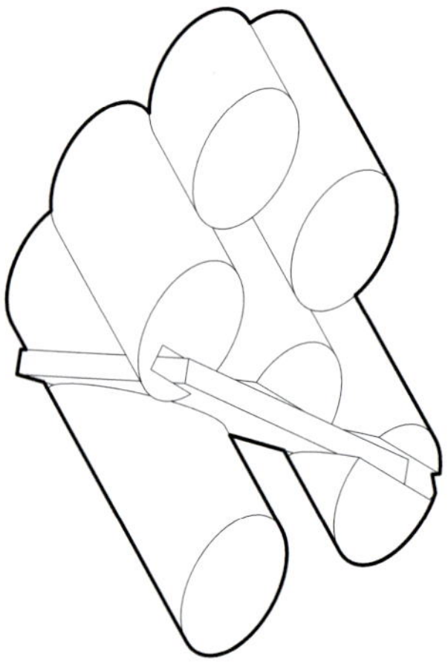

PY . FO/ST . LA/ME . HD 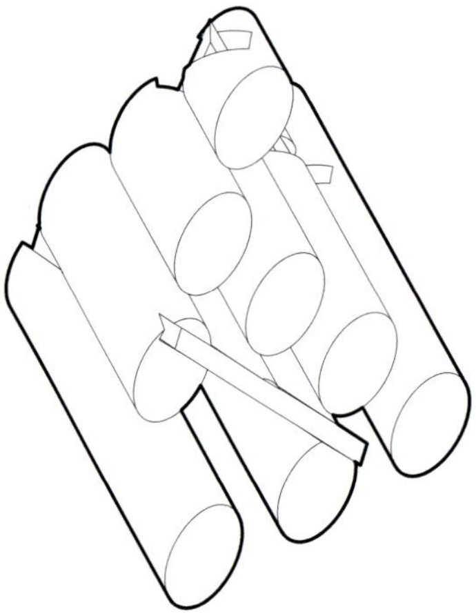
PY . FO/ST . LA/ME . HD 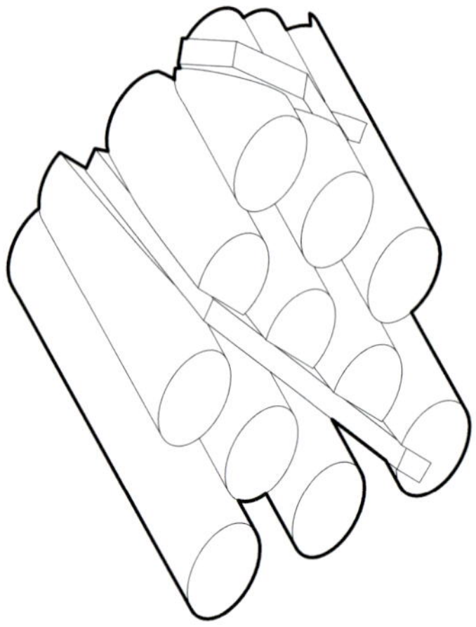
PY . FO/ST . LA/ME . HD

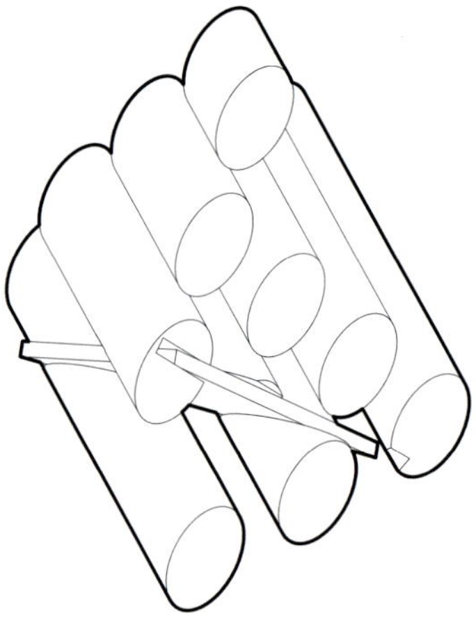

PY . FO/ST . LA/SM . HD 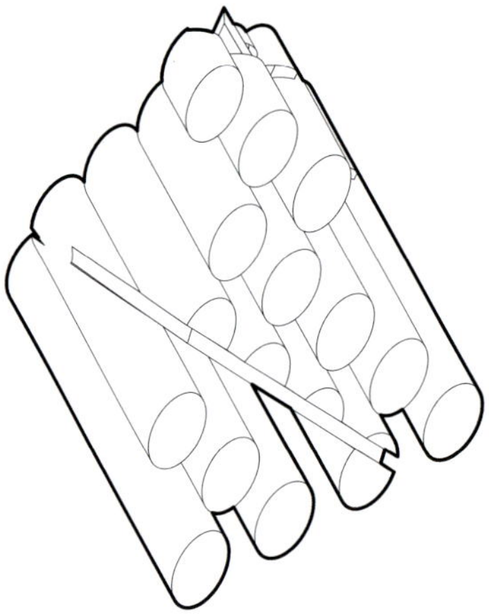
PY . FO/ST . LA/SM . HD 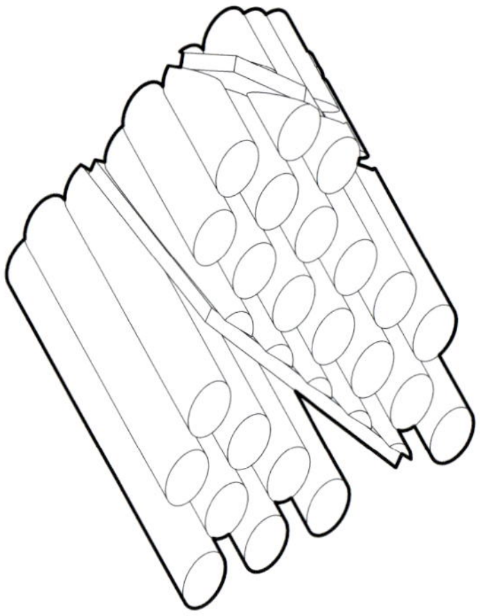
PY . FO/ST . ME/SM . HD

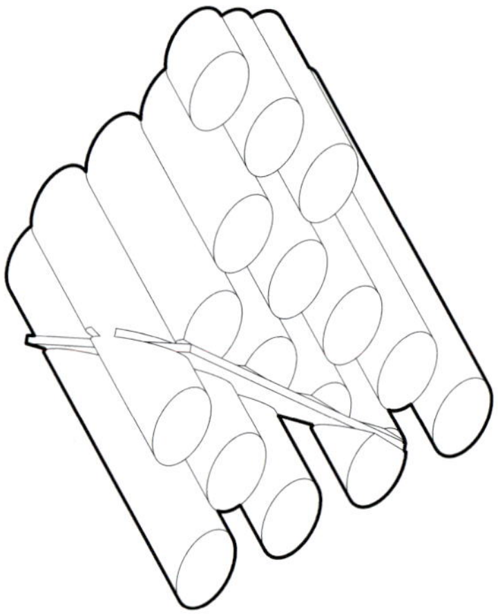

PY . FO/ST . ME/SM . HD
PY . FO/ST . ME/SM . HD 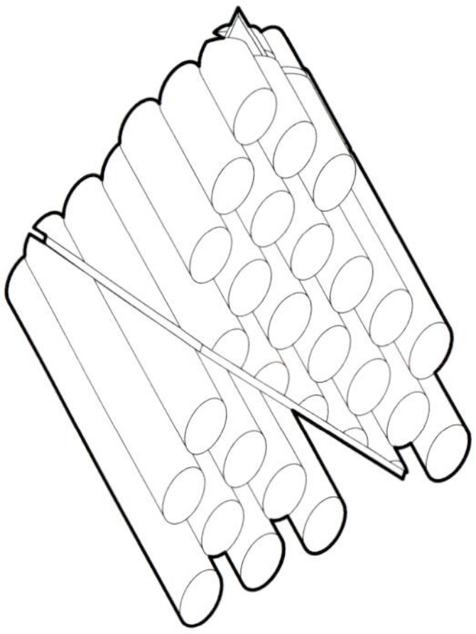
PY . FO/ST . ME/SM . HD 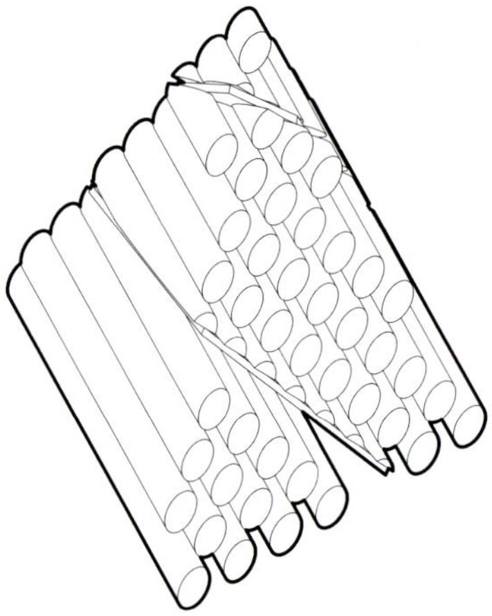

198   **3.4** HYBRID H1 SOLID PLANE **VARIATIONS**

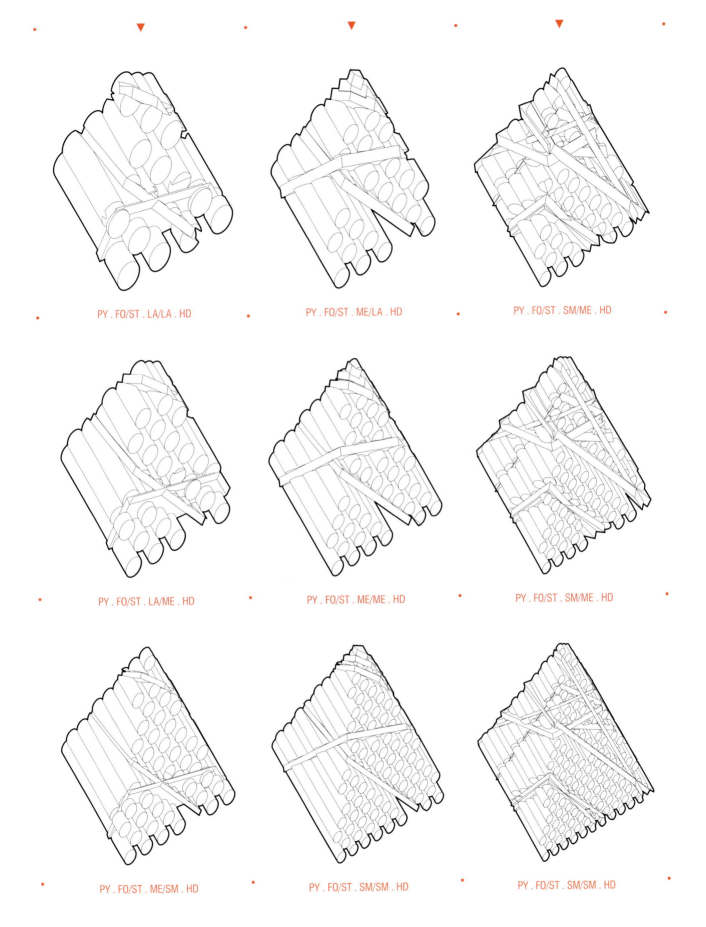

H2 FRAME SOLID

1. Create cube
2. Get 3 edges of cube on X Y Z
3. Divide X Y Z edges with planes
4. Cull first and last plane
5. Get Z vectors from planes
6. Get border curves
6A. Clean and explode into X Y Z branches
7. Create surfaces from border curves
8. Get intersection points
8A. Create profile curve domain
8B. Define thickness of boolean cutting object by the thickness of frame element
9. Create curves between points from step 8
10. Explode initial intersection curves and create a flat data tree
10A. Extend curves
11. Merge boolean cutting extrusions
12. Boolean difference cutting extrusions from base cube geometry
13. Get first and last frame of each base curve from step 10
14. Create profile for frame elements
15. Create frame elements
16. Randomly reduce solid elements
17. Preview both geometries

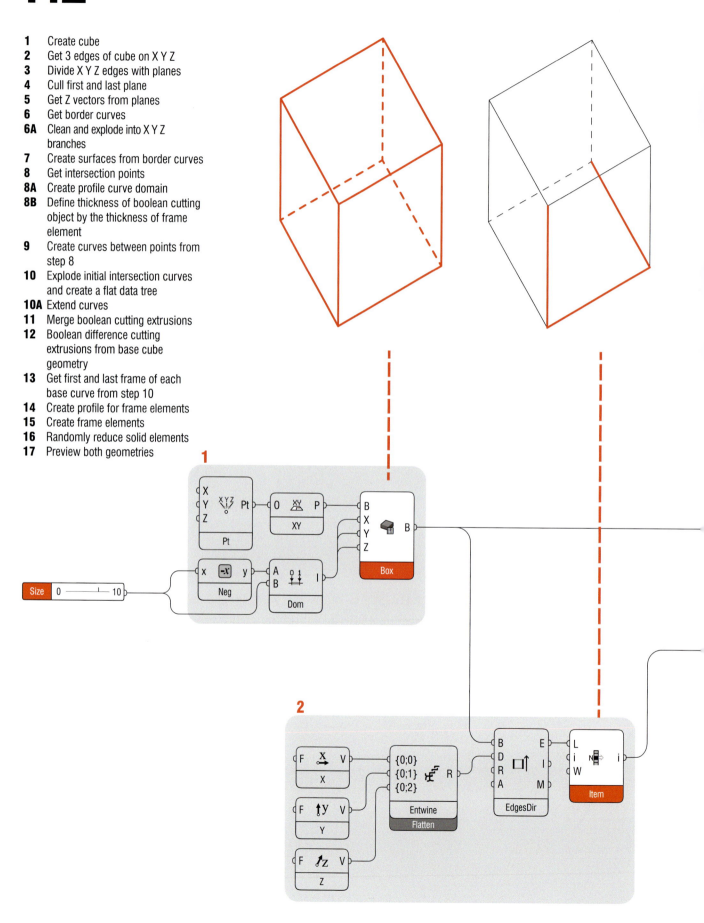

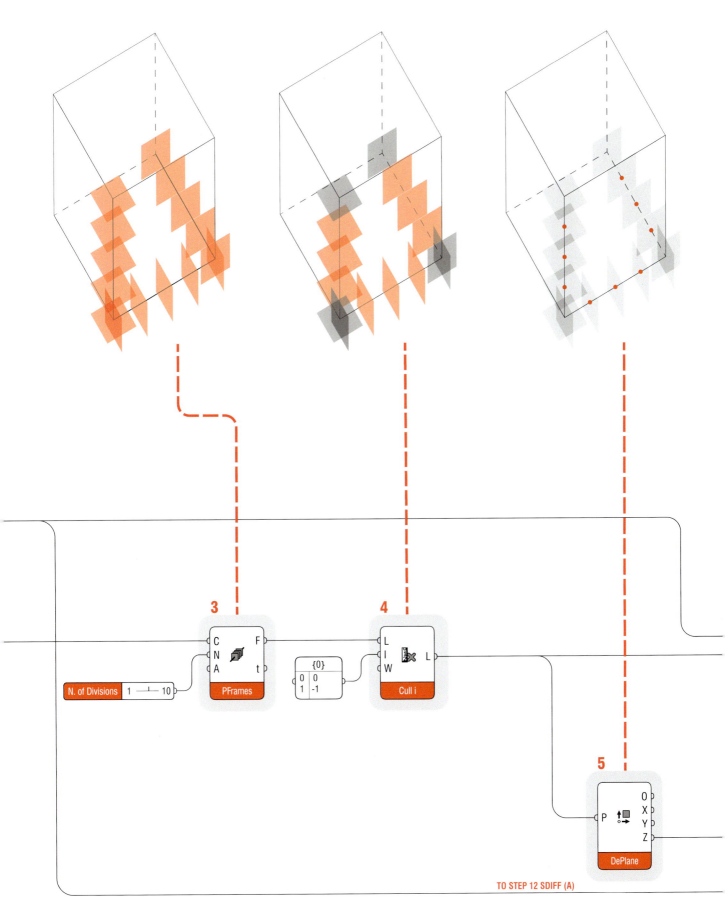

FRAME SOLID HYBRID H2 **3.4**

H2

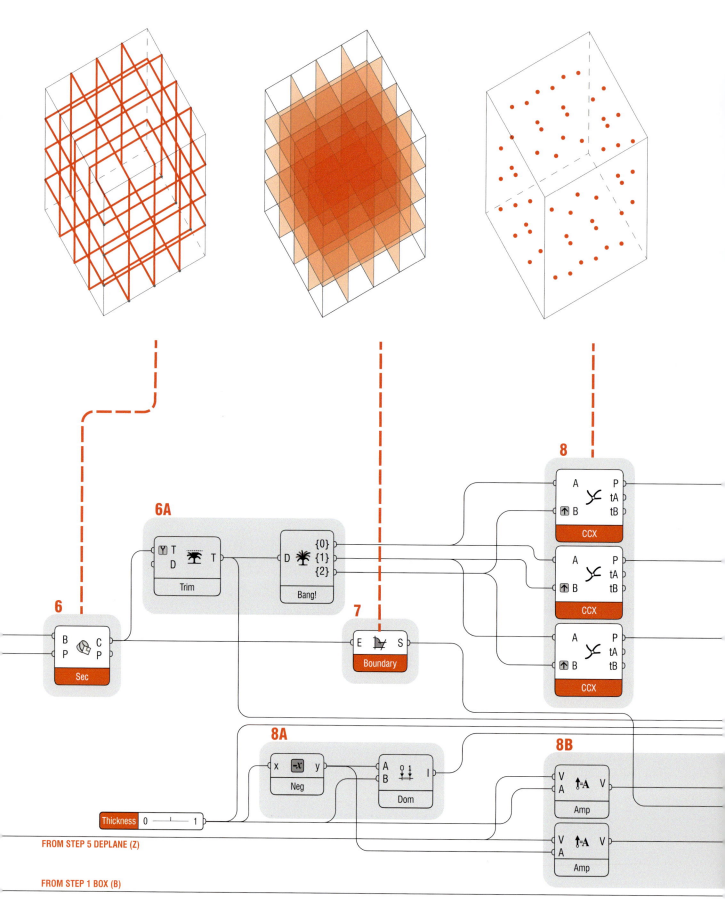

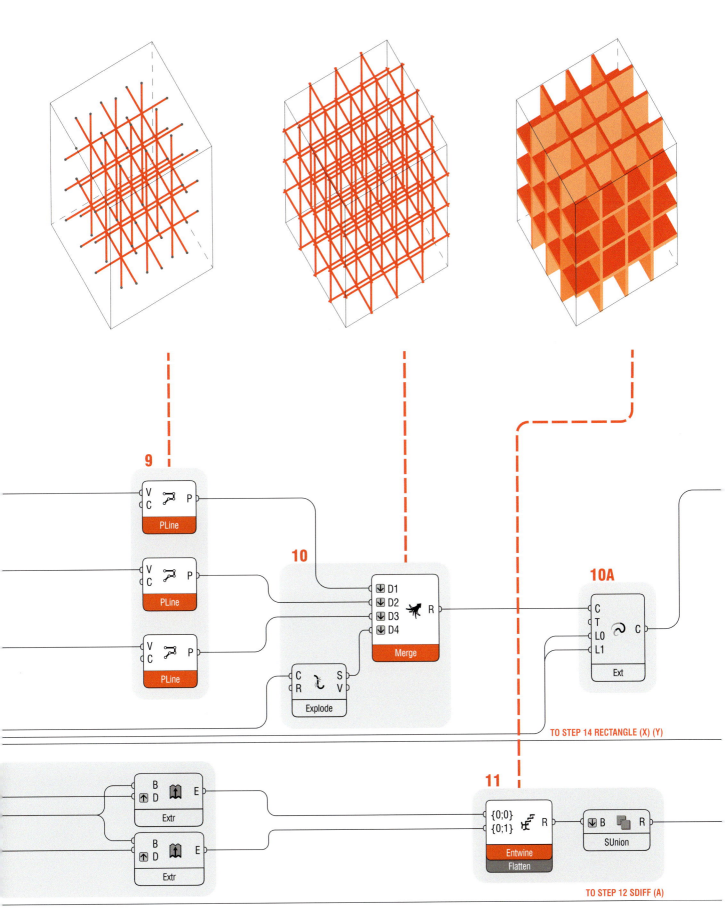

FRAME SOLID HYBRID H2 **3.4**

H2

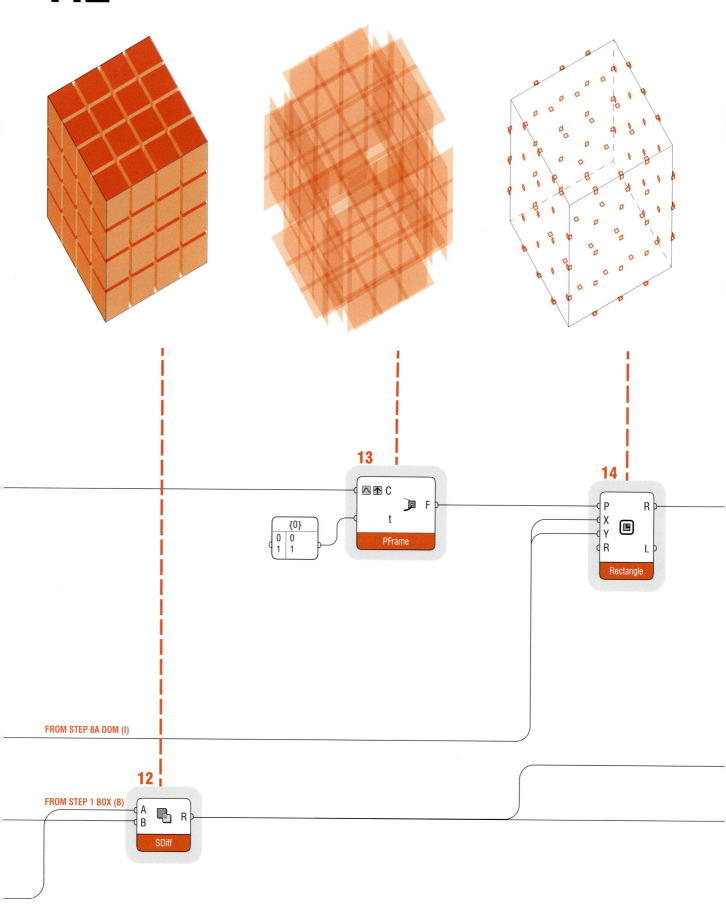

204 3.4 HYBRID H2 **FRAME SOLID**

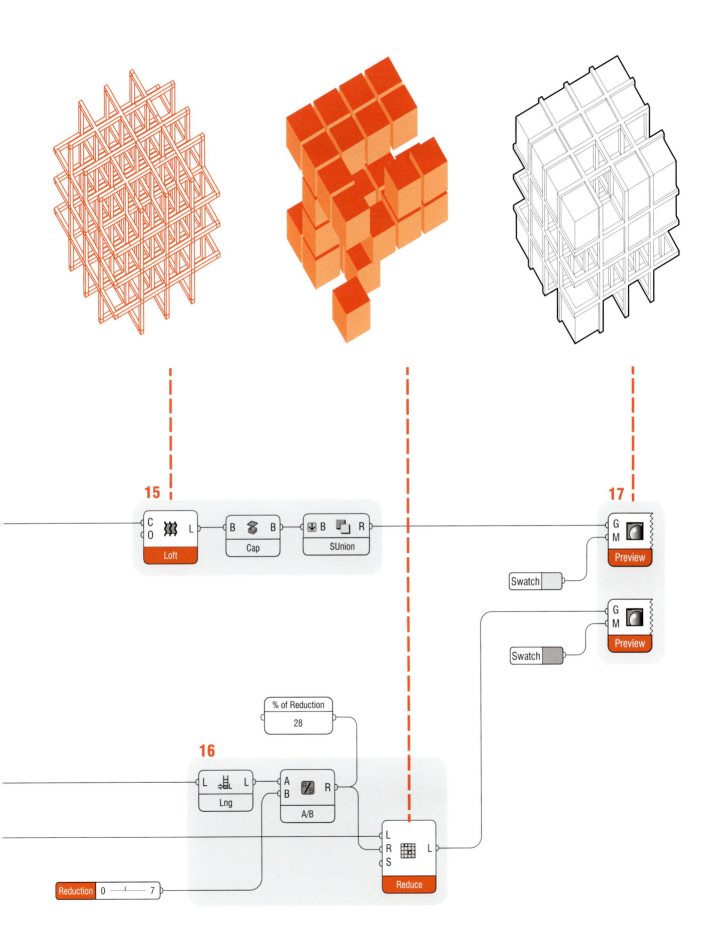

FRAME SOLID HYBRID H2 **3.4**

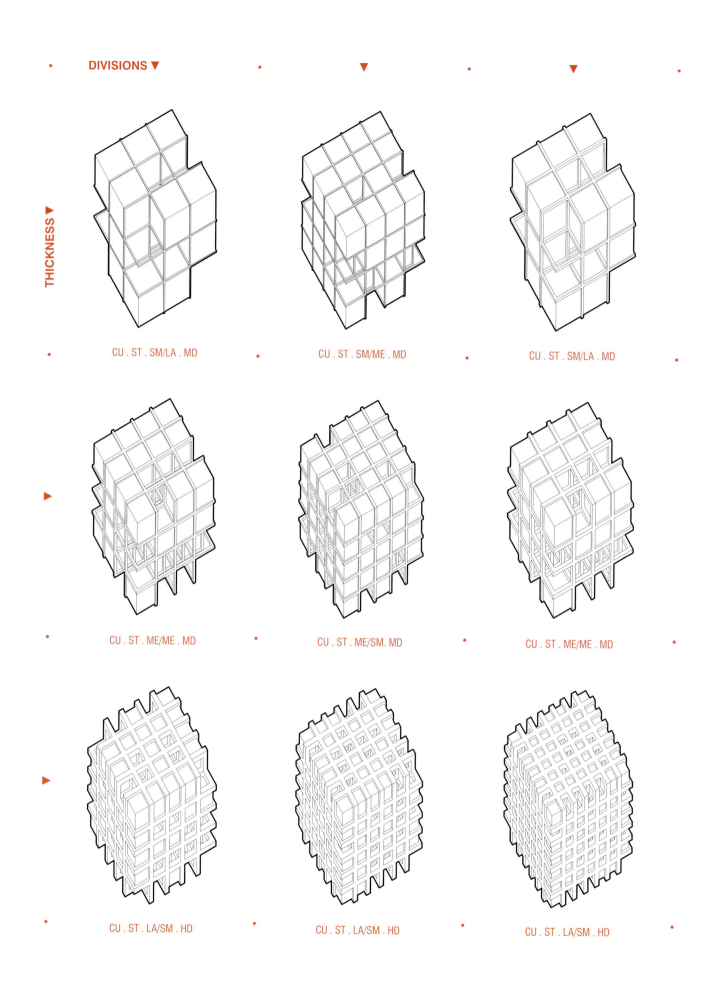

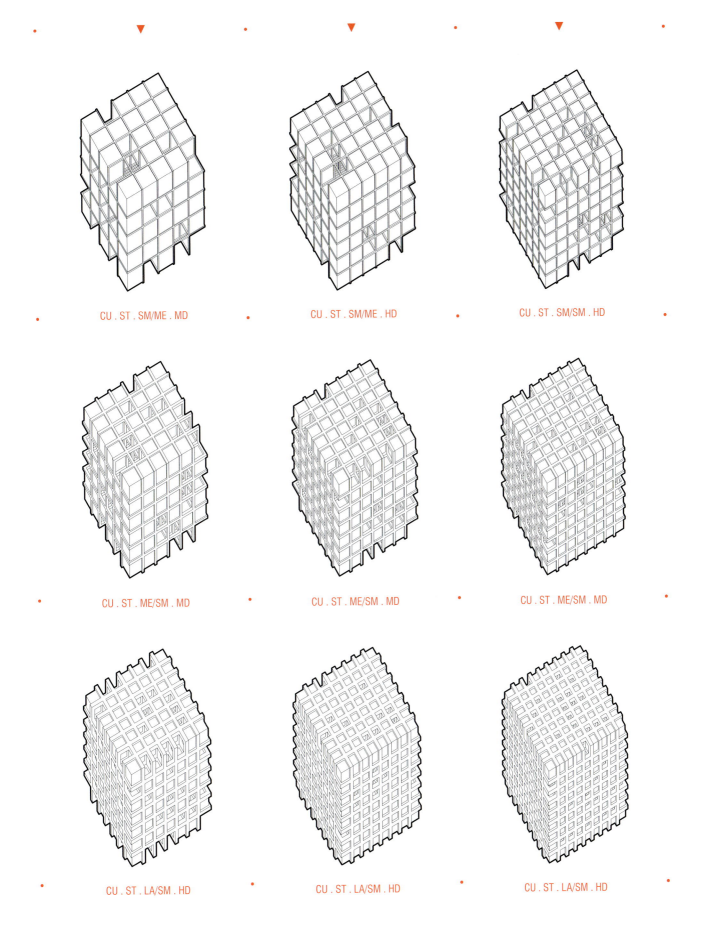

H3 FRAME PLANE

1. Create cylinder
2. Create vertical axis and get the seam on cylinder
3. Translate the vertical axis
4. Divide vertical axis in three parts
5. Create one data tree
6. Define the curved line from vertical axis control points
7. Get central segment of vertical axis
8. Create outside frame element for outside planes with curved line from step 6
9. Mirror curved line
10. Create a base plane for outside plane elements
11. Divide center segment of vertical axis from step 7 with planes
12. Get the intersection points
13. Divide translated vertical axis
14. Get frames at the points
14A. Find closes point on curved line from step 6
14B. Define base curve thickness
15. Intersect the base plane with frames from step 14 and split base plane from step 10
16. Get midpoints of split base planes and sort data
17. Define shape and size of center frame elements
18. Create center frame elements
19. Define pattern for outside planes
20. Define half plane thickness and create half outside plane elements
21. Mirror plane elements about axis from step 2 to create full plane element thickness
22. Polar array outside planes
23. Subtract intersecting outside planes from outside frame elements from step 8
24. Polar array outside frame elements
25. Combine all frame elements
26. Preview both plane and frame elements

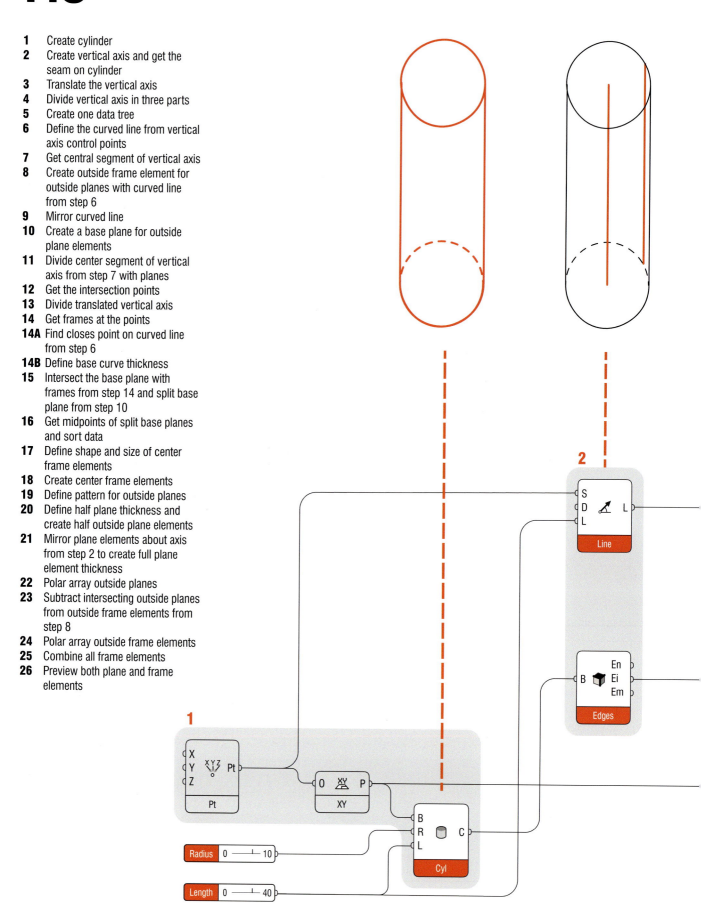

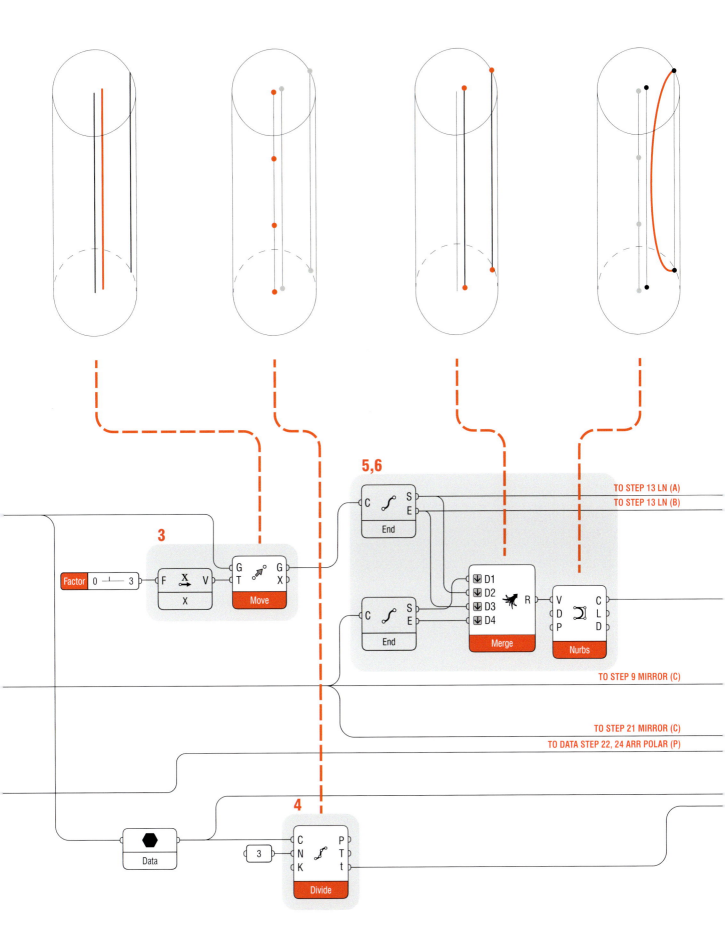

H3

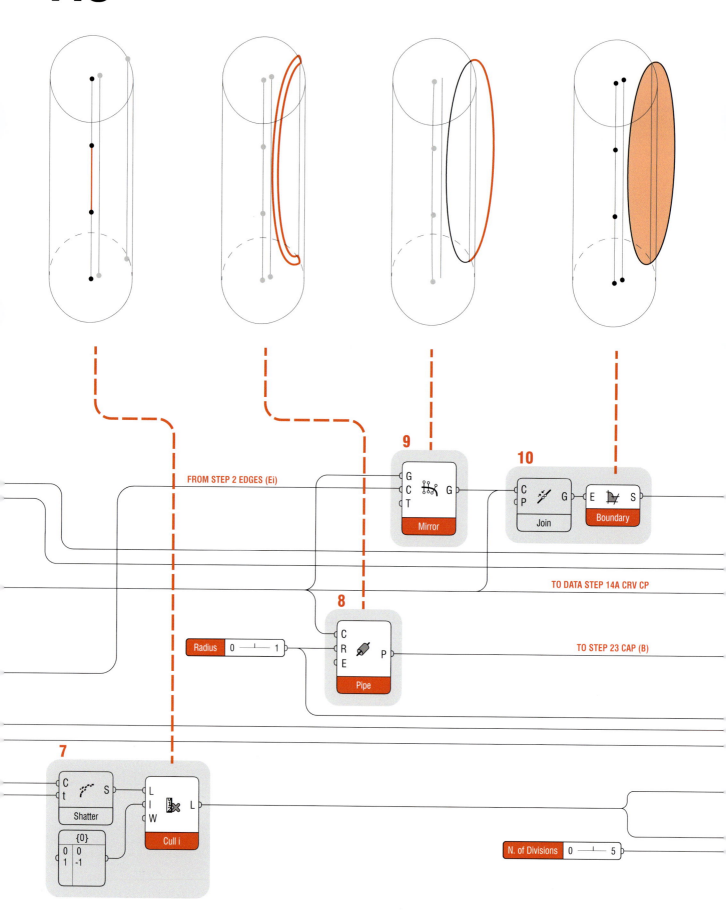

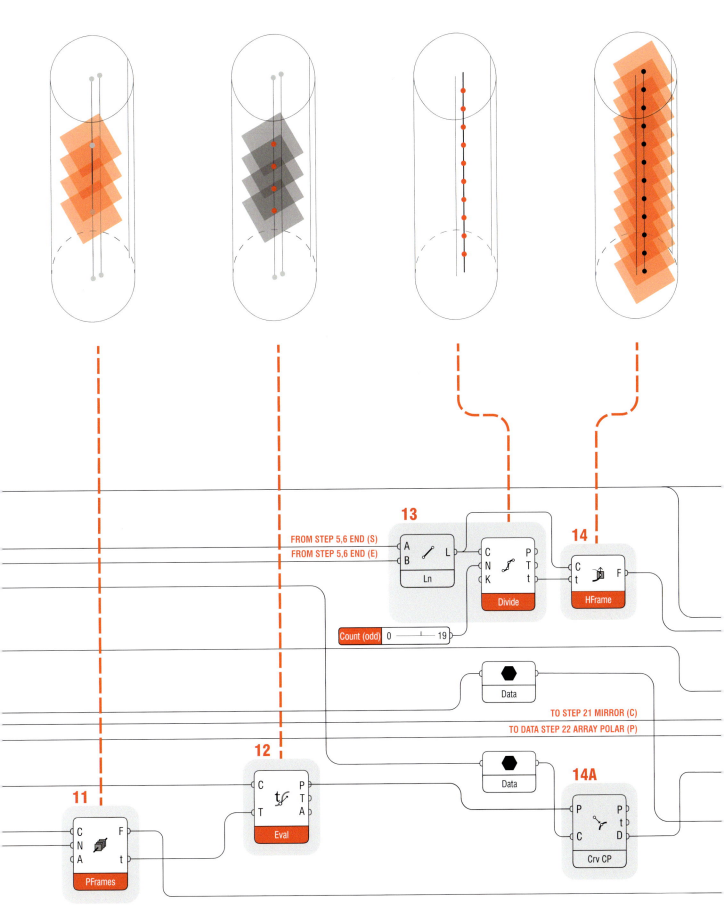

H3

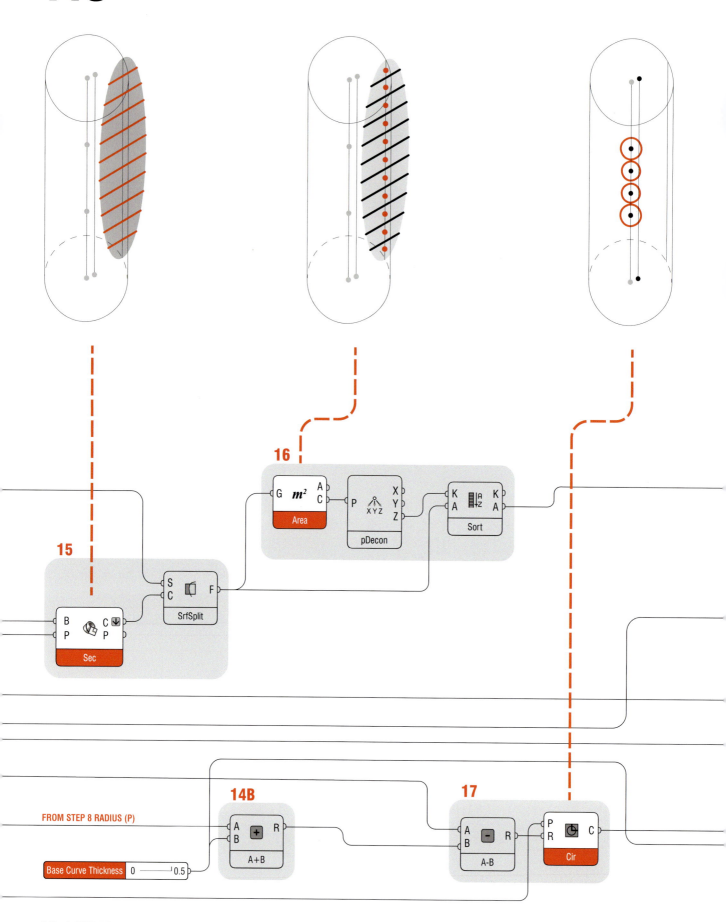

212 3.4 HYBRID H3 **FRAME PLANE**

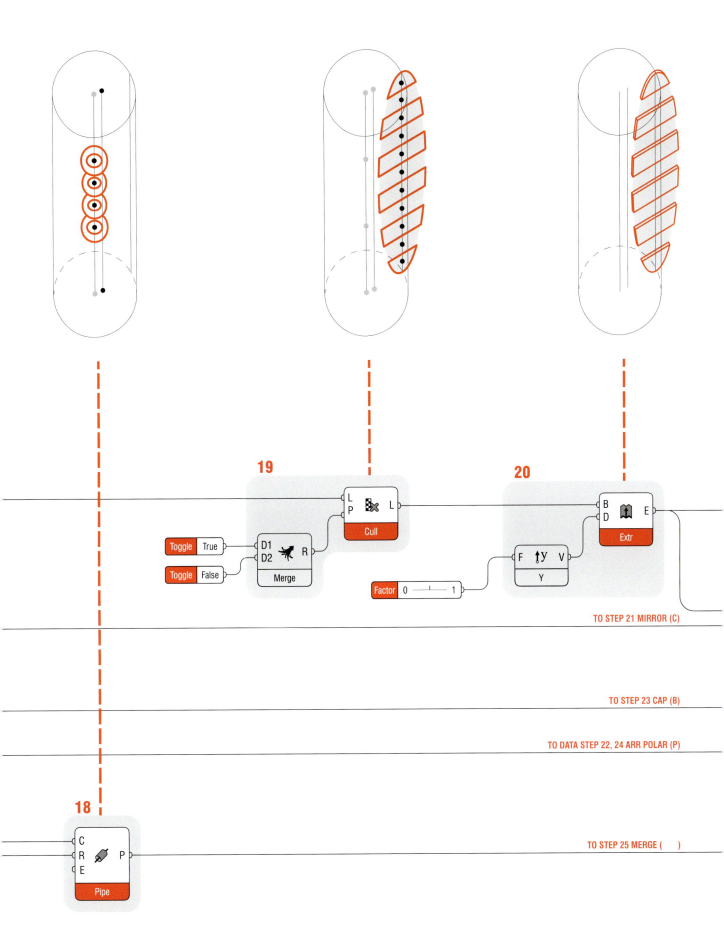

H3

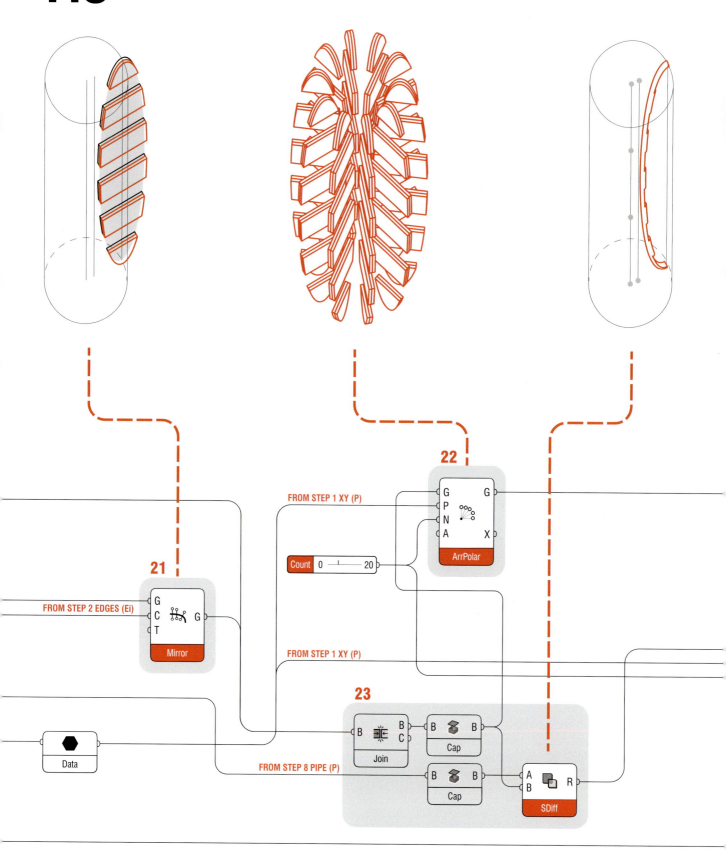

214   3.4 HYBRID H3 **FRAME PLANE**

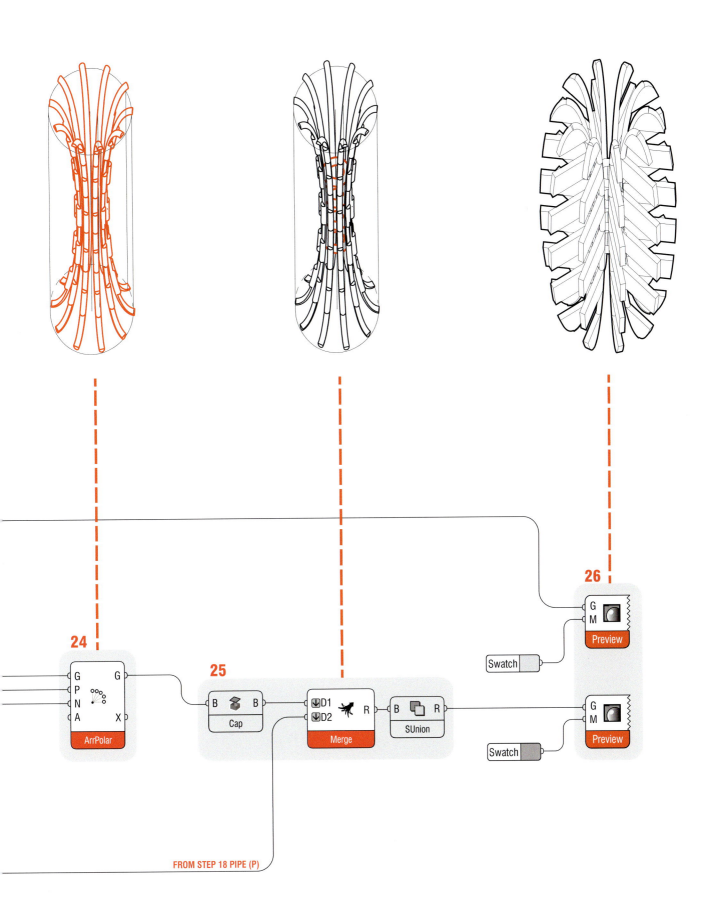

DIVISIONS ▼

THICKNESS ▼

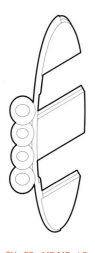
CY . FO . ME/ME . LD

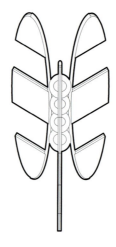
CY . FO . ME/SM . LD

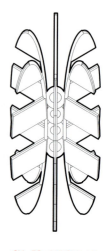
CY . FO . ME/SM . LD

CY . FO . ME/ME . LD

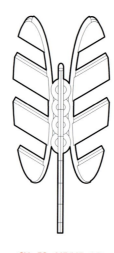
CY . FO . ME/ME . LD

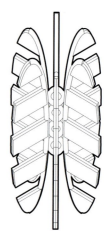
CY . FO . ME/ME . MD

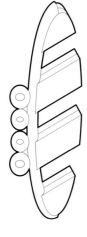
CY . FO . LA/LA . LD

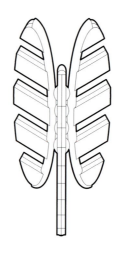
CY . FO . ME/LA . MD

CY . FO . LA/ME . MD

216　**3.4** HYBRID H3 FRAME PLANE **VARIATIONS**

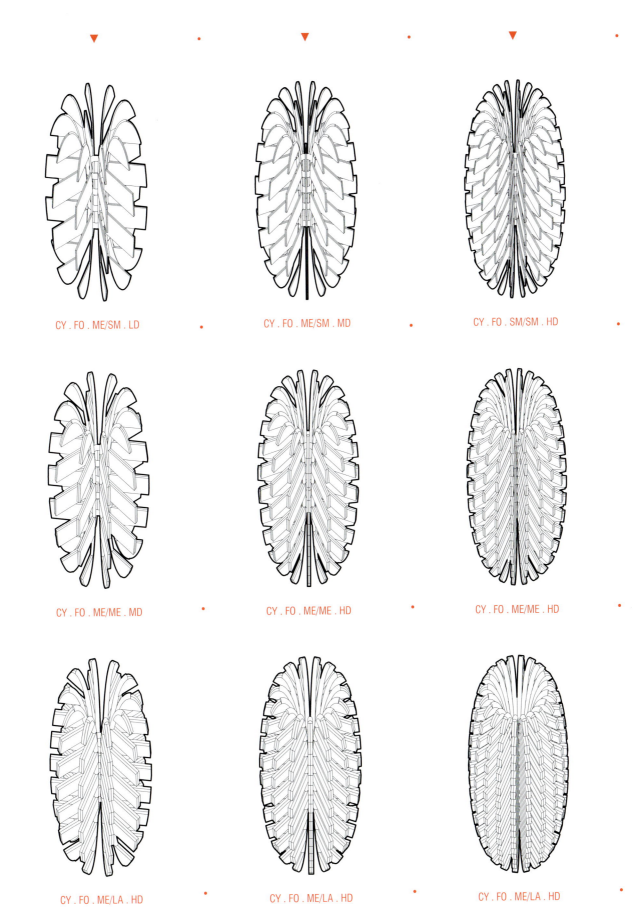

H4 SOLID FRAME

1. Select a closed brep
2. Get bounding box
2A. Divide XYZ domain
2B. Get dimensions of voxel on XYZ
3. Create 3D grid based on XYZ domain divisions
4. Create voxels
4A. Convert voxel boxes to mesh and get vertices of voxel meshes
4B. Define the removal of voxels that have vertices outside of the base brep boundary
5. Get voxels inside the base brep boundary as breps
5A. Define percentage of voids
6. Mix data list
7. Get edges of brep
8. Extend edge curves, search for first and last plane at each edge curve
9. Create profile curve for frame elements
10. Create frame elements
11. Define a solid element
11A. Map solid element into voxels
12. Preview frame and solid elements

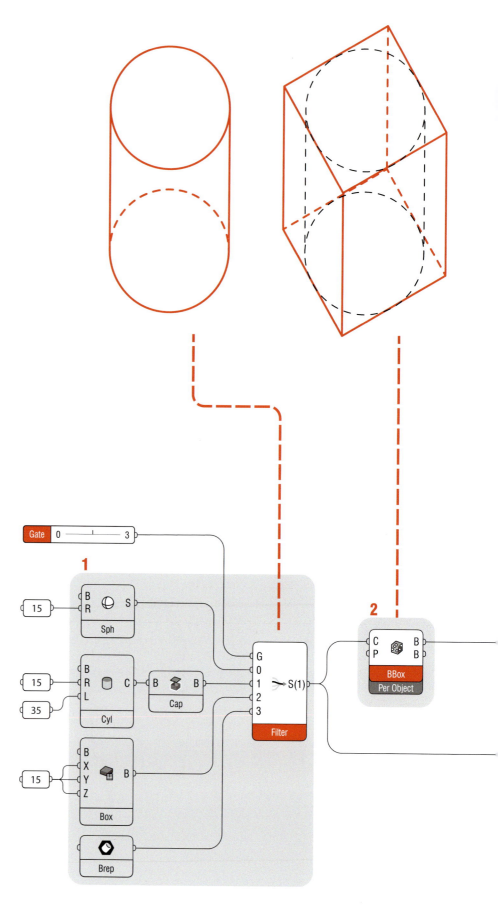

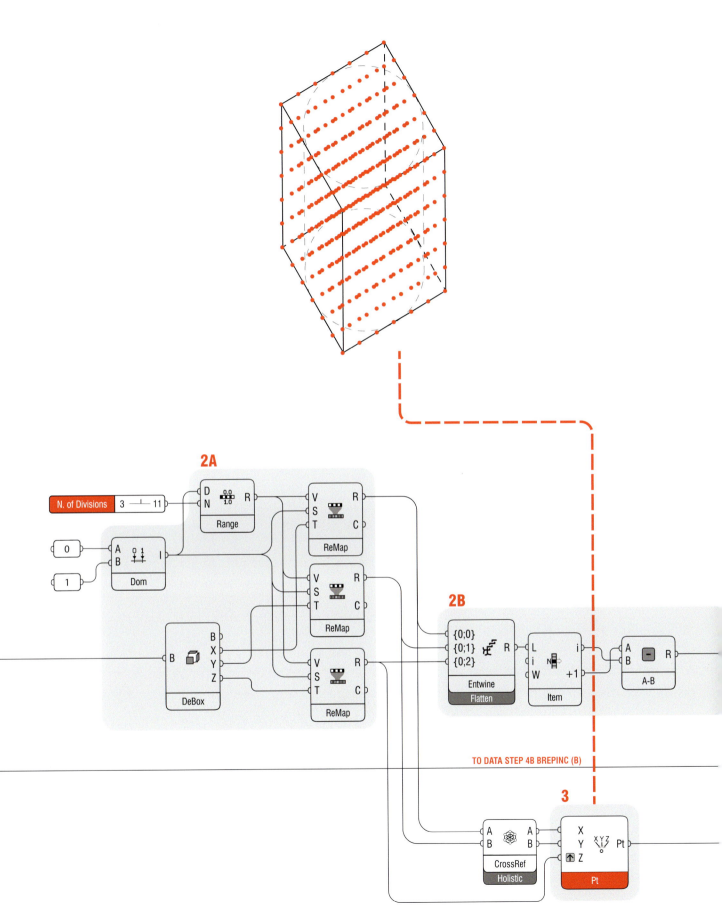

H4

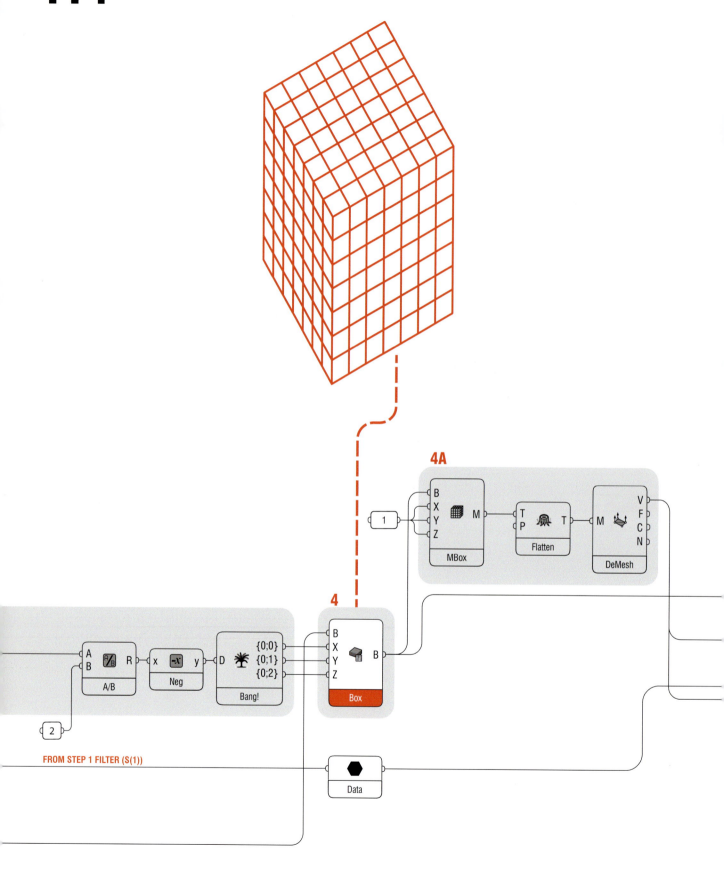

FROM STEP 1 FILTER (S(1))

220 3.4 HYBRID H4 **SOLID FRAME**

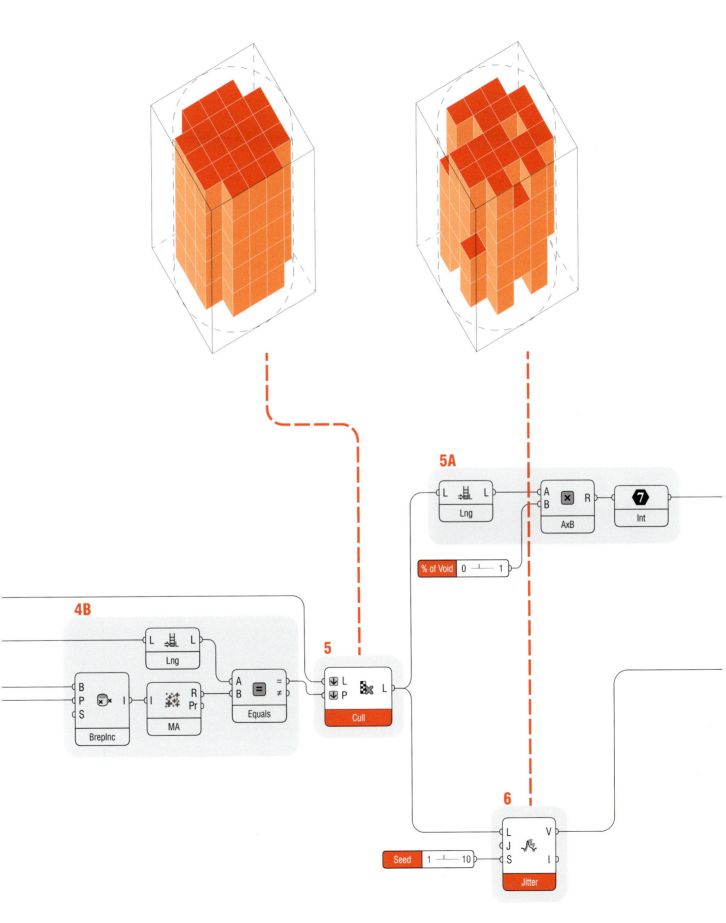

SOLID FRAME HYBRID H3 **3.4**

H4

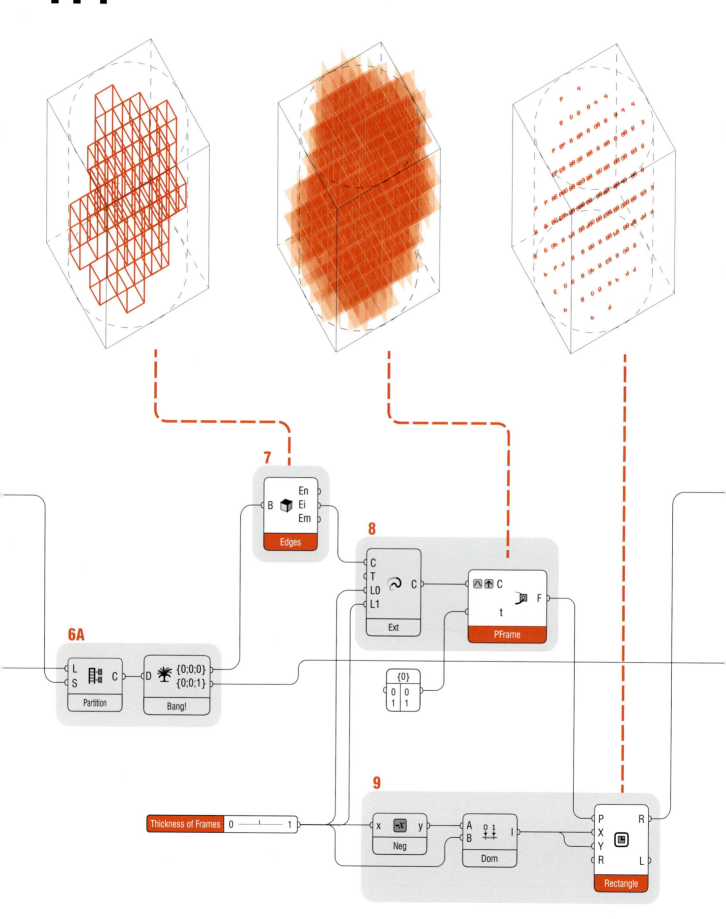

222 3.4 HYBRID H4 **SOLID FRAME**

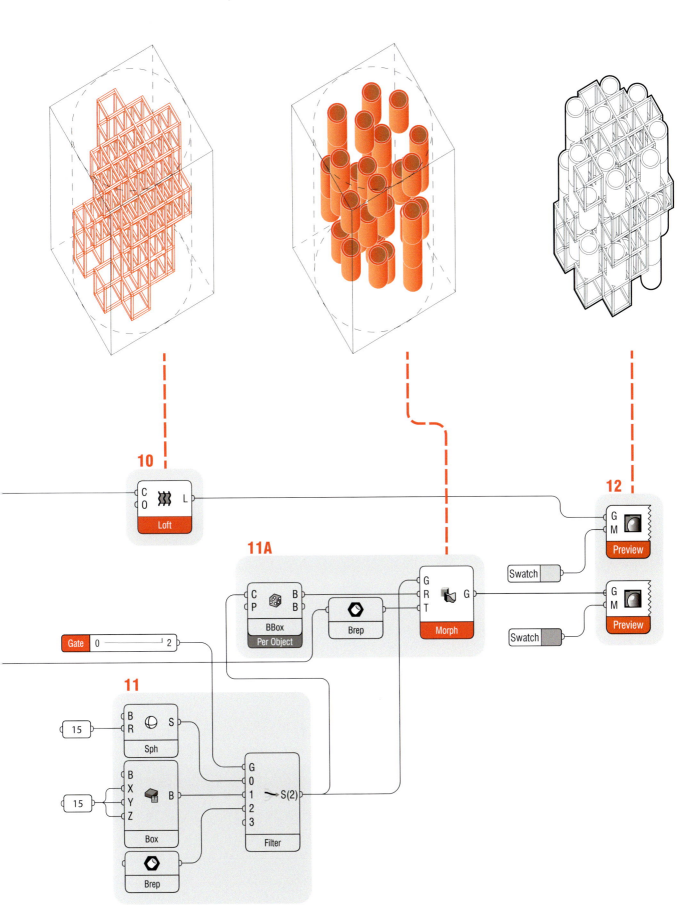

DIVISIONS ▼

SHAPE ▼

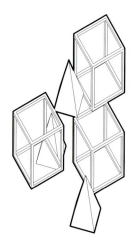
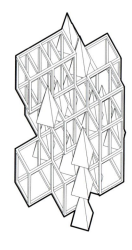

CU/PY . ST . ME/LA . LD   CU/PY . ST . SM/ME . LD   CU/PY . ST . ME/SM . MD

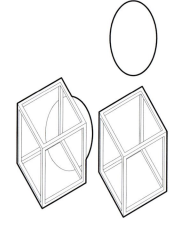
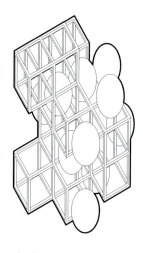
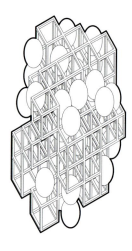

CU/SP . ST/FO . ME/LA . LD   CU/SP . ST/FO . ME/ME . MD   CU/SP . ST/FO . ME/SM . HD

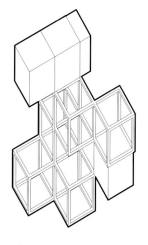
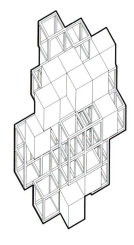
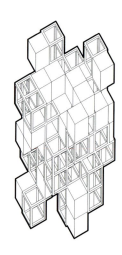

CU/CU . ST/ST . ME/ME . MD   CU/CU . ST/ST . SM/SM . MD   CU/CU . ST/ST . SM/SM . MD

3.4 HYBRID H4 SOLID FRAME **VARIATIONS**

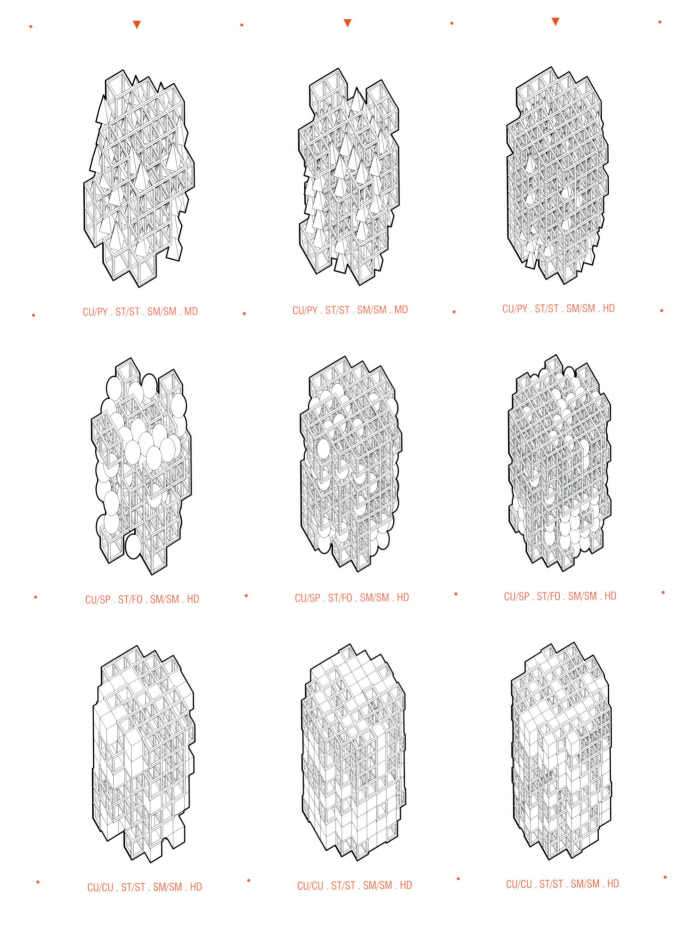

4 MORPHOLOGIES

In the **MORPHOLOGIES** section of the book you will operate on the objects you learned to create in the **CONSTRUCTIONS** section, submitting them to various morphological transformations based on the following verbs: bend, stretch, twist, branchoff, implosion, shatter, inflate, droop, pinch, carve, decompose, and merge. These verbs will be paired with their equivalent parametric operations in Rhino/Grasshopper in order to mutate individual objects thereby altering their tectonic qualities, emotive effects, and taxonomic category. As you work through the **MORPHOLOGY** definitions, see how far you can push the form. Can you push it so far that it no longer looks as though it is in the same family? What can you add to the definition that you have been introduced to in previous lessons in the books?

M1   Bend
M2   Stretch
M3   Twist
M4   Branchoff
M5   Implosion
M6   Shatter
M7   Inflate
M8   Droop
M9   Pinch
M10 Carve
M11 Decompose
M12 Merge

M1 BEND

In this exercise you will be taking the definition you worked on within Constructions / Frame Objects / F1 and morphing it such that it creates a bent figure. Bending the frame object changes its rigid nature, creating a playful fluidity and plasticity. On the right facing page are the steps that you underwent in exercise F1. Use the definition from F1 and add to it as shown on the spread that follows. Test the limits of the bend definition, see if you can break it by attempting to get the figure to bend in on itself. Watch closely as to how the nature of the object changes as you move the sliders.

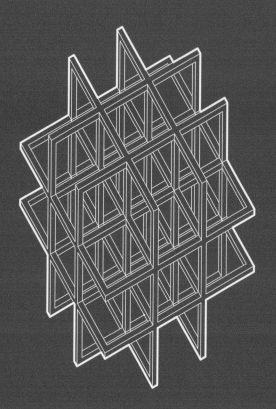

11 Group geometries
12 Get the boundary box
13 Get centroid and Z dimension
13A Get the size of the box in Z
13B Create a base point and get of distortion
14 Find endpoints of arc
15 Move midpoint of arc
16 Create arc
16A Position the middle point of the arc
17 Bend following the arc

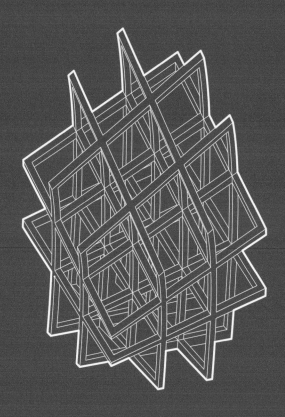

M1

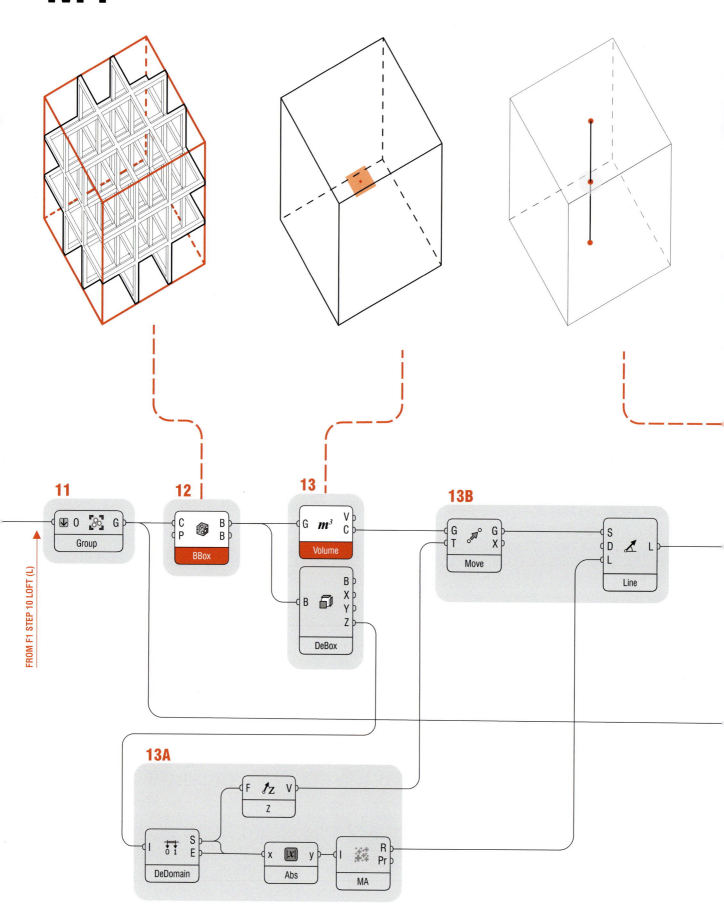

230 4 M1 BEND

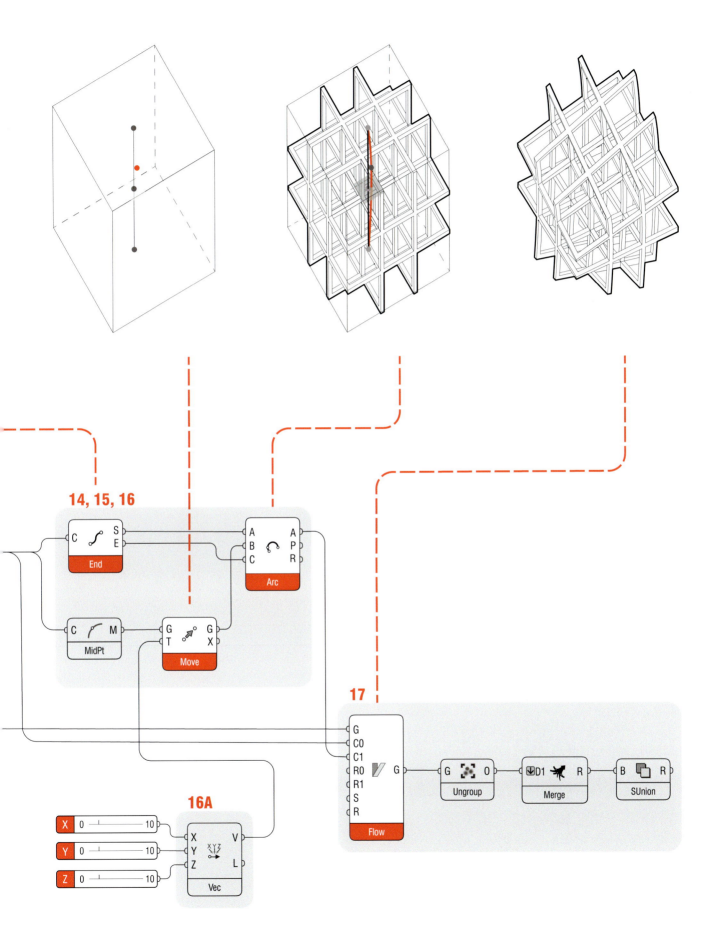

DIVISIONS ▼

THICKNESS ▼

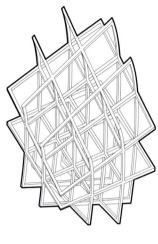

CU . ST . SM . LD

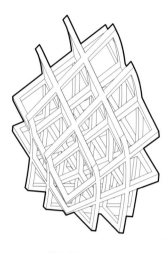

CU . ST . ME . LD

CU . ST . ME . MD

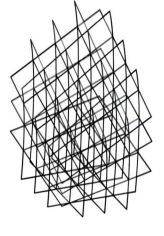

CU . ST . SM . LD

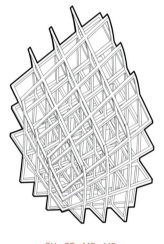

CU . ST . ME . MD

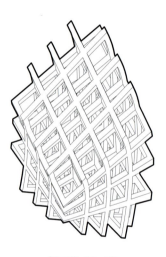

CU . ST . LA . HD

CU . ST . SM . MD

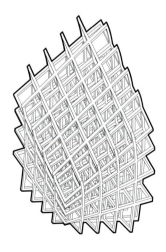

CU . ST . ME . HD

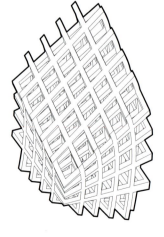

CU . ST . LA . HD

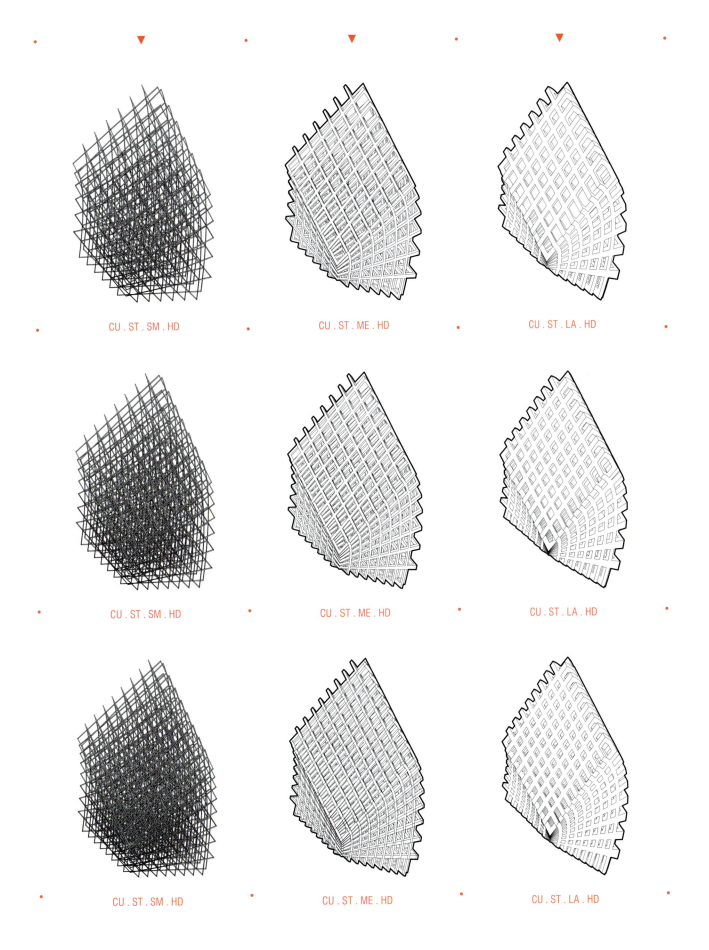

M2 STRETCH

In this exercise you will be taking the definition you worked on within Constructions / Frame Objects / F2 and morphing it such that it creates a stretched figure. Stretching the frame object changes its rigid nature, creating a playful fluidity and plasticity. On the right facing page are the steps that you underwent in exercise F2. Use the definition from F2 and add to it as shown on the spread that follows. Test the limits of the stretch definition, see if you can break it by attempting to get the figure to stretch into strange shapes. Watch closely as to how the nature of the object changes as you move the sliders.

ORIGINAL FRAME OBJECT

13 Group geometries
14 Get centroid of bounding box
14A Get Z dimension of bounding box and move base point of vector
14B Define vector for stretching
14C Preview stretch vector
15 Create axis to set direction of distortion
16 Stretch

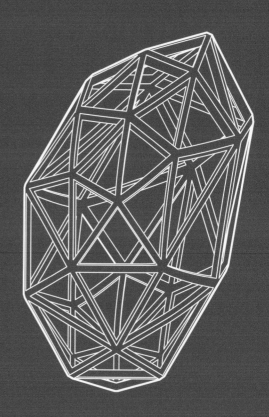

STRETCHED FRAME OBJECT

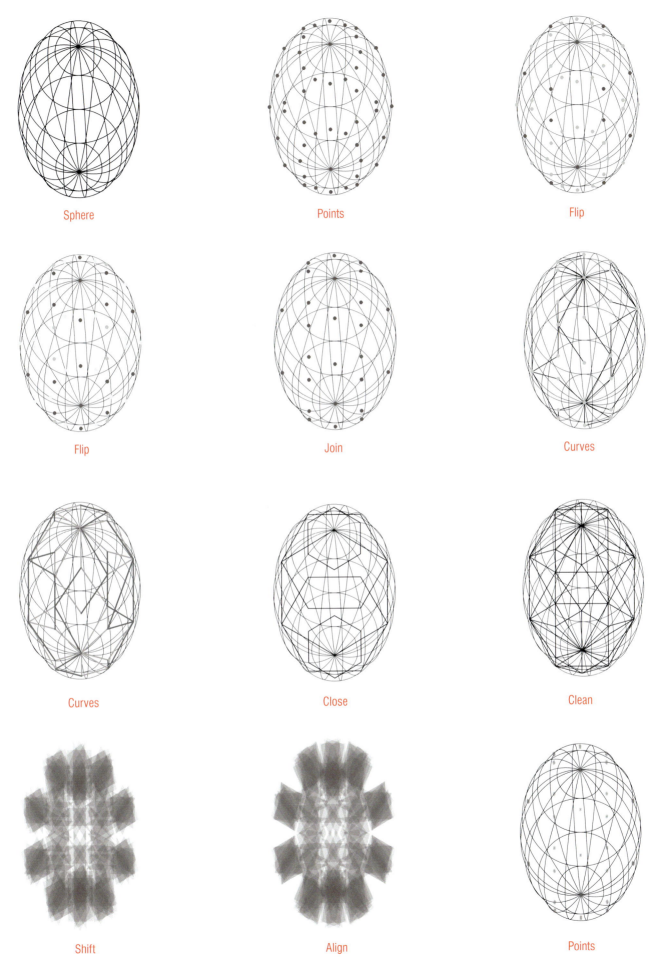

M2

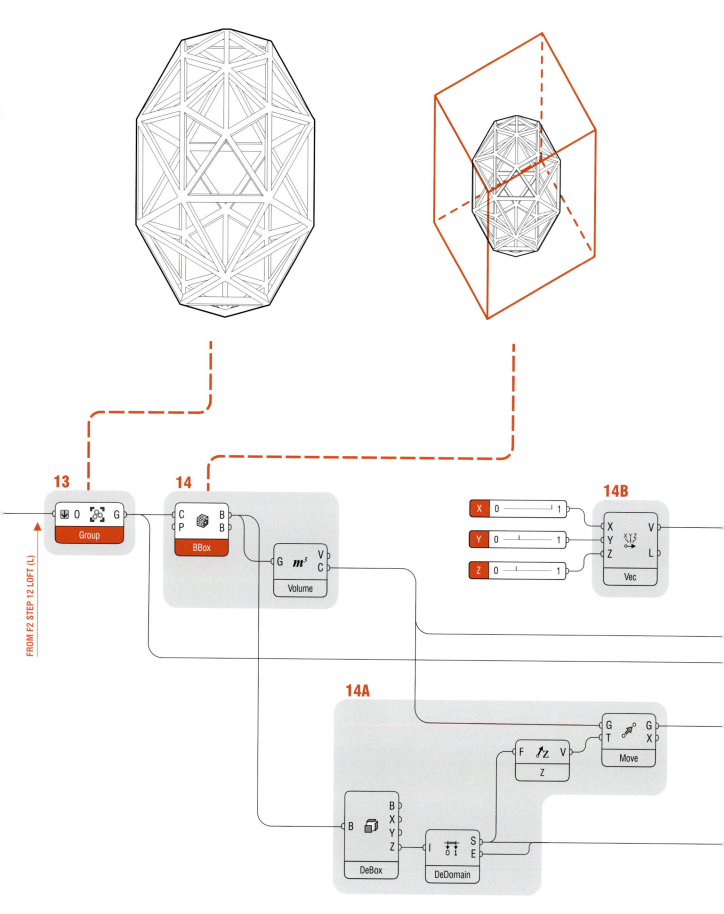

236 4 M2 STRETCH

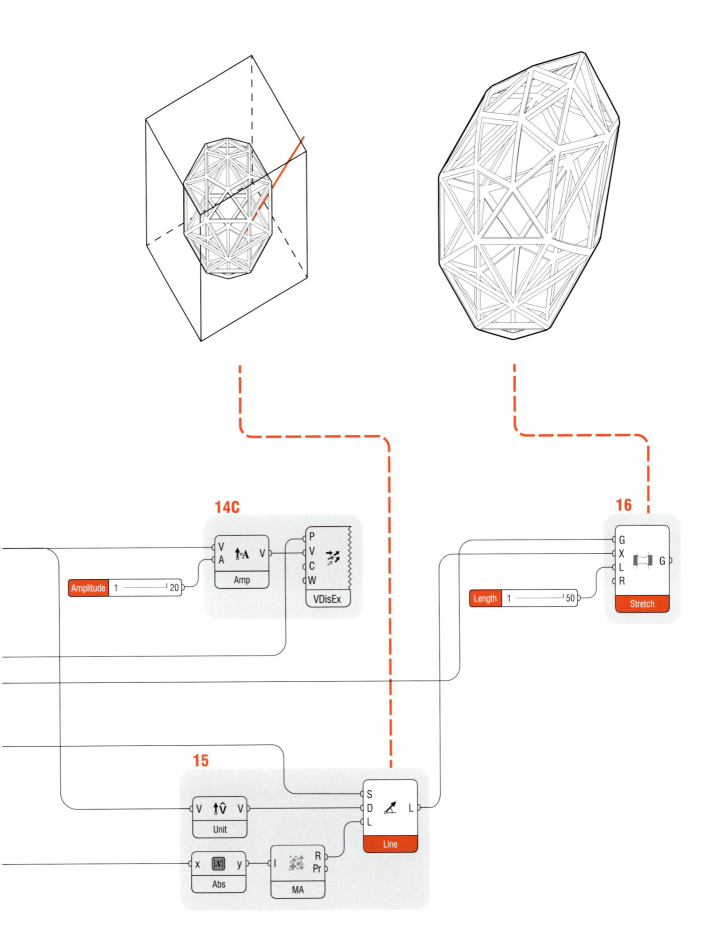

DIVISIONS ▼

THICKNESS ▼

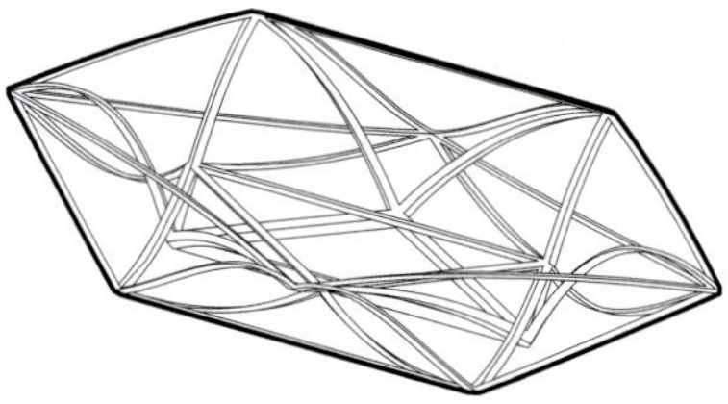

SP . ST . SM . LD

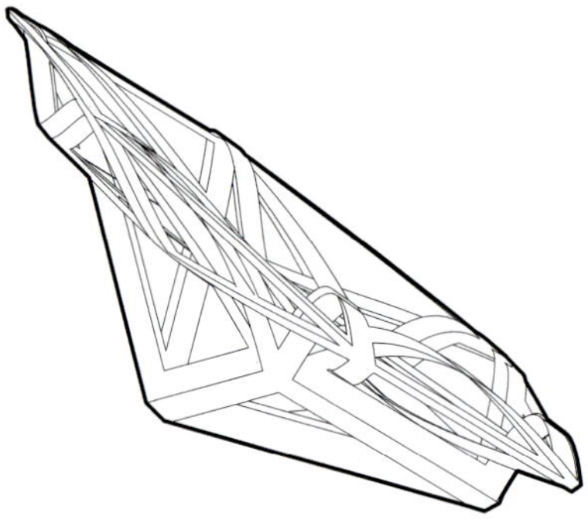

SP . ST . ME . LD

SP . ST . LA . MD

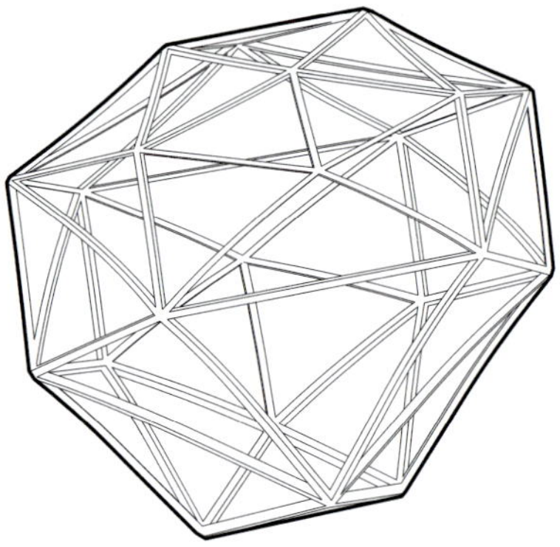

SP . ST . SM . LD

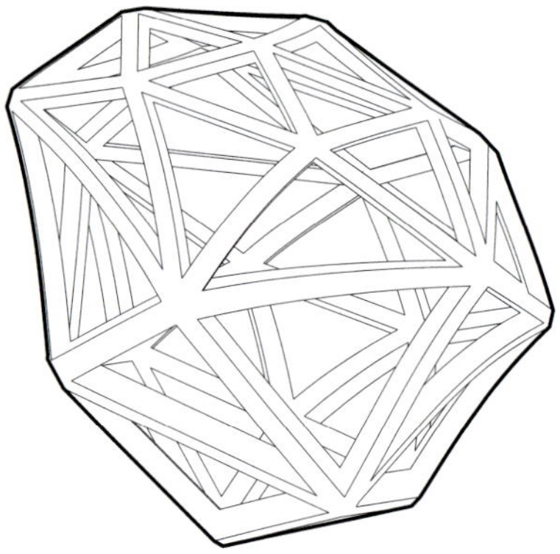

SP . ST . ME . MD

SP . ST . LA . HD

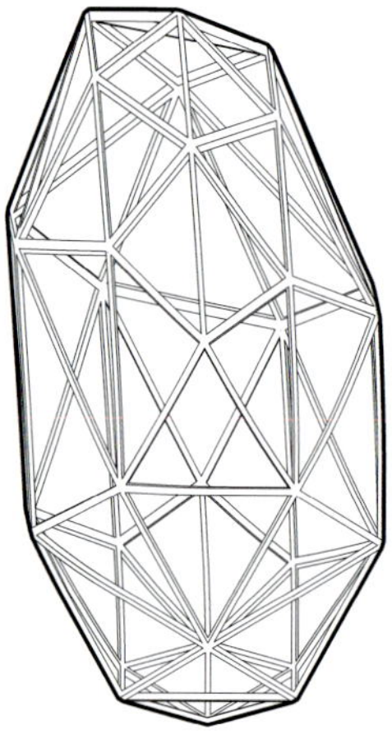

SP . ST . SM . LD

SP . ST . ME . MD

SP . ST . LA . HD

4 M2 STRETCH VARIATIONS

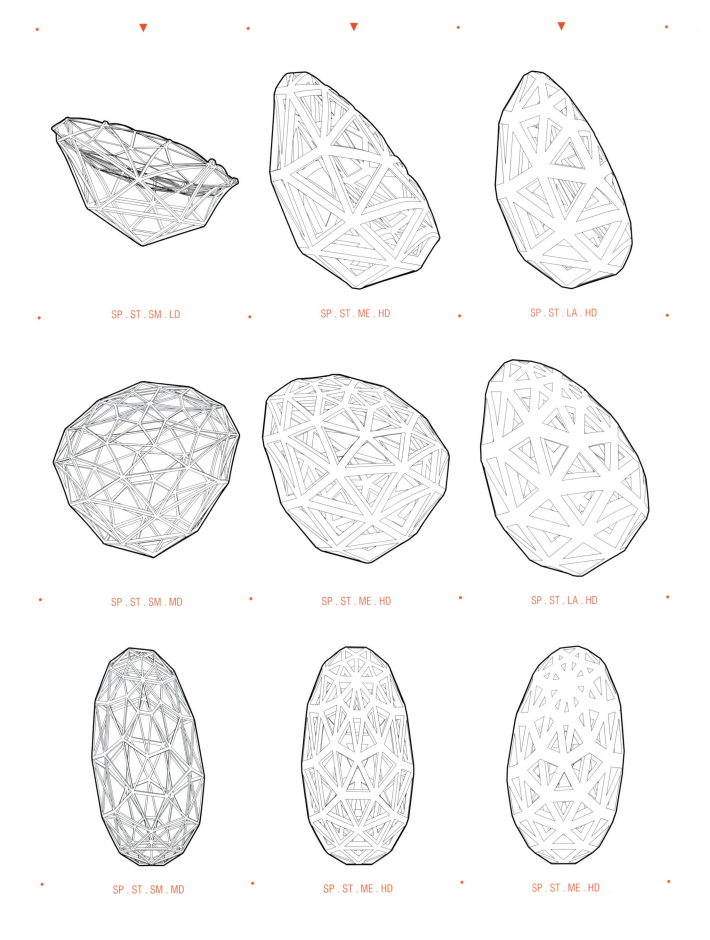

M3 TWIST

In this exercise you will be taking the definition you worked on within Constructions / Frame Objects / F3 and morphing it such that it creates a twisted figure. Twisting the frame object makes the individual frame elements act as a fluid. On the right facing page are the steps that you underwent in exercise F3 and the short morphological definition used to create the twist. See what you can create by modifying both the original frame definition and the new definition for twist. Can you make objects that look completely different than one another, that don't feel as though they belong in the same typological family?

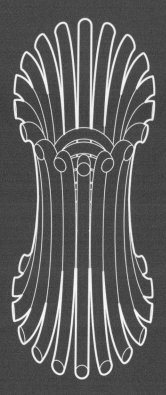

ORIGINAL FRAME OBJECT

13 Insert geometry
14 Twist geometry

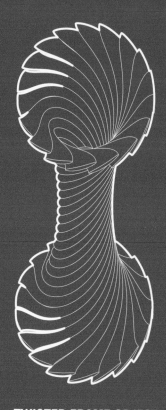

TWISTED FRAME OBJECT

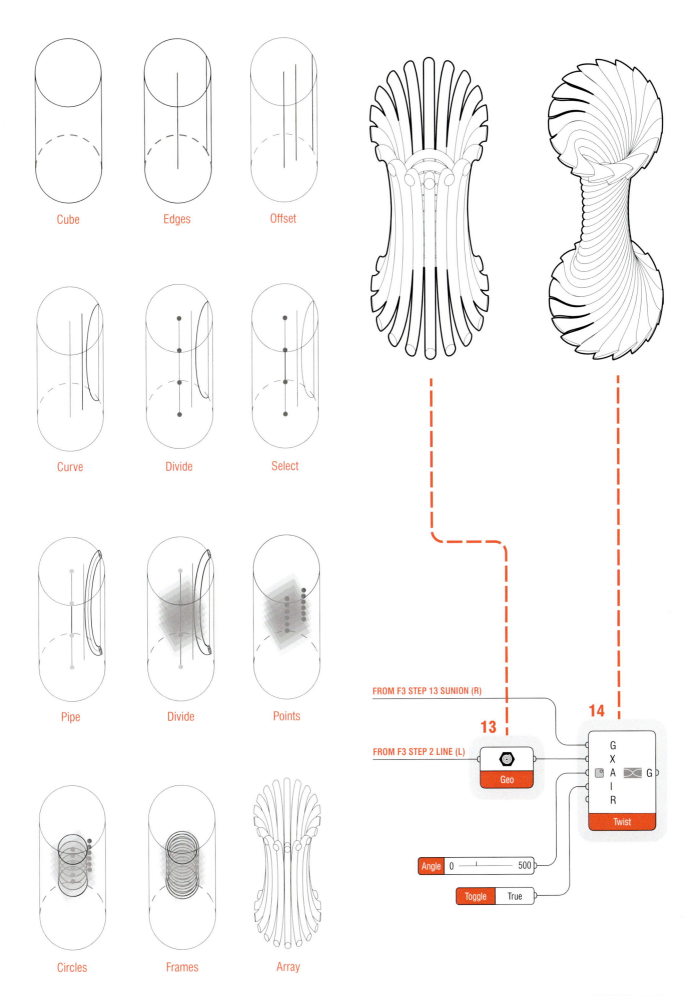

DIVISIONS ▼

THICKNESS ▼

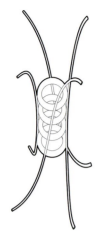
CY . FO . SM/ME . LD

CY . FO . ME/ME . LD

CY . FO . LA/ME . LD

CY . FO . SM/ME . LD

CY . FO . ME/ME . LD

CY . FO . LA/ME . MD

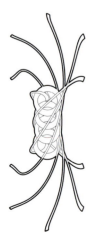
CY . FO . SM/ME . LD

CY . FO . ME/ME . MD

CY . FO . LA/ME . MD

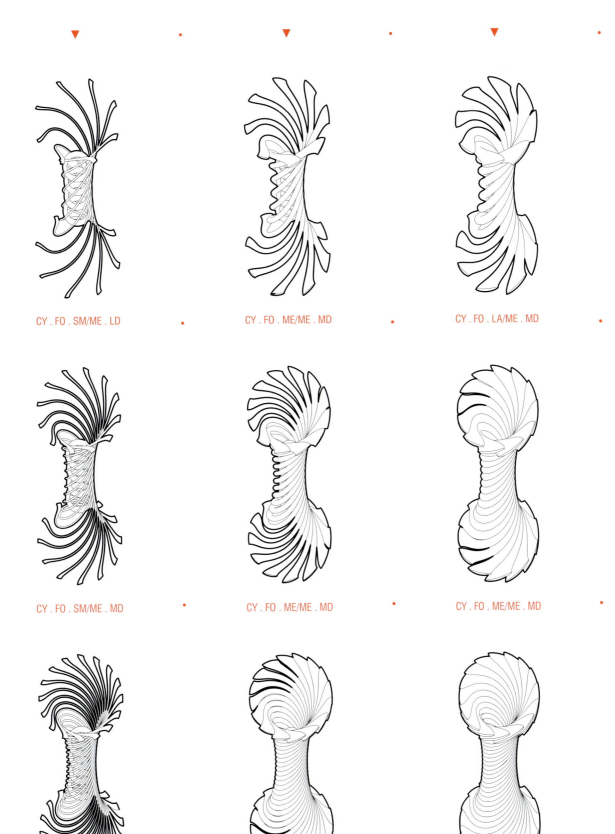

CY . FO . SM/ME . LD   CY . FO . ME/ME . MD   CY . FO . LA/ME . MD

CY . FO . SM/ME . MD   CY . FO . ME/ME . MD   CY . FO . ME/ME . MD

CY . FO . SM/ME . MD   CY . FO . ME/ME . MD   CY . FO . ME/ME . MD

M4 BRANCHOFF

In this exercise you will be taking the definition you worked on within Constructions / Frame Objects / F4 and morphing it such that it creates a branching pattern. Branching patterns are a fundamental aspect of how life is made and grows. On the right facing page are the steps that you underwent in exercise F4. Use the definition from F4 and add to it as shown on the spread that follows. Play with the complexities you can create by changing the nature of the original definition, adding frames to each axis, and then test the definition with those variants.

9A Get start points
10 Use GH Python Script to create branches
- **First** - Change default input (x) to initial_point, (y) to depth, add additional inputs, start_thickness and thickness_step
- Change default output (a) to branches, add additional output, thickness_arr, (see glossary for how to add input/output)
- **Second** - Right click on inital_point / Type Hint / Point 3d
- **Third** - Right click on depth / Type Hint / Int
- **Final** - Copy Python script, reference Rosettacode for base script and fill in code information, run test and ok (see below)

11 Rotate branches around axis, using F4 Step 9 RotAx, Connect GH Python Script into RotAx
12 Make branches into pipes
13 Revolve branches around axis
14 Preview original frame and branch object

GH PYTHON SCRIPT

"""Fractal script based on Rosettacode. See https://www.rosettacode.org/wiki/Fractal_tree#Python"""

```
import math
import random
import Rhino as rh
def draw_tree(x1, y1, angle,
   depth, arr, z, thickness, thickness_arr):
   fork_angle = 20
   base_len = 1.0
   if depth > 0:
      x2 = x1 + int(math.cos(math.radians(angle)) * depth * base_len)
      y2 = y1 + int(math.sin(math.radians(angle)) * depth * base_len)
      thickness-=thickness_step
      pt1 = rh.Geometry.Point3d(x1, y1, z)
      pt2 = rh.Geometry.Point3d(x2, y2, z)
      line = rh.Geometry.Line(pt1, pt2)
      if line.IsValid:
         thickness_arr.append(thickness)
         arr.append(line)
      draw_tree(x2, y2, angle - fork_angle, depth - 1, arr, z, thickness, thickness_arr)
      draw_tree(x2, y2, angle + fork_angle, depth - 1, arr, z, thickness, thickness_arr)
branches = []
thickness_arr = []
x, y, z = initial_point.X, initial_point.Y, initial_point.Z
start_angle = 0
draw_tree(x, y, start_angle, depth, branches, z, start_thickness, thickness_arr)
```

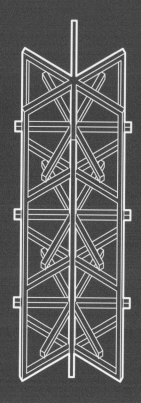

ORIGINAL FRAME OBJECT

BRANCHED FRAME OBJECT

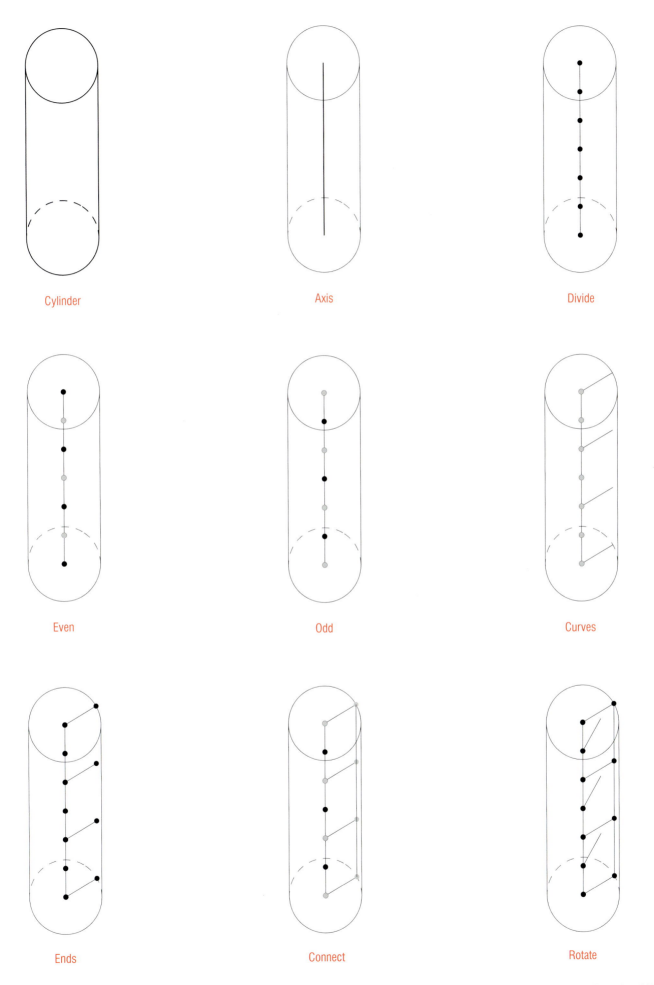

M4

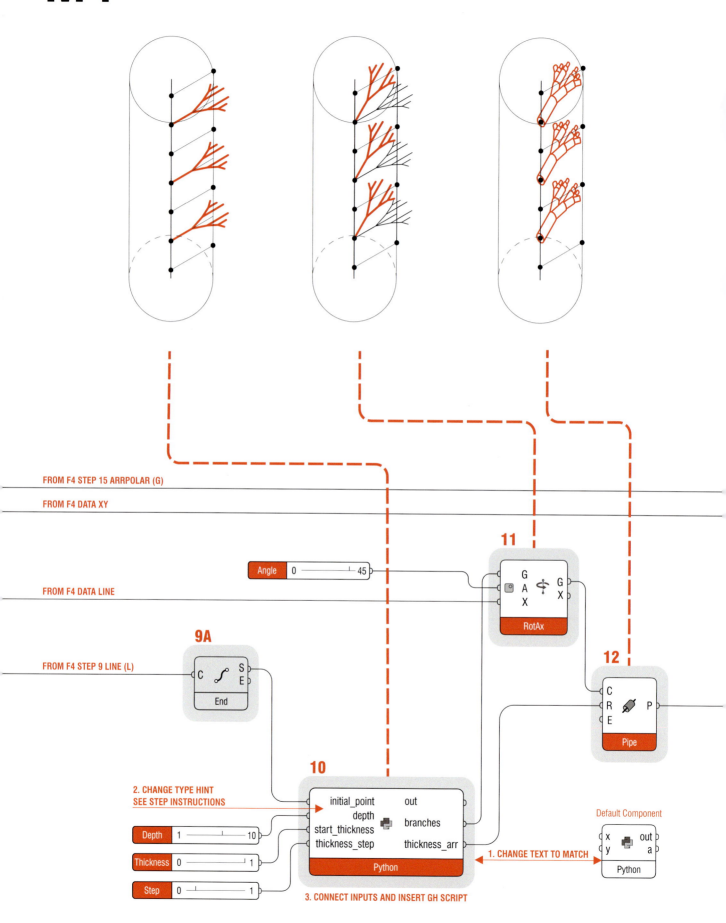

246 4 M4 **BRANCHOFF**

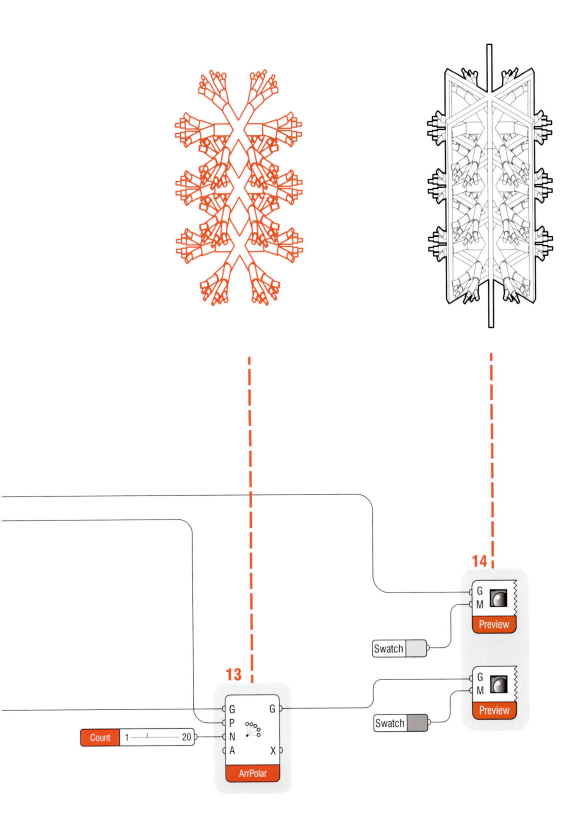

THICKNESS ▼

DIVISIONS ▼

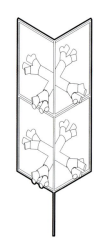
CY . ST/FO . SM/ME . LD

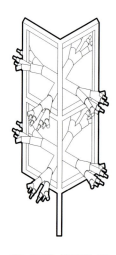
CY . ST/FO . ME/ME . LD

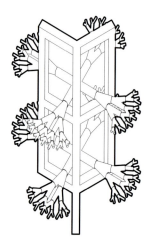
CY . ST/FO . LA/ME . LD

CY . ST/FO . SM/LA . MD

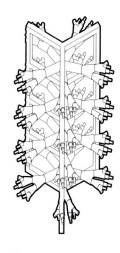
CY . ST/FO . ME/LA . MD

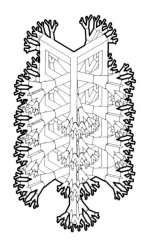
CY . ST/FO . LA/LA . HD

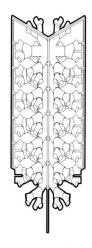
CY . ST/FO . SM/LA . MD

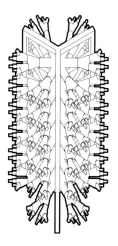
CY . ST/FO . ME/LA . MD

CY . ST/FO . LA/ME . HD

248   **4** M4 BRANCHOFF **VARIATIONS**

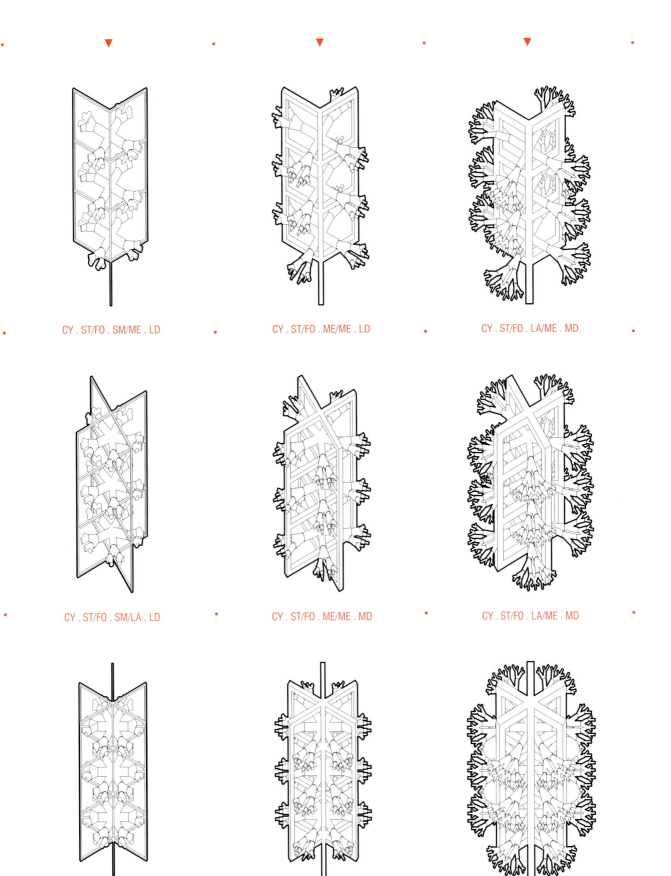

M5 IMPLOSION

In this exercise you will be taking the definition you worked on within Constructions / Plane Objects / P1 and morphing it so that it implodes. Because the implosion includes a randomizing feature, you will notice strange forms emerging as you adjust the definition's sliders. On the right facing page are the steps that you underwent in exercise P1. Use the definition from P1 and add to it as shown on the spread that follows. Can you combine the morphological implosion with some of the boolean difference operations you have learned?

ORIGINAL PLANAR OBJECT

15 Get Geometries
15A Get z vector to move geometries to xy plane
15B Move and convert geometries to raw meshes and get mesh edges
15C Get clothed and naked points
15D Kangaroo Goal 1 - 4, preview, same edge length, move point to become coincidents, and anchor points
15E Kangaroo solver
16 Get mesh

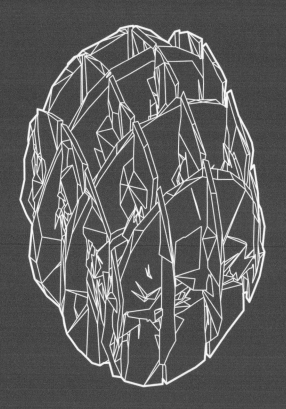

IMPLODED PLANAR OBJECT

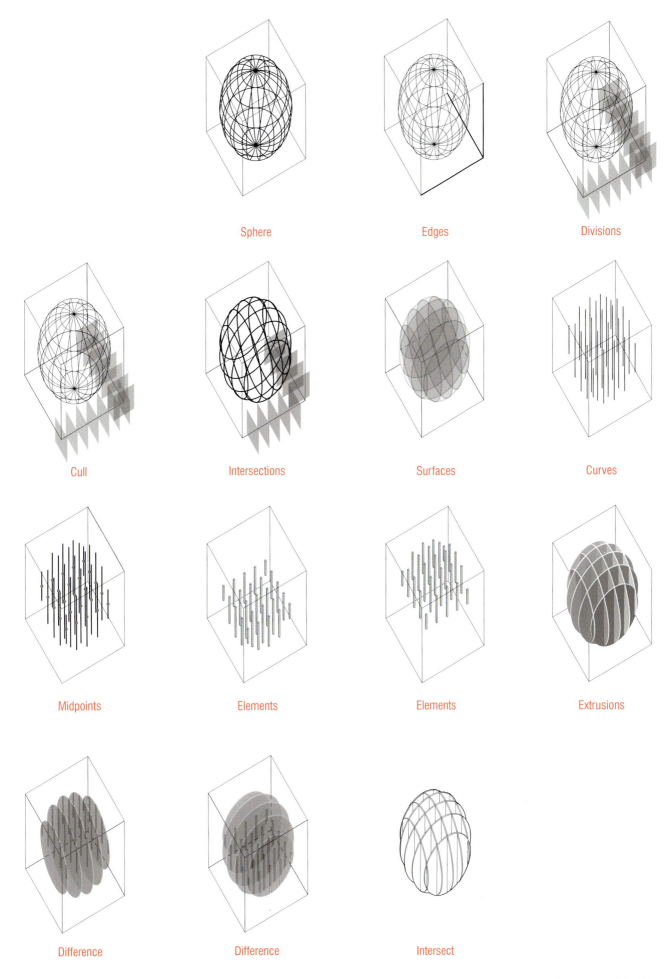

M5

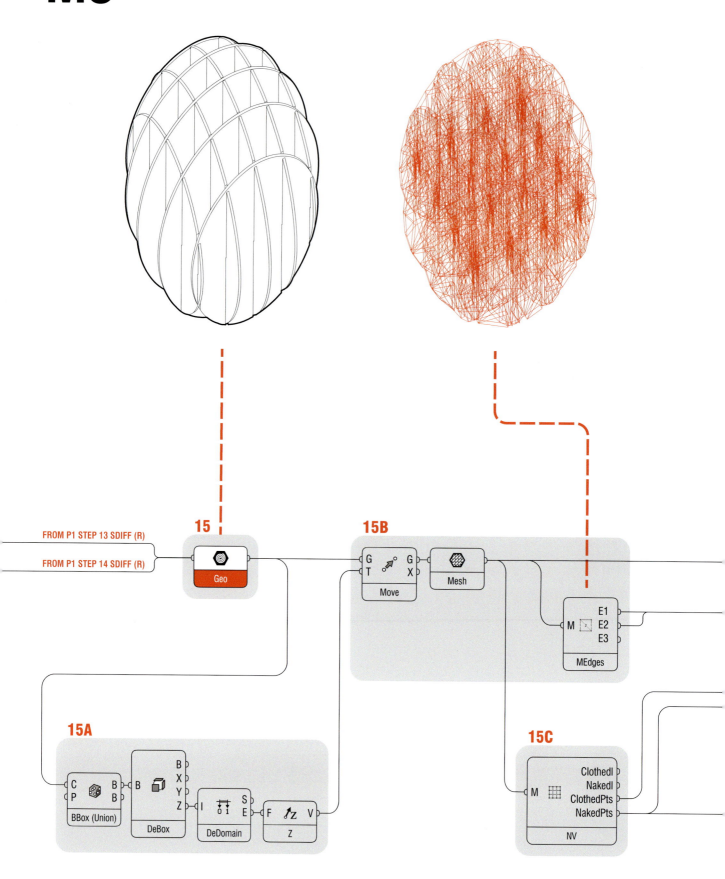

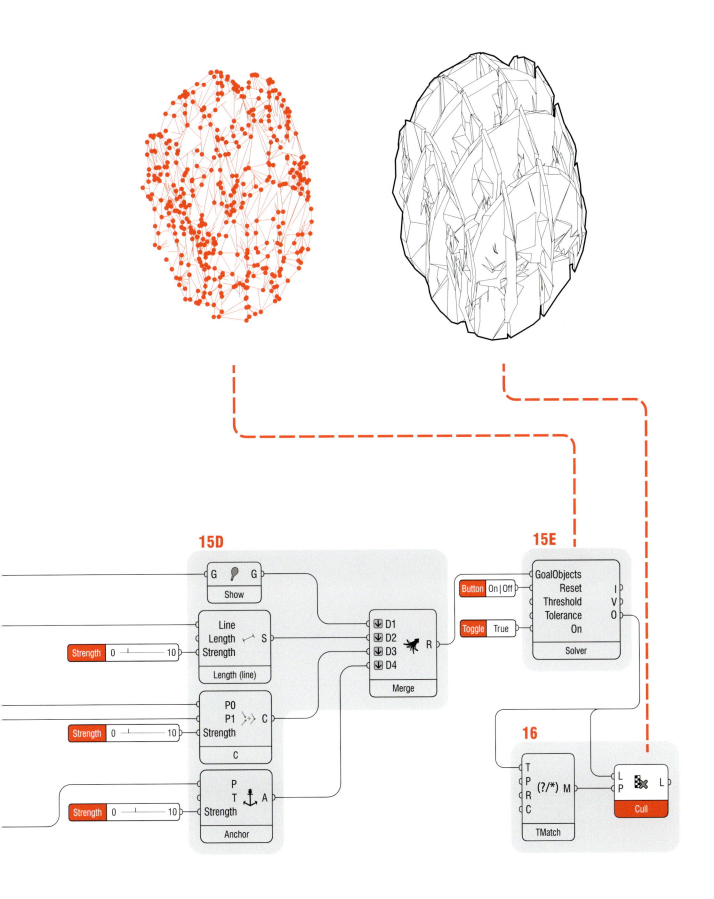

IMPLOSION M5 4 253

DIVISIONS ▼

THICKNESS ▼

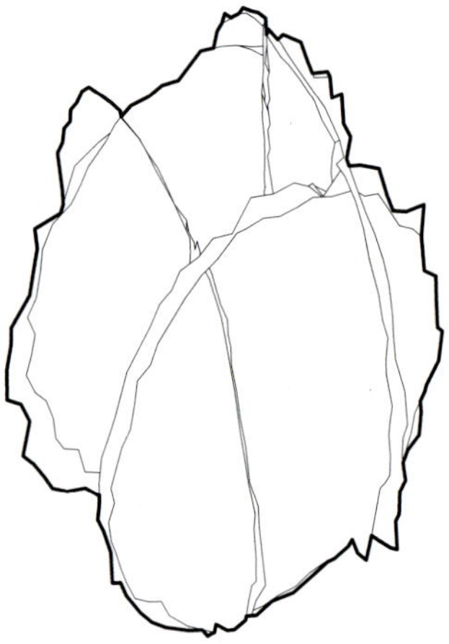

SP . FO . SM . LD    SP . FO . ME . LD 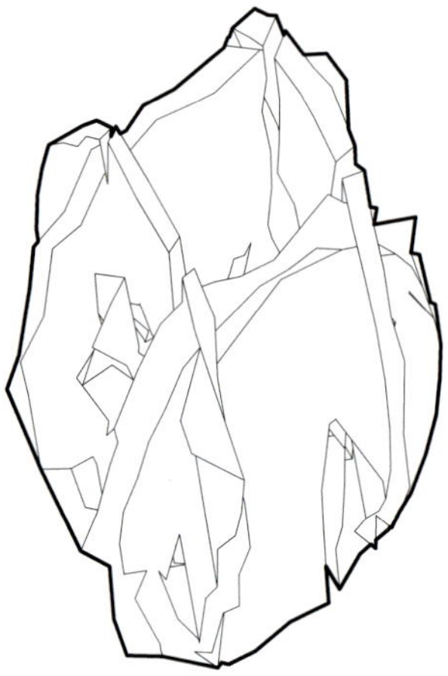   SP . FO . LA . LD

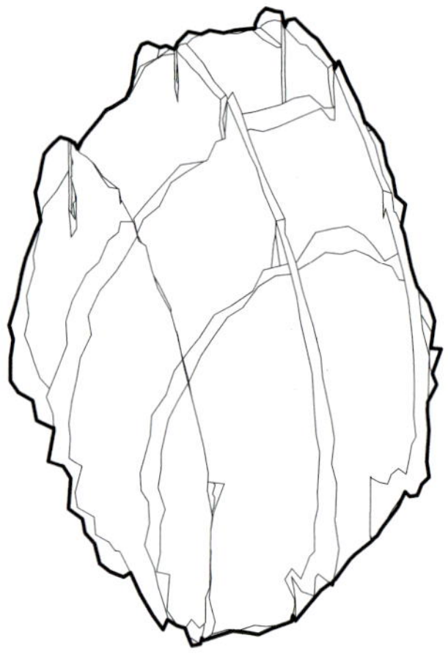

SP . FO . SM . MD 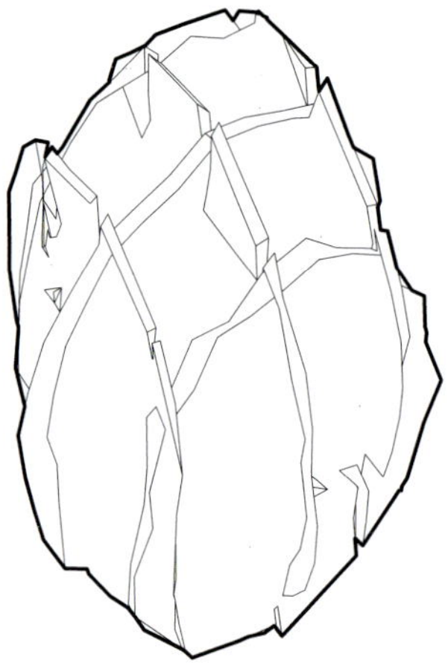   SP . FO . ME . MD 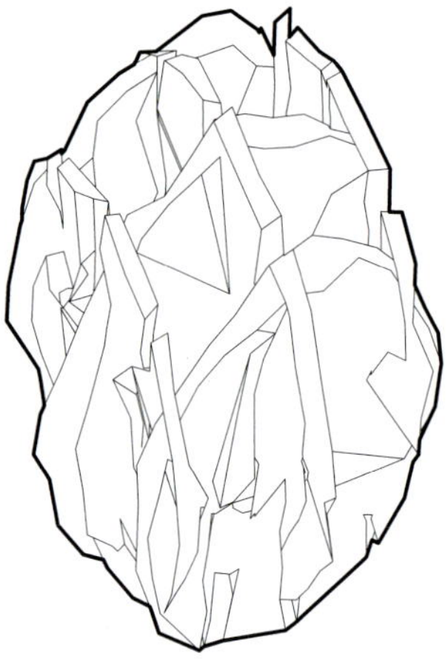   SP . FO . LA . HD

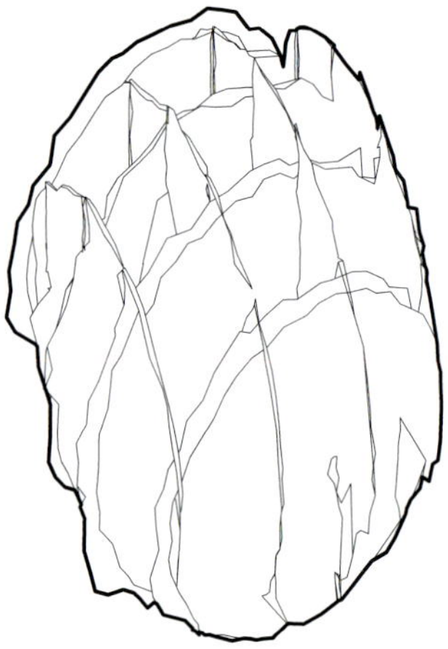

SP . FO . ME . HD 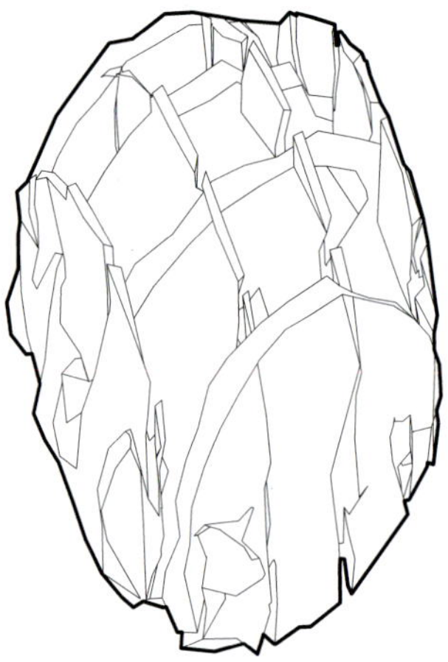   SP . FO . LA . HD 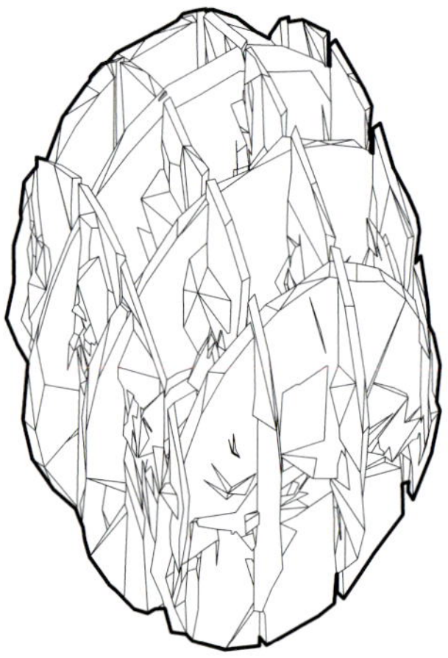   SP . FO . ME . HD

254 **4** M5 IMPLOSION **VARIATIONS**

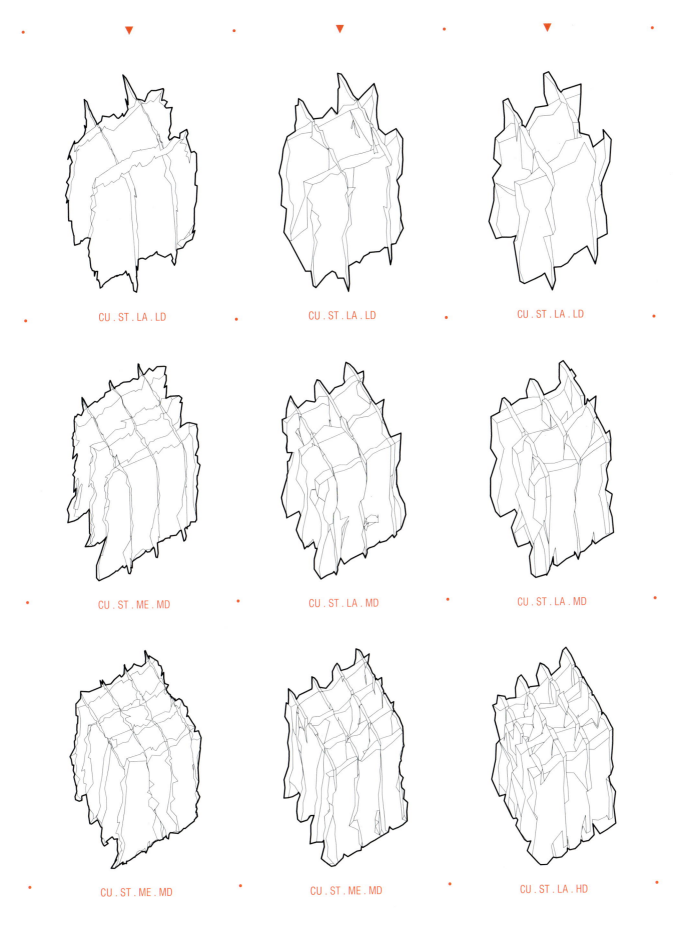

M6 SHATTER

In this exercise you will be taking the definition you worked on within Constructions / Plane Objects / P2 and morphing it such that it creates a shattered figure. Shattering the plane object surface dynamism through diagonal voids that reveal planar layering. On the right facing page are the steps that you underwent in exercise P2. Use the definition from P2 and add to it as shown on the spread that follows. Test the limits of the shatter definition. How much can the object be shattered while maintaining its essence as a singular form? How would you rejoin the shattered planes were you to physically construct the object?

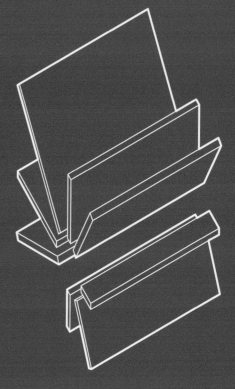

ORIGINAL PLANE OBJECT

16 Flatten tree
17 Create planes for shatter action
18 Create random points for division
18A Thickness of planes
19 Shatter the planes
   To create expression, right click on the input x and change to L , change y to P, then double click on component and replace the default expression text to read as shown, select ok
19A Get the right number of pieces to remove
20 Cast to integer and remove pieces randomly
20A Create random vector magnitudes and apply magnitude to move pieces
21 Move shattered pieces

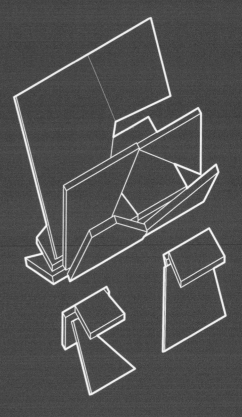

SHATTERED PLANE OBJECT

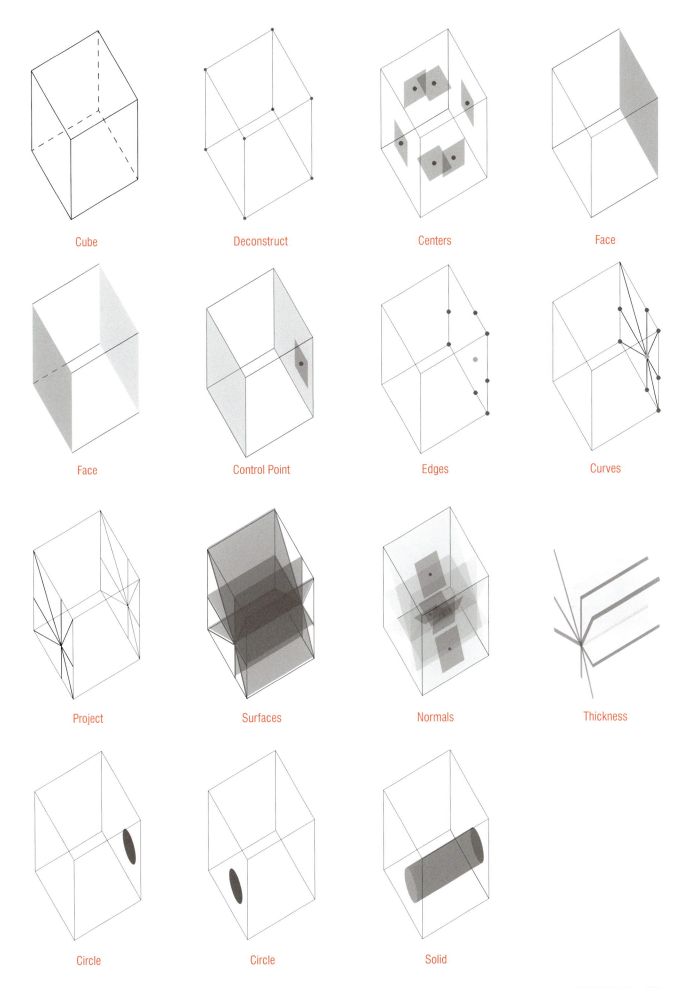

M6

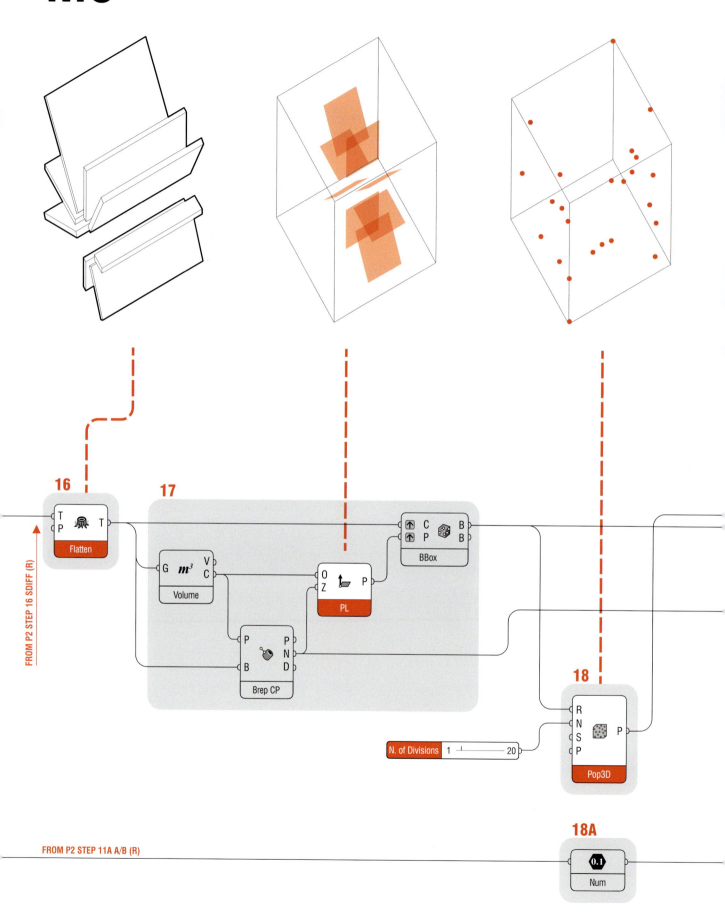

258   4 M6 **SHATTER**

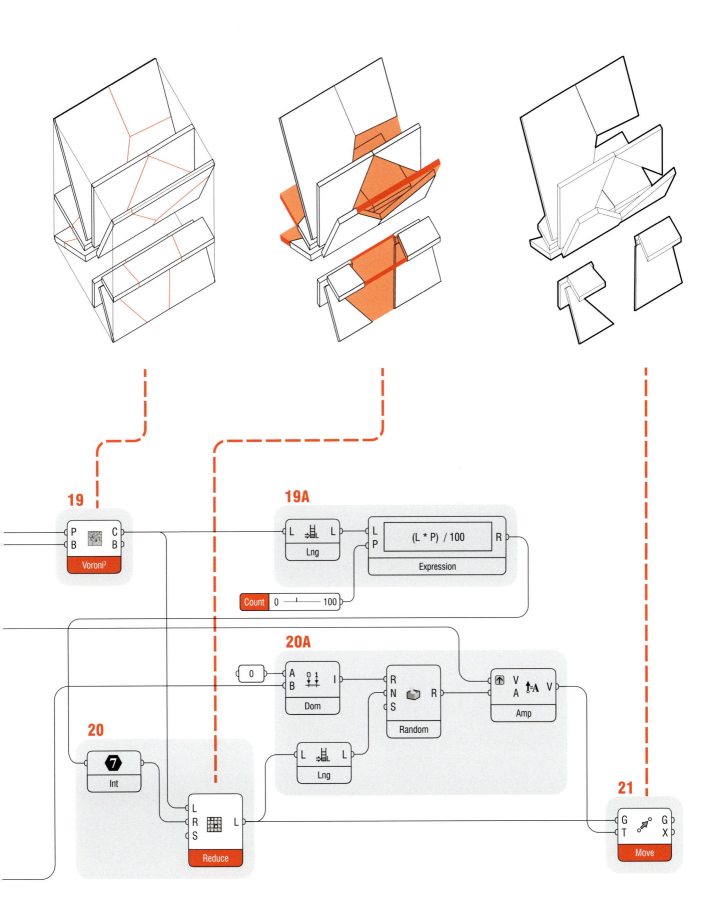

THICKNESS ▼

DIVISIONS ▼

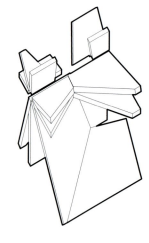
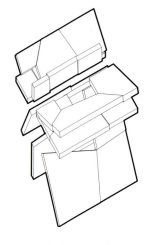
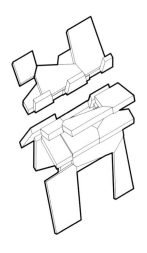

CU . ST . ME . LD   CU . ST . ME . LD   CU . ST . ME . LD

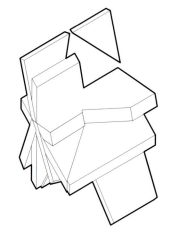
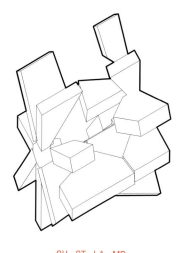
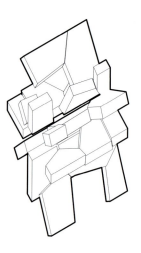

CU . ST . LA . MD   CU . ST . LA . MD   CU . ST . LA . MD

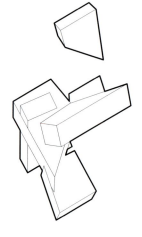
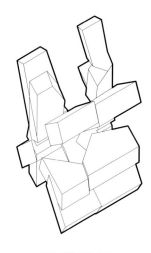
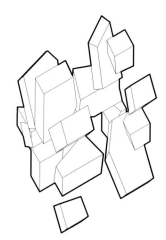

CU . ST . LA . LD   CU . ST . LA . MD   CU . ST . LA . MD

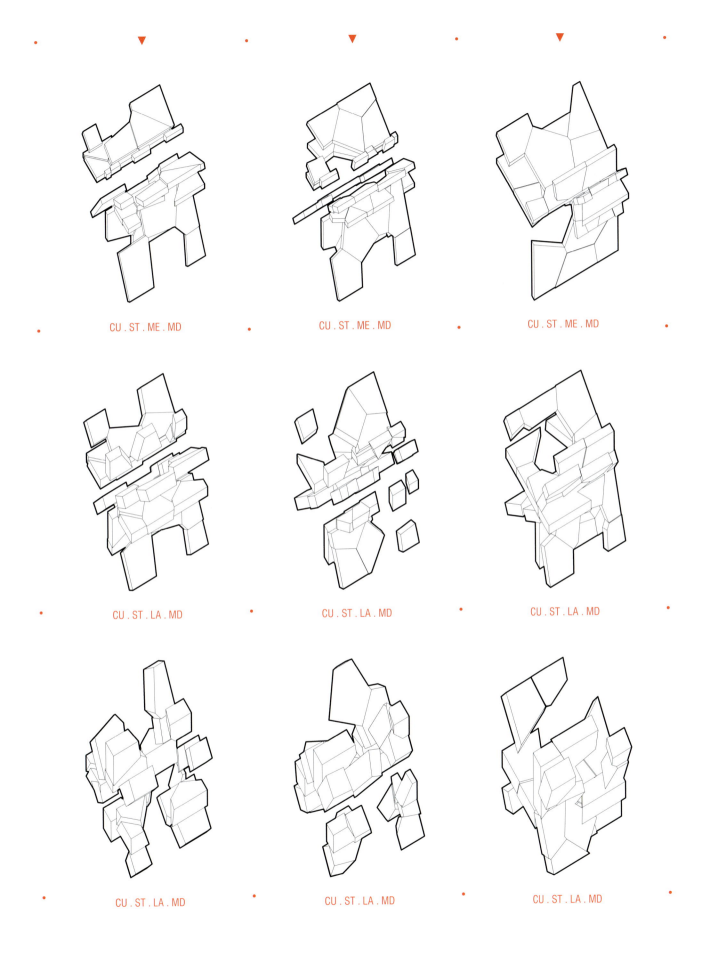

M7 INFLATE

In this exercise you will be taking the definition you worked on within Constructions / Plane Objects / P3 and morphing it so that it inflates. Watch how the inflation changes the nature of the object from a hard-edged entity to one with soft qualities. On the right facing page are the steps that you underwent in exercise P3. Use the definition from P3 and add to it as shown on the spread that follows. How much can you inflate this object until it becomes unidentifiable from its original? What new forms and shapes are made through this act of inflation?

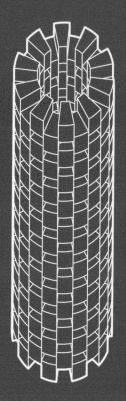

ORIGINAL PLANE OBJECT

10 Triangulate mesh with TriMesh
11 Clean the mesh and get mesh edges
11A Kangaroo Goal 5 - 6, direction and anchor points
11B Kangaroo Goal 1 - 4, preview, set pressure, keep edge length, and plastic deformation
12 Kangaroo solver
13 Display result

INFLATED PLANE OBJECT

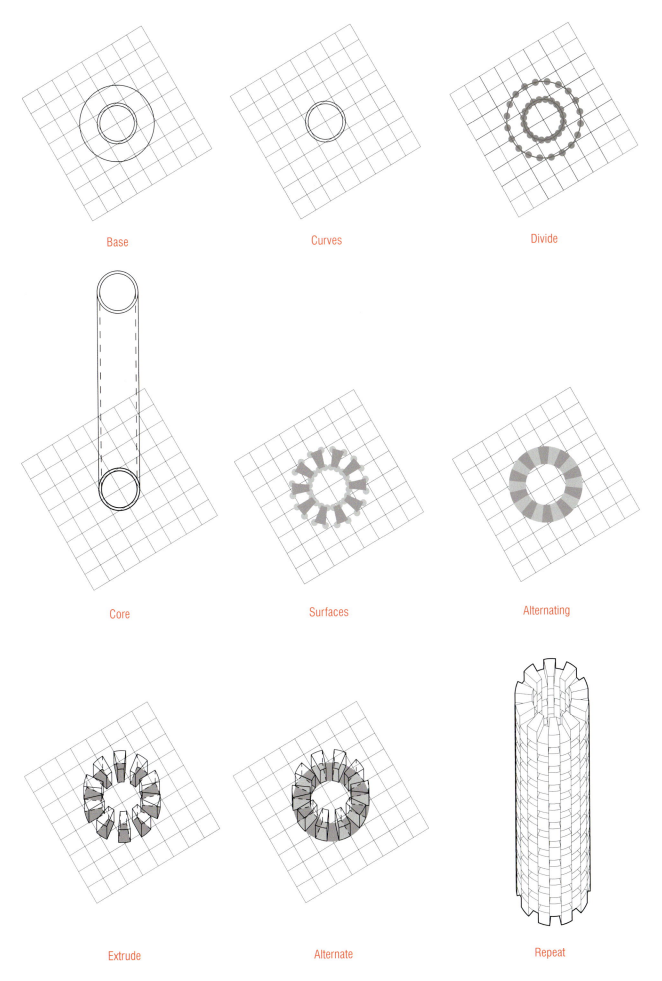

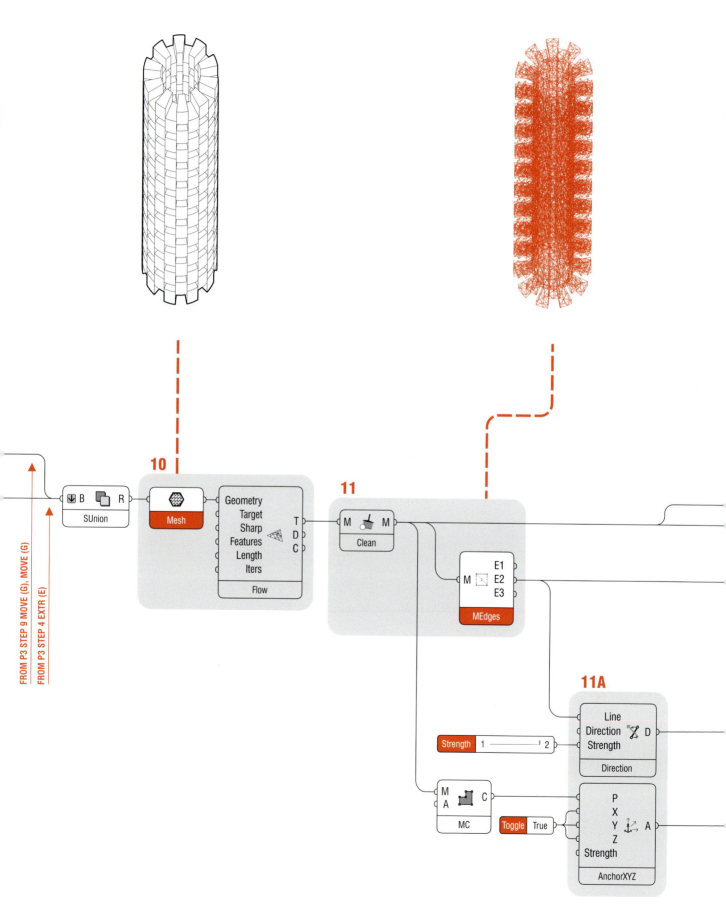

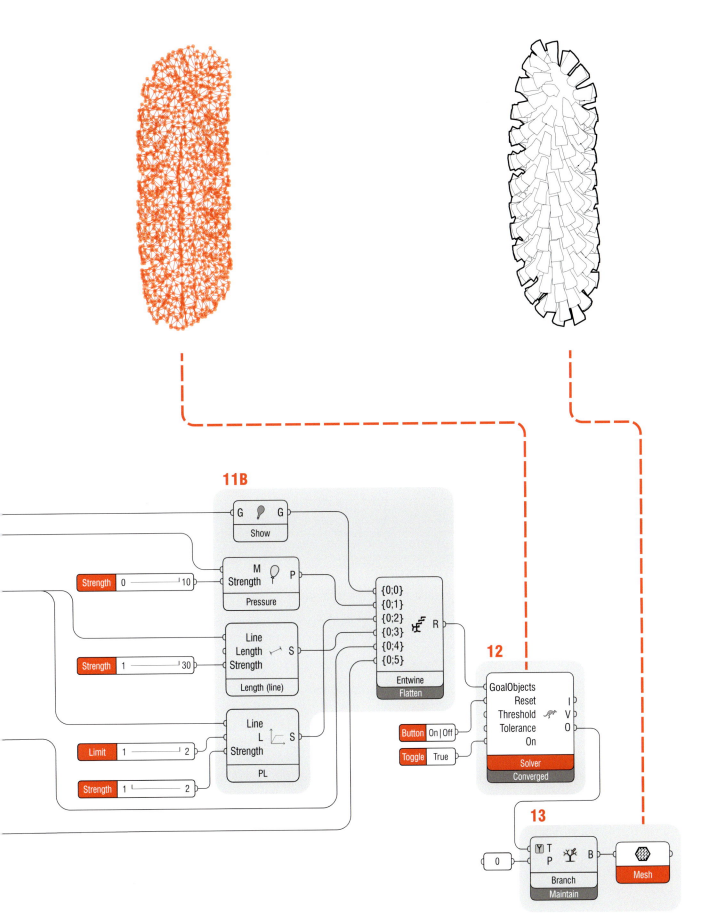

DIVISIONS ▼

DIVISIONS ▼

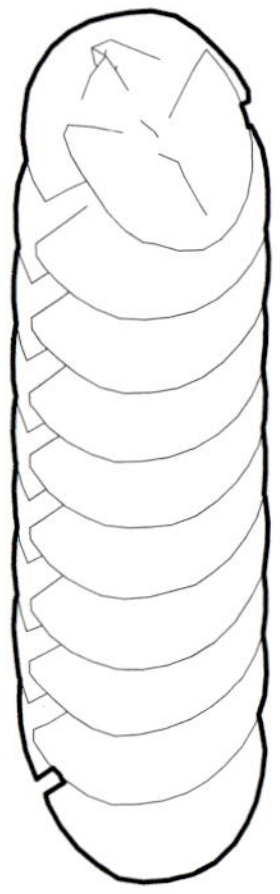

CY.FO.ME.MD	 CY.FO.ME.MD	 CY.FO.ME.HD
 CY.FO.ME.MD	 CY.FO.ME.HD	 CY.FO.ME.HD
 CY.FO.ME.MD	 CY.FO.ME.HD	 CY.FO.ME.HD

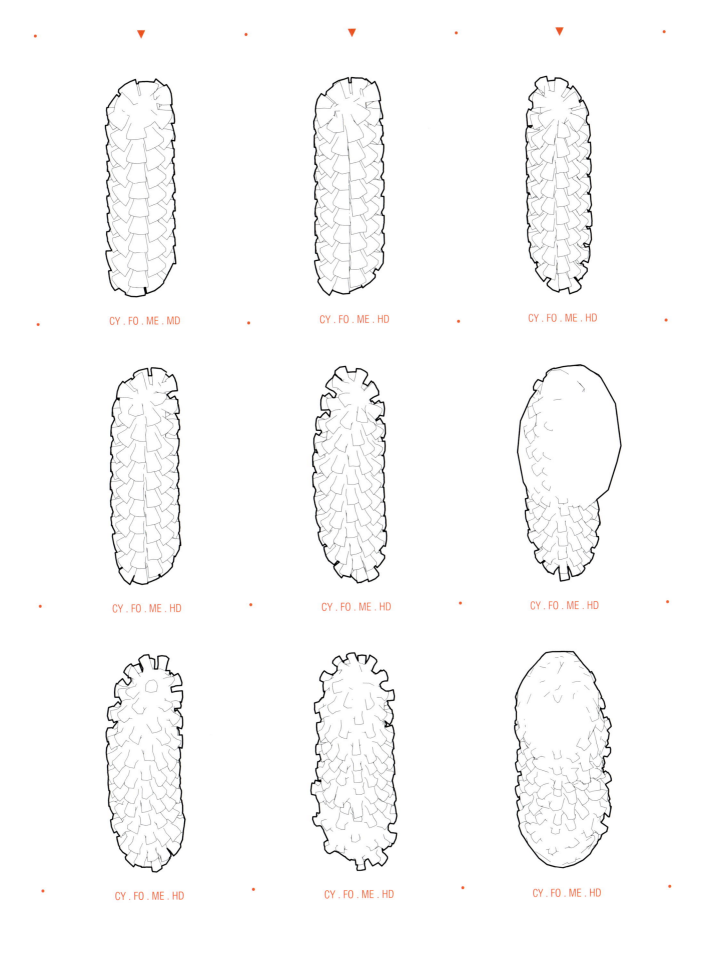

M8 DROOP

In this exercise you will be taking the definition you worked on within Constructions / Plane Objects / P4 and morphing it so that it crumples. As the object crumples you will see what might happen to this material entity when subject to gravitational force over time. On the right facing page are the steps that you underwent in exercise P4. Use the definition from P4 and add to it as shown on the spread that follows. How much can you crumple this object until it becomes unidentifiable from its original? What new forms and shapes are made through this act of crumpling?

ORIGINAL PLANAR OBJECT

7 Convert geometry to mesh
8 Align the geometry with the world XY plane
9 Get edges
10 Get vertices
10A Kangaroo Goal 1 - 3, preview, negative fields, and keep the same edge length
11 Move the cube inside the mesh up
11A Kangaroo Goal 4 - 6, keep the same start volume, soft collide among parts, and anchor points
11B Kangaroo Goal 7, floor
11C Kangaroo Goal 8 - 9, collision with planes and keep the edge angles
11D Put in a tree
12 Kangaroo solver
13 Final form

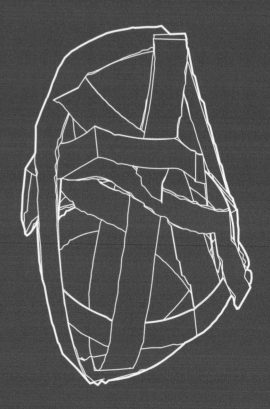

DROOPED PLANAR OBJECT

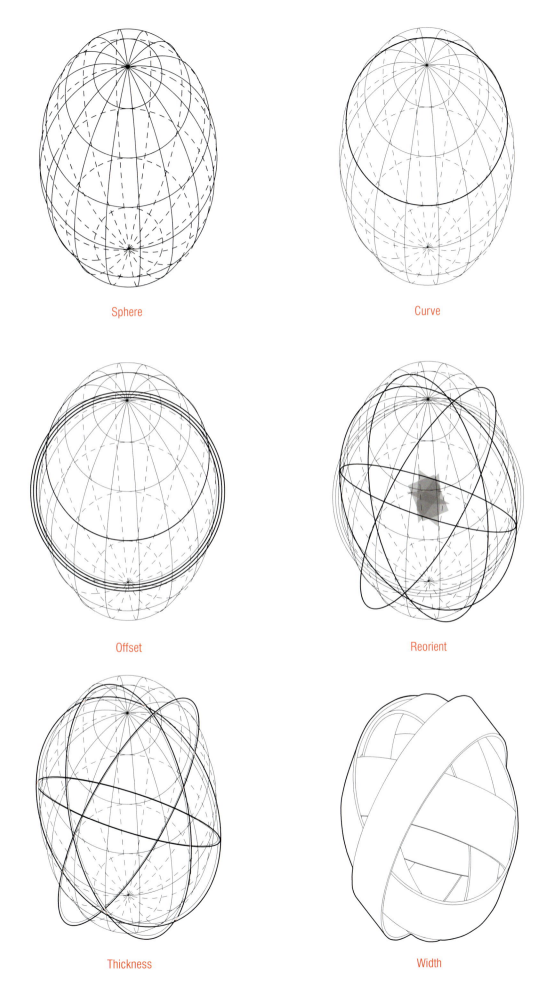

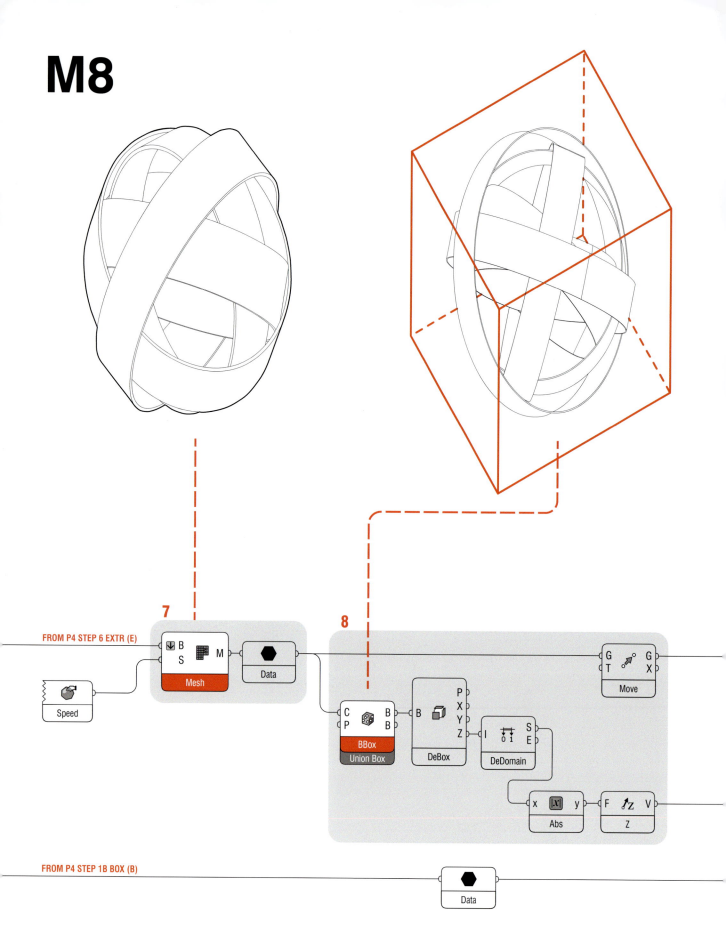

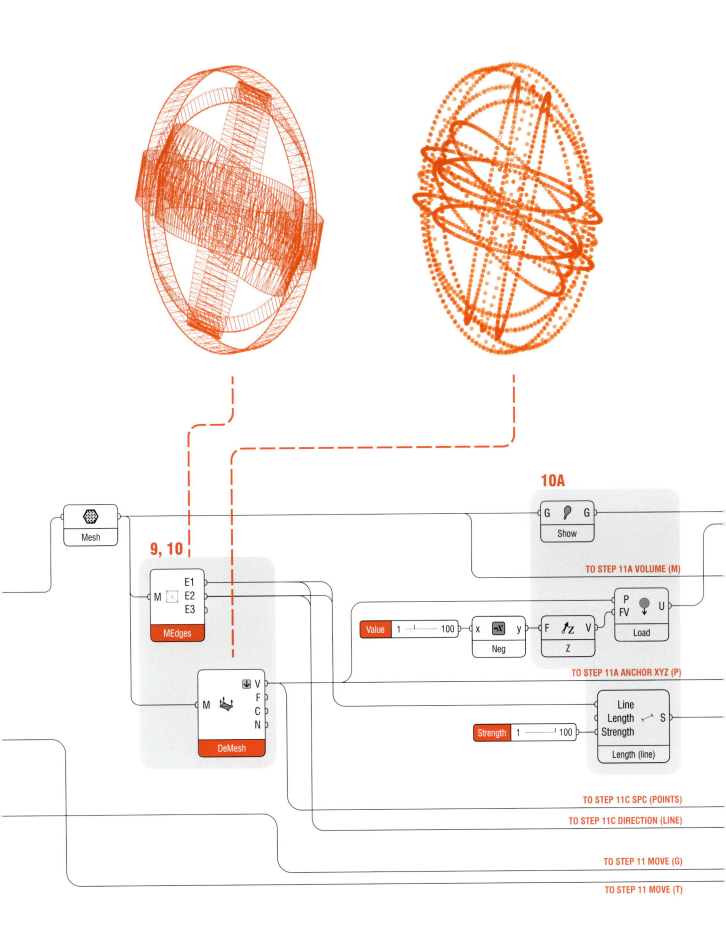

M8

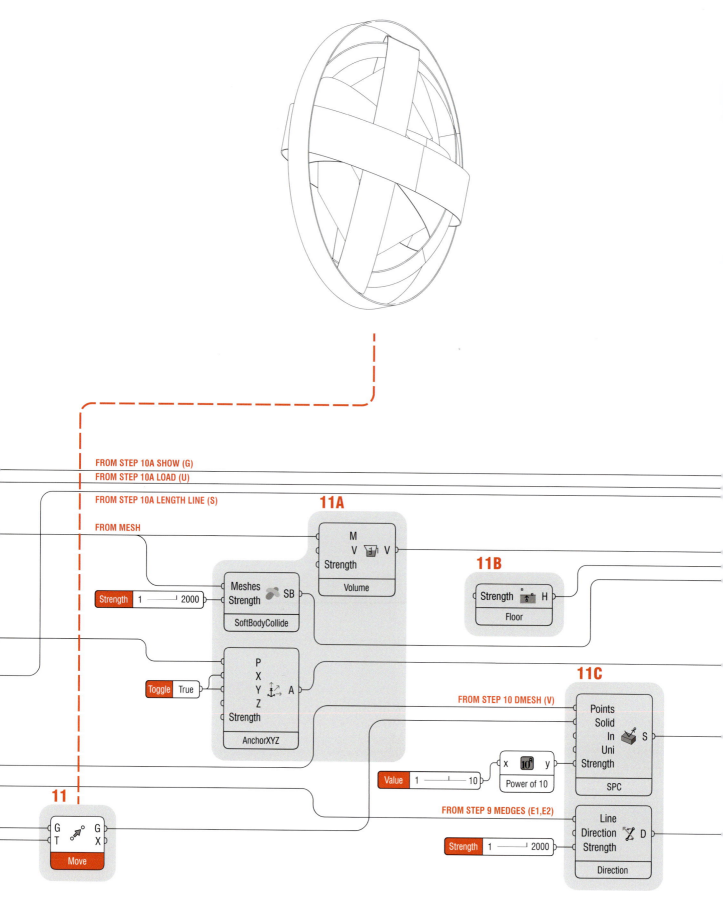

272   4 M8 **DROOP**

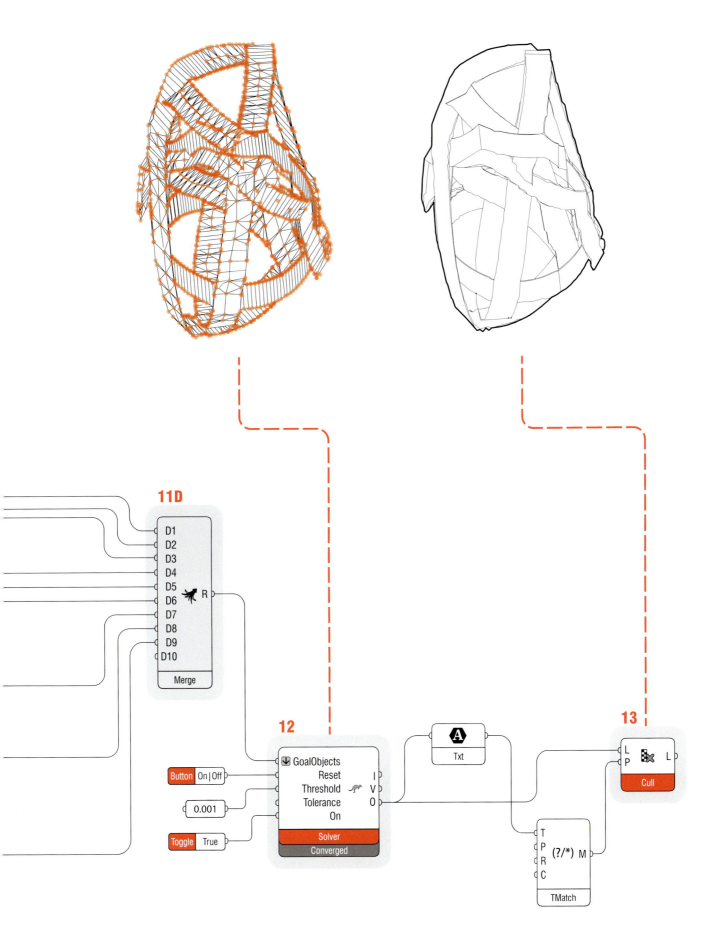

DIVISIONS ▼

THICKNESS ▼

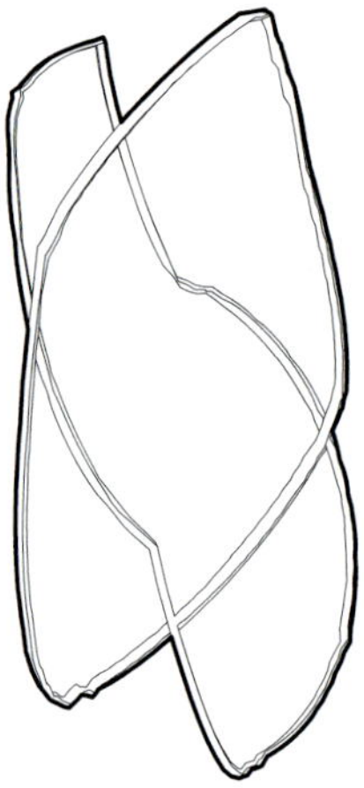

SP . FO . SM . LD

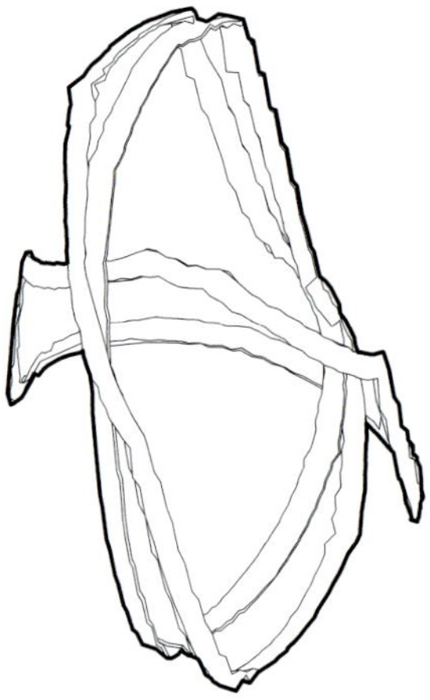

SP . FO . ME . LD

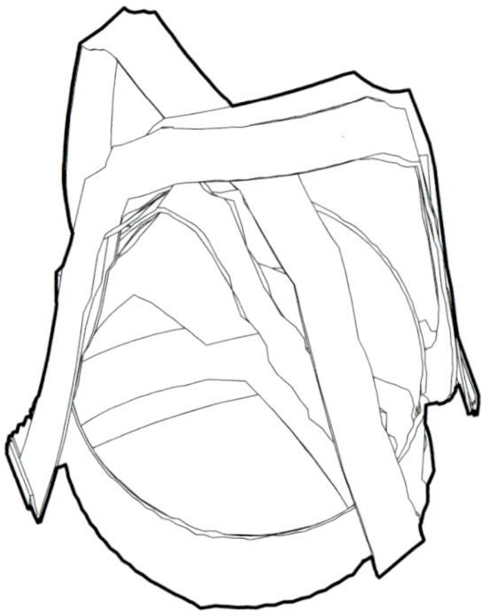

SP . FO . LA . LD

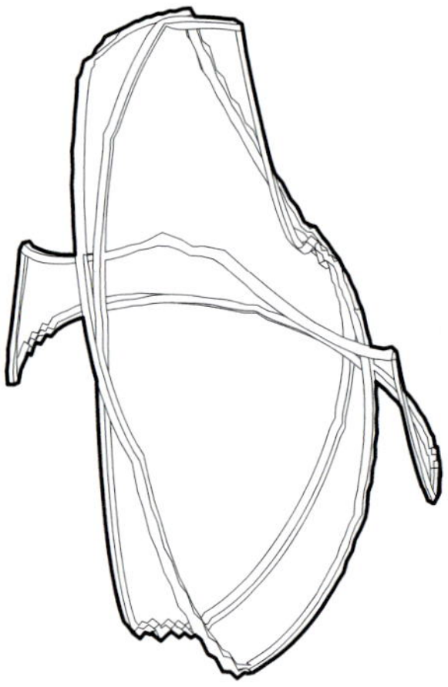

SP . FO . SM . LD

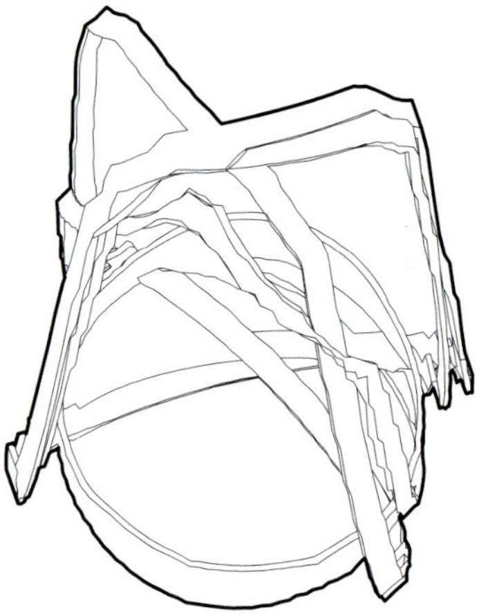

SP . FO . ME . LD

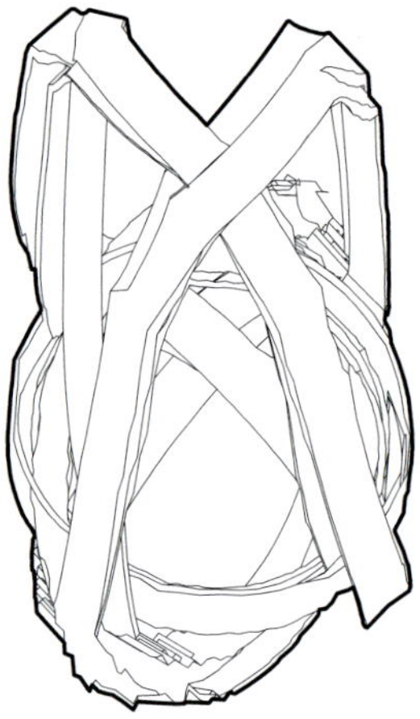

SP . FO . LA . MD

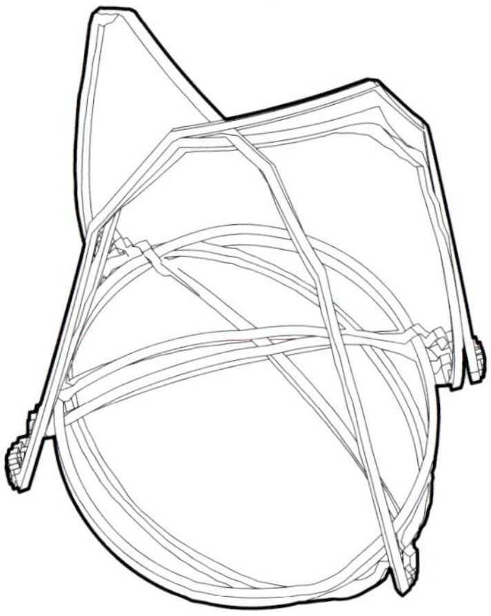

SP . FO . SM . LD

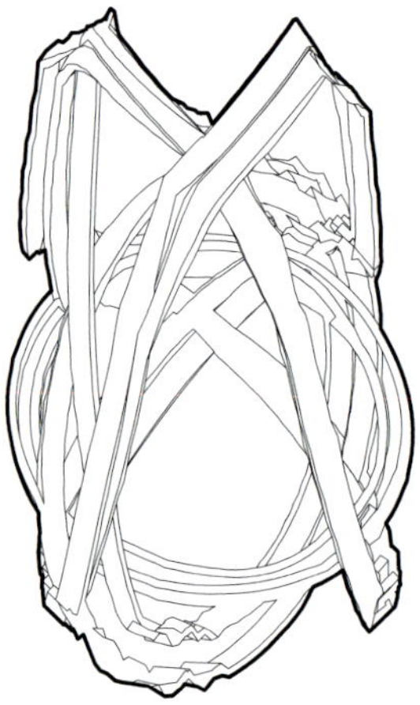

SP . FO . ME . MD

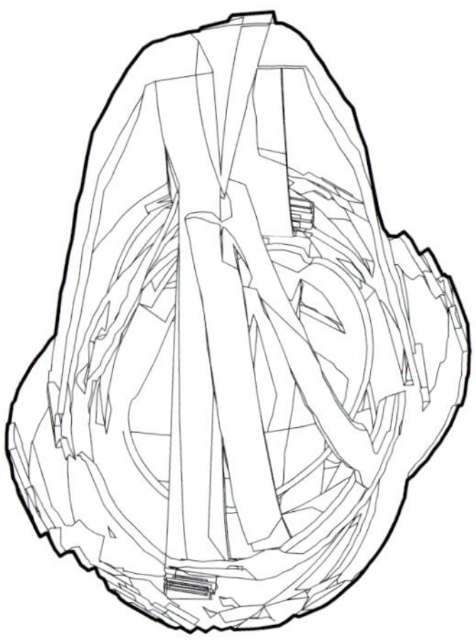

SP . FO . LA . MD

274 4 M8 DROOP **VARIATIONS**

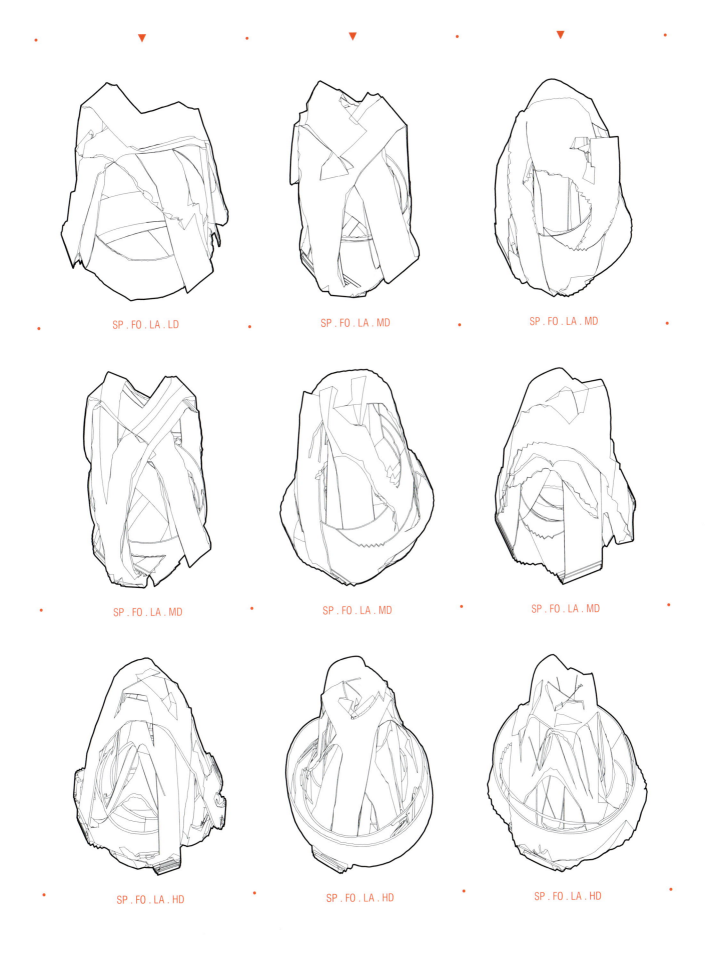

M9 PINCH

In this exercise you will be taking the definition you worked on within Constructions / Solid Objects / S1 and morphing it such that it creates a pinched figure. Pinching the solid object creates curvature near the midpoint and reveals a clear force enacted upon the object. On the right facing page are the steps that you underwent in exercise S1. Use the definition from S1 and add to it as shown on the spread that follows. Play with the pinch definition, notice how it transforms the voxels.

ORIGINAL SOLID OBJECT

8   Get centroid and plane vectors. Create plane for ring of fields
9   Circle to Place Vectors
10 Create a series of vectors for transformation
10A Vectors to use. Set vector magnitude
11 Pinch effect

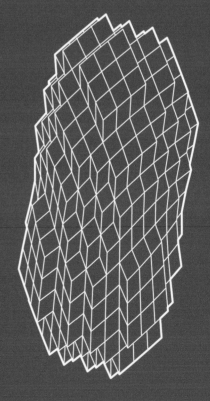

PINCHED SOLID OBJECT

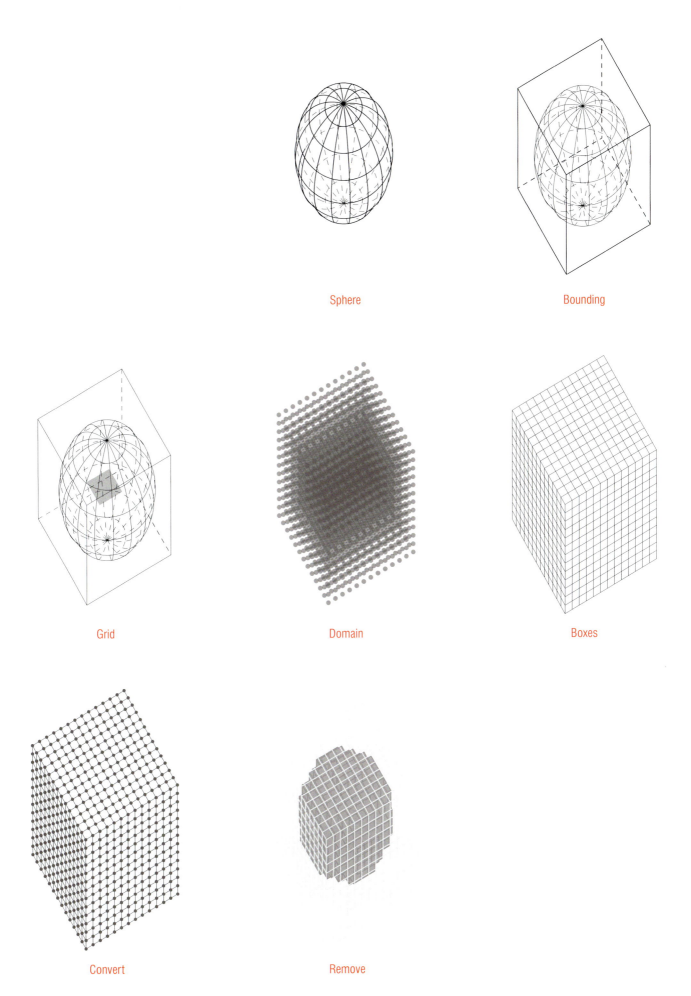

M9

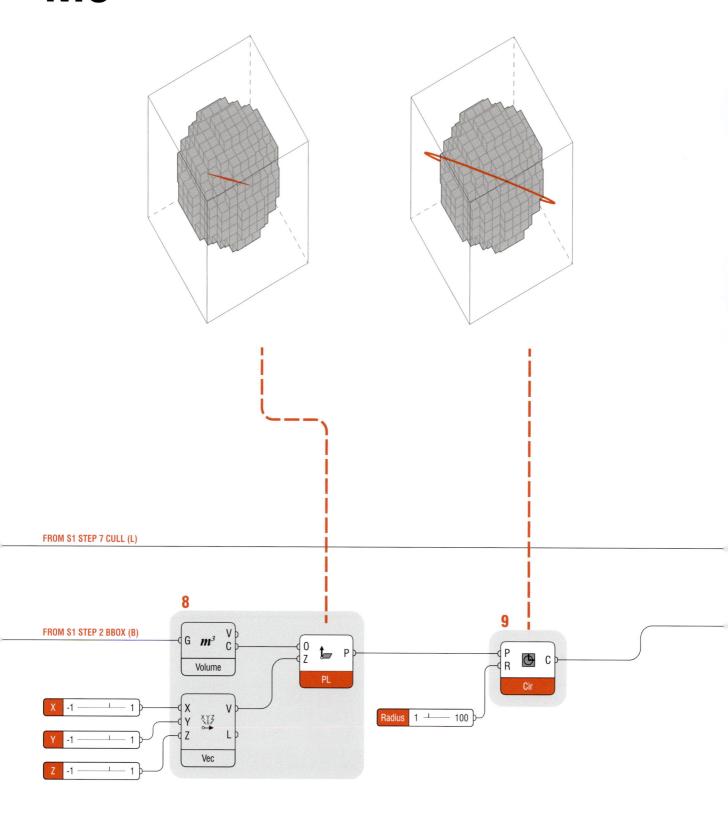

FROM S1 STEP 7 CULL (L)

FROM S1 STEP 2 BBOX (B)

278   4 M9 **PINCH**

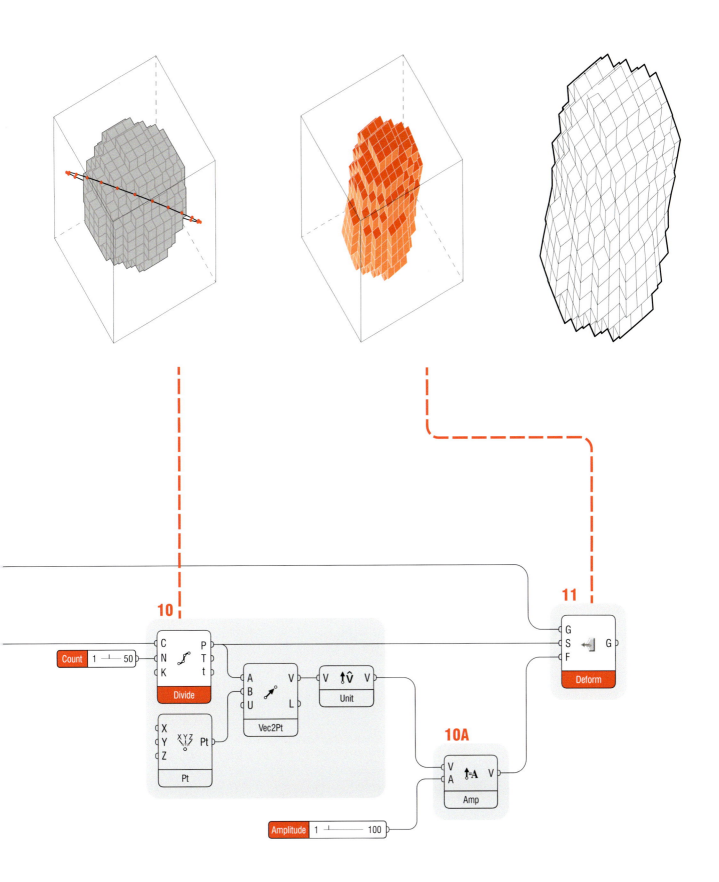

THICKNESS ▼

DIVISIONS ▼

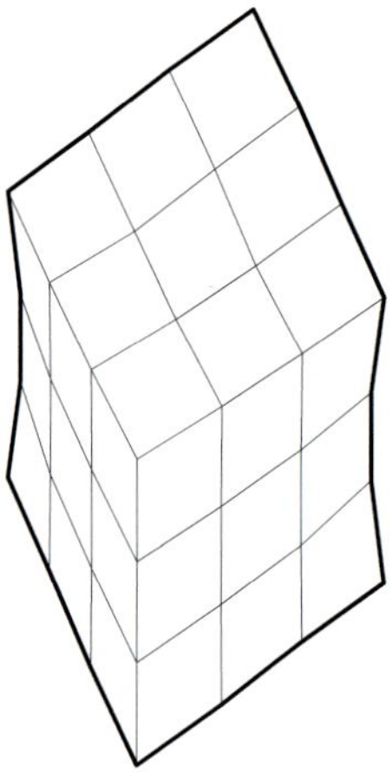

CU . ST . LA . HD

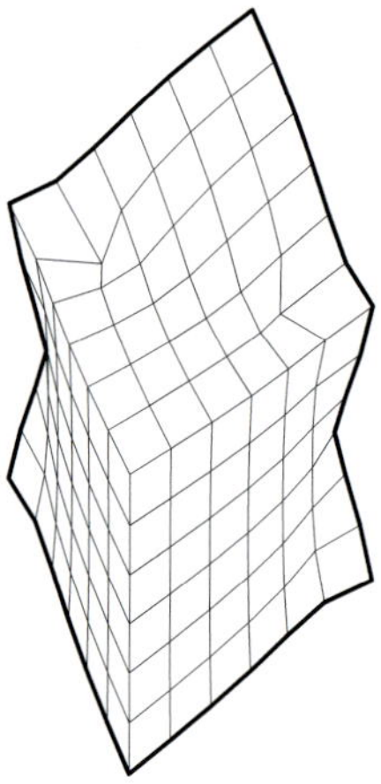

CU . ST . ME . HD

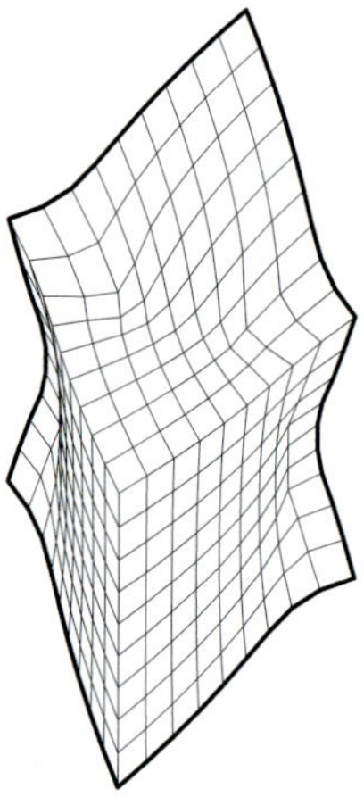

CU . ST . SM . HD

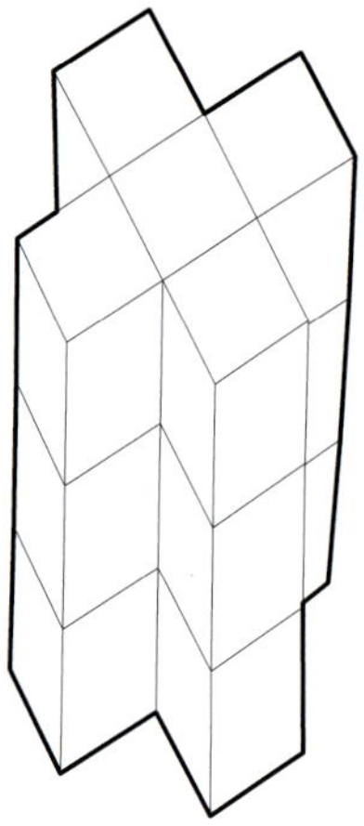

CU . ST . LA . LD

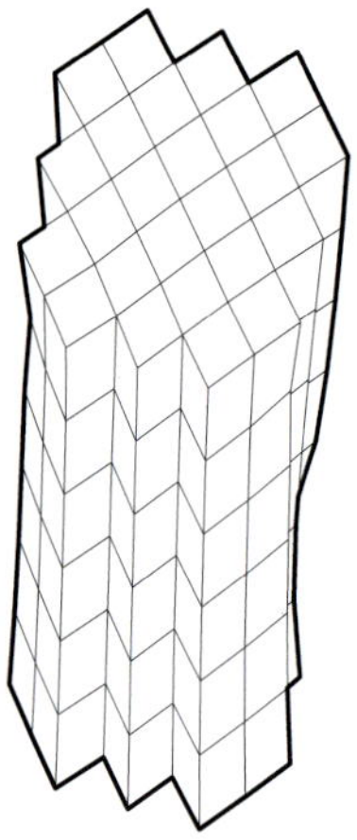

CU . ST . ME . MD

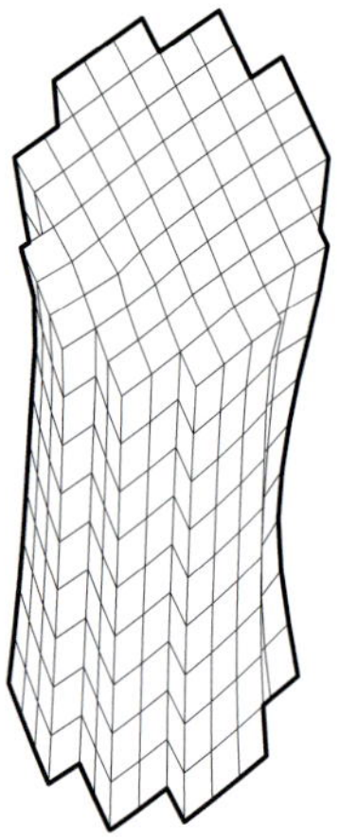

CU . ST . SM . MD

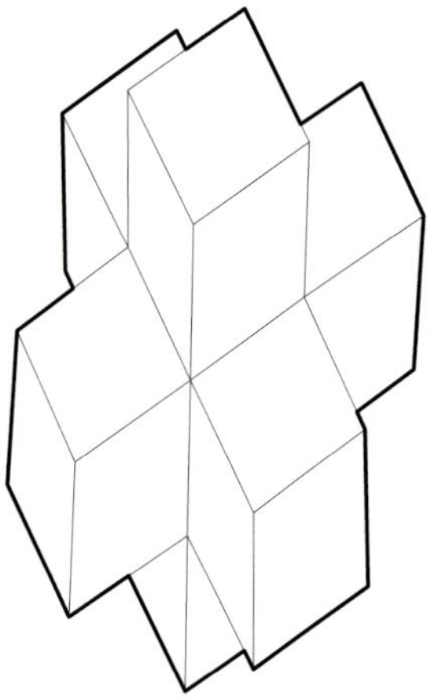

CU . ST . LA . MD

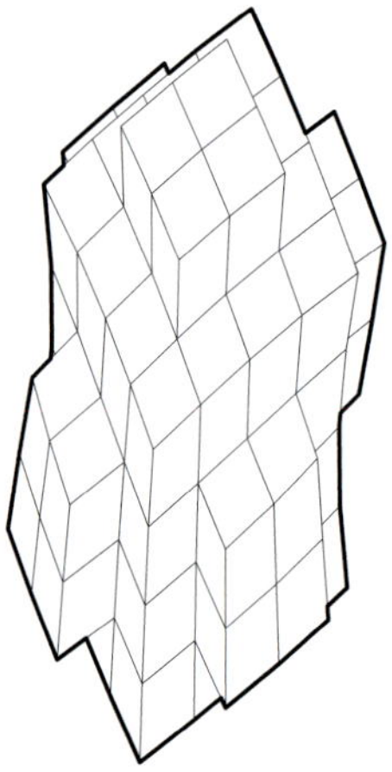

CU . ST . ME . MD

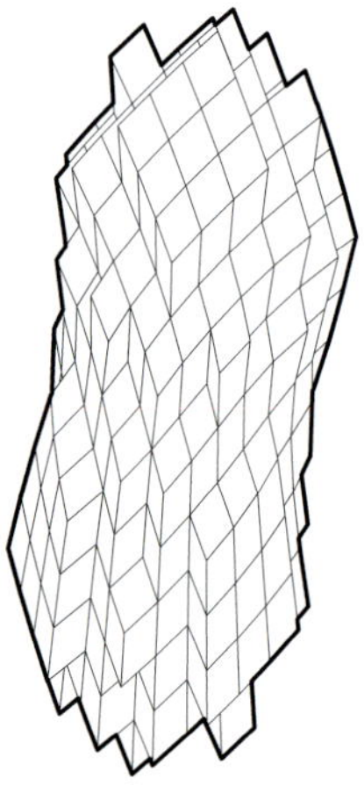

CU . ST . SM . MD

280   4 M9 PINCH **VARIATIONS**

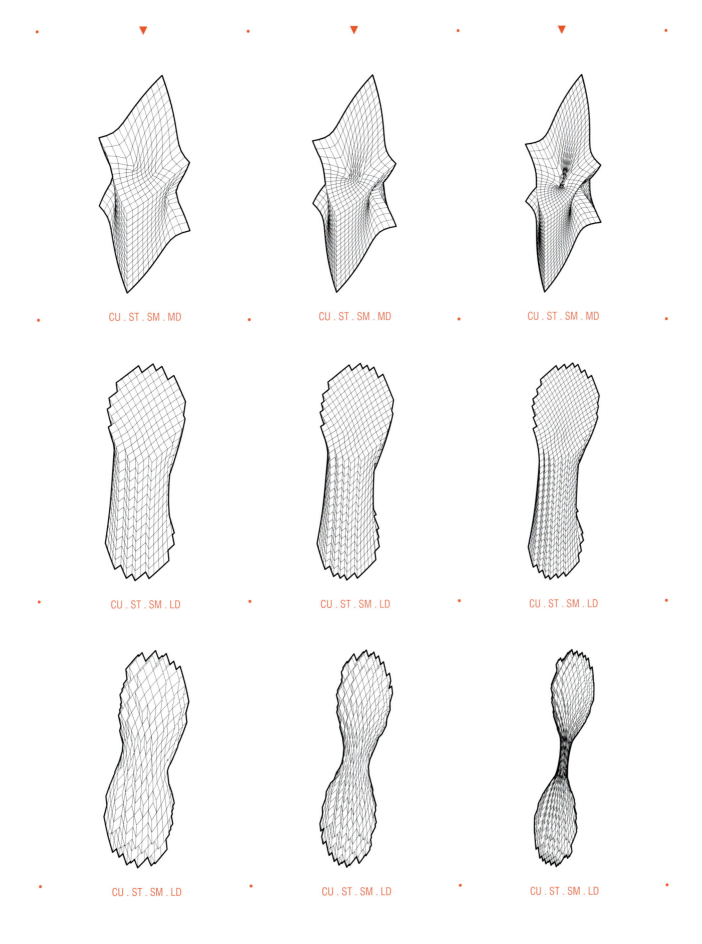

M10 CARVE

In this exercise you will be taking the definition you worked on within Constructions / Solid Objects / S2 and morphing it so that it can be carved. Carving, known as boolean differencing within Rhinoceros, is a great way to create space within an otherwise solid object. On the right facing page are the steps that you underwent in exercise S4. Use the definition from S4 and add to it as shown on the spread that follows. Notice how the nature of the object changes toward Frame when its density is decreased and Solid when its density is increased. Changes the nature of the original object will greatly affect the impact of the carving.

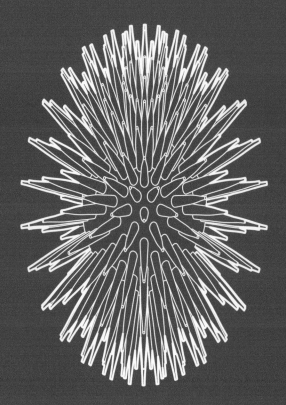

ORIGINAL SOLID OBJECT

9 Get last points and mix them
10 Select 8 random points from list
10A Get random size values from a range
11 Create spheres
12 Perform boolean operation
12A Sphere wireframe
13 Geometry preview

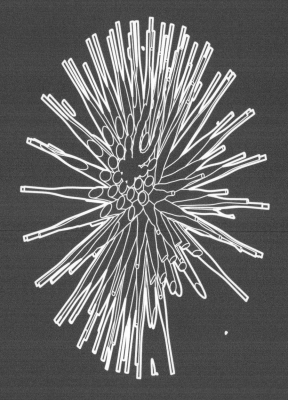

CARVED SOLID OBJECT

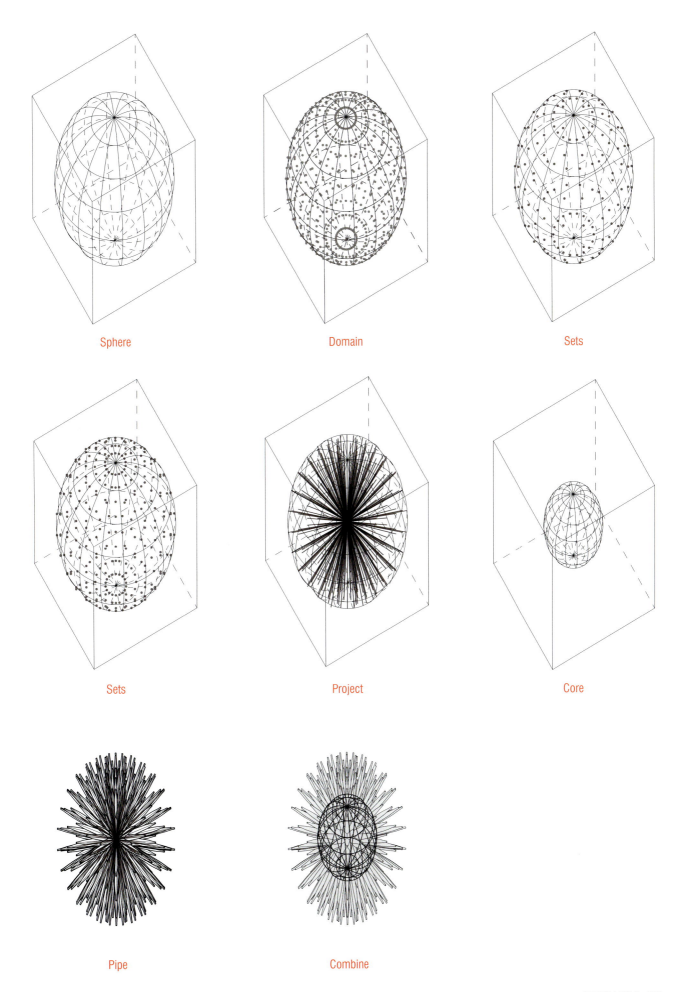

M10

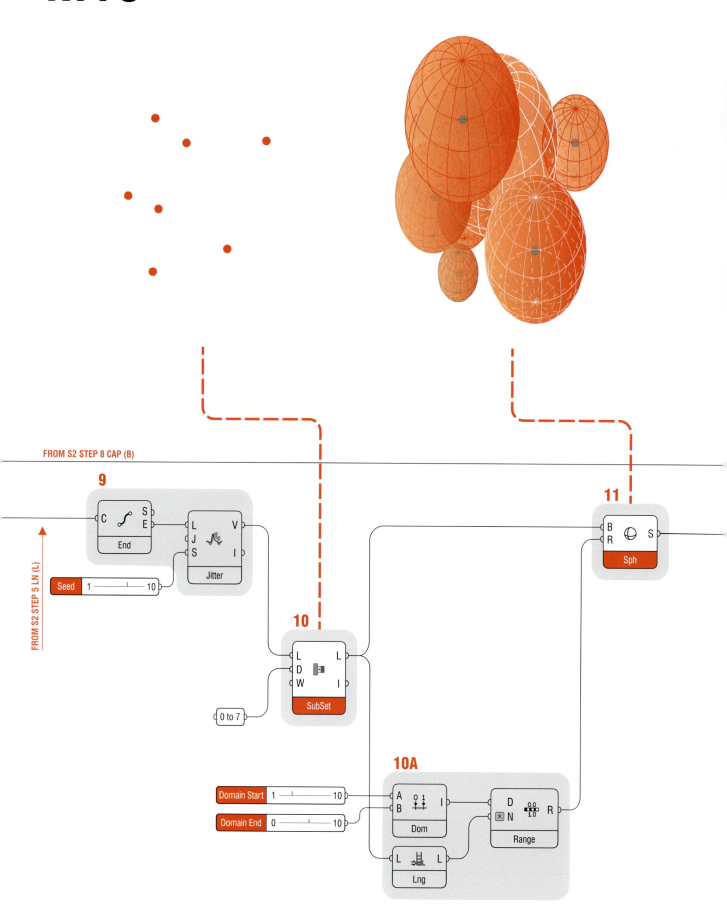

284 4 M10 **CARVE**

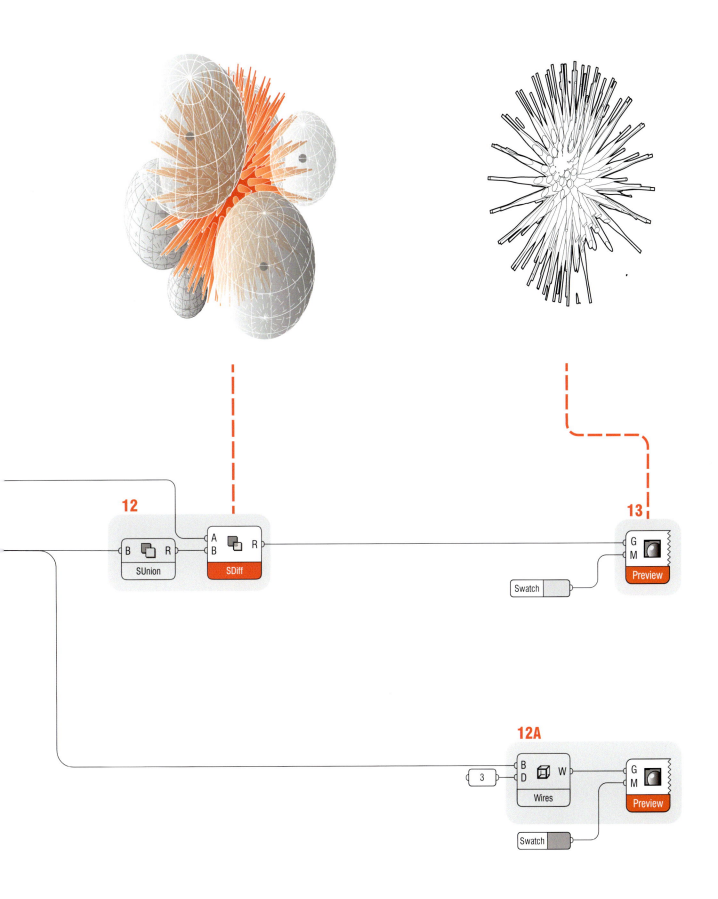

DIVISIONS ▼

DIVISIONS ▼

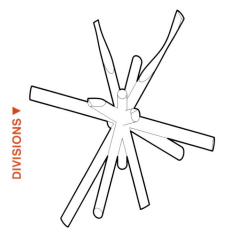
SP . FO . ME . LD

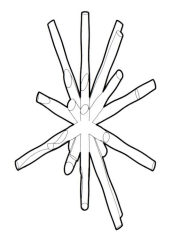
SP . FO . ME . LD

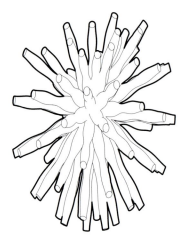
SP . FO . ME . MD

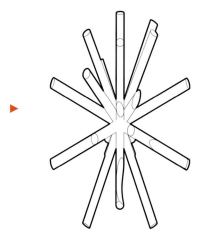
SP . FO . ME . LD

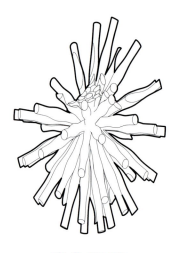
SP . FO . ME . MD

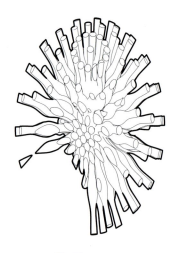
SP . FO . ME . HD

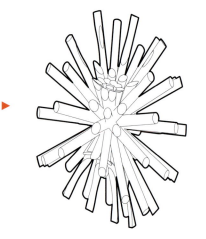
SP . FO . LA . MD

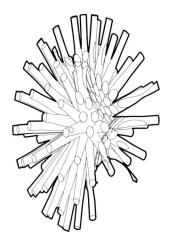
SP . FO . ME . MD

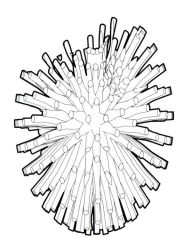
SP . FO . SM . HD

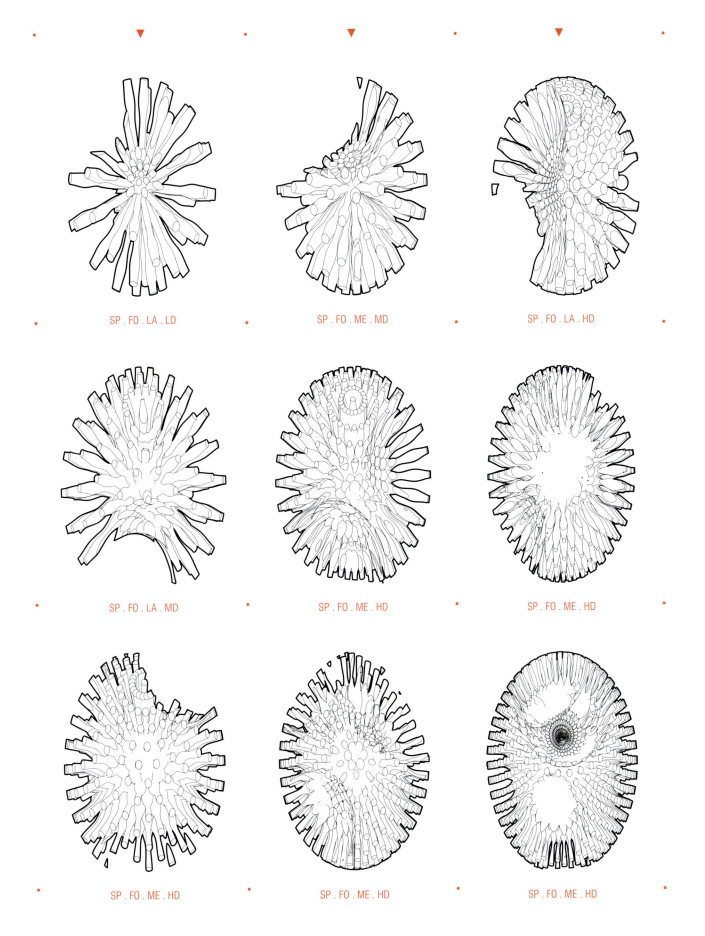

M11 DECOMPOSE

In this exercise you will be taking the definition you worked on within Constructions / Solid Objects / S3 and decomposing it using a spherical boolean difference. Think of this as a way of creating the perception of material erosion within the object. On the right facing page are the steps that you underwent in exercise S3. Use the definition from S3 and add to it as shown on the spread that follows. Experiment with different intensities of decomposition. Test how much decomposition is needed in order to make the object unrecognizable from its original.

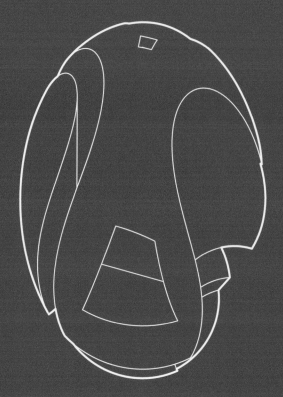

ORIGINAL SOLID OBJECT

5 Get random points inside the boundary box
6 Project points on base sphere
7 Create spheres
8 Decompose form using the spheres

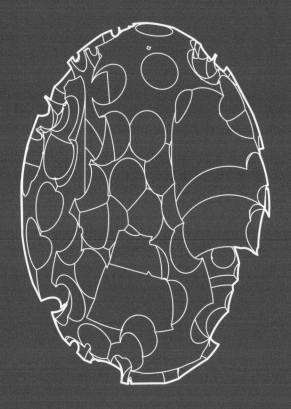

DECOMPOSED SOLID OBJECT

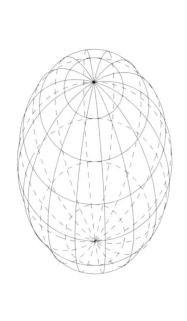

Points

Project

Spheres

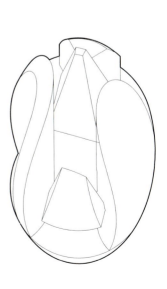

Decompose

M11

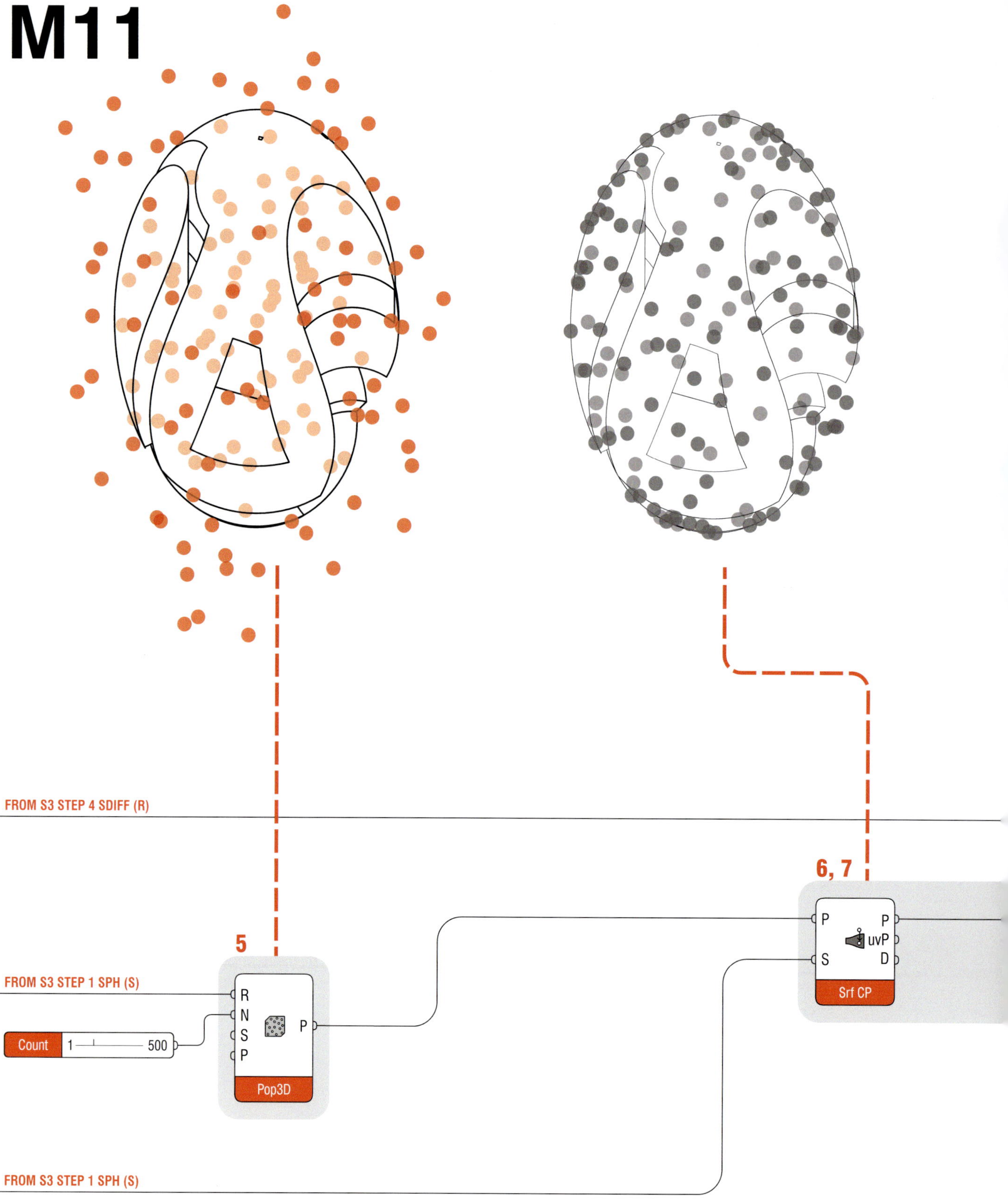

FROM S3 STEP 4 SDIFF (R)

5

FROM S3 STEP 1 SPH (S)

Count 1 — 500

Pop3D
R N S P → P

6, 7

Srf CP
P S → P uvP D

FROM S3 STEP 1 SPH (S)

290 4 M11 **DECOMPOSE**

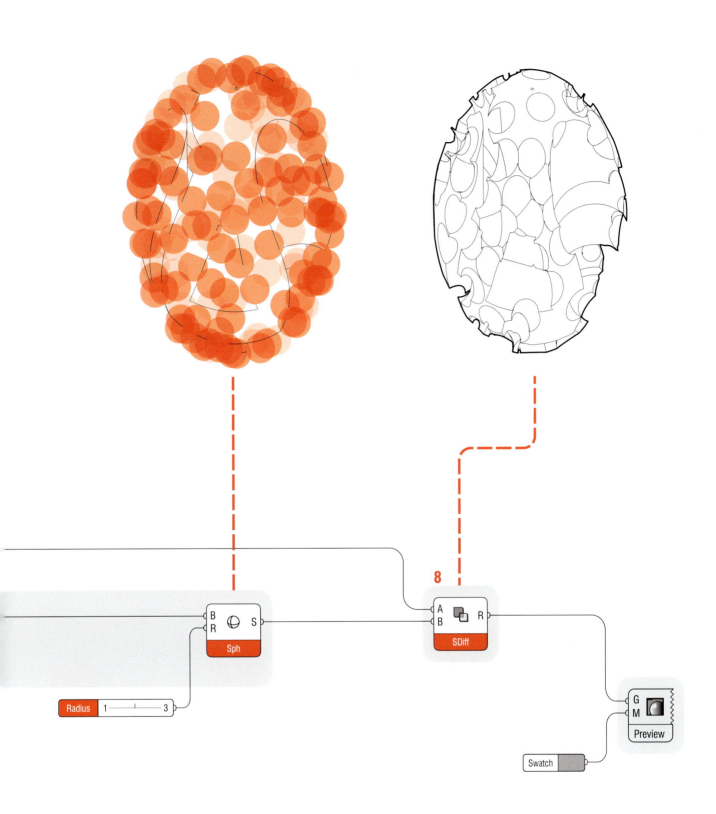

DECOMPOSE ▼

DECOMPOSE ▼

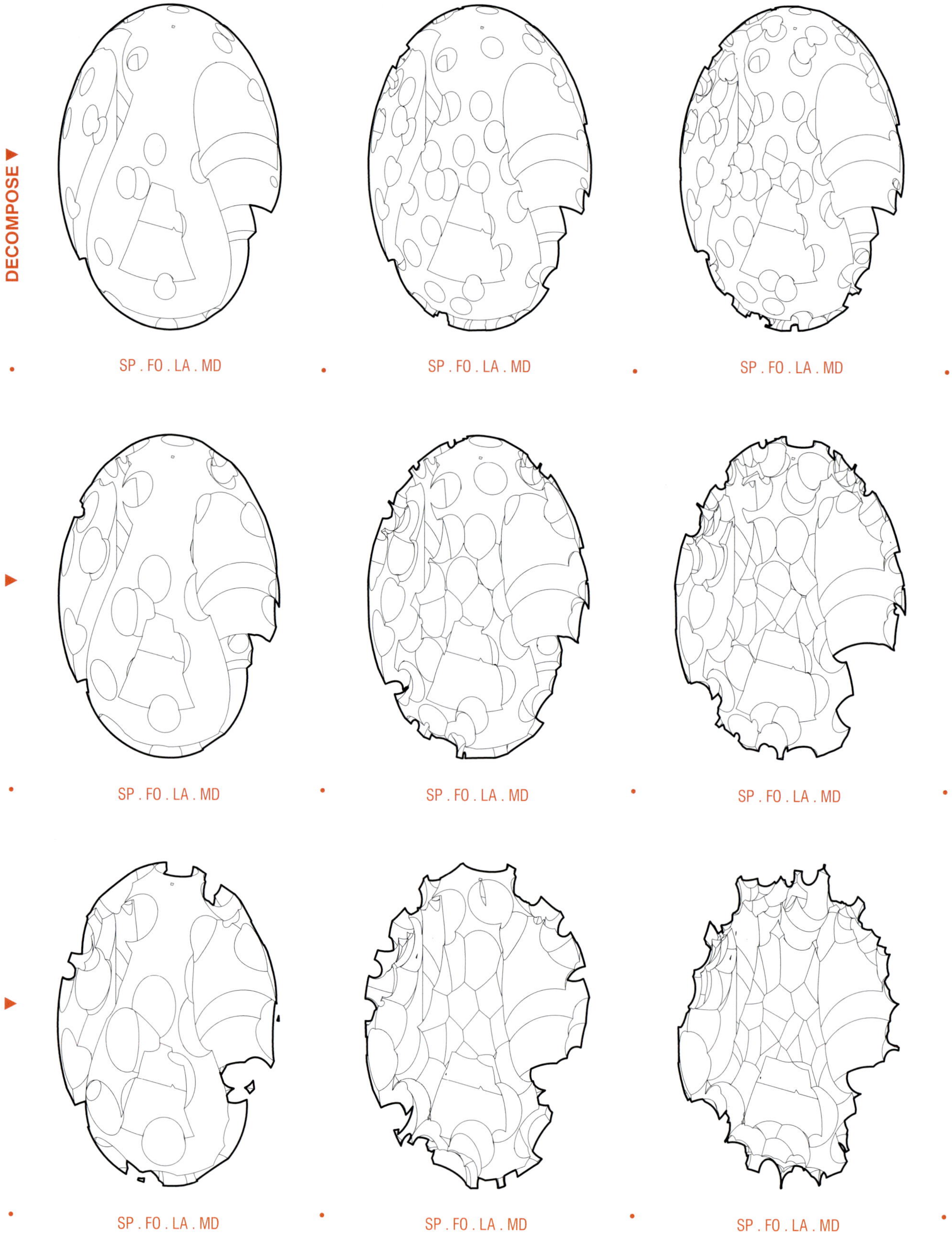

SP . FO . LA . MD

SP . FO . LA . MD

SP . FO . LA . MD

SP . FO . LA . MD

SP . FO . LA . MD

SP . FO . LA . MD

SP . FO . LA . MD

SP . FO . LA . MD

SP . FO . LA . MD

292   4 M11 DECOMPOSE **VARIATIONS**

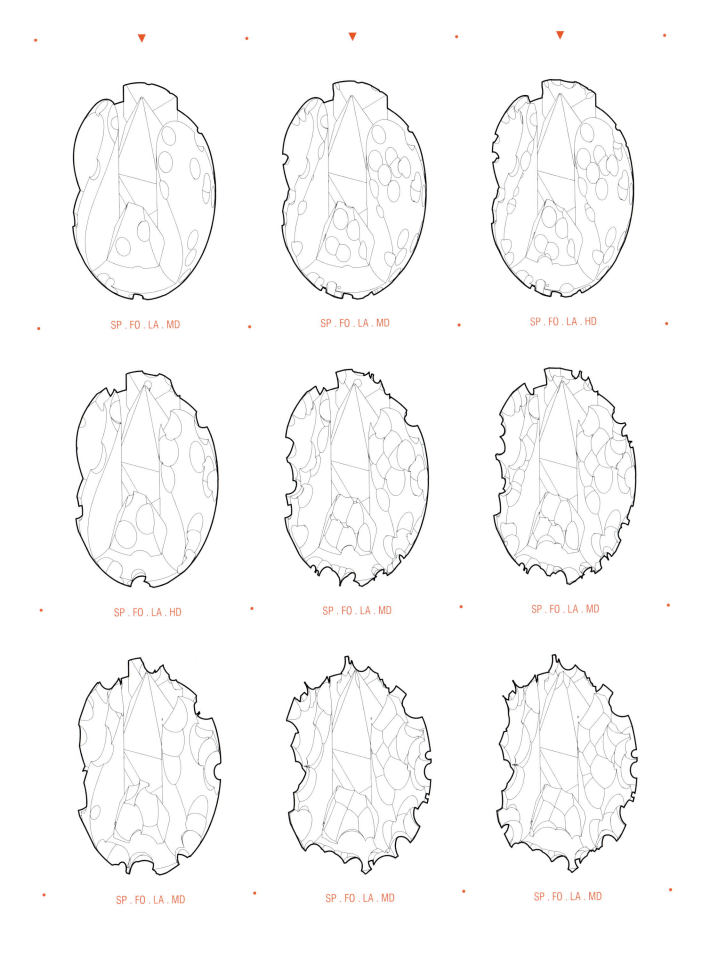

M12 MERGE

In this exercise you will be taking the definition you worked on within Constructions / Solid Objects / S4 and morphing it such that it creates a merged figure whose individual elements bend. Merging the frame elements of which the solid figure is constituted will alter its rigid, regular order. On the right facing page are the steps that you underwent in exercise S4. Use the definition from S4 and add to it as shown on the spread that follows. Test the limits of the merge definition, see what happens when you exaggerate the slider quantities. Watch closely how the nature of the object changes.

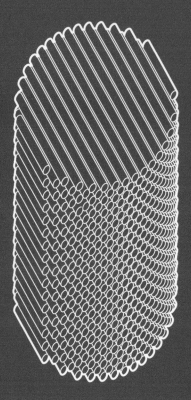

ORIGINAL SOLID OBJECT

7	Base curves
8	Divide curves
8A	Get numbers based on a mathematical rule (sine wave distribution, Graph Mapper)
8B	Remap to a target linear domain
9	Generate curves
9A	Rotate from 0 to PI
10	Rotate curves randomly
11	Force existing pipes to follow the new curves

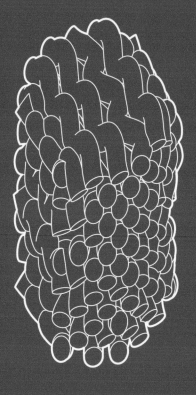

MERGED SOLID OBJECT

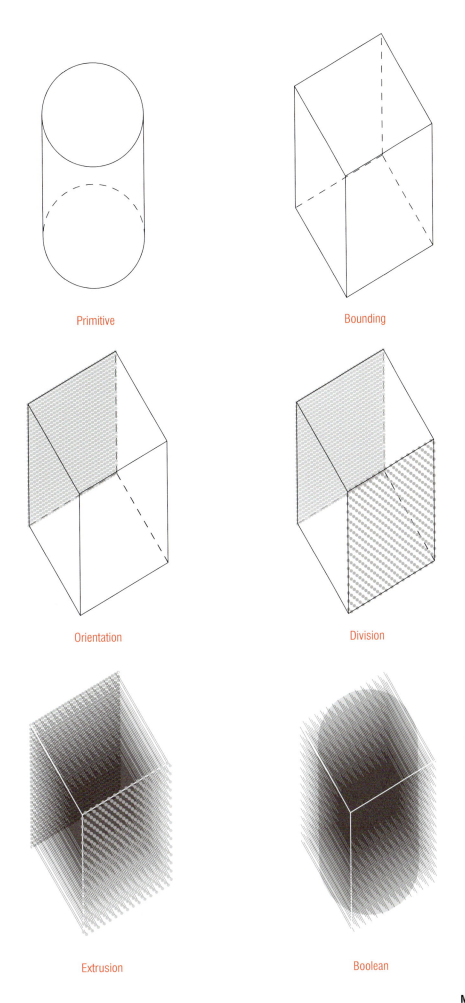

M12

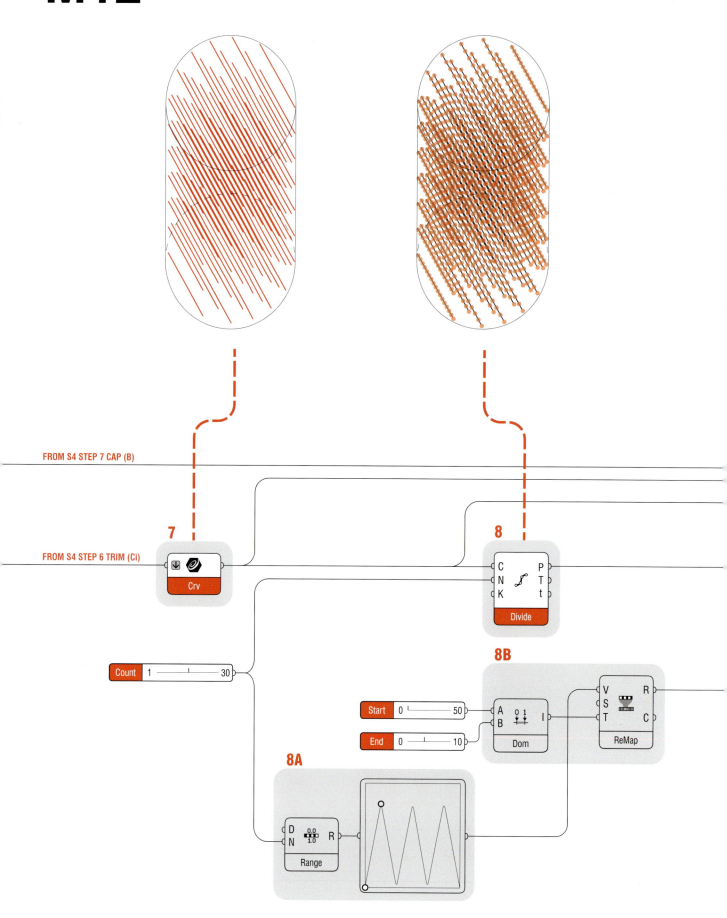

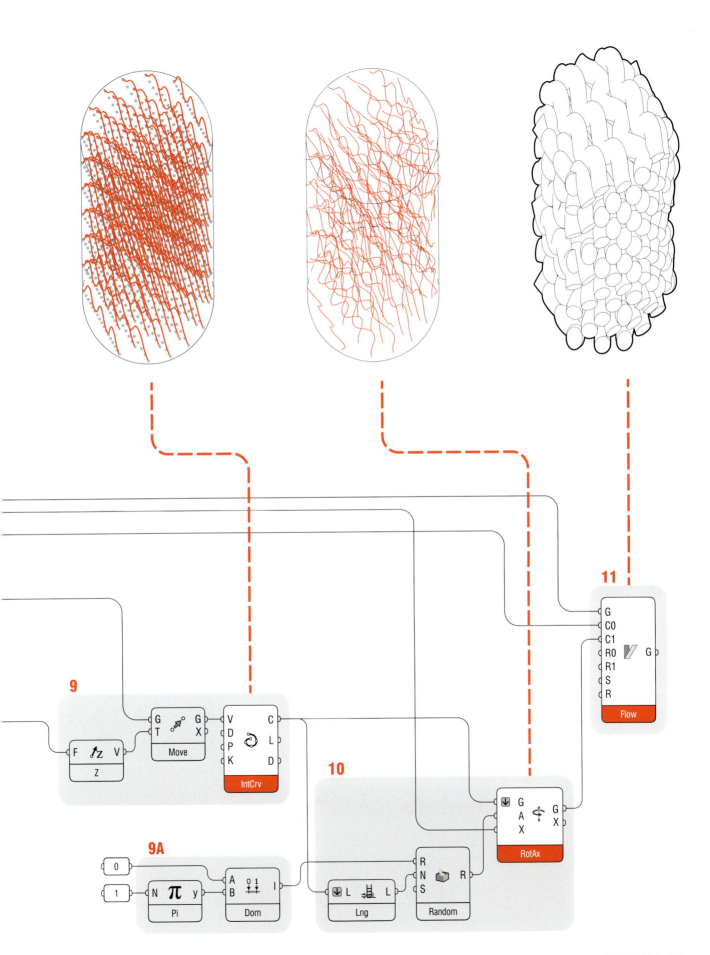

DIVISIONS ▼

SHAPE ▼

SP . FO . LA . MD	SP . FO . ME . HD	SP . FO . SM . HD
CY . FO . LA . MD	CY . FO . ME . HD	CY . FO . SM . HD
CU . FO . LA . MD	CU . FO . ME . HD	CU . FO . SM . HD

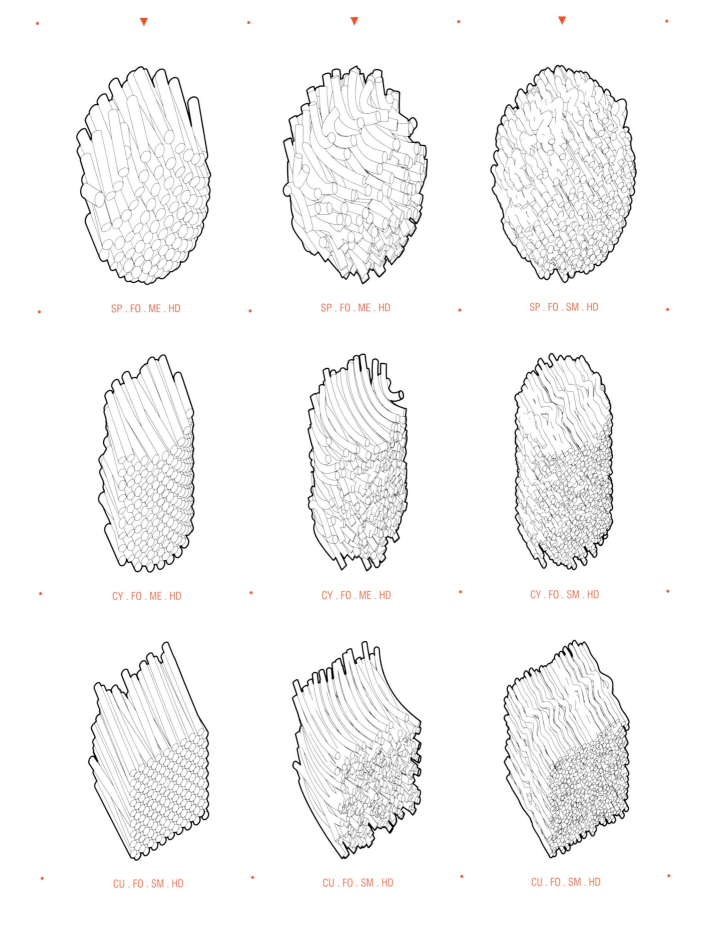

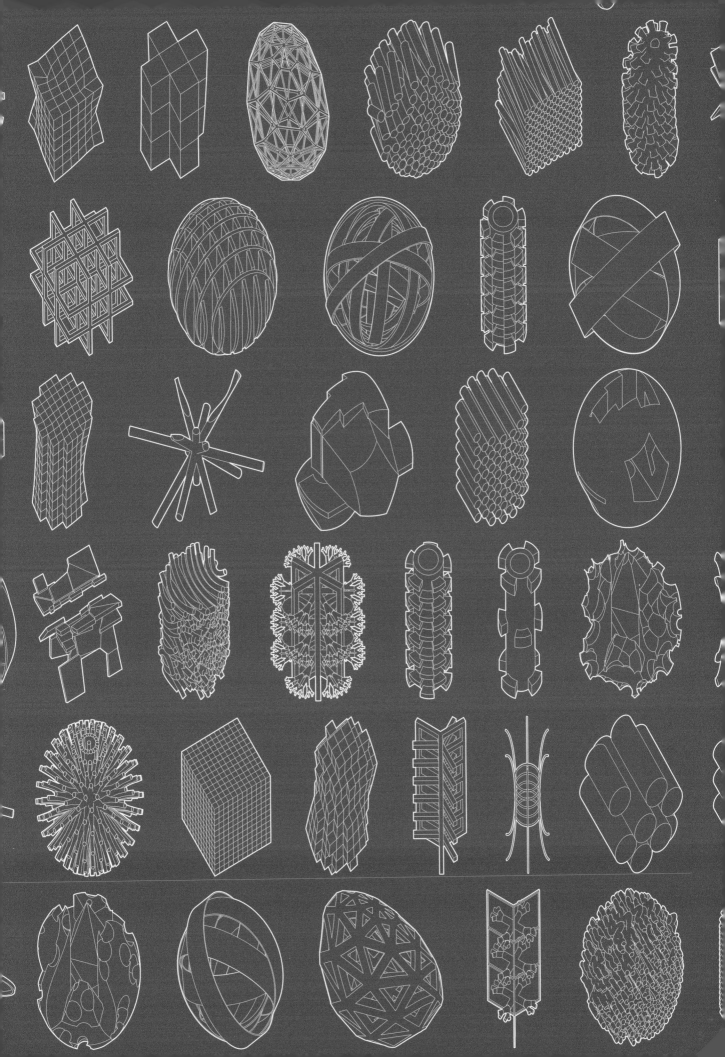

INDEX

3D models 68–70, 71
3D printing 39, 41–4, 49, 66
3D scanning *see* reality capture

Additive Manufacturing 39
additive materials 64, 66, 71
Alberti, Leon Battista 50
Antonelli, Paola 39
array 89; 1D scale reduce 90–2; axial 128–33; rotate 93; toggle 3D scale split 94–5
art autre movement 46
artificial intelligence 72–9; definition 76
augmented reality (AR) 73–5
Autocad 58, 62
Autodesk 57, 58
automotive design 21–2, 62
aviation design 12
axial array 128–33

B2 building 64, *64*
balance 33
Banham, Reyner 45–6
Barclays Center 63, 64, *65*
base element 88
bend transformation 226–31
bespoke objects 5, 15, 66
Bézier, Pierre 62
Boids 19
Boolean differencing 136, 280–6
Boolean solid 178–81
Borromini, Francesco 50
Botswana Innovation Hub 63, 64, *68–9*
bottom-up approach 11
bounded objects *32*, 33
branching 22–3
branchoff transformation 242–7
brittleness 12, 29, *29*
building codes 17, 20, 76
Building Information Modeling (BIM) 48, 57, 58
bundled solid 182–7
Butterfly 59

C# 57, 73
Carpo, Mario 41, 42
carve transformation 280–5
cast materials 65–6
CATIA 48, 62, 64
cellular automata 24–5, *24*
centric intersection 144–51
centric ordering systems 30–1
Chitham, Robert 53
classical architecture 48–54, *see also* Roman architecture
climate change 55–6
Climate Studio 58
Club of Rome 56
CNC machines 41
color 33
Colosseum 49
complex systems 12, 19
Composite order 49
computational fluid dynamics (CFD) analysis 22, 59
computer numerical control (CNC) 62, 63, 64–6
computer vision 74, 75–6
computer-aided design (CAD) 48, 62, 73
computer-aided design and drafting (CADD) 56
computer-aided manufacturing (CAM) 62, 63, 68
concrete 12, 65, 66
Configured Product 38
constructions 4, 104–223
convolutional neural network (CNN) 76
Conway, Horton 24–5, *24*
Corinthian order 49
curtain walls 67

Davis, Daniel 9, 12
decay of plants 19, *20*
decompose transformation 286–91
deep learning 74, 76–8
delayed decisions 12–13
density *31*, 32–3, 172–7

Desargues, Girard 51
design modifications 7, 11–13, 15, 27, 62
digital fabrication 14, 76
Digital Project 48, 62
DIVA 58
division of boundary 108–13
Doric order 49
Drift Lamp 39–41, 45
droop transformation 266–73
Dynamo 58

economic considerations 12, 14, 37, 41, 42–3
ECOTECT 56–7
element curve divide orient 102–3
element populate orient 100–1
elements 4, 80–103
embedded logics 19
emergence 19
environment *see* sustainable design
equivalence 34, 51
ergonomics 22
Evolutionary Solvers 58–9
extrusions 30, *30*, 64–5, *66*, 67

Ferris, Hugh 21
Fibonacci sequence 18, *18*
field conditions 30
fingerprints 73
Firefly 5
flocking 18–19
Floor-Area Ratios (FAR) 20–1, *21*
Flora, Jim 44
Flotsam & Jetsam 66
fractals 22, 23–4
Frame Elements 28–9, *28*, 32, 106, 188, 238, 292
Frame Objects 1, 26, 28–33, *28–9*, *31*, 104, 106–33; axial array 128–33; bend transformation 226–31; branchoff transformation 242–7; division of boundary 108–13; Frame Plane 206–15; Frame Solid 198–205; revolve 122–7; Solid Frame 216–23; stretch transformation 232–7; tessellation 114–21; twist transformation 238–41

Galapagos 58, 59
"Game of Life" 24–5, *24*
Gehry, Frank 48, 62
generative adversarial network (GAN) 76
Genetic Algorithms 58–9

Goldhar, Joel D. 39
Grasshopper for Rhino 5, *45*, 52–4, 57, 58, 59, 62; constructions 4, 104–223; elements 4, 80–103; Frame Objects 106–33; glossary 82–3; Hybrid Objects 188–223; morphologies 4, 224–97; Plane Objects 134–63; Solid Objects 164–87
Greek cities 20, 49
Guarini, Guarino 51

Hadid, Zaha 48, 57
hard symmetry 34
Haring, Keith 44
Harouni, Lisa 39
Head-Mounted Displays (HMDs) 74
Hybrid Objects 104, 188–223

IES VE Gaia 58
Imperiale, Alicia 51
implosion transformation 248–53
industrial design 21–2
inflate transformation 260–5
Ionic order 49
irrational numbers 50
irregularity 31–2, *31*

Joinville Soldier Walking 19

Kahn, Louis 16
Kangaroo 5, 248, 260, 266
Karle, David 11
Katz, Ralph 39
Keats, Ezra Jack 44
Kelly, Brian 11
Kepler, Johannes 17
King, Alexander 56
Koch, Helge von 23
Koch Snowflake 23–4, *24*

Ladybug 5, 57, 58, 59
Laiserin, Jerry 48
lamp production 39–41, 45
land use patterns 21
LEED environmental 59
Lego Group 38–9
Lei, David 39
Levi Strauss 39
LiDAR (Light Detection and Ranging) 75
Life Cycle Assessment (LCA) 59
Lindenmayer System (L-System) 22–3, *23*
line 33, 34
linear ordering systems 30–1, 33

machine learning 76
Mackey, Chris 57
McNeel, Bob 57
Maeda, John 73
Mandelbrot, Benoit 23
Marey, Jules Etienne 19
Marsh, Andrew 56
Maslow, Abraham 72
mass customization 5, 14, 37–47, 63–4
masses *see* solids
material 33
Mazria, Edward 55–6
Menges, Achim 42
merge transformation 292–7
metadesign 37–47
The Metropolis of Tomorrow 21
modular growth 152–7
modular housing 63–4
monolithic materials 64, 66
Moretti, Luigi 51–2
morphologies 4, 224–97
multi-objective optimization 58
murmurations 18–19

natural systems 17–19
network ordering systems 30–1
neural networks 76, *77*
nFold Table *13*, 44–5, *45*
Nunzio, Antonello Di 59

Octopus 58
OneClick LCA 59
OpenFOAM 59
ordering systems 30–1, *31*
Oxman, Neri 42

Palladio, Andrea 50
parallel string rewriting system 22
Parameterized Product 38
parametric equations 8–9
Pareto-Principle for Multiple Goals 58, 59
patterns 17–18
Peccei, Aurelio 56
performance 51
pinch transformation 274–9
Pine, Joseph 38
placeholders 13
Plane Objects 1, 28–33, *28*, *32*, 104, 134–63; centric intersection 144–51; droop transformation 266–73; Frame Plane 206–15; implosion transformation 248–53; inflate transformation 260–5; modular growth 152–7; shatter transformation 254–9; Solid Plane 190–7; waffle 136–43; wrap 158–63
Platform-Based Design 21–2
Platonic solids 17, *17*
point line plane solid 84–5
populate point curve 96–7
Pro/ENGINEER 62
production, parametrized 39–44
proportion 33–4
punch-card systems 62
Python 57, 73, 83, 242

RABBIT plug-in *23*, *24*
Rael, Ronald 41–2
reality capture 75
recursion 22, 23
regularity 31–2, *31*
Revit 57, 58, 73, 78
revolve 122–7
Reynolds, Craig 18–19
Rhino *see* Grasshopper for Rhino
rhythm 33, 34
Roman architecture 20, 49, 50, 52–4, *52–3*, 60, *60*
Roudsari, Mostapha Sadeghipour 57
rules-based approaches 5, 16
Rutten, David 58–9

safety 76
San Fratello, Virginia 41–2
scale 33
Scamozzi, Vincenzo 50
Schumacher, Patrik 48–9, 57
Sefaira 58
self-organizing systems 18–19
shape 33, 34
shatter transformation 254–9
sheets *see* planes
SHoP Architect 63, 64–6, 70
Shumacher, Patrik 51
SKETCHPAD 62
SketchUp 58
Smith, Rick 12
snowflakes 23–4, *24*
soft symmetry 34
Solemma 58
Solid Objects 28–33, *28*, 104, 164–87; Boolean 178–81; bundled 182–7; carve transformation 280–5; decompose transformation 286–91;

density 172–7; Frame Solid 198–205; merge transformation 292–7; pinch transformation 274–9; Solid Frame 216–23; Solid Plane 190–7; voxel 166–71
space 33, 34
spatial computing 73, 74–5, 78
Standardized Product 38
sticks *see* frames
stone 66
stretch transformation 232–7
Summerson, John 49–50
surface line plane solid 86–7
surface subdivide 98–9
sustainable design 55–61
Sustainable Development Goals (SDGs) 55
Sutherland, Ivan 62
swarming 18–19, *19*
symmetry 33, 34
Syracuse University National Veterans Resource Center 63, 66, *67*, 70, *70*
System Design 67–9

Tapie, Michel 45–6
terracotta 65, *66*
tessellation 22, 114–21
texture 33
Thompson, D'Arcy Wentworth 17
timber 66
Toolkits for User Innovation 39
Toyota 38

twist transformation 238–41
Type Chair 42–3, *42*, *44*, 45

Ulam, Stanislaw 24
unbounded objects *32*, 33
UNISURF 62
United Nations 55
urban form 20–1

Vasari 57
ventilation 59
versioning 13–14
Vignola 50
virtual collaboration 75
virtual reality (VR) 73–4, *74*, 75
visual scripting 73
VisualBasic 57
Vitruvius 49, 50
von Hippel, Eric 39
von Neumann, John 24
Vought Corporation 39
voxel 166–71

waffle 136–43
WAVE/CAVE 65, *65*, *66*
Wolfram, Stephen 24
wrap 158–63

Zevi, Bruno 51
zoning regulations 20–1